From Romanticism to Critical Theory

Literary theory is now perceived by many people as being in crisis, because some of its dominant theoretical assumptions are proving hard to sustain. *From Romanticism to Critical Theory* offers a new view of literary theory, seeing it not as a product of the French assimilation of Saussurian linguistics and Russian Formalism into what we term 'deconstruction', but rather as an essential part of modern philosophy which begins with the German Romantic reactions to Kant, the effects of which can be traced through to Heidegger, Benjamin and Adorno.

Andrew Bowie argues that, contrary to many current assumptions, the central question in contemporary literary theory is really the question of truth. He begins by showing how Kant's and F.H. Jacobi's reflections on grounding truth in modern philosophy form the background to the exploration of the relationship between literature and philosophy in early German Romanticism. The importance attached by Friedrich Schlegel, Novalis and Schleiermacher to questions of literature for philosophical approaches to language is seen as playing a crucial role in the genesis of modern hermeneutics, as well as being significant for issues raised in contemporary analytical semantics. Romantic ideas are also used to argue against the cultural materialist view of literature as merely a form of ideology. The book makes clear links between the Romantic philosophical tradition, Martin Heidegger's approaches to art and truth, and the related work of Benjamin and Adorno.

From Romanticism to Critical Theory argues that key problems in contemporary literary theory are inseparable from the main questions of modern philosophy after Kant. In addition to offering detailed accounts, based on many untranslated texts, of major positions in German literary theory since the Romantics, this controversial new approach to literary theory makes fascinating and important links between hermeneutics, analytical philosophy and literary theory, and will be a vital point of reference for future work in these areas.

Andrew Bowie is Professor of European Philosophy at Anglia Polytechnic University in Cambridge. He is the author of *Aesthetics and Subjectivity: From Kant to Nietzsche* and *Schelling and Modern European Philosophy*.

From Romanticism to Critical Theory

The philosophy of German literary theory

Andrew Bowie

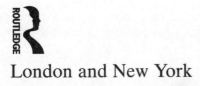

London and New York

First published 1997
by Routledge
11 New Fetter Lane, London EC4P 4EE

Simultaneously published in the USA and Canada
by Routledge
29 West 35th Street, New York, NY 10001

© 1997 Andrew Bowie

Typeset in Times by Keystroke, Jacaranda Lodge, Wolverhampton
Printed and bound in Great Britain by Clays Ltd, St. Ives PLC

British Library Cataloguing in Publication Data
A catalogue record for this book is available from the British Library

Library of Congress Cataloging in Publication Data
Bowie, Andrew, 1952–
From romanticism to critical theory: the philosophy of German
literary theory / Andrew Bowie.
Includes bibliographical references.
1. Criticism – Germany – History. 2. German literature – History and
criticism – Theory, etc. 3. Criticism – Philosophy – History. 4. Literature
and philosophy. I. Title.
PT73.B69 1996
801′.95′0943–dc20 96–7703

ISBN 0–415–12762–9 (hbk)
ISBN 0–415–12763–7 (pbk)

Contents

Preface and acknowledgements

'Literary theory' has been regarded by some of its practitioners as a wholly novel approach to language, literature and interpretation, and by many of its opponents as either 'poor man's philosophy' or as a renunciation of the proprieties of literary scholarship. There is some justification for the views of both sides. On the one hand, literary theory has undoubtedly revealed aspects of the philosophical understanding of language and literature which the Anglo-American traditions of analytical philosophy have tended until recently to ignore; on the other, though, it has itself often ignored many of the insights into art, truth and language that are the concern of the German hermeneutic tradition and of analytical philosophy. This book tries to mediate between these positions, and positions in more conventional literary studies, by taking a new look at a still fairly neglected area of literary theory, namely that initiated by the early German Romantics, which eventually leads to Heidegger and to the 'Critical Theory' of the Frankfurt School. It does so in order to suggest via this tradition that there is a much greater scope for dialogue between differing contemporary philosophical, theoretical and philological traditions than seems to be apparent to many of those working within these traditions.

The creation of such dialogue can often result from a revaluation of the emergence of the differing traditions, and this book tries to offer such a revaluation. This can, though, lead to a particular narrowing of perspective, which I have been concerned to avoid. One of the aims of the book is, therefore, to exemplify an approach in which the critical rewriting of aspects of the history of philosophy is seen as offering as much opportunity to establish important philosophical arguments as an exclusively analytical approach. This does, however, bring certain dangers. Any book which tries to mediate between so many opposing positions runs the risk of either levelling important differences or of failing to create a really enlightening dialogue between those positions. I leave to my readers the judgement on my success in avoiding these dangers, but if, for example, post-structuralist literary theorists, analytical philosophers and traditional literary critics, particularly in German studies, find something substantial to engage with in the book, I shall probably have achieved my main aims. My previous work on German aesthetics and on Schelling has been criticised by hermeneuticists for failing to remain within the historical context of the theories I am examining, and by analytically oriented philosophers for being too concerned with history at the expense of argument. This actually seems to me about the right place to be these days, if one is to avoid both the tendency towards the merely 'monumental' history of ideas characteristic of some work in hermeneutics and the unconscious philosophical amnesia of much analytical philosophy. Inevitably, though, in a book that covers so much ground, many of the issues considered can only be dealt with superficially, and there is a limit to one's engagement with the secondary literature in many areas: I therefore apologise here to those whose work is not mentioned but whose ideas may well have played an important role in what I have to say.

Various bits of the book have appeared or will appear, usually in a very different form, in *Radical Philosophy*; in the *Publications of the English Goethe Society*; in Simon Critchley and Peter Dews' *Deconstructive Subjectivities* (Albany: SUNY Press 1996), and in other essays: in the era of the hard disk it becomes difficult to detail such limited borrowings from oneself. The book has benefited greatly from discussion after papers given at a wide variety of institutions and organisations, notably the network 'Literature and Romanticism' at the University of Copenhagen, the universities of Bergen, Tübingen, Bradford, Cambridge, Derby, East Anglia, Lancaster, Middlesex, Nottingham, Southampton, Sussex, the Architectural Association, the English Goethe Society, the Goethe Institute in London, the Institute of Contemporary Arts, the Slade College of Art, and the Centre for Research in Hermeneutic and Analytical Philosophy at Anglia Polytechnic University.

My thanks go to the British Academy, whose excellent Research Leave Scheme allowed me, with matching support from Anglia Polytechnic University, to complete the book in a far shorter time than would otherwise have been possible. The Alexander von Humboldt Foundation Research Fellowship which I held at the University of Tübingen in 1991–2 allowed me to do much of the preparatory thinking and work which eventually resulted in the present book. I am, once again, very grateful indeed to Manfred Frank, whose own work in this area, and whose friendship, motivation and support have been, as ever, indispensable. David Isaac's great skill in organising the Philosophy Division at Anglia so as to create the opportunity for its members to do serious research has been vital, as have the friendship and philosophical discussions with my colleagues Alison Ainley and Neil Gascoigne, and the students at Anglia's interest in the questions of the book. Simon Critchley, Peter Dews, Roger Frie, Steve Giles, Nick Jardine, Neil Leach, Peter Middleton, Peter Osborne, Jonathan Rée, Julian Roberts, Kiernan Ryan, Birgit Sandkaulen-Bock, Simon Schaffer, Martin Swales, Nick Walker, and too many others to mention by name, helped me to arrive at what I wanted to say. T.J. Reed's somewhat extravagant reply in *Oxford German Studies* to my attempt at explaining the value of German literary theory to him supplied motivation of a rather different kind. Adrian Driscoll at Routledge helped to initiate the project and gave his usual excellent editorial help. My parents accepted with characteristic patience my misplaced desire to finish the book while I was on holiday with them in the Western Highlands of Scotland, and were as supportive as ever. Finally, Liz Bradbury's love, insight, encouragement and acute criticisms provided the most essential inspiration.

Andrew Bowie, Cambridge 1995

Introduction
Renewing the theoretical canon

THE ROOTS OF LITERARY THEORY

The history of worries about the point of the study of literature, and about how to establish the meaning of literary texts, is a very long one indeed:

> PROTAGORAS: In my view, Socrates, the most important part of a man's education is to become an authority on poetry. This means being able to criticise the good and bad points of a poem with understanding, to know how to distinguish them, and give one's reasons when asked. (Plato, *Protagoras* 339)

> SOCRATES: Conversation about poetry reminds me too much of the wine parties of second-rate and commonplace people.... No one can interrogate poets about what they say, and most often when they are introduced into the discussion some say the poet's meaning is one thing and some another, for the topic is one on which nobody can produce a conclusive argument.
> (Plato, *Protagoras* 347)

Questions about 'poetry' and literature are in fact inseparably connected to the history of Western philosophy, including, as we shall see, aspects of that philosophy, like analytical philosophy, which generally have little direct concern with literature. The starting point of this book is the emergence at a decisive point in the intellectual development of the modern world of theoretical concern with the status of the notion of 'literature'. Indeed, I shall later argue that 'literature' itself comes into existence in the period in question, because, prior to the growing dominance of non-theological conceptions of language in the second half of the eighteenth century, what it is that makes a particular text a 'literary' text is not necessarily an issue of any wider significance. The rise of 'literature' and the rise of philosophical aesthetics – of a new philosophical concern with understanding the nature of art – are inseparable phenomena, which are vitally connected to changes in conceptions of truth in modern thought. It is this latter aspect of the question of 'literature', which has been too often neglected in literary theory based on the assumptions of French structuralism and post-structuralism, that will be central to this book: hence my desire to give an account of the philosophy of German literary theory rather than just of 'German literary theory'.

Why, though, should there have been such sustained world-wide attention to the theory of literature in recent years? No doubt the justified feeling that the academic study of literature can get rather too close to what goes on at the 'wine parties of second-rate and commonplace people' was a factor in the rise of literary theory at the end of the 1960s. However, the motivations behind the differing positions in literary theory have been so diverse that it is difficult to see any common denominator between them. Motivations have ranged from the scientistic desire to prove that one can make empirically testable truth claims about literary texts of the same kind as can be made about physical phenomena (in certain versions of structuralism), to the desire to unmask class or gender ideology in even the most admired products of Western literary culture (in the most varying versions of Marxist and Feminist theory). Despite this diversity of aims most such positions have at least shared the need to establish stronger legitimations for literary study, either by reflecting upon just what it is trying to achieve in its existing forms or by suggesting that it ought to concentrate on doing something else. Literary theory is, then, usually bound up with the perceived need to legitimate the study of literature, or, perhaps more significantly, with the suggestion that such legitimation is now lacking. One of my major concerns here is to show how the analysis of some of the attempts to legitimate literary study necessarily takes us into key areas of modern philosophy. The need to integrate the disciplines of literary study and philosophy in new ways is, I propose, vital to the longer-term health of both disciplines: there *is* for most of us in the developed Western world no *immediately* important social and political point to the revelation of the ideological aspects of major bourgeois literary works, and it is time that radical critics finally admitted this fact. Important work needs to be done, though, in showing how issues which emerge in relation to literature are, when connected to important developments in contemporary philosophy, germane to issues concerning our self-understanding which do potentially play an important role in engaging with virtually any area of modern society.

Despite the enormous success and influence of the literary theory which began in the late 1960s there is now a growing suspicion, even among some of its practitioners, that literary theory itself is in crisis. The signs of this suspicion have, of course, been eagerly seized upon by those who never engaged in literary theory in the first place. Despite the threadbare nature of the arguments of many traditionalist opponents of literary theory, it is becoming clear that some of the more ambitious claims for literary theory are in need of revision and that some of the more extreme versions of post-structuralist theory in particular cannot be defended. This book is intended, then, in the light of the decline of the euphoria that inevitably follows any fundamental reorientation in an academic discipline, to provide new impetus for theoretical work in all areas of the humanities by changing the focus of the theoretical debate in the direction of a more informed philosophical consideration of the issues. It is also intended to show that the extreme form of the opposition to literary theory is simply mistaken, because the essential bases for such reflection have been with us at least since the German Romantics and form part of mainstream philosophy. In this respect the very fact that literary theory has, because of its deeper historical roots, not been quite such a controversial issue in Germany as it has been in Britain, France, and the USA, should give pause for thought to those who are so implacably opposed to it. This difference in perception also has to do with the differing perceptions of the role and nature of philosophy in the intellectual culture of these countries.

Why, then, write a book which focuses on the German tradition of reflection upon literature?[1] The initial answer is that the German philosophical traditions I shall be exploring are the historical and theoretical 'condition of possibility' of the new wave of theory which developed from the 1960s onwards in the work of Roland Barthes, Michel Foucault, Jacques Derrida, Paul de Man and others. It will become apparent, though, that the German traditions in question have yet to be understood in sufficient depth, a fact which must affect our understanding of recent French theory.[2] A further obvious legitimation for such a book is the fact that many people in German studies, especially in Great Britain, have failed to engage with French and American literary theory, let alone with German theory. Many students in German studies will read some Immanuel Kant or some Friedrich Schlegel, or even some Walter Benjamin, but there is too little awareness that the theoretical issues with which these thinkers were engaged are very close to the issues that make certain eminent figures in German studies and other areas of the humanities so hot under the collar when they are attached to the name of Jacques Derrida. As we shall see, an apparently dead piece of the history of German ideas, like the 'Pantheism controversy' which began in 1783, involves many of the questions that eventually lead both to post-structuralism and to some of the dilemmas of contemporary analytical philosophy. Rather than these issues being the product of a new fashion, then, they actually involve a history which goes back at least as far as the beginnings of German Romanticism. The importance of this tradition will also be shown from a different direction: approaches in analytical philosophy to questions of meaning have, until very recently, seemed very distant from questions posed by the tradition of German hermeneutic philosophy whose origins play a major role in what I have to say here. The fact is, though, that some of the most interesting developments in contemporary American philosophy, in the work of Donald Davidson, Hilary Putnam, Richard Rorty and others, come remarkably close to aspects of a tradition which, with the exception of Kant, is never even mentioned by most analytical philosophers.

LITERATURE, AESTHETICS AND IDEOLOGY

What, then, do I actually mean by 'literary theory'? Am I not failing to see that, if the fuss over theory is to be explained, something radically new must have emerged at the end of the 1960s which changed so many people's approaches to literature? It all depends, though, upon what is understood as the real innovation in literary theory. In his invaluable *Literary Theory*, Terry Eagleton cites the Russian Formalist Viktor Shklovsky's 1917 essay 'Art as Device' as the decisive moment in the development of what would come to be known as literary theory (Eagleton 1983 p. vii). In that essay Shklovsky attempted to establish ways of analysing literary texts which freed the reading of the text from the attempt to interpret its meaning in terms of the biography of its author, the history of the time of the text's production, or other factors beyond the text. For Shklovsky and the other Russian Formalists, the linguistic techniques in the literary text which 'de-familiarised' our habitual perceptions became the criterion of 'literariness'. By concentrating upon verifiable features of the *language* of the text this approach moved the focus of interpretation away from the idea that one is reconstructing the author's intended meaning to the idea that textual meaning is not primarily constituted at the level of the intentions of the author at all. What we understand are the words on the page, which do not require knowledge of what was intended by the person who wrote those words for them to be comprehensible: we understand via the rules and contexts of the language into which we are socialised, not by access to the inner mental acts of others. A related approach to meaning will, of course, come to be shared by the tradition of analytical philosophy which develops via Gottlob Frege, and others, parallel with the early manifestations of literary theory such as the work of Shklovsky.[3] The vital aspect of this shift in understanding for literary theory was, then, the change in the locus of meaning from author to text, a shift which also leads to attention to the role of the interpreter in the constitution of textual meaning.

In the light of the importance for the emergence of literary theory of this change of focus towards language and away from the author, it might seem to be rather stretching the point to suggest that the real founders of literary theory are the Romantic thinkers Friedrich Schlegel, Novalis (the pen-name of Friedrich von Hardenberg) and F.D.E. Schleiermacher, in their work from the 1790s onwards. This work was, of course, written before the development of the kind of linguistics supposedly capable of establishing binding norms of everyday language which Shklovsky thinks literary texts transgress. Indeed, many approaches to literary theory have seen the hermeneutic tradition which develops as part of German Roman-ticism as the source of precisely the kind of interpretation which locates meaning in the individual author qua creator of the text and therefore leads literary criticism to search for that meaning by attempting to reconstruct the contexts of the author's internal and external world. If literary theory depends upon the move *away* from this hermeneutic paradigm, why claim it begins with the early German Romantics?

The reasons for my version of the story of literary theory become clearer if one considers Shklovsky's essay from another perspective. Rather than seeing the essay predominantly in terms of linguistics and textual theory, and therefore regarding it as a prototype for structuralist and post-structuralist theories of the text, one can see its argument as really an argument about aesthetics. The 'aesthetic' aspect of the literary text can here be understood simply as that which is not bound by existing linguistic and formal rules, which is significant precisely because it is not rule-bound. The vital point is that a proper understanding of the role of aesthetics in literary theory enables one to see many aspects of the work of Derrida and others as a continuation of a tradition in modern philosophy, not as a wholly novel (let alone disreputable) way of approaching philosophy. In Russian Formalism the text takes on aesthetic status if it reveals the already known world in a new light, thereby rendering the familiar unfamiliar. The analysis of such revelation is admittedly at the level of deviation from linguistic norms, and literary theory has generally tended to rely upon particular – sometimes questionable – conceptions of language, deriving in particular from Formalism and from Saussurian linguistics. What interests me here, though, is how this revelation itself is to be understood. This is a question about the relationship of the notion of literature to aesthetics, rather than to linguistics. Underlying many of my subsequent arguments will be the premise that without this change in orientation towards the aesthetic literary theory will end up without a valid way of talking about 'literature', with consequences I shall discuss below.

Eagleton justifiably maintains that defamiliarisation is a possibility inherent in any use of language at all. This can either mean that we give up the notion of defamiliarisation as a means of reliably identifying literature, or – a point which Eagleton largely ignores – that its becoming significant in the discussion of literature may turn out not to be primarily a linguistic issue at all. Much here will turn upon what one thinks language is, and I shall spend some considerable time on this issue in the following chapters. The fact that defamiliarisation need not be understood solely in linguistic terms is evident in all kinds of aesthetic experience: for example, a painting or a piece of music can also be understood as 'defamiliarising' habitual perceptions. Linguistic defamiliarisation can therefore be seen as only one form of what Martin Heidegger termed the 'world-disclosing' capacity of art, art itself being understood as that which 'discloses' the world in new ways: in this context Manfred Frank (1989b) cites Paul Klee's dictum that art 'renders reality visible', rather than copying or representing what is known to be already there.[4] The examples of wordless music and non-representational visual art can suggest why the capacity for world-disclosure has to be understood in more than the restricted sense involved in linguistic defamiliarisation. Although we may not always be able to say exactly what it is that is revealed or articulated to us by a piece of music, that does not mean that the piece is not meaningful in some important sense. The same, as we shall see later, also applies to new metaphors, which are not amenable to definitive paraphrase. The implications of this aspect of aesthetics have too often been obscured in many existing approaches to literary theory, because of the desire to unmask what are seen as the reactionary tendencies of the understanding of art and literature in the Western bourgeois tradition. I shall argue that this evaluation of the tradition of aesthetics in modern European thought is, both in terms of progressive politics and in terms of a workable account of interpretation, a serious mistake.

Thus far we have not got much closer to a satisfactory account of what is meant by 'literature' than the suggestion that it is linked to questions about what might be meant by art. This could look more like a regression to older problems than a potentially new approach, but I want to suggest that the issues of aesthetics are still very much with us. Eagleton claims that 'There is no "essence" of literature whatsoever' (Eagleton 1983 p. 9), precisely because any use of language which deviates from established linguistic practices can be said to involve defamiliarisation. It is, he maintains, a question of ideologically interested judgement as to what counts as 'literature', a fact which is reflected in the battles over the changing membership of the 'canon' of socially and academically accepted literary works. Literature is, as such, a functional term which is used in relation to certain texts deemed to be worthy of cultural approval within a particular society or class. The vital question here, though, is how the notion of judgement itself is to be understood. Eagleton's case depends upon making a clear distinction between kinds of judgement, in which aesthetic judgements are inherently linked to ideology. The fact that all judgements – be they cognitive, moral or aesthetic – necessarily involve evaluation rightly does not trouble Eagleton. What matter are the further consequences which are drawn from the functioning of evaluation in specific historical contexts. Eagleton sees 'literature' as inextricably implicated in the legitimation of forms of social power and control, most notably those of the modern European bourgeoisie. It has no 'essence' because the functioning of these forms of social power is so diverse that the very fact of regarding 'literature' as *au-dessus de la mêlée* would, by hiding their ideological roots, actually contribute to the ideological function of those texts that are valued at certain periods under the name of literature.

However, the failure to identify literature as being 'a distinct, bounded object of knowledge' (ibid. p. 205), in the same way as, say, the chemical elements are bounded objects of knowledge, is a less persuasive argument for subsuming literature into a theory of ideology than Eagleton tries to make it. It is evidently wrong to underestimate the ideological functions of what a society or class honorifically terms 'literature'. The danger, though, is that the notion of ideology can become hopelessly vague, because any cultural artefact can be seen as functioning ideologically if it has effects on the perceptions and understandings of the members of a society. Important discriminations must therefore be made here if the notion of ideology is not to become vacuous. Eagleton's claim is that literature ties in with the existing forms of domination in the society of its origin. However, even at this level the identification, for example, of the possible stabilising ideological function of Theodor Fontane's novels in relation to fears about social unrest in the Wilhelmine period may obscure other ways in which those texts could also have subverted the dominant ideological perspectives of their time.[5] This kind of interpretative ambiguity already poses the question as to whether differing possible readings are merely ideologically at odds, or whether one of the readings may invalidate the others, because it tells us more about the work's capacity to reveal the world. It also points to the fact that one of the most vital features of a text qua literature may be that it provokes certain significant kinds of interpretative ambiguity.[6] This alone does not give us a sufficient criterion for literature – and the very notion of criterion, as I show below, may be itself problematic with regard to literature – but it is arguable that texts which retain a productive ambiguity in thoroughly differing contexts over long periods seem to be those to which the name literature is now often attached. It may be that other texts would have been equally able to do this, had they not been excluded from attention by dominant cultural valuations, but the fact that the history of culture involves the distressing waste of works of great value does not mean that the works that have the luck to survive *only* do so because they fit into dominant ideological expectations. This would anyway be a circular argument which no one could validate unless they were beyond ideology, a location which Eagleton's theory itself cannot allow.[7]

A perhaps even more important danger of Eagleton's position for a radical approach to literature is that interpretation of a text in terms of its ideological functions within its own era may render the text inert for its readers today. This can then lead to a surrendering of the text to those who wish to mobilise it for their own ideological ends. If the Left (wrongly) insist that Shakespeare was ideologically a proto-Tory, the Right will thank them for handing him over to them as a part of their heritage which can make most of the Left's approved cultural icons look puny in comparison (on this see Ryan 1995). In that case, though, what on earth should the Left do with figures like Richard Wagner? The failure to engage with the most powerful works of bourgeois culture, like those of Wagner, beyond revealing their indisputable relations to barbarism, means we do not understand why such works are enduringly powerful in ways which cannot finally be grasped by the category of ideology and which cannot be merely a function of their roots in barbarism. Although great works of art almost invariably involve aspects which must repel critics concerned with human emancipation, it is fatal to reduce them to these aspects.

Underlying such questions is the very simple question of why one is bothering with these particular works in the first place, especially when one is primarily concerned with unmasking their ideological functions. If this really is one's primary concern, one must already have judged that the works exercise such an ideological influence via their aesthetic power that the unmasking is essential. This assumption itself already seems to concede a lot to the aesthetic, in so far as the attention of radical critics to works in the 'canon' of classics either rests on the blunt fact that they are rightly or wrongly what gets read and studied, which would seem to obviate the need to worry about them so much, or upon the fact that the classics *are* somehow different, despite the ideological shadow which they also cast. Often the fact of ideological misuse is so patent, as in the reception of the work of Goethe or Hölderlin by the Nazis, that it is hardly difficult to show that it *is* misuse.[8] The fact of ideological misuse does, though, raise the vital issue of whether the revelation of that misuse is achieved from a position which is not itself merely another ideological perspective – so that one person's misuse is merely another person's use. I shall be looking at these issues in more detail later, particularly in Chapter 5, but it is important already to see the inherent complexity they involve for a radical approach to literature. The fact that Goethe's works are still important could be and sometimes is the result of their bolstering reactionary and patriarchal ideologies – think of the sexism evident in the different fates of Gretchen and Faust at the end of *Faust* Part II – but to begin with this assumption is already to lose the battle, because trying to reveal what else they have meant and may yet come to mean can then only be a secondary concern. Without an orientation towards understanding the truth-potential in art that is more than ideology, many of the most essential issues concerning the significance of art cannot even be discussed. The vital task here is to develop an account of truth which enables such issues to appear at all: this will be a constant concern in what follows.

Eagleton tends to assume that because cultural evaluations are continually being transformed they are best dealt with via the category of ideology. Hidden behind this is the assumption that 'truth' would be that which is not thus subject to continual transformation and not linked to the exercise of power, and that truth's task would be to grasp the 'essence' of the object. Eagleton cites Marx's famous dilemma, given the assumption that the stage of social and economic development of a society must relate to its degree of cultural development, over the 'eternal charm' of Greek art, suggesting that it is mistaken to see this charm as eternal, because social and cultural conditions might change and our positive judgements of Greek art might be wholly revised at some point in the future. He thus implies that our present interest in Greek art is predominantly a product of our particular culture. In one sense this is a truism: if our culture were not at least minimally interested in it we would have no access to it anyway. It may indeed turn out to be the case that Greek tragedy will become wholly distant to some future society (as it no doubt already contingently is in many already existing societies), but we do not *know* if it will, which makes Eagleton's argument mere supposition. In contrast, if one considers the real historical change in the significance of Greek tragedy in Schelling's and Nietzsche's shocking reorientation of the interpretation of tragedy away from the ideas of the Good, the True and the Beautiful towards tragedy as the expression of an inherently riven 'Dionysian' cosmos, a much more substantial basis for argument than Eagleton's questionable counterfactual suggestion is revealed.[9] In this perspective the decisive question is how these texts can undergo such a radical shift in significance, while yet remaining alive for their differing recipients.[10]

Eagleton's position here is based on a false alternative. His concern is to get away from the idea of an entity called 'great literature', which is supposed to be an expression of eternal human values, in order not to ignore the evident historical relativity and ideological interestedness of such evaluations. Consequently he deconstructs the very notion of a unified 'thing called literature' by revealing the disparate genealogy of the notion. His suspicion is primarily of literature 'in the sense of a set of works of assured and unalterable value' (Eagleton 1983 p. 11). This, though, is by no means the only way the word 'literature', which Eagleton admits is the best available term we have at present for what he is talking about, has been used. The value attached to Greek tragedy qua 'literature' has been radically *different* for differing cultures throughout history. As such the real question is why radically differing – and even wholly opposed – interpretations continue to emerge in relation to these works rather than others. This, as T.W. Adorno, Heidegger, Gadamer and others have realised, necessarily connects questions of literature to central philosophical questions concerning art and truth.

Eagleton's assertion that there is no 'essence' of literature means that there is no criterion which can reliably be employed to identify whether a text is literature or not, as opposed, say, to the concept of oxygen, which can usually be employed to establish whether a gas is oxygen or not. He invokes the notion of the 'eternally given and immutable', which, he says, cannot apply to 'literature', thereby seeing literature in relation to more reliable concepts, such as those in the natural sciences. It is, though, arguable that *no* particular knowledge is 'eternally given and immutable', because all particular knowledge continually changes its status in relation to the world within which it is understood, and inherently requires interpretation for its validity. Though we *may*, for example, mean the same as Lavoisier when we talk of oxygen, it is another matter altogether to assert that what we think oxygen is is the same as what Lavoisier thought it was (it almost certainly is not). This topic is far too complex to be dealt with appropriately here, but it is worth noting how contentious it has been in recent analytical philosophy.[11] Furthermore, in another perspective, the very lack of a stable concept of the literary can actually be used to *defend* the notion of literature rather than eliminate it.

In this view the literary text is precisely that kind of text which resists being categorised in terms of the attributes which it shares with other texts. Schleiermacher claims 'There can be no concept of a style', in the same way as Eagleton claims there can be no stable concept of literature. Schleiermacher does so, though, as we shall see in Chapter 5, in order to defend the significance of the literary. This way of talking about the literary is in one sense necessarily indeterminate: the important attributes cannot be 'identified' in the strict sense of the word, which entails subsuming those attributes under an already existing concept, or attaching the appropriate predicate to them, because they must be unique to particular texts. The sense that Kafka's style is ultimately inimitable, but yet exclusively and identifiably *his* style, is one factor in what makes his texts aesthetically significant. There are clearly problems with this position, but it does do justice to one of the most widely shared intuitions concerning literary works, namely that they are immune to paraphrase in ways that non-literary texts are not.[12] The conception suggested here does not entail establishing the 'essence' of literature, because what is a unique literary style when it emerges in the work of an author at one point in time might (and often does) subsequently become part of an established, identifiable repertoire of stylistic means. 'Literature' here becomes understood via transformations of language, not via the notion of a set of approved fixed cultural artefacts. The presence of the 'literary' is consequently not confined to certain kinds of text, but is, as Eagleton himself suggests, a possibility in any text when it reshapes linguistic and conceptual possibilities. Classification at differing historical periods of certain kinds of text as 'literature' is therefore to be understood as only one part of a wider process whose significance cannot be circumscribed by a theory of ideology. The decisive issue is *why* value comes to be attached to linguistic and formal innovation in this way, and the theories at issue here will be used to suggest answers to this question which affect much more than just the question of literature.

One alternative to this approach to the question of 'what is literature?' is to give up altogether on reflection about the nature of the literary, and simply to 'get on with the job' of literary criticism. This position, which is still the norm in many areas of literary study, seems to me to be intellectually dishonest, especially in the light of the cogent attacks, like those of Eagleton, on many of the dominant conceptions in literary study. Reflection on what literature is relates to the need constantly to show anew why literature matters: once one fails to do this and just carries on working in an established mode of literary criticism an essential dimension of the motivation for literary study can be lost. The decline of the study of literature in many modern languages subjects is not just to be explained by students' burning, career-driven interest in 'area studies', or whatever marketable alternative modern linguists have thought up to keep Philistine governments at bay. English studies have few such problems and have been given a new lease of life by the controversies generated over literary and cultural theory, and European philosophy continues to grow in popularity despite the formidable intellectual difficulties it entails. Clearly it is undesirable to become involved in meta-reflections at every point of one's work in the study of literature; it is, though, even more undesirable to pretend that established approaches to literary scholarship are self-legitimating. That is the route to the final demise of the subject which one purports to love.

In a very important sense, though, most study of literature is pointless: there is no unanimous goal towards which it is oriented. Although the most obvious point of reading literary texts would seem to be the 'pleasure of the text', for example, it is worth noting how little academic work on literature has anything convincing to say about this pleasure and how little sense of that pleasure is really allowed to penetrate into academic discourse. Scholarly journals are full of new interpretations of the classics and of a range of other texts deemed worthy of academic attention. However, the biggest *mistake* of traditional literary criticism, I would suggest, is just to assume that its goal is to establish the meaning or meanings of literary texts. Regarding this as a mistake might sound rather odd. No doubt concern about the meaning of a literary text is vital to our engagement with it, but one of the main achievements of literary theory has been to force a reconsideration of what constitutes the meaning of a text. Consider the following: if the goal of reaching the meaning of the text were to be achieved, the discipline of literary criticism could presumably abolish itself, at least in relation to those texts where there was final consensus over their meaning.[13] The traditional interpretative attitude to the text feeds upon one way in which people respond to the challenge of texts whose meaning is not immediately apparent to them, by suggesting that research, especially into the life and times of the author, can reveal what that meaning really is, or add to and deepen the initial intuitions one has about that meaning. At the same time such criticism, whose partial validity is, as far as I am concerned, incontrovertible, fails to come to terms with crucial other aspects of literary experience, such as the sense of the text's *resistance* to being clearly understood, despite its apparent meaningfulness. The notion that the latter experience ought really to be converted into the former fits the classic model of Cartesian rationalism: the critical task is understood in the form of a move from indistinct personal impressions of the text, to clear and distinct ideas which can be shown to be publicly valid by use of evidence from the text and its contexts.

Varying versions of this model have tended to and largely still do form one important basis of literary studies as an academic discipline.[14] The easiest way to see what might be wrong with the model is to ponder what it is supposed to do with the recalcitrant elements of a modernist text, such as a Kafka short story (on this issue see Menke 1991, Bowie 1992b). If the recalcitrant elements can be definitively interpreted in discursive language, then the point of the critical task would seem to be a game of 'hide and seek the meaning', which comes to an end when the interpreter has found the real meaning cowering behind the cellar door of the text. At this point the literary text is safely rendered into discursivity, but, of course, thereby becomes thoroughly pointless, because we no longer need the literary text itself to communicate what it really means. Now, as we shall see in the following chapters, the notion of pointlessness is vital to aesthetics, but *this* kind of pointlessness would obviate art altogether.[15] The 'Cartesian' model is historically very recent and is in some measure the result of the perceived need for humanities subjects to reach the level of rigour that was assumed to be present in the natural sciences, an attitude which, as we shall see in Chapter 6, is associated with Wilhelm Dilthey. Furthermore, the obvious fact about the 'Cartesian' approach to texts is that it can be applied to any text of any kind, which actually leads it into a strange convergence with Eagleton's position.

The radical alternative to the complacency of the literary critical consensus is the complete renunciation, in the manner of Eagleton, of the notion of literature, based on the fact that most existing attempts to give an adequate account of what literature is end up in the kind of difficulties he so effectively reveals. Interestingly, the traditional critic tends to end up agreeing with Eagleton despite himself, because he does not in fact possess a defensible way of approaching the literary. The traditionalist claim that the interpretation of 'forms, structures, images, allusions, symbols, conventions and their transgression', which are the 'means that literature has developed to offset or bypass any limitations of the bare linguistic medium'[16] (Reed 1992 p. 209), is the object of literary study must first deal with the problem that the elements to be interpreted are not particular to literature. Indeed, ancient rhetoric requires attention to almost exactly the same elements – Eagleton suggests that a new version of rhetoric is one of the directions in which the study of literature should move once it has ceased to be solely about privileged texts. Reed insists that we do not need philosophy to carry on literary study, but he locates that study in relation to a range of topics which are the bread and butter of a whole series of philosophically oriented disciplines: the establishing of the conventions which literature transgresses was, as we have already seen, a product of the particular conception of linguistics which fed Russian Formalism, and helped form the basis of structuralist textual theory. Do we, then, give up the notion of literature after all, because it can either be subsumed into ideology or because there are no actual criteria on offer to show us what it is? It should already be plain that I think this renunciation of the term is a significant mistake, which derives from a characteristic misunderstanding of the role of aesthetics in modern philosophy. Both the dominant literary critical consensus and Eagleton's view can be most appropriately questioned by reinterpreting aspects of the German tradition in the light of issues which have become apparent in contemporary theory.

For many people, the worrying aspect of my position will lie in its reliance upon a notion of judgement which makes no claims to the kind of certainty that could be achieved either by arriving at more stable definitions, relying on well-established criteria of literary criticism, or by seeing literature as simply a subset of other ideological formations. In this context it is important to see, however, that much recent philosophy, both European and analytical, has increasingly moved away from the idea that there are fixed boundaries between areas of judgement, towards the idea that all claims to validity inherently involve interpretation. These strands of contemporary philosophy thereby echo issues from the origins of German literary theory. Kant already regarded the question of judgement as perhaps the most important issue in our very understanding of truth in any area, not just in relation to literature or other art. In his later work he did so particularly with regard to aesthetic judgements, thereby setting in motion one of the main traditions of German literary theory. Issues from this tradition, from Romanticism to Heidegger and the Frankfurt School, to the present, will form the object of the following chapters. The fact is that Romantic philosophy initiates a vital but often misunderstood transformation in modern philosophy, which is linked to the development of Romantic philosophy's particular notion of literature. Both Eagleton's theory and the literary critical approach cannot adequately articulate this notion of literature, which can be used to open up new perspectives on themes that have re-emerged in recent literary theory.

THE ROMANTIC HERITAGE

What, then, does the Romantic approach offer which the other positions we have so far looked at do not? Eagleton regards Shklovsky's founding essay as particularly significant because it moved literary study away both from the categories of 'creativity' and 'imagination', and from the notion that literature 'represents' the social world, towards the study of linguistic techniques and to a conception which does not regard literature as the representation, the 'copying' or 'imitation' in language, of a world constituted in the mind of the individual author or reader. He thinks this move revokes the legitimacy of theories of literature that are attached to the ideas of representation and imagination, in favour of a theory of ideology and rhetoric. The theory of ideology links the production and reception of literature to wider collective political and social questions; the theory of rhetoric concerns itself with the pragmatic effects which texts, as 'discursive practices', can have in historical and social contexts. Such a move away from the 'imagination' might seem to make my projected story even less convincing, in so far as creativity and imagination are evidently central to Romantic thought. It is, though, a mistake to think that the everyday understanding of these terms exhausts what they meant in Romantic theory.

A central aim of early German Romantic thought was to bring together in a new synthesis the increasingly specialised knowledges that were developing in both the natural and the human sciences at the end of the eighteenth century. This synthesis would counter the increasing divergence of these particular knowledges by integrating them into a world-view in which the activities of free human beings and the law-bound nature investigated by the sciences were not rigidly opposed. The Romantic synthesis was to replace the discredited scholastic and early Enlightenment picture of a world whose unity was a priori divinely guaranteed. The work of art, understood as the manifestation of a unification of necessity and freedom not possible in any other realm of human activity, played a vital role in Romantic approaches to such a synthesis.[17] This, however, already points to one of Eagleton's major contentions against Romantic thought. The emergence in this period of the idea of a realm of human activity which unites necessity and freedom would seem inherently ideological, because that realm will fail to confront the real antagonisms in the society which gave rise to it, in which the most basic forms of freedom are denied to most of the members of that society – we are talking, after all, about the world which drove many of its most socially and politically aware members to despair, madness or suicide. In the Romantic conception art can be regarded as reconciling in the realm of appearance what is unreconciled in reality, and thus as a form of ideology.[18] Art does so, though, because it grants freedom to the imagination, allowing it to move beyond the world of what there is to a world of as yet unrealised possibility. There is therefore, in the strict sense of the word, a 'utopian' aspect involved in the understanding of art.[19]

Understanding this utopian aspect of art prevents a one-way interpretation of art as ideology. The initial question here is whether one regards the work of the imagination as merely a substitute for something more solid or 'real'. Clearly the imagination can produce omnipotence fantasies of the kind manifested in the worst of Hollywood: that the imagination is the prime object of ideological manipulation is beyond question. But consider the following: if there were no realm in which images of an as yet non-existent freedom became available to the oppressed in a society it would become hard to see how any hope for a better world could even be *understood*. The fact is that the argument that art merely reinforces the ideological superstructure is essentially the same as the 'Young Hegelian' argument, common to both Feuerbach and the early Marx, that religion is an obstacle to real social progress because it offers images of a non-existent after-life. Religion and art are in this view providers of only apparent solutions to real problems – which is, of course, also the function of mythology. In this respect the Romantic enthusiasm for art has generally – and in some senses rightly – been understood as part of the attempts to fill gaps left by the process of secularisation and rationalisation in Western societies.

It is crucial, though, to understand the complexity of the decline of theology, and the relationship to art of that decline. Even Marx did not see religion in a one-sided manner: the 'opium of the people' is a real and justifiable necessity when the pain of life is intolerable and cannot immediately be redeemed. Furthermore, the power of theology as a source of meaning is not obliterated when belief in God comes to be undermined. Indeed, one can argue that much of the Marxist tradition, particularly that current which leads, via Romanticism, from the early Marx to the work of Adorno, Ernst Bloch and Benjamin, is actually concerned with trying to come to terms with the demise of theology while not surrendering the resources offered by the theological tradition for human emancipation. Jürgen Habermas, the most distinguished contemporary heir of this tradition, has recently insisted that

> As long as religious language brings with it inspiring, indeed indispensable semantic contents, which (for the time being?) withdraw themselves from the power of expression of philosophical language and still await translation into discourses of legitimation (*begründende Diskurse*), philosophy will, even in its post-metaphysical form, neither be able to replace or repress religion. (Habermas 1988 p. 60)

By connecting this conception of religious language to the question of aesthetics and literature we can better begin to understand what is at stake in Romantic philosophy. The semantic contents of those forms of language which are not reducible to any other type of discourse are precisely what is at issue in the Romantic conception of art. Stanley Cavell has suggested that 'the activity of modern art, both in production and reception, is to be understood in categories which are, or were, religious' (Cavell 1969 p. 175): the failure to understand how this is the case is one root of many of the invalid attempts to reduce literature to ideology.

Romantic thought, as we shall see, was driven by the insights of Kant's philosophy and by an understanding of language which was linked to the emergence of interest in the integrity and diversity of other cultures characteristic of the second half of the eighteenth century in Europe. As well as expressing fears both about the dangers inherent in the rise of deterministic conceptions of the natural world, of the kind summarised in the title of La Mettrie's book *Man the Machine*, and about the processes of rationalisation in society that form part of the rise of capitalism, this opening of perspectives on to the diversity of human languages also related to the increasingly rapid death of the rigid ideologies of feudalism, including the ideology of established religion. The resultant theory was often eclectic, refusing to accept definitive boundaries between apparently differing intellectual spheres. This was both its strength and its weakness: sometimes the imaginative creation of analogies between differing areas of knowledge took over completely from scientific or other kinds of validation.[20] At the same time the use of analogy and metaphor to connect apparently disparate phenomena did lead to real scientific advances and to ideas which still command our attention. Even at this level of generality the links of Romantic theory to aspects of literary theory should begin to be apparent. The combination of aesthetics and new approaches to language leads to a loosening of rigid demarcations between areas of knowledge. It is this reorientation of established approaches to knowledge which makes both literary theory and Romantic philosophy so controversial.[21]

Literary theory is itself a hybrid rather than a unified discipline, combining resources from philosophy, linguistics, psychoanalysis, feminism, social theory and other areas of the humanities, in order to question basic assumptions about the understanding of texts and other bearers of truth and meaning in both the human and the natural sciences. Like Romantic philosophy, literary theory can be understood as part of a growing reaction against the separation of the everyday 'life world' from the systemically determined spheres of science, technology and modern bureaucracy. By crossing boundaries between subjects it attempts to reveal the repressions involved in the specialisation of knowledge into discrete cultures of experts. The fact that objections of the kind made to Romantic thinking have resurfaced in recent objections to literary theory can further suggest ways in which they are closely related. The fundamental attribute which Romantic philosophy shares with literary theory is, then, a questioning of the borders between differing disciplines, including those between the humanities and the sciences.

By reducing the theory of literature to a theory of ideology Eagleton's version of the story of literary theory pays too little attention to questions of aesthetics which emerge in the Romantic re-examination of knowledge in all spheres that results from the decline of traditional theology. For Eagleton, 'literature' becomes, as we saw, one of the ways in which a particular social class attempts to make its own self-legitimation into the universal form of legitimation, a trait it shares with the dominant bourgeois conceptions of other forms of high art.[22] For the Romantics literature and art are actually linked to a much more complex sense of the nature and value of human knowledge than Eagleton's theory can countenance.

THE TRUTH OF LITERATURE

If the tension between the conception of the text as bearer of the ideology of its class and era, and the conception of the text as a work of art which, because of its claim to truth, cannot be reduced to its ideological functions is not sustained, a whole dimension of our understanding of the significance of modern art and literature in relation to other forms of knowledge and expression becomes obscured. Perhaps the most significant dimension of the theory we shall be considering, which plays virtually no role at all in Eagleton's account, is, therefore, the emergence via Romantic theory of the idea that works of art are bearers of truth. For this to be the case a change away from the notion of truth as 'representation', as the adequacy or correspondence of mental concept or proposition to its object, a notion which probably dates back at least as far as Aristotle, must take place. This change in the concept of truth is linked to the move away from a conception of art as mimesis towards the idea of art as a revelation or 'disclosure' of the world. In a representational theory of truth a statement is true because it corresponds to the way the world already is 'out there', which means that what is true pre-exists its being able to be said that it is true. The difficulty of sustaining this conception lies in the fact that we have no obvious warrant for claiming that the truth of a proposition already exists in this way, without begging the question as to what makes the proposition true by pre-supposing the conception which is at issue in the first place. The move away from representational conceptions creates a tension in the modern notion of truth which underlies many of the debates over truth and ideology in Marxism and elsewhere, and which has become important in various areas of contemporary philosophy, both European and analytical. I want to argue that without a proper understanding of this tension literary theory is likely to continue pursuing some paths which are already proving to be dead ends. By attending to this tension in the history of Western philosophy literary theory can and should be led closer to the wider discussion which is developing between the analytical and European traditions of philosophy. The further benefit of this approach to these issues is that it gives one much stronger methodological legitimations for the study of literature, by suggesting that truth is not that which is confined to the verifiable and instrumentally applicable sciences. At the same time such an approach will acknowledge that the *academic* study of literature can only be more substantially legitimated by its being brought into new contact with other disciplines: although the aesthetic reasons for reading literature seem to me in many senses the vital reasons, it is questionable whether they alone prove the case for the necessity of an *academic* study of literature.

In order to elucidate what is at issue here let us, then, very briefly and schematically consider two paradigmatic modern notions of truth, one from analytical philosophy and the other from the hermeneutic tradition.[23] A central task in analytical philosophy has been the clarification of the status of propositions. This clarification has often been undertaken via the exploration of what is entailed by the convention of the logician Alfred Tarski that '"Snow is white" is true if and only if snow is white' (which is also often couched in the form '"*Schnee ist weiß*" is true if and only if snow is white', in order to suggest how truth is possible between differing natural languages). Removing the quotation marks from 'Snow is white' points to the relationship between a sentence (the words 'Snow is white' or '*Schnee ist weiß*') and the conditions under which it is held to be true (its being the case that snow is white). This kind of analysis is, in some versions at least, concerned with how our everyday use of assertions functions via what Donald Davidson, the most significant contemporary theorist of truth in analytical philosophy, has called our 'general and pre-analytic notion of truth' (Davidson 1984 p. 223), the notion which we require both for everyday communication and for the most sophisticated scientific theories. For Davidson, understanding what it is that makes 'Snow is white' true is understanding its meaning, the two being basically identical.[24]

An important part of the hermeneutic tradition which derives from Romanticism, on the other hand, takes an apparently very different tack by linking truth to art, via the claim that art reveals the world in ways which would not be possible without the existence of art itself – a version of this view can be ascribed to Schlegel, Novalis, Schleiermacher, Heidegger, Benjamin, Adorno and Gadamer. This view is connected to a very different conception of language, which begins to develop with Rousseau and Herder. Truth is here seen in terms of the capacity of forms of articulation to 'disclose' the world. However, the conceptions of truth as warranted assertability and truth as revelation or 'disclosure' are, despite appearances, not wholly separable. Once this is established many of the major themes in recent theoretical discussion begin to look different. Heidegger suggested the link of the two conceptions of truth in his demonstration that the ability to make assertions must be preceded by the 'disclosure' of the state of affairs that is to be asserted. Wittgenstein's famous example of the 'duck-rabbit' drawing can, for example, be seen as lines on paper, or as a duck, or as a rabbit. There is no one answer to 'what it is', and one could easily see it as something other than these three obvious descriptions. The truth 'disclosed' in the proposition that 'This is x' does not consist for Heidegger in that proposition's correspondence to a direct apprehension of 'objective' reality – the apprehension of lines, or a rabbit, or a duck – but rather in its expressing a state of affairs in which something is understood *as* something. It is in this dimension of understanding, which is not a registering of pre-existing truth-determinate objects 'out there' in the world independent of what we say about them, that the potential aesthetic aspect of our relationship to language becomes apparent. The structure of 'seeing-as' is fundamental both to knowledge claims in the sciences, and to the experience of literary or other art works, because it is the basis of how the contents of our inner and outer world become articulated.[25] What something is 'seen as' is historically variable, in ways which cannot be circumscribed by a definitive scientific description of what the thing 'really is'. This approach begins to suggest good theoretical reasons why 'literature' might continue to be a major source of the ways in which we make sense of the world, a fact that has, for example, become increasingly important in recent work in the history of science. Once one moves away from the presupposition that there is a final fact of the matter 'out there', the question of interpretation, of how we understand the world through language, becomes the crucial issue.

The relationship between the propositional and the aesthetic conceptions of truth becomes particularly interesting when linked to the attempt to establish a workable notion of literature. A vital aspect of the history of modern art can most effectively suggest the dimension missing from Eagleton's analysis in *Literary Theory* (which is also largely absent from his subsequent book on aesthetics). Perhaps the most important artistic devel-

opment linked to German Romantic theory was the change in the status
of music, the least representational form of art, from being regarded as a
subordinate form of art to being regarded as the highest form of art.[26] The
rise of the idea of 'absolute music', music which does not accompany a text
and does not require a text, and the emergence of a workable conception
of literature are simultaneous phenomena in Germany at the end of the
eighteenth century.[27] Questions concerning music's relationship to ideology
are therefore clearly linked to ambiguities concerning the aesthetic status
of literature. In Thomas Mann's *The Magic Mountain* Settembrini, the
democratic rationalist and admirer of 'literature' as a vehicle of progressive
ideology, is ironically presented as suggesting that music is 'what is half-
articulated, dubious, irresponsible, indifferent'. Even when music is 'clear'
it is not, Settembrini claims,

> real clarity, it is a dreamy, insignificant clarity which does not commit
> one to anything. . . . I have a political aversion to music. . . . Music is
> invaluable as the last means of arousing enthusiasm, as a power which
> drags one upwards and forwards, if it finds the mind prepared for its
> effects. But literature must precede it. Music alone will not move the
> world forwards. Music alone is dangerous. . . . I am not exaggerating if I
> declare it to be politically suspect. (Mann 1972 pp. 120–1)

Settembrini's suspicions are echoed in Eagleton's desire to be rid of
an aesthetic notion of literature in favour of a theory of discursive practices,
and in Eagleton's claim that the alternative to his approach leads to a
reactionary mystification of our understanding of language in literary texts.
Now music is clearly not inherently an ideology-free means of articulation,
as Adorno, despite his belief in the centrality of great music for understanding the underlying truth of developments in modern society, will make
very clear. There is already an ideological dimension, even to wordless
music, when it repeats, rather than transforms, the patterns of music produced solely for commercial and functional ends, or when the manner of
performance, including of great music, leads to the mere creation of effect,
rather than to the illumination of the work. This suggests, though, how
important it is to be able to judge the ideological as of a different order
from what is aesthetically valid. Eagleton's desire to abandon the notion
of literature begins to look more problematic when, as it is in Romantic
theory, literature is linked to music.

Music clearly shares certain attributes with verbal language, consisting
in the articulation of sounds (or inscriptions) in patterns, according to
underlying (but shifting) rules whose exact status seems elusive. Furthermore, music has a capacity to affect how we see something: the example of
film music most obviously illustrates this. The music which accompanies a
scene in a film can do more than transform the mood of what is shown: it can
actually change what we see. The decisive difference between music and
verbal language is usually established at the level of semantics: music lacks

'meaning'. Meaning is, of course, a notoriously difficult term to define, but one recent (if questionable) definition of meaning can help make a basic point clear. Richard Rorty, claiming to follow aspects of Donald Davidson's theory seen above, usefully summarises some of the recent discussions in American philosophy by defining meaning as 'the property which one attributes to words by noting standard inferential connections between the sentences in which they are used and other sentences' (Rorty 1991a p. 13), so that 'Snow is white' will tend to occur when other sentences of a certain kind recur. The crucial aspect of this definition here is that 'meaning' is not constituted by standard relationships of words to objects – of the kind where the word 'table' 'represents' the object out there upon which my computer is sitting – because what an object is *said* to be depends upon discriminations within language itself, rather than upon already existing discriminations in an objective world.[28] The idea should also be familiar from recent literary theory, where it generally derives from Saussurian linguistics, which maintains that the relationship of word to object is not a relationship between pre-existing entity and signifier, because the *determinacy* of differentiations between entities (but, one should add, not necessarily the differentiations themselves) depends upon linguistic differentiations.[29]

Rorty uses his sense of 'meaning' to claim that the creativeness evident in literature is just a special case of the

> ability of the human organism to utter meaningless sentences – that is, sentences which do not fit into old language games, and serve as occasions for modifying those language-games and creating new ones. This ability is exercised constantly in every area of culture and daily life.
>
> (Rorty 1991b p. 125)

He does not, though, offer us any kind of explanation as to *how* it is that meaningless utterances can take on meaning. This problem relates in part to his exclusion of the subject from meaning-creation, an exclusion which I shall consider in other thinkers in the following chapters. It also relates to questions concerning the very ability of philosophy to give a definitive account of any aspect of language. Hilary Putnam has, for example, pointed out that Rorty's 'dichotomizing human thought into speech within "criterion governed language games" and speech "outside" language games' (Putnam 1995 p. 64) offends against Rorty's own claims to be a pragmatist by introducing an essentially metaphysical distinction between kinds of language: from what location is one to judge what is within and what is outside the language game? Davidson, whose conception Rorty claims to be developing, has himself suggested that all language (not just metaphors) can in fact 'make us notice' things in ways which are not analysable in terms of the conception of meaning seen in Tarski's convention. In the convention the meaning of the utterance is circumscribed in the act of understanding whether it is true, whereas what the statement

'Snow is white' can make us notice cannot be thus circumscribed. In the present context the statement may make us notice things about the functioning of statements in diverse contexts, for example, rather than telling us about the properties of snow.

The function of 'making us notice' can, of course, also be attributed to music, which is able to make us notice things in much the same ways as language, and whose 'meaning' cannot be semantically determined.[30] The interesting historical fact is that the relationship of language to music becomes particularly significant once the idea that language primarily represents objects in the world begins to be abandoned. This move – away from the notion of language as representation[31] – can be clearly located at the beginning of what is now usually termed 'modernity', around the middle of the eighteenth century.[32] The change in the understanding of language which takes place during this period is obviously linked to the decline of theological views of the world, in which language, to put it crudely, was regarded as God's naming of the furniture of the universe. Michel Foucault argues in *The Order of Things*, for example, that a shift in the nature of language occurs in Europe at the beginning of the nineteenth century, such that 'words cease to intersect with representations' (Foucault 1970 p. 304. On this see also Bowie 1989, and 1990 Chapter 7). Significantly, although Foucault does not link this shift to music, he does link it to the rise both of 'literature' and of modern philology. Literature and philology are, for Foucault, the dialectical opposites of each other: for there to be literature there must, he claims, be that which attempts to explain language, a science of language. The perceived need for such a science clearly becomes more pressing when the theological understanding of language loses credibility. Literature therefore becomes the realm of language which 'arises for its own sake' and which is not bound to representation. The notion of language which 'arises for its own sake' already shows how this conception of language is connected to the wider issue of aesthetics, which from Kant onwards involves the idea of the object which is valuable for its own sake, as opposed to being valuable in terms of its abstract commodity value. Kant's setting the agenda of modern aesthetics is, of course, contemporaneous with the rise of Foucault's 'literature'.

In this light the Russian Formalist criterion of the literary can be seen as the result of an attempt to marry a scientific analysis of language, which provides rules for discriminating between kinds of language – the realm of Rorty's 'meaning' – with an aesthetic understanding of language, which points to usages that cannot be subsumed under existing rules. The proximity of Foucault's description of literature to a description of music is fairly obvious. In this view literature also enacts the problem inherent in language's attempt to circumscribe itself in a science. If literary language involves the creation of new, previously 'unheard' meanings, language cannot be finally describable. For it to be thus describable would require new meanings already to exist prior to their articulation, leaving the problem of how one could assert that they do so exist without just invalidly assuming that they do. It is this realisation which has led Davidson more recently to suggest that there is no such thing as a language 'if a language is anything like what many philosophers and linguists have supposed' (Lepore 1986 p. 446) – i.e. an already existing entity which can be theoretically circumscribed, as opposed to being the endlessly changing praxes of real speakers. The consequences of the realisation that words cannot be said to intersect with things are, then, vital both to literary theory and to contemporary philosophy. Foucault's account offers one way of looking at a fundamental issue in modern thought, namely the tension between the attempt to explain the functioning of language in a science of language and the awareness that such an explanation involves the necessary circularity of using language to explain itself. This tension, I will contend, is at the heart of the development of the modern idea of literature.

The importance of the necessary circularity entailed in language's self-explanation can be suggested by a later example, which has undoubted links to Romantic philosophy. The 'linguistic turn', the turn towards language, rather than the mind, as the primary object of philosophical investigation, which is usually seen as the product of the twentieth century, is a consequence of central aspects of Romantic philosophy. Wittgenstein actually claimed in the *Tractatus* that language *is* able to represent reality (a view he was later to repudiate). He goes on to add, though: 'The proposition can represent the whole of reality [thus of the 'sayable'] but it cannot represent what it must have in common with reality in order to represent it' (Wittgenstein 1961 p. 50). To achieve this representation one would have to place oneself 'outside the world' (ibid.). If the world is mirrored by or in language, what guarantees *outside* of language that the reflection is really of the world? Nothing that can be said – *in* language – could *identify* what is *beyond* language as identically reflected in language. The conceptions of language as re-presentation of the world which preceded this realisation about (or change in?) the nature of language relied on an explicit or unconsciously theological link between word and object, in which the object is given a name by God or derives its name from a Platonic realm of essences, the *universalia ante res* ('universals which precede the things' – the Platonic table, for example, as opposed to the one in front of me). If this link is broken, radically new ways of understanding language become inevitable, which must take new account of the constitutive role of language in the worlds people make for themselves. One of the new ways of understanding language that emerged at the end of the eighteenth century linked attempts to grasp language to a form of language which was semantically indeterminate: to music. Semantic indeterminacy can be interpreted either as rendering a form of articulation inferior, as primitive cries or animal cries are usually taken to be, or as pointing to a higher form of expression *beyond* semantically determinate language. It was the latter conception which played the vital role in Romantic philosophy. If language cannot finally say how it relates to the world, a means of articulated expression such as music takes on a new significance, because it may tell us what verbal language cannot – either by complementing what verbal language can do or by enabling something to be understood in a non-verbal manner. It is at this point that probably the most defensible modern notion of literature, which regards it as that which tries to 'say the unsayable', becomes possible. The implications of this perhaps rather mystical sounding conception of 'literature' will be considered in the following chapters, where it will become evident that a series of major philosophical issues emerge from it.

The conception of language at issue here depends, then, on those aspects of verbal language which have no 'meaning'. If 'meaning' requires inference from standard contexts, those uses of language which do not allow such inference because they do not fit into standard contexts do not have 'meaning' in Rorty's particular sense. The most obvious examples of such lack of 'meaning' are new metaphors, which rely upon unfamiliar combinations of the familiar. We understand the individual words and the syntax in a metaphor like Schopenhauer's 'a geometrical proof is a mousetrap' (an example discussed by Max Black and Donald Davidson) but we cannot give a definitive analysis of what it means.[33]

The underlying question here – which has played a major role in the controversies over the work of Derrida – is whether determinacy of meaning is given priority over those aspects of language which are not determinable. The mistake of those who think concentration on indeterminacy – or, better, undecidability – is a move towards mere linguistic anarchy lies in their failure to see that the relationship is always being re-negotiated between the relatively stable elements of everyday language – 'meanings' – which make possible the functioning of social life by solving problems and co-ordinating action, and the metaphorical, 'world-disclosing' aspect of language. One of the main loci of that process of negotiation is our modern understanding of 'literature' and its relationship to other kinds of articulation, such as music. The most significant aesthetic theorists in the German tradition attempt to find ways of understanding the relationships between those aspects of articulation which can be determined in a stable manner in terms of their truth-value, and those which cannot be thus determined, but which still play an essential role in the constitution of the worlds we inhabit. The shift in the understanding of language outlined above depends upon the awareness of the freedom that results when the notion of language as representation of a pre-existing fixed reality is rejected. It is this perceived freedom which gives rise to the modern conception of literature, of language which can rewrite rules and thereby open up new aspects of the world.

The capacity of literary discourse to rewrite the rules crucially also extends to the formal constitution of the work, whose very aesthetic status is often regarded as being dependent upon its ability to establish its own rules, upon its 'aesthetic autonomy' qua work of art.[34] Adorno suggests how this change in the status of language is essential to the question of literature:

> No word which becomes part of a literary work completely gets rid of the meanings which it has in communicative speech, but in no literary work, not even in the traditional novel, does this meaning remain untransformed and the same as the word had outside the work. Even the simple 'was' in a report of something that was not gains a new formal quality (*Gestaltqualität*) by the fact that it was not. (Adorno 1965 p. 111)

From what we saw earlier it can be argued, as does Eagleton, that any word in any text has its significance transformed by its context. Once again, though, merely registering this fact threatens to level the kinds of discrimination that a proper account of judgement should be most concerned to preserve. Eagleton pays too little attention to the extent to which great literary works involve much more diverse ways of transforming meaning than other texts. This is again a matter of degree, but differences of degree are the basis of forms of judgement in any realm, as I have already suggested. Giving a theoretical account of the difference between a literary text and a non-literary text is difficult, and depends upon interpretative evaluation which may not achieve consensus. A view which thinks consensus over such evaluation is inherently doomed to failure is, as I shall show in Chapter 5, the product of a creeping positivism that only wishes to allow cognitive validity to judgements that supposedly do not require interpretative consensus.

What we usually term literary form, which can, to take only a very few elements, be the rhythmic patterns of the sentences – rhythm in the sense of repetition of signifying elements of any kind, be they semantic or musical – the distribution of line or paragraph lengths, or a whole variety of larger-scale structural echoes, is no doubt made up of aspects inherent in all language, but the crucial factor is how the new forms of combination give rise to something which, although it may not be the integrated organic totality of some Romantic conceptions of the work of art, is more than the sum of the particular aspects of the text. Furthermore, it is at the level of the irreducible particularity of the organisation of great works that form is most significant, precisely because it cannot be reduced to general rules.

Discussion of literary form is notoriously contentious, because identification of formal constituents of a work depends upon the vagaries of interpretation: in this sense there are as many formal aspects of a work as there are different interpretations of that work. While such interpretations are always open to revision, this fact is only a problem for those who raise the mythical standard of hard data that are independent of interpretation, a standard whose validity is increasingly impossible to defend. The question is, then, not *whether* one can, but *how* one interprets the significance of formal aspects of a text, a question which relates to the status of the text qua work of art. Clearly mere formal coherence is not what is at issue: the most tedious form of regular verse will provide this. Adorno's point is that it is in relation to works where existing meanings are most decisively transformed, indeed to the point of the *destruction* of those meanings, that the significance of form really becomes apparent: clearly this is more the case in late Hölderlin than in a regular sonnet by a minor poet.

Underlying Adorno's argument is a vital aspect of Romantic aesthetics already encountered above: the essential model for his conception of aesthetic form is Viennese classical music, itself a product of the period in which the conception of literature at issue here was first articulated. Adorno's insistence on the notion of the autonomous work of art, an insistence that is – mainly because of the inherently non-representational aspect of music – easier to defend in the case of music than of literature, is the precondition of his notion of form. The point of aesthetic autonomy is that the configuration of the elements of the work brings about an irreducible transformation of those elements, which are therefore regarded as bound only by their own law. The literary text can in this respect also become the locus, not of the constitution of new meaning, but of the manifestation of language's capacity to resist conversion into 'meaning'. This fact is vital in understanding why questioning the nature of literature is important at more than a merely theoretical level. The history of modernist literature (and other arts) has often been seen as a continual negotiation with 'nonsense', because radical new articulation may be either revelatory of new sense or actually devoid of any explicable sense at all. The proximity to nonsense of modernist literature is, of course, a further way in which literature becomes connected to music.

At the most basic level music qua acoustic phenomenon consists, like language, of series of differentiated frequencies, of the kind which also occur in nature. Both musical and verbal forms are built up out of elements which have moved from being merely occurrent to being significant, and have been subsequently reshaped in traditions of musical praxis and verbal communication which necessarily involve sedimented elements of already existing significance. The use of received forms in new contexts is inherently an aspect of all forms of art from the very beginning of the history of art, as the work of Mikhail Bakhtin and others has demonstrated. The specifically modern awareness of language at issue here, in which meaning comes to be understood as transformable by re-contextualisation, rather than as ultimately residing in the divinity, or some other fixed order, allows one to construct a bridge between differing forms of modern art. Links between literature and music cease to be mere analogies if the borderline between language and music is made more permeable. When, for example, Brahms (in his First Symphony) and Bruckner (in his Fifth) suddenly interpolate a Lutheran chorale into the climax of the conclusion of the work, one kind of potential significance, the liturgical significance of the chorale, is transformed into something else, which has then to be understood via the context of its occurrence. When Alban Berg later uses a Bach chorale in his violin concerto the intervening changes in music make the interpolation signify differently again. Interpreting the significance of the musical element from the past necessarily leads into the realm of metaphor, because there cannot be a definitive account of what the mixture of existing, historically significant, material and a new context 'really means': the new context uses the old material as part of its novelty. It is at this level that the significance of aesthetic autonomy and its links to the question of literature become most obviously apparent.

The above example can itself be used as a metaphor for the functioning of language in literary texts: it involves a version of what has come to be referred to as 'intertextuality', the inherent dependence of texts upon preceding texts. The difference of literary intertextuality from the everyday repetition of historically sedimented linguistic praxes in differing contexts is never absolute, and the significance of what difference there is depends upon interpretative judgement. This dependence is, though, precisely the aspect of literary theory which has so far often been neglected, on the basis of some of the assumptions I wish to question in this book. The mistake of much literary theory which works with notions like intertextuality has been to stress the dependence of the text on the already existing resources of other texts while failing adequately to characterise the aesthetic transformations brought about by the new formal configuration of those resources. It is the reconfiguration of existing linguistic elements to release new semantic potential, or to destroy existing meanings, that makes literature a vital fact in the self-understanding of modernity, not the fact that all texts are parasitic upon other already existing texts. The condition of possibility of 'literature' is, then, connected to the fact that even the most sophisticated semantic theory is unable to account for the transformation of meanings brought about by the recontextualisation of words in a text.[35]

The fact that there is no stable boundary between transformed and untransformed meanings, thus between Adorno's 'communication' or Rorty's 'meaning', and those aspects of a text which refuse communication in terms of established meanings is only a problem for those who think that the only kind of judgement that is 'real' has to be fitted into a theory which can be validated empirically in terms of already established concepts. Novalis makes the striking statement, whose theoretical consequences will be examined in the following chapters, that 'Criticism of literature (*Poesie*) is an absurdity. It is already difficult to decide, yet the only possible decision, whether something is literature or not' (Novalis 1978 p. 840). There is no fixed concept for such a decision, and it may be that works cease to be literature if their semantic potential or their resistance to interpretation becomes exhausted – think, for example, of some of the now clearly dead nineteenth-century realist novels. However, if one accepts that the crucial aspect of the literary is its irreducibility to conceptuality, then Novalis' insistence on such judgement – what he terms the 'aesthetic imperative' – makes the notion of literature as a source of truth a vital philosophical issue.

Before we embark on the account of some of the ways in which these issues have manifested themselves in modern German philosophy and literary theory, it is important to remind ourselves what is really at stake in the debates over the status of literature in modernity. The process of secularisation which gives rise to the new conceptions of language and art in question here is also, as Nietzsche, Max Weber and many others will suggest, a process of 'disenchantment' of reality, which can and does lead to the threat of complete meaninglessness or 'nihilism'. The differing ways in which literature and other art in the modern period confront the dangers of meaninglessness which are an inherent part of the post-theological world are mirrored in the differing approaches to literary theory from the Romantics to post-structuralism. The particular political and historical involvement of the thinkers to be considered here, such as Heidegger's membership of the NSDAP, and the links of other theorists such as Benjamin and Adorno to political opposition to Nazism and to the ravages of modern capitalism, can connect the theoretical issues to central questions about the direction of the modern world, thereby rendering consideration of 'literary theory' vital to a whole series of other interpretative and cognitive disciplines, from history to social theory. The crucial linking factor will be the understanding of the relationship between truth and art.

Even in a book as extensive as this one, there will necessarily be major omissions: I shall only mention one here. For a variety of reasons I have not included a chapter on Nietzsche. One reason is that the whole book is in a way directed against some of the more extreme Nietzschean conceptions of truth that have fed into certain areas of literary theory. I have already suggested in the Conclusion of Bowie (1993) that the Nietzschean critique of truth is only startling if one assumes that all previous versions of truth are correspondence theories: this book shows that suspicion of the notion of correspondence was already part of philosophy at the end of the eighteenth century. At his best Nietzsche does come close to some of the approaches I try to show here are the central aspects of Romantic thought. At his worst, though, he becomes a crass reductionist (see Bowie 1990 Chapter 8), and sometimes worse than that. My further major reason for not devoting a whole chapter to Nietzsche is personal: I actually think he is overrated. Nietzsche may indeed be the most influential thinker of modernity, but he is also one of the most hectoring, derivative, self-obsessed and generally reactionary modern theorists to put pen to paper. In short, this book simply wants to suggest that there are more interesting theorists out there, who may now have more to offer than Nietzsche.

1 Philosophical origins
Kant, Jacobi, and the crisis of reason

NEW FRAMEWORKS

It is increasingly apparent that we lack an appropriate archaeology of contemporary 'literary theory'. This chapter will begin to establish aspects of such an archaeology by investigating philosophical arguments whose relevance to and influence on subsequent theory will only become fully evident in later chapters. I trust the reader will bear with me in this trip through the 'icy wastes of abstraction': exploration of these philosophical arguments will help us both to understand what differentiates literary theory from other approaches to literature, and to see how the issues associated with literary theory play an ever more important role in contemporary philosophy. The figures of Immanuel Kant and his contemporary F.H. Jacobi (1743–1819) appear in virtually any book on the *Goethezeit*, as participants in the debates which lead to Romanticism, but they are hardly ever seen as being inextricably connected to ideas that have recurred in the work of Derrida and in other areas of contemporary philosophy. This recurrence can suggest how intellectual traditions which diverged in the course of the nineteenth and throughout much of this century have now begun again to converge, for reasons which will become apparent in the course of this book.

The initial importance of making clear what differentiates literary theory from other approaches to literature is apparent in the fact that the practice of 'literary theory' in the widest sense has been around at least as long as Aristotle's *Poetics*. Aristotle's descriptive and prescriptive move beyond consideration of particular epic, dramatic and lyrical works, to a theorisation of the general constituents of a successful work of what is now termed 'literature' created the framework for nearly all subsequent attempts at such theorisation, and, indeed, for much literary criticism. Had recent literary theory remained within this framework it would never have generated the degree of controversy which it has. The roots of this controversy lie in the late eighteenth century, when vital philosophical assumptions that had obtained throughout the history of what Martin Heidegger and his successors term 'Western metaphysics' began to come under fire.

The need to move beyond many of the questions in Western thought posed by the dominant strands of Greek philosophy and carried on in Christian theology's adoption of the Platonic and Aristotelian traditions is, as we shall see later, one of the most influential themes in Heidegger's work. Heidegger, who, along with Saussure and Nietzsche, is perhaps the most significant influence on contemporary literary theory, came to attribute a vital role to literature in his later attempts to redefine the task of philosophy in the modern world. He did so because he thought that literature offered access to truth of a kind which the dominant forms of truth in the modern world had obscured. Without understanding the history of which Heidegger is only one part we will fall into the trap of much recent literary theory, which relies on an untenable account of modern philosophy that is too dependent upon Heidegger's own selective account.

It has been noticeable in recent years that many strands of philosophy have moved away from the totalising claims associated with the rise of a notion of Western rationalism which has been too readily associated by Lyotard and others with the philosophy of modernity as a whole.[1] Oddly, at a time when it would appear that the application of modern scientific methods is unifying human knowledge across the globe, a universalistic notion of 'Reason' based on the model of natural science is now actually regarded with suspicion in many quarters. In the work of Derrida, Lyotard, Rorty and others the idea that there is an overarching conception of reason which can accommodate the sheer diversity of different world-views and evaluations in the contemporary world has come under severe attack, not least in Rorty's contention that philosophy needs to see itself as a kind of literature if it is to escape its failed Platonic obsession with Truth. Truth with a big 'T' is, for Rorty, what would bind together all the ways in which we think things to be true in a grand philosophical theory which showed how thinking and being correspond to each other. The initial sources of this kind of attack on universalising notions of reason lie in the period now to be examined. Furthermore, there are many other issues in recent debates that have their counterpart in the philosophical movements which begin in the second half of the eighteenth century. This chapter will look at one particular and very influential theoretical constellation – there are many other related sources of the issues – which most clearly exemplifies the shift that eventually leads, via Heidegger and others, to the questions of contemporary literary theory. What I term 'literary theory' should therefore be understood here in the widest sense, and it includes approaches, like Lyotard's, which contend that we have reached a 'post-modern' era beyond the universalist rationalism of 'modernity' (see the Introduction to Bowie (1990) for another account of the basic debate). The reasons for my wide application of the term relate, as we shall see, to the Romantic critique of Enlightenment universalism and its links to literary theory, as well as to the broad use of the term in much contemporary American debate. Because I do not wish to divorce literary theory from mainstream philosophy, such a broad usage should not be regarded as misguided: the problems of literary theory are the problems of modern philosophy and do not constitute some wholly new area of study.

The theme which preoccupied many major thinkers in the second half of the eighteenth century in Germany was the increasingly questionable status of human reason. In the light of the more and more evident difficulties for theology posed by new approaches in philosophy and the emerging modern natural sciences, new legitimations had to be sought for the idea of reason.[2] It is, as we shall see, at the moment when reflections upon the status of reason become linked to increasingly secularised conceptions of language that certain key preconditions of literary theory are fulfilled. To understand why, we need first to understand some of the questions concerning the legitimation of reason more thoroughly than has been the case in most recent accounts, such as Lyotard's, of the perceived failures of Western rationality. Both Kant and Jacobi questioned the legitimation of reason in ways which have echoes in all subsequent attempts to understand reason in modernity, and which form important links to literary theory. Their differing responses to the question of reason thereby offer two useful models which can orient our understanding of the history of literary theory. By concentrating on a very few particular theoretical aspects of their work the main themes which will concern us from now on should become easier to grasp.

The overall intellectual context at issue here is, of course, the critique of the Enlightenment and the rise of German Idealism and Romanticism. If we insist on such labels, though, it is too easy to slip into another familiar version of the history of ideas or into a reductive Marxist contextualisation of the issues,[3] both of which can tend to remove the issues from their connection to the state of theory for us now. The aim here is to see the historical issues, not as exhibits in an intellectual museum, but as the very material of our contemporary self-understanding. These ideas are clearly related to the historical and social upheavals of their own time, but they cannot be reduced to or fully explained by their historical and social contexts. If that were possible their new significance for contemporary theory would become hard to understand. By showing how the issues to be presented here have, in differing forms, underlain most of the major theoretical debates in literary theory we will be better placed to judge the real contributions of that theory.[4] The extremity of the reaction against the work of Jacques Derrida in both Britain and America was, for example, not least a result of the failure to see just how much his work directly and indirectly owes to issues we are about to consider. Why, then, is Kant so central to these issues?

KANT AND THE CRITIQUE OF THE 'READY-MADE WORLD'

It is too often forgotten that the perception of Kant by many of his contemporaries was of a dangerous iconoclast. Indeed, Jacobi linked consequences which he saw in Kant's philosophy to the wider danger of what he termed 'nihilism'.[5] As we shall see, Jacobi regarded nihilism as the inevitable result of the failure of philosophy to explain the fact that the world exists or is manifest at all. Kant, who himself avowedly believed in God, was regarded as a threat in his own time because he rejected the idea that philosophy can have access to the (theologically) inbuilt structure of reality. However this aspect of Kant's thought is understood, it evidently puts into question the idea that the ultimate truth of the world is accessible and therefore constitutes the knowable goal of philosophy or natural science. The idea of such accessibility must rely upon some form of the presupposition that the fact of the matter is already out there to be discovered in the world. This presupposition will turn out to be very difficult to defend, as I have already suggested in the Introduction when considering 'representational' conceptions of truth. Rather than being a mirroring of what Hilary Putnam has termed a 'ready-made world' (Putnam 1983) whose structure can be said to pre-exist our knowing it, for Kant *knowledge* of the world became the product of the activity of the knower.

Kant's revolutionary thought was, as is well known, primarily occasioned by David Hume's assertion that the notion of causality gave us no warrant for claiming that the world was *inherently* bound by fixed causal laws. All the causal laws we know are, for Hume, the result of repeated observation, which gives us no right to predict that the connections of empirical data we happen to observe on one occasion will, because the world is really like that independently of our seeing it, always recur in the future. By arguing in this way Hume took a step which, so to speak, began to remove the theological glue from the structure of the knowable universe, rendering that structure a contingent product of observation. In trying to overcome the sceptical consequences of Hume's position, while acknowledging the undeniable force of Hume's initial objections to a metaphysical interpretation of causality, Kant was led to explain successful scientific theories like Newton's theory of gravity in a different manner from all previous philosophy.

Kant's 'Copernican turn' is founded on the claim that all previous philosophy had assumed that 'our cognition has to follow objects' (*KrV* p. B XVI), which led to the problem of how we could arrive at any firm foundations for knowledge if our access to objects involved the sort of empirical contingencies which Hume had revealed. 'Metaphysics', the attempt to arrive at 'a priori' knowledge, which was not subject to the vagaries of each individual's shifting empirical perceptions, seems impossible if it is to 'follow objects', given that Hume had restricted our access to objects to their contingent effects on our sensory apparatus. Instead, Kant suggests, we should assume that 'objects follow our cognition': this would still entail a priori foundations, but ones which are located in the way we necessarily apprehend the world, rather than in the world itself. The aim of philosophy was still to explain 'objective truth', of the kind that the new natural sciences were now so successful in providing, but objectivity takes on a wholly different sense. An object for Kant is that concerning which a subject can make a true judgement, not something which is true independently of its appearing to the subject. The world of judgements becomes a world of 'syntheses', in which the subject brings together ideas (*Vorstellungen*) which are in one sense different, but in fact are judged to be the same. By relying solely upon the certainties which can be generated by the conditions of our own necessary cognitive activity, such as the ability to constitute identities between differing experiences, Kant thinks that he can get round Hume's objections to a priori knowledge, which therefore becomes dependent upon the subject, not upon the object.

The further result of Kant's position, though, which will trouble Jacobi and nearly everyone else who engages with it, is that the world 'in itself' becomes inaccessible to human cognition. Once this move is made the constitution of the truth about the world is necessarily bound up with our capacity for judgement, rather than being assumed to exist independently of this capacity. The ramifications of such a conception are emphatically still with us in modern philosophy, not least because the beginnings of the critique of the idea of truth as representation are present in it.[6] Manfred Frank suggests of Kant's account of the constitution of the object-world by the understanding: 'If objects only come about at all via synthetic acts of the understanding [in judgements], the understanding cannot be made into the imitator of objects' (Frank 1989b p. 175). As such, truth cannot pre-exist the cognitive activity of the subject. The link to questions of art of Kant's conception lies in the way cognitive activities associated with the aesthetic, such as the invention of new metaphors, can play a role in the establishing of truth in the cognitive domain, as well as playing a role in the way we constitute the meaningfulness of the 'life-world'.

If the world were known to be ready-made, as opposed to being constantly articulated via the cognitive activity of the subject, then we would already have our destiny inscribed within us in such a way that science would ultimately be able to tell us what we are and why we are. It was this deterministic view of existence that had informed what became, via Jacobi's influence in the so-called 'Pantheism controversy', which began in 1783, the most important metaphysical system for late eighteenth-century Germany: Spinoza's *Ethics*. Both Kant and Jacobi see much the same danger in Spinoza, the danger of a world which operates in a deterministic manner and thereby renders human freedom and moral responsibility merely illusory, but they draw significantly different conclusions about how to respond to that danger. The structures which trouble them are, as I shall now show, the foundation of the traditions in modern philosophy which lead to literary theory and to many of our contemporary philosophical concerns.

Kant's ultimate aim is to establish the goal of human existence once the idea of a theological order can no longer be presupposed: the law-giver in both the cognitive and the moral realm now becomes ourselves, rather than anyone or anything else. Famously, Kant was therefore led, via his wish to square the determinism of natural phenomena with our sense of moral duty, to split the human world into the law-bound realm of appearances and the free world of the inner 'intelligible' self, which he locates in the realm of the 'in itself'. Clearly the two realms must be in some way related, because we ourselves are both physico-chemical machines and autonomous beings. The question was how such a relationship could now be established without invoking access to a ready-made world in the manner which Kant had shown to be invalid.

This much is probably familiar to many readers, who may well by now be asking how it all connects to literary theory.[7] The fact is that it will be problems in epistemological foundationalism, even in the more modest version proposed by Kant in the *Critique of Pure Reason*, which lead to the story of aesthetics and the beginnings of literary theory which I wish to tell here. As we shall see in Chapters 2 and 3, the significance of 'literature' and art for the thought of Kant's period relates precisely to the awareness that epistemology cannot complete the job it is intended for. It was Jacobi who was one of the first to claim he could show why.[8]

The epistemological problems whose consequences both Kant and Jacobi confront put into question the very status of Western philosophy's attempt to reach the truth of the world, if that truth is understood to be 'ready-made' and awaiting its adequate 're-presentation'. The problems with the model of truth as representation began to be apparent in the light of the problems which Kant sought to answer. One fundamental way of seeing the issue will, as we shall see, recur in differing forms right until the present day, hence my concentration upon it here. The world of the laws of nature for Kant is a world of 'conditions', in which the explanation of something depends upon seeking its prior condition, such that z is conditioned by y is conditioned by x, etc. This leads to a regress, because any particular judgement will be reliant upon a potentially infinite series of prior conditions. By locating the conditions of possibility of knowledge in our minds rather than in the world of things, Kant wished to avoid the infinite regress necessarily entailed in attempting to ground any empirical judgement by tracing all of its conditions. In the 1787 Introduction to the first *Critique* Kant maintains that, although reason must postulate the 'unconditioned . . . in all things in themselves for everything conditioned, so that the series of conditions should thus become complete' (B, p. XX), by restricting *knowledge* (the product of understanding) to appearances, rather than 'things in themselves', the contradiction of seeking conditions of the unconditioned can be avoided. Previous 'dogmatic' metaphysics, such as Spinoza's, had relied upon the idea that the totality of conditions could be made accessible to philosophy by constructing the necessary system of internally related conditions.

Spinoza summed up his manner of establishing what something is in relation to the totality in his dictum that 'All determination is negation'. The table of elements, for example, as we now see it, is constituted in terms of the *relations* of the elements, each of which is therefore defined by its dependencies upon the others: copper is not sulphur, is not, etc.[9] In Spinoza's system the totality of conditions which constitute the laws of nature forms the very structure of what he calls 'God', who thus includes all the relations as the structure of Himself. For Spinoza, the fact that the idea of conditions can be construed as leading to the idea of the totality of conditions reveals the inherent intelligibility of the world, because it shows that everything must ultimately relate to everything else in a complete internally linked system. Things are explicable because they embody the intelligibility of God. For Kant, such a system ignores the Humean restrictions on metaphysical claims to be able to extend our *cognitive* access to the world beyond what is given to us in sensory experience.

In Kant's view we therefore have no way of *knowing* that there *is* a totality in Spinoza's sense. Science may try to postulate this totality and work towards it, but philosophy cannot assert positively that it exists, because the only way we can move towards it is by the continuing determination of the laws of nature in scientific investigation, a process which need not ever come to an end. Our only other way of understanding it, at least for the Kant of the *Critique of Pure Reason* and the *Critique of Practical Reason*, is via our sense of higher purpose evident in moral duty, which he links to the sense of the totality of the universe as a meaningful whole, in his famous invocation of the 'starry sky above us and the moral law within us'.

The decisive point, which will eventually lead to a growing suspicion of the attempt to defend the representational conception of truth, is that we can never arrive at final certainty with regard to the totality in a cognitive manner, because we would not recognise when we have reached the end of the investigation unless we already knew what it is that we are looking for. If the truth we are to arrive at is to be a representation of the world in itself it also, as we already saw, entails the assumption that what we are seeking pre-exists our way of thinking about it *and can be known to do so*.[10] Kant, as we shall see later, realised the need to confront this issue more appropriately in the *Critique of Judgement* of 1790. However, it was Jacobi who probably made the underlying problem clearer than anyone else. Jacobi's contentions became of considerable public concern because they signalled the failure of the philosophy of the Enlightenment in the tradition of Leibniz and Christian Wolff, as it was exemplified in the work of Moses Mendelssohn.[11] Jacobi's fundamental insight, whose echoes are still with us, deeply affected the course of German philosophy, and particularly affected the work of the Romantics.[12]

JACOBI: 'BEING' AND THE CRITIQUE OF METAPHYSICS

The 'Pantheism controversy' began because Jacobi claimed that the greatest literary figure of the German Enlightenment, G.E. Lessing, had told him that he was a Spinozist.[13] The shock this involved for many people at the time can only be understood if one remembers that Spinozism was usually equated with atheism, because Spinoza's God was devoid of the features of a personal, providential cause of the universe, being merely the ground from which the interrelated laws of nature necessarily ensued.[14] The fact that the views put forward by Jacobi forced the already frail Mendelssohn into precipitately working on a critique of Spinoza which probably hastened his death added a degree of intensity to the controversy, and rendered a fair assessment of the arguments at the time even more difficult. It is quite evident, though, that the fraught nature of the controversy also lay in the fact that what was at issue went very deep indeed. I shall concentrate on the main philosophical aspects of Jacobi's contribution, in his *On the Doctrine of Spinoza in Letters to Herr Moses Mendelssohn* which was first published in 1785, followed by the more significant revised and extended version of 1789, and in other texts such as *Jacobi to Fichte*.

It has been a commonplace of much literary theory that 'Western metaphysics', particularly in its Cartesian and post-Cartesian forms – and the assumptions about meaning and interpretation which ensue from that metaphysics – depends upon the transparency to itself of the thinking and writing subject, upon what is often termed 'self-presence'.[15] The move to the post-modern era is often seen as an acknowledgement of the subversion of the 'self-present' subject by the language which pre-exists it and by the unconscious which is its never directly accessible ground. What is too often forgotten is that the notion of the 'subverted' subject is very evidently already part of theological traditions that have a massive influence on the development of modern thought from Pascal to Kierkegaard and beyond. The importance of Jacobi in this respect is evident in his declaration in the Introduction to the second edition of the *Letters* of 1789 that

> The decisive difference of my way of thinking from the ways of thinking of the majority of my philosophical contemporaries lies in the fact that I am not a *Cartesian*. I begin like the Orientals (*Morgenländer*) in their conjugations with the third, not with the first person, and I believe that one simply should not put the *Sum* after the *Cogito*. I needed a truth which was not *my* creature, but whose creature *I* would be.
>
> (Scholz 1916 p. 52)

The Cartesian model which Jacobi rejects forms the foundation of Enlightenment conceptions of reason which are too often associated with the philosophy of modernity as a whole.

The Enlightenment thinking which Jacobi, like Kant, rejects holds the necessities of thought evident in mathematics and logic to be imbued in the very nature of things, so that the task of thinking is to construct the whole pattern of reality on the basis of these indisputable a priori foundations. Descartes' philosophy relies on establishing the link between the one certainty in thought he believed he had established – the fact that even if I doubt the reality of my thoughts I must yet exist in order to doubt that reality – with the 'ontological' proof of the existence of God. Both arguments depend upon a necessary relationship between existence and essence. In the *cogito* the essence of the thinking I lies in the fact that, however mistaken it may turn out to be about *what* it thinks, it must exist, even in order to doubt itself; the ontological proof results from the claim that God's essence as 'necessary being' (how could *God*'s existence be contingent?) must coincide with His existence. In both cases, therefore, necessities within *thought* are used to establish absolute foundations for the truth about the *world*, including the existence of what gives rise to or is the ground of the world.[16]

This is precisely what Jacobi rejects in his critique of Cartesianism.[17] We already saw how Kant questions aspects of this conception by locating these foundations only in our necessary ways of seeing the world, not in the world in itself.[18] Kant, though, still hangs on to the idea that cognitive foundations can be established via a more modest version of a rationalist project. Jacobi has an ambivalent relationship to both Kant and Spinoza. In his perhaps most influential statement on Kant, the essay 'On Transcendental Idealism', Jacobi claims, on the basis of Kant's separation of appearances and things in themselves, and in line with his reading of Hume, that 'all our knowledge is nothing but a consciousness of linked determinations of our own self, on the basis of which one cannot infer to anything else' (Jacobi 1787 p. 225). He suggests that, even in order to establish what Kant claims to have established, Kant would have to transcend the relationship between appearances and things in themselves:

> For even if according to [Kantian philosophy] it can be *admitted* that a transcendental something *may* correspond as *cause* to these merely subjective beings (*Wesen* [by which he means 'appearances']), which are only determinations *of our own being*, it yet remains hidden in the deepest obscurity *where* this cause and what the nature of the relation it has to its effect is. (Jacobi 1787 p. 224)

Jacobi's vital point is that this kind of cause cannot be articulated within philosophy and must be located within a theology which transcends what philosophy can demonstrate. The responses to his contentions in both German Idealism and Romanticism are attempts to avoid this way of understanding the consequences of Kantian philosophy.

Jacobi tries to explore the ground of our thinking which cannot be established in terms of thinking itself. He suggests against Spinozism's claim to establish a complete philosophical system in the light of Descartes that Spinozism rests on a 'misunderstanding, which always has to be *sought* and artificially *produced* if one wishes to explain the *possibility* of the existence of a universe in any manner', which 'necessarily ends by having to discover *conditions* of the *unconditioned*' (Scholz 1916 p. 51). While each particular aspect of the world of experience can be seen to be linked to its condition, and its condition in turn to its own conditions, 'being' itself, the ground of all the conditions, cannot be regarded in the same way. In arguing in this manner Jacobi already establishes one version of what Heidegger will term 'ontological difference', the difference between an account of something in terms of a particular science (in which the thing is seen as what Heidegger terms '*Seiendes*', as an 'entity'), and the fact of that something's existing prior to its being subsumed into an explanatory account (which leads to what Heidegger terms '*Sein*', 'being', the very fact of the world's being intelligible at all). The relationship between the being of a particular 'this or that', such as a tree, and the being which the tree shares with everything else which exists reveals a difference in the sense of 'being' that has troubled philosophers at least since Aristotle, and which Heidegger tried to overcome with his new way of understanding being.[19] Jacobi will try to overcome ontological difference via his theology, but his way of showing the difference is not open to the same criticisms as his theological attempt to overcome it.

Jacobi's phrase concerning the '*conditions* of the *unconditioned*' signals his central thought in relation to Spinozism, which, even though he thinks it at this time the most important philosophical system, he regards as entailing a fatalism that reduces our thinking to mere passivity. In Spinozism, thinking's 'only business is to accompany the mechanism of the effective forces' (ibid. p. 81) as a spectator which represents the truth of the world. Like Kant, Jacobi rejects the assumption that the realm of freedom, in which he expressly includes the realm of scientific invention *and* artistic creation – as well as the freedom to *disobey* the dictates of reason – can be reduced to the causally determined processes in our organism. Jacobi's insistence on the reality of this aspect of our conscious life leads him, though, to question the very foundations of the scientific world-view, especially as they are presented by Spinoza. In Jacobi's interpretation Spinoza, like many contemporary 'physicalist' philosophers such as Daniel Dennett, effectively turns the mind, including our affective self, into a digital computer, in which the same functions give rise to the same thought processes (see Bowie 1995c). Jacobi sees this model as the basis of 'nihilism', in which the world of thinking is reduced to a solipsistic self-contained functioning: he does not exempt Kant from a related accusation, because of the separation of thinking and things in themselves. The question is, though, what alternative Jacobi offers to the explanation of the world of conditions, which is, after all, still the dominant way of conceiving of the world in modern science. The fact is that his position becomes an overt rejection of all *philosophical* attempts to make being intelligible.[20] The effects on some of Jacobi's contemporaries of what is implied by this position will be evident in their turn to questions of aesthetics, and, by extension, to questions of literature. To understand Jacobi's disturbing insight it is essential to grasp the following aspect of Spinoza's account of God.

Henry Allison maintains that Spinoza conceives of

> the causal relationship between God and the world in terms of the logical relationship between ground and consequent. God functions in Spinoza as the logical ground of things. The latter follow from his nature in precisely the same way as the conclusion of a valid argument follows from its premises. (Allison 1987 p. 64)

Jacobi regards this understanding of God as mistakenly seeking the '*condition* of the *unconditioned*', because the ability to assert that there is such a relationship between the world and its ground fails to acknowledge a crucial difference: that between 'ground' – *Grund* – and 'cause' – *Ursache*. He uses the words in an unusual manner: the word 'ground' derives, for Jacobi, from Leibniz's 'principle of sufficient reason', the principle that *Nihil est sine ratione*: 'nothing is without reason/cause/ground', which Jacobi reformulates as 'everything *dependent* is *dependent upon* something' (Scholz 1916 p. 271).[21] A ground is, then, a part of a chain, which is therefore itself dependent on other parts of the chain, and belongs to Heidegger's '*Seiendes*', in the sense of an entity which is explained in a theory. One uses grounds for 'explanation', but this is not all we do in understanding the world because *what* we explain cannot be accounted for by theoretical judgements alone. Jacobi maintains, thereby already suggesting a clear link to questions of aesthetics, that:

> In my view the greatest achievement of the researcher is to disclose (*enthüllen*) and to reveal (*offenbaren*) existence (*Daseyn*). . . . Explanation is a means for him, a path to the goal, the proximate, but not the final purpose. His last purpose is that which cannot be explained: that which cannot be dissolved, the immediate, the simple. (ibid. p. 90)

The roots of the explicit division between 'explanation' and 'understanding' ('*Verstehen*'), which will become, via Dilthey and others, a central theme of twentieth-century philosophy, and which has played a vital role in the question of the relationship of the arts to the sciences, are already present here. The irreducibility of understanding to what can be explained in causal terms remains, as we shall see, one of the central themes of hermeneutic philosophy, particularly in Heidegger's account of *Verstehen*. Even Jacobi's choice of words is reminiscent of Heidegger's concern with 'world-disclosure', as that which must precede cognitive truth claims. Jacobi is led by this view of the limits of explanation to his conception of a personal creator-God, who is understood as being the ultimate 'cause' of the manifest world. In this sense he refuses (probably for very personal reasons)[22] really to take on the consequences of what his philosophy suggests, but it is the moves on the way to this theological conception that still matter.

Jacobi claims that there is a necessary circularity involved in all truth claims: without this circularity all knowledge would be subject to the endless regress which Kant tries to escape by limiting knowledge to the syntheses of appearances by the subject. He therefore makes the apparently startling claim that 'Every path of demonstration ends in fatalism', because completing any explanation, particularly of human action, would have to reveal that it could not have been otherwise. To show this would require access to the totality of the conditions of the action, a notion which Spinoza finds unproblematic, but which Kant also had to regard with suspicion. Jacobi takes the Kantian suspicion in his own direction: 'We can only demonstrate similarities (*agreements, relatively necessary truths*), progressing in statements of identity. Every proof presupposes something which has already been proved, whose principle is *revelation*' (ibid. p. 178).[23] What has already been proved will, if *its* truth is to be finally demonstrated, again lead to a regress, because it depends upon the proof of something else, etc. *ad infinitum*. For Spinoza this leads us back to the grounding necessity of God, as suggested in Allison's remark above. Jacobi argues, though, that the fact of scientific knowledge means we must always rely on something immediate – 'revelation' – in order to make knowledge claims at all,[24] rather than being able to understand the nature of God by understanding how everything is interdependent.

Jacobi terms this immediacy '*Glaube*', 'belief' or 'faith'.[25] Belief, what Jacobi terms 'holding as true' ('*Fürwahrhalten*'), cannot itself be demonstrated, because the condition of demonstrating conditions cannot itself be a condition in the same way as what it demonstrates. The idea that truth involves an 'intuitive' aspect, as suggested in Jacobi's notion of 'belief', is becoming more and more current in contemporary philosophy, forming a link of insights from the tradition at issue here, which are developed by Heidegger and others, to recent philosophy which has emerged from the analytical tradition. Donald Davidson, for example, talks of our 'general and pre-analytic notion of truth' (Davidson 1984 p. 223) and of an 'intuitive grasp we have of the concept' (ibid. p. 267), which means we cannot finally give a theoretical description of truth, because we always already rely upon it in order to describe or understand anything at all. Jacobi's demonstration of the necessarily 'immediate' basis of truth is the location of his attempt to provide a theological response to the problem of grounding knowledge, by claiming he can escape via a '*salto mortale*', a leap of faith, that results precisely from the failure of explanation to explain itself. Despite its importance at the time and later in the nineteenth century, this theological move is not the most important aspect of his argument in this context.[26]

Jacobi reveals an inherent tendency for any conception of reason to become narcissistic, to be able only to see the truth in terms of what it itself presupposes, because what it claims must result from reflection upon its own internal necessities. The route to what is outside those subjective necessities is not available unless reason surrenders its desire for total explanation – hence Jacobi's *salto mortale*. His most disturbing insights for his contemporaries, which recur in a variety of guises in later thinkers – such as in Nietzsche's famous contentions about the aesthetic aspect of truth in 'On Truth and Lie in the Extra-Moral Sense'[27] – are summarised by the following from the *Letters*, which is worth citing at length:

> Among the means of preservation of life ... we know none which proves itself more powerfully than language. The close link between language and reason is recognised by everyone; and just as much that we have no conception of a life higher than that which exists through reason. More complete perception and a greater multiplicity of combination creates in limited beings the need for abstraction and language. In this way a world of reason arises, in which signs and words take the place of substances and forces. We appropriate the universe for ourselves by tearing it apart and making (*erschaffen*) a *picture*-, *idea*- and *word*-world which is appropriate to our capabilities, and completely unlike the real world. What we make in this way we understand, to the extent to which it is our creation, completely; what cannot be made in this way we do not understand; our philosophical understanding does not reach beyond its own production. But all understanding takes place by our *positing* differences and *negating* them again [i.e. by establishing conditions, which leads into the 'chain of conditions']. (Scholz 1916 p. 265)

As such 'the real existence of a successive world that consists of single finite things which produce and destroy each other in turn cannot *in any way* be made comprehensible, i.e. be explained *in terms of nature*' (ibid. p. 272), and the investigation of that existence necessarily takes one beyond the world of nature as the realm of causal laws. Consequently 'all the things which reason can bring out by dissection, linking, judging, concluding, and grasping again are simply things of nature, and reason itself belongs as a limited being with these things' (ibid. p. 274). All knowledge is therefore located as part of a 'chain of conditioned conditions' (ibid. p. 276). The 'unconditioned' cannot therefore be an object of knowledge, although we arrive at the fact that there must be more than the world of conditions when we realise the necessarily self-contained status of any system of reason. The links of the limitations of explanation to the need for ways of escaping the world of fatalism will, as we shall see, play a vital role in the conceptions of art and literature which emerge at this time.

It might now seem as if Jacobi has merely manoeuvred himself into an indefensibly sceptical position, which was precisely the objection Lessing, who claimed to be happy to take on the Spinozist refusal to accept anything in the world beyond the laws of nature, made to him. The vital point is, though, that Jacobi has begun to make moves which undermine any attempt to arrive at final epistemological foundations, moves which are usually associated with Nietzsche, Heidegger, Derrida, Rorty and others in the 'post-modern' canon. By arguing as he does, then, Jacobi sometimes arrives at startlingly prescient insights, which we will repeatedly encounter in other thinkers. In the *Letters*, for example, he historicises philosophy in a quite remarkable manner, in which defining themes of hermeneutic and Marxist philosophy are already prefigured:

> Philosophy cannot create its material; the material is always there in present or past history . . . the actions of people must not be deduced from their philosophy, but rather their philosophy from their actions . . . their history does not emerge from their way of thinking, but their way of thinking from their history. (ibid. pp. 188–9)

Jacobi thereby already announces the theme of the 'end of philosophy', the rejection of the search for the Platonist timeless world of Truth, which, via the 'Young Hegelians', Marx, Nietzsche, Heidegger, Derrida, Rorty and others has become a crucial aspect of our contemporary theoretical landscape. What is at issue in all these thinkers is the tendency of philosophy to think it can establish some kind of self-supporting view of the world which would explain the truth, of the kind most classically represented in Spinoza, and later in Hegel's system. Analysing the relationship of the idea of 'post-metaphysical thinking' to the concept of literature is one of the best ways of understanding what is at stake in contemporary debates about literary theory.

Lest this seem an exaggerated claim for Jacobi, I want to move in the concluding section of this chapter to a consideration of perhaps his most remarkably prophetic attack on the idea of philosophy. This will help us to grasp the significance of Jacobi for the emergence of Romantic ideas and suggest the roots of a further dimension of Kant's philosophy which we will consider in Chapter 2: its concern with the aesthetic and with the 'free play' of our cognitive faculties.

'PURE REASON LISTENS ONLY TO ITSELF': FROM METAPHYSICS TO LITERARY THEORY

After Fichte had been accused of atheism in 1798 Jacobi wrote and published a letter defending him (Jacobi 1799), while making very clear how their positions differed. His presentation of this difference is an exemplary account of one of the pivotal issues in modern philosophy. The role of Fichte in the genesis of Romantic philosophy and literary theory is crucial. Fichte's essential moves should be readily comprehensible in the light of the discussion so far.[28] If, as Kant acknowledged, the world of 'conditions' leads to the problem of the 'unconditioned', any aspect of ourselves which can itself be seen as unconditioned must be central to a philosophy which accepts Kant's attacks on 'dogmatic' metaphysics. In Kantian terms the 'intelligible' self, which can, in 'practical reason', act counter to the promptings of natural determinism, is 'spontaneous', not subject to any prior cause.

That which is not externally caused must in one sense be ground of itself. Fichte takes up Kant's suggestion that even the cognitive self must be understood as a 'spontaneity', because it cannot be of the same order as the world of conditions, of which it constitutes the cognitive cognition of possibility. Kant had offered no clear indication of what kind of access we have to the transcendental subject, given that it could not itself be construed as part of the world of appearances. Fichte's claim is that, because both the cognitive and the ethical self must be understood as 'spontaneities', the activity of the 'I' in practical reason was the key to the notion of the I in both theoretical and practical reason: the subject was, namely, a self-generating 'deed-action' ('*Tathandlung*'), rather than a determinate entity.

Fichte's answer to the problem of the unconditioned was, then, that the I was itself the absolute ground, from which the intelligibility of the world ensued: 'It is . . . the ground of explanation of all facts of empirical consciousness that before all positing in the I the I itself must previously be posited' (Fichte 1971 p. 95).[29] Taken in this manner the I itself did not require a further ground. Any such ground would make it subject to a prior condition, etc., and thus would contradict the most fundamental fact about the I: its spontaneity. Despite their doubts about Fichte's conception, the Romantics were highly attracted by the sense that what Fichte was striving to understand, the I, as that which revealed nature, could not be understood in the objectifying terms which had dominated Western philosophical thinking's relationship to the natural world until this period. This soon led, in Schelling, Hölderlin, Schlegel and Novalis, to the notion that the I might best be understood by aesthetic means.

Jacobi was convinced that Fichte reproduced the difficulties we have already encountered in Kant and Spinoza. Like some of the later critics of metaphysics, such as the later Heidegger, or Rorty, Jacobi thinks the problem lies in the philosophical enterprise itself. He goes so far as to say that his own position is no longer philosophy – he terms it '*Unphilosophie*' – because it has renounced the idea that knowledge can be finally grounded within a system. Any such grounding, of the kind suggested by Fichte's 'I', will entail a narcissism on the part of reason:

> In everything and from everything (*In Allem und aus Allem*) the human mind, by making concepts, only seeks itself to find itself again; continually tearing itself away from the momentary, determined existence which, so to speak, wants to swallow it, in order to save its being-itself and being-in-itself, in order to carry on this being via its own activity and to do so with freedom. (Jacobi 1799 pp. 10–11)

He agrees with Fichte that the 'science of knowledge' should strive to be complete, but thinks the completion of the science of knowledge will reveal that what really matters lies outside the domain of 'knowledge', the realm of the 'conditioned'.[30] How, then, does one arrive at what is outside 'knowledge'?

Jacobi's formulations concerning the grounding of reason have been echoed almost verbatim in some of the contemporary critiques of foundational philosophy which are so essential to literary theory. Consider the following, which should now make the direction of my broader argument much clearer. Jacobi's case against Fichte begins from the following view of 'philosophy' in Fichte's sense, meaning a self-supporting system based on the autonomy of reason:

> A *pure*, that is a *thoroughly immanent* philosophy; a philosophy made only of *One* piece; a true *system* of reason is only possible in the Fichtean manner. Obviously everything must only be given in and through reason, in the I as I, in *egoity*, and already be contained in it, if pure reason alone should be able to deduce everything from out of itself alone.
>
> The root of reason (*Vernunft*) is listening (*Vernehmen*). – Pure reason is a listening which only listens to itself. Or: Pure reason listens only to itself. (Jacobi 1799 p. 14)

The paradigm case of a '*thoroughly immanent* philosophy; a philosophy made only of *One* piece; a true *system* of reason' will, of course, be Hegel's system, which was developed from the 1807 *Phenomenology of Mind* onwards, not least as an attempt to overcome the sort of consequences for a conception of philosophy which wishes to be complete in itself which Jacobi revealed to his contemporaries, including to Hegel himself.[31] In Hegelian philosophy everything which appears opposed to something, such as thought and its object, is eventually revealed as being dependent upon its relationships to what it is not, so that it is inseparable from this Other. For Hegel, the metaphysical system is completed by the subject's realisation of its final identity with what seemed other to it, the object world, in the most emphatic and totalising form of 'self-presence'. The truth of the world turns out to be the world's articulation of itself – hence Hegel's dictum against Spinozism that the 'substance is subject': the substance is alive and can develop, rather than having a fixed essence. In Hegel's 'Absolute Idea', thought and the world are finally shown to mirror each other via the explication of the moving structure of what he terms *Geist*. In these terms language, which Hegel termed the 'existence of *Geist*', is itself revealed as the product of thought's '*self*-reflection', as that which allows thought to know itself.

It is because of this that Jacques Derrida, echoing Jacobi's claim that 'Pure reason listens only to itself', has termed metaphysics in the Hegelian sense the 'absolute desire to hear oneself speaking' (Derrida 1967a p. 115). Hegelian metaphysics explains all knowledge as the result of a process of reflection between thinking and being. Derrida tries, in one of the decisive moves in recent literary theory, to subvert this notion by showing how the means of signification inherently prevents such a mirroring – 'hearing oneself speaking' – because it leads into the sort of regress we have already encountered in the notion of the chain of conditioned conditions. In language each signifier depends upon other preceding and succeeding signifiers for its identity, which means that it cannot be present to itself and as itself, because the chain cannot come to an end: this failure of the sign ever to be finally determinable is the result of what Derrida calls '*différance*', the 'deferral' of final meaning occasioned by the differential constitution of the sign. As we shall see, a related, though not identical, conception is central to thinking about literature in Romantic philosophy, where it emerges as a result of the links between the Spinozist ideas observed here and aspects of Kant's notion of the 'free play' of the imagination in aesthetic experience.

Derrida, like Rorty and other radical anti-foundationalists, has often been regarded as a sceptic: philosophy based upon the endless dynamic recontextualisation of particular linguistic and other praxes cannot in this view make claims about truth and meaning which could transcend the context of those praxes and claim to be founded in anything other than those contingent praxes. Jacobi similarly suggests that his '*Unphilosophie*' 'is essentially non-knowledge' (Jacobi 1799 p. 1), as opposed to the transcendental claims of Fichte's 'knowledge', which is derived from the absolute activity of the subject. However, although he adopts a kind of sceptical position with regard to the claims of 'knowledge', Jacobi startlingly insists upon a very emphatic conception of what he terms 'the true'. Indeed, he makes 'the true' ontologically prior to whatever may become 'knowledge' within science or philosophy. Once again the ultimate intention of the argument is theological, but the import of the argument need not be understood theologically and will lead us to a vital issue concerning the notion of literature.

Jacobi's underlying fear is the fear of what he comes to term 'nihilism', which began to surface in the *Letters*. If philosophy were able to encompass the constitution of the manifest world, then 'The ground of all coming into being and being, right from the lowliest beast up to the most elevated saint and *nearly-God* would be – a merely logical enthusiasm' (ibid. p. 23), because it would be determined a priori by the necessities of the philosophical system, as, Jacobi claims, it is in Fichte and Spinoza. As with the rules and tricks of a simple game like solitaire, which, once learned, render the game meaningless, knowing the answer in philosophy would render each new piece of knowledge merely the result of the new combination of elements within an already constituted game. The capacity for generating truths from axioms and theories may be infinite, but, Jacobi suggests, this makes existence meaningless, because truths which can be generated by philosophy do not take us beyond the confines of what we have already presupposed. 'The true' cannot, therefore, be encompassed by reason, because reason depends upon it as its ground:

> I understand by the true something which is *before* and *outside* knowledge; which first gives a value to knowledge and to the *capacity* for knowledge, to *reason*.

Listening presupposes what can be listened to; reason presupposes the *true*: it is the capacity to presuppose the true. A reason which does not presuppose the true is an abomination. (Jacobi 1799 p. 27)

Jacobi's unmotivated move, as a way of overcoming the fear of nihilism, from the true to the idea of the Higher Being cannot invalidate the basic thought that the prior ontological ground of the knowledge that follows from presuppositions is the fact that the world is disclosed to us and intelligible at all.

Significantly, aspects of Jacobi's theological contentions can be translated into the assumptions that will be central to the hermeneutic philosophy which begins to develop around this time in the work of Schleiermacher,[32] and which forms a vital and frequently misunderstood aspect of the history of modern literary theory in question here. As Jacobi repeatedly suggests, the attempt finally to ground theoretical claims always either comes up against a regress or has to rely on some kind of presupposition which cannot further be grounded.[33] When Jacobi says of any access to God, who is the ground of the 'true', that 'we cannot seek or investigate what we are not already familiar with in some way or other' (ibid. p. 45), he makes the necessarily circular structure of interpretation apparent, even though we may question his claim to familiarity with God. The same assumption of a necessary circularity can, as modern hermeneutics will suggest, be made in relation to any object of inquiry, be it in the natural or the human sciences. In a classic passage in *Being and Time* of 1927 Heidegger suggests how deeply this issue affects our conceptions of truth, when, in line with Jacobi's assumptions, he reveals how the ground of any explanation cannot itself be grounded, and thus how all scientific proof involves a necessary circularity:

Scientific proof is not supposed already to presuppose what its task is to give grounds for. But if interpretation must always already move in that which has been understood and must nourish itself from it, how should it bring about scientific results without moving in a circle, especially if, moreover, the presupposed understanding moves in an everyday knowledge of man and the world. (Heidegger 1979 p. 152)

This always already existing everyday pre-understanding, without which questions about understanding could not even be put, is the ground of truth, and is the initial source of access to what Heidegger means by 'being'.[34] We will see in Chapter 7 how Heidegger connects this insight to questions of art and literature, not least when he realises that his own version of the insight in *Being and Time* may still fall prey to what is in fact Jacobi's essential contention. For the moment it is important to see how certain fundamental questions about the status of truth, knowledge and reason, of the kind raised by Jacobi, lead beyond a conception of philosophy which relies on establishing foundations within itself for establishing the truth, and towards the concerns of aesthetics and literary theory.

The theological conclusions of Jacobi's position are clearly unsatis-
factory, but the structure of the alternative he offers in relation to Fichte
will be echoed in numerous ways in subsequent theory:[35]

> man loses himself as soon as he refuses to find himself, in a manner
> which is incomprehensible to his reason, in God as his maker, as soon
> as he wishes to ground himself *in himself alone*. Everything then
> dissolves into his own nothingness. But man has the following choice,
> and only this choice: *nothingness* or a *God*. If he chooses nothingness he
> makes *himself* into God; that means: he makes God into a *phantasm*
> (*Gespenst*); for it is impossible, if there is no God, that man and all that
> surrounds him should not be merely a *phantasm*. (Jacobi 1799 pp. 48–9)

One need not accept Jacobi's bluntly theological alternative to be able to
see the validity of the objection to the attempt to demonstrate how
self-consciousness grounds itself in its own activity: the vital question will
be how to take on this issue without sharing Jacobi's dogmatic recourse to
theology. Jacobi's claim that the result of refusing the theological alternative is nihilism will, of course, be echoed in Nietzsche's attacks towards
the end of the nineteenth century on the belief that the notions of truth and
reason can be grounded in any more than the 'will to power', the universal
drive for domination of the Other which Nietzsche sees as the underlying
condition of all forms of identity. Both the positions at issue here – Fichte's
initial grounding of the world's intelligibility in the spontaneity of the I,[36]
and Jacobi's grounding of reason in a God who is outside what philosophy
can articulate or explain – take crucial aspects of the post-Kantian investigation of reason to their extreme. The extremes between which these
positions are located – and the ways in which the positions are yet related
– offer a productive framework for understanding a whole series of issues
in literary theory.

Consider the following admittedly reductive argument: if the author of a
text is understood as the absolute authority over or origin of the meanings
of that text, he or she plays a similar role to the 'self-positing' subject in one
interpretation of the early Fichte. The spontaneous, self-caused act of the
creative subject gives rise to an artefact which should be wholly transparent
to the author of that artefact. Without this sense of transparency the very
notion of that which is self-caused is invalidated by the revelation of its
dependence on an 'Other' which, as Jacobi maintains, must be its ground
or cause. In his notion of God Jacobi insists against Fichte that: 'my motto
and the motto of my reason is not: *I*; but, *more* that I! *Better* than I! – a
completely *Other* (*ein ganz Anderer*)' (Jacobi 1799 p. 30). The problem is
how this 'Other', which blocks the subject's ultimate transparency to itself,
is to be understood: the varying ways in which it comes to be understood
are at the root of many of the major positions in literary theory and post-
structuralism.

The question of the 'Other' of the writing subject plays a central role in undermining the notion of authorial intentionality in recent literary theory, and is, in differing versions, a central concern of those contemporary philosophies which no longer conceive of meaning in terms of the inner intentions of the thinking and speaking subject. In one of his attacks on what he perceives to be the predominant conception of interpretation, for example, Jacques Derrida contrasts 'two interpretations of interpretation': one 'seeks to decipher, dreams of deciphering a truth or an origin that escapes the play and the order of the sign, and lives the necessity of interpretation like an exile'; the other 'affirms play and tries to go beyond man and humanism' (Derrida 1967b p. 427). The contrast which concerns Derrida emerges from a fundamental metaphysical conflict of the kind we have observed between Fichte and Jacobi.[37] In 'Fichtean' terms the transparent truth or origin is the self-positing subject, conceived of as that which freely intends and produces the textual meanings which the interpreter tries to reproduce. A hermeneutics which would come to terms with this conception of meaning-production would have to assume a 'congenial' or empathetic capacity for meaning-production on the part of the interpreter, which he or she shares with the author, if this origin is to be reached. This is roughly the position proposed, *c.* 1808, by Friedrich Ast, that Schleiermacher will reject in his work on hermeneutics, and which still informs much work in literary studies.[38] Although such a position is clearly indefensible, its inversion, in which the subject has no serious control over the meanings of the 'discourse of the Other', because that discourse is always already prior to the subject who is 'inserted' into it, will turn out to be equally indefensible. Derrida's move beyond 'man and humanism' is a move beyond the idea of the self-present spontaneous subject that is invoked to explain the real meaning behind the 'play' of the text. The potential for this move is already latent – albeit only if one subtracts the theological let-out – in Jacobi's sense of 'alterity', 'otherness', in the undermining of the certainties of self-consciousness and the revelation of the dependence of human reason on the 'true', thus on an origin which cannot be discursively explicated. The crucial factor here is how language and the true are understood to relate to each other. In both Derrida's and Jacques Lacan's versions of this argument the 'Other' – language itself – prevents the initial self-presence which might then be recovered in interpretation, because meanings can only be produced via pre-existing signifiers which are, in one sense, external to the subject.[39] The origin of language is never transparent to the individual user of that language, and meanings are, as such, never finally controllable by that user: the meaning of the text can therefore never be grasped in any final manner beyond the always differing ways in which we may subsequently articulate it.

Seen in this way, then, the now familiar theoretical conflict between an intentionalist hermeneutics based on the recovery of what the author meant and a structuralist conception of meaning-production as a result of the functioning of the linguistic system, rather than of the intentions of speakers, can be related to one of the major metaphysical conflicts in early modernity. At the same time, however, these positions can actually be shown to mirror each other. The idea that meaning can be understood in terms of its origin in the meaning-intentions of the subject in fact shares the presupposition of a transparent origin with a structuralist (as opposed to a post-structuralist) account of the genesis of meanings. In the structuralist account meaning is founded in the supposed pre-existing structures of the signifying system as a whole, so that the meaning of a myth, for example, exists independently and can be analysed independently of what the individual members of the society that uses that myth think the myth may mean.[40]

Jacobi's position suggests how these positions might actually mirror each other when he claims that Fichte's transcendental idealism is in fact an 'inverted Spinozism' (Jacobi 1799 p. 4). Each aspect of the Spinozist system gains its identity from its relationships to the other aspects within the whole, just as in structuralism the signifier can only be what it is via its relations to other signifiers. Whereas Fichte's transcendental idealist position establishes its system via the absolute 'positing' of the I, the Spinozist system establishes it on the basis of the 'substance', which, Jacobi asserts, is, like Fichte's I, 'nothing but the unintuitable [in the sense of 'intuition' which means that it is not available to the senses] absolute identity of subject and object which can only be proved by conclusions, upon which the system of the new philosophy, *of the independent philosophy of intelligence* [thus of the 'I' in Fichte's sense] is grounded' (ibid. p. 3). The point is that both theories circumscribe the truth in an internally grounded system of relationships that is founded in what is both subject and object – the 'I' or Spinoza's substance – and thus, in the last analysis, fully transparent to itself. Derrida's affirmation of 'play' in the second conception of interpretation is, then, his way of suggesting that this origin cannot be made transparent, that reason cannot be sure that it 'hears *itself* speaking' because meaning is not finally determinable via access to an absolute origin or via the articulation of the totality of a system of relations. It is suspicion of this absolute origin which underlies many key assumptions in those versions of literary theory which are informed by both critical hermeneutics and post-structuralism.

This linking of Jacobi's view of Fichte to the contemporary questioning of ways of grounding textual meaning might appear merely as an argument from analogy. The fact is, though, that the questions raised by the work of Kant, Fichte, Jacobi and others demonstrably lead in Romantic philosophy to exactly the kind of questions about truth and interpretation which are – often via the mediating figure of Heidegger – the basis of recent literary theory.[41] Furthermore, the re-emergence of these questions in contemporary literary theory is part of a neglected history of modern philosophy which has become increasingly significant in the light of the contemporary critique of representational notions of truth. The investment during the post-Kantian period in the special status of art, the change in the status of music, and the emergence of the notion of literature which we discussed in the Introduction derive at least in part from doubts as to whether philosophy is any longer able to give satisfactory answers to the problem of grounding revealed by Jacobi.[42] The new approaches to language which originate towards the end of the eighteenth century can clearly be connected to this kind of questioning of the ground of reason, as one final ramification of Jacobi's arguments can begin to suggest.

Jacobi insisted on the 'true' as that 'which first gives a value to knowledge' (Jacobi 1799 p. 27). This insistence on the value of knowledge points to a crucial question for the understanding of modern metaphysics. If the relations between differential elements within a system are all there is, then value is based merely on those relations and equivalences: one element becomes of value merely via what it is not, and thus is not valuable for its own sake. This is one root of Jacobi's notion of nihilism, which will be adopted in many different forms in subsequent philosophy. Jacobi sees the problem with 'mediation', the constitution of 'value' by relations alone, as follows:

> if all philosophical knowledge (*Erkenntnis*) is effected in accordance with the principle of sufficient reason, thus by *mediation*, and thus is necessarily always only a *mediated* knowledge, then it is easy to understand why we cannot arrive at any philosophical knowledge either of the Highest Being or of our own personality and freedom.
>
> (Jacobi 1789 p. xxii).

Such mediation, which determines what anything is via what it is not, is completely indifferent to the content of what is mediated: establishing relationships between aspects of the world is a possibility which is always present, however valueless the results may be. The specific awareness of this problem that develops at the end of the eighteenth century will have very wide-ranging consequences, linking issues from metaphysics to literary theory as well as to ethical and political matters. The problem of the ground, which Fichte answers in terms of the subject and Jacobi in terms of God, is essentially a problem of value and how it is established. Clearly any assault on the theological ground of value, for which the world in itself is essentially valuable because it is God's creation, leads to the dilemmas which Jacobi reveals in his critique of Pantheism, while trying to conjure them away again via his theology.

Kant illustrates a vital instance of the problem when, in the *Foundation of the Metaphysics of Morals*, he makes the distinction between that which has a 'price', which can be exchanged via the principle of equivalence, and that which has what he terms a 'dignity', which is 'not just a relative value, i.e. a price, but an inner value' (Kant 1974 p. BA 78). Beings who are capable of autonomy, who are therefore not 'conditioned', *are* their own purpose and thus have an intrinsic value which is not derived from relating them to anything else. The use of the notion of price makes it clear that Kant is already aware of the implications of the rise of modern European capitalism, within which, as Marx will argue, the principle of exchange-value can render everything, including an autonomous being, merely relative to what it can be exchanged for.

The fact is – and here we encounter a central issue for the coming chapters – that there is a crucial homology between the constitution of metaphysical systems via the principle of determination as negation, the idea of language as a system of differences without positive terms, and the economy of negatively related exchange values.[43] The ways in which these three areas are understood as interconnected will determine many of the theoretical positions to be examined in the following chapters, from the Romantic conceptions of language, art and philosophy, to Adorno's demand that art and literature should give us access to what he terms 'non-identity', to that which is not finally comprehensible in terms of existing cognitive or economic ways of determining the world. This problem is a critical factor in the self-understanding of modernity. In all three areas the constitution of the system leaves what is really of value outside the system itself, via an inversion, in which the form of the system comes to take priority over the content which it is supposed to represent. Similar thoughts are present in the doubts about rationalisation and bureaucracy in the work of Max Weber and his successors, which Adorno links to the way Hegel makes his philosophy into a completed system. As has been frequently noted, Saussure often links the structural conception of linguistics to political economy, thereby himself suggesting the historical significance of what may initially appear to be merely a metaphorical relationship: the linguistic element which can only have linguistic value via its relations to other elements is understood in analogy to the commodity, whose exchange value can only be expressed via other commodities. This raises the question of whether there is anything which is valuable in and for itself and how such a value could be established outside of its location within a relational system.

Kant gives two examples of intrinsic value: autonomous beings capable of giving the law to themselves in practical reason, who have 'dignity', and, in the *Critique of Judgement*, the aesthetic object which is valued for its own sake without any interest in appropriating it. The two are related by Kant, because the only empirical access to the 'intelligible' ethical basis of the rational being will be via 'aesthetic ideas'. These offer images – which them-selves can be 'intuited' – of what can never be intuited, such as the quality of 'goodness'. In order to find a bridge between the causally determined world of appearances and the realm of reason, the realm of 'purposes' led by moral imperatives, Kant has to appeal to an aspect of the world of appearances which cannot be finally subsumed into conceptual judgements. The vital question is how the awareness that systems of relations can both repress and articulate leads to the revaluation of that which cannot be understood in terms of those relations.

A classic example of this awareness occurs in *Concluding Unscientific Postscript* of 1846, when Kierkegaard, in the guise of Johannes Climacus, maintains in a discussion of Pantheism and Hegelian philosophy, based precisely on Jacobi's *Letters*, that:

> every such system fantastically dissipates the concept *existence*. But we ought to say this not merely of pantheistic systems; it would be more to the point to show that every system must be pantheistic precisely on account of its finality. Existence must be revoked in the eternal before the system can round itself out. (Kierkegaard 1968 p. 111)[44]

Like Jacobi, Kierkegaard thinks that 'mediation', the integration of the particular into a system, simply reduces the essential nature of individual existence to its relationships, in order that the system be able to complete itself by making the individual a determinate aspect of the whole. In its most emphatic version, in Hegel's system, this means that being itself is subordinated to the relationships generated in thinking.

The playing out of the tension between a system and what resists integration into that system is the underlying motif of many of the aspects of literary theory to be considered in subsequent chapters. The change in the understanding of language towards the end of the eighteenth century – which Foucault, as we saw, characterised in terms of the simultaneous rise of linguistics and 'literature' – is connected to an analogous suspicion of the reduction of everything particular to a system. The rise of the modern idea of literature can in part be understood as the product of a reaction against the idea that language and meaning can be grounded in merely relational identities. Saussure's analogy of linguistic structures to economic structures contributes to a conception of language which seems to make meanings independent of the individuals who use language.[45] In this context Jacobi's objection to both the Spinozist and the Fichtean systems – that, via their concern to complete the system, they failed to come to terms with the 'true' – is, minus the theology, echoed in those views of language from Schlegel and Schleiermacher, to the early Heidegger, to Davidson's remark we cited in the Introduction, that 'there is no such thing as a language . . . if a language is anything like what many philosophers and linguists have supposed' (Lepore 1986 p. 446). In differing ways these thinkers all regard the attempt to circumscribe and ground language in a theory as failing to come to terms with the fact that such a theory is grounded in what the theory itself can never finally explain. If one has to invoke truth as part of the explanation of one's theory of language, at the same time as presupposing truth in order to arrive at such a theory, some kind of circularity of the kind suggested by Jacobi seems inevitable.[46] The implications of this situation begin to emerge when ideas deriving from Kant's reflections on art become linked in Romantic philosophy to questions of language and music. The diverse modern understandings of language, in which language can be an object for systematic determination in a science, a means of revelation or world-disclosure, and the medium of true assertion, form the force-field within which the modern notion of literature is constituted. In Chapter 2 we will consider how the metaphysical issues discussed in this chapter contribute to the emergence of Romantic literary theory.

2 Shifting the ground

'Where philosophy ceases literature must begin'

'THE PHILOLOGY OF PHILOSOPHY' (FRIEDRICH SCHLEGEL)

If recent literary theory has irritated those primarily concerned with literary history and literary interpretation because of its insistence on raising philosophical issues, it has equally irritated many philosophers because of its introduction of questions derived from the study of literature into philosophy. The roots of this dual irritation lie, as I shall demonstrate in this and Chapter 3, in the insights of early German Romanticism.[1] The effects of the interference between philosophy and literature, which began in its modern form with early Romanticism, have again become central to important developments in contemporary philosophy.[2] In the *Athenäum Fragments* of 1798 Schlegel declares that: 'Many of the complex disputed questions of modern philosophy are like the tales and the Gods of ancient literature. They return in every system, but always transformed' (Schlegel 1988 (2) p. 145). Recent debates between 'philosophers' and 'literary theorists' – the terms cannot, of course, be easily separated – such as the debate between John Searle and Jacques Derrida over conceptions of meaning, can be interpreted as re-articulations, and thus as transformations, of issues that first emerged with Romanticism. Understanding why this recurrence of Romantic concerns has taken place, and how our contemporary questioning differs from that of the Romantics, will be vital to the future development of both philosophy and literary theory.

In *On the Study of Greek Literature* of between 1795 and 1797 Friedrich Schlegel claims:

> The borders (*Gränzen*, which also means 'limits') of science and art, of the true and the beautiful are so confused that even the conviction that those eternal borders are immutable has almost universally been shaken. Philosophy poeticises and poetry philosophises.
>
> (Schlegel 1988 (1) p. 68)

Later, in the *Ideas* of 1800, he maintains 'Where philosophy ceases literature (*Poesie*) must begin. . . . One ought, for example, not just oppose unphilosophy, but also literature, to philosophy'[3] (Schlegel 1988 (2) p. 226).

The reference to 'unphilosophy' is an explicit reference to Jacobi's conception of the failure of philosophy to ground itself, which led Jacobi to his theology – and to his prescient insights – in the manner we saw in Chapter 1.[4] Schlegel thinks that this failure should be responded to by a reinterpretation of the relationships between philosophy, art and religion. Underlying this reinterpretation is the problem of grounding, be it at the epistemological level, or – and this will be the crucial new departure – at the level of language. As we already saw, the problem of grounding points to the new conceptions of truth which are the principal issue in the history of literary theory being reconstructed here. Schlegel, then, explicitly sees truth as an issue both for philosophy and for literature.

In his 'Philosophical Fragments' from the *Notebooks on Philosophy*, which he begins writing in 1794, Schlegel even reveals a significant ambiguity concerning the status of philosophy in the wake of Kant's critiques: 'The critique of philosophy = philology of philosophy, they are One and the same. Since philosophy has criticised so much, indeed has criticised almost everything in heaven and earth, it can now tolerate itself also being criticised' (Schlegel 1988 (5) p. 18). The constellation suggested by Schlegel is fundamental to the threat which Romantic theory – and its successors in literary theory – are seen as posing to many received conceptions of the role of philosophy. His claim would, though, seem to undermine itself. If philosophy is concerned with the truth, or at least with a theory of the truth, what position could be adopted from which to criticise the activity which is concerned with the truth, without that position itself just being another, 'higher' kind of philosophy? This then leads to a regress of 'meta-philosophies', each of which requires a further philosophy to establish its own truth. Schlegel's 'philology of philosophy' criticises the love of wisdom via the love of the historically developed 'logos' in which that wisdom is embodied, thereby posing the question as to the priority of the disciplines. The main problem will be exactly *how* language plays this new critical role, which is why 'literature' becomes so important, and, indeed, why the very notion of literature in a modern sense might be said to develop at all.

In his essay on Georg Forster of 1797, Schlegel asks:

> Why does one wish to demand everything of everything! – If philology is to be carried on as a strict science and a real art, then it requires a quite particular organisation of the mind; no less than real philosophy, where it is long overdue for one to begin to realise that philosophy is not for everyone. (Schlegel 1988 (1) p. 205)

Schlegel's ambiguity with regard to philosophy, which runs through much of his work, is a symptom of a series of broader issues. This is evident in the way it is echoed by Richard Rorty's contemporary attempts to say farewell to 'philosophy' – in the sense of that which would ground our knowledge of the world – in the name of 'literature', of the creation and exploration of new vocabularies with which to articulate our world. The significance of the work of the early Romantics for the development of literary theory is, as I suggested in the Introduction, the result of a particular historical constellation, in which the relationships between philosophy, the natural sciences and the arts were being established in their modern form. These relationships are further developed by the foundation of new kinds of university in Germany at the beginning of the nineteenth century, a process in which the Romantics played a major initiating role.[5] The decline of philosophy in modernity, from the role of highest science into which all other sciences were subsumed, to a subsidiary role of often very questionable status, will be in part a consequence of these divisions. The question posed by this decline is, however, whether the increasing specialisation of the differing sciences might not lead to a world which lacks any sense of human purpose or orientation, and which falls prey to what Jacobi meant by 'nihilism'. In this sense it is interesting to note Jürgen Habermas' recent suggestion, which is wholly in the spirit of a Romanticism of which he is generally suspicious, that philosophy today might 'at least help to set in motion again the frozen interplay between the cognitive-instrumental, the moral-practical and the aesthetic-expressive, which is like a mobile that has become stubbornly entangled' (Habermas 1983 p. 26).

Kant's philosophy, which was primarily directed against what Jacobi most feared, exemplifies the new perspectives emerging at this time, via its search for particular legislative procedures for grounding the cognitive, ethical and aesthetic approaches to the modern world. The essential aspect of the early Romantics' relationship to Kant, which was crucially influenced by their reception of Fichte – and by their relationship to Jacobi – lay in their attention to those parts of Kant's account of his new approach to the modern 'spheres of validity' which implied that the divisions he established were less stable than they might at first appear. Whereas Kant begins by wishing to circumscribe the spheres of legitimacy, so that the cognitive, the ethical and the aesthetic become distinct domains, the Romantics follow the indications in Kant that the aesthetic is inextricably bound up with the cognitive and the ethical, and that the *relationship* between the domains may be the most important factor in the new philosophy.[6] The vital work of Kant's in this respect, from which so many of the major issues of subsequent philosophy derive, is the 1790 *Critique of Judgement*, and it is the ramifications of the question of judgement which provide the methodological linking factor between the philosophical concerns investigated in Chapter 1 and the rise of literary theory in Romantic philosophy.

Schlegel's argument that one should oppose literature to philosophy can initially be understood as follows: if what grounds reality cannot be included within the philosophical system which tries to encompass it, then a medium in which the revelation of the failure to arrive at the final ground – at the 'unconditioned' – is in some way constitutive may be more apt for comprehending the nature of existence and truth than a self-contained philosophical system. The medium will, of course, be art.[7] This position has too often been understood as either a regression into an aestheticising mysticism, or as a surrender of the proper goal of philosophy, the goal of truth. In Jacobi the renunciation of a ground which could be articulated within philosophy was the route to a non-rationalist conception of theology, the beginning of a theology of 'alterity'. Is the aesthetic response, then, not just the attempt to turn art into religion, by suggesting that the highest insight cannot be discursively articulated and that it must therefore be disclosed via the symbolic means available in art? Although such views do play a significant role in Romantic philosophy, the Romantic position at issue here has a much more strictly philosophical pedigree, which does not rest upon the idea of art as a substitute for theology. The source of the position lies in Kant's own problems over the genesis of truth, which begin with a central aspect of the *Critique of Pure Reason* that is further explored in the *Critique of Judgement*. This aspect of Kant's philosophy will haunt modern philosophy in a variety of guises, and has, often unconsciously, been at the root of many of the most common positions in literary theory (see e.g. Caygill 1989).

JUDGEMENT, SCHEMA AND LANGUAGE

We arrive here at another case in which the concept of literature in the modern period cannot be understood without attention to questions of epistemology. In a subsequently much criticised section of the *Critique of Pure Reason*, 'On the Schematism of the Pure Concepts of the Under-standing', Kant had tried to overcome a version of the problem examined in Chapter 1. By grounding truth in the subject's capacity for judgement, rather than in the world 'in itself', Kant sought to avoid the regress which resulted from trying to complete the sequence of conditions required finally to ground any empirical judgement. This capacity, however, actually gives rise at another level to a structurally analogous problem to the one seen in Jacobi.

Knowledge depends, for Kant, upon rule-bound judgements on the part of the knowing subject, which subsume recurrent connections of appearances under concepts. Once such rules are established they can be repeatedly employed to make a knowledge-claim. Having learned a rule we can judge that x is a case of it, thereby arriving at cognitive certainty. However, this actually leads to the threat of another regress. In order to avoid this regress Kant invokes an ability of the subject which itself does not allow of a further grounding, because such grounding would lead to a regress involving the necessity of rules for the application of rules, and so on:[8]

> If judgement wanted to show universally how one is to subsume under these rules, i.e. distinguish whether something belongs under the rule or not, this could only happen via a further rule. But because this is a rule

it requires once more an instruction by judgement, and thus it is shown to be the case that the understanding is admittedly capable of being instructed and equipped by rules, but that judgement is a particular talent which cannot be given by instruction but can only be practised. (*KrV* B p. 172, A, p. 133)

The 'talent' required to prevent a regress of rules for rules depends on a 'hidden art in the depths of the human soul' which will, Kant maintains, probably remain inaccessible to us.[9]

He terms this 'art' (which has the Greek sense of '*techne*')[10] 'schematism', which belongs to the 'productive imagination' (although what he says about it in this passage makes its location between the receiving of sense data and the organisation of those data unclear (cf. *KrV* B, pp. 181–2, A, p. 142)). Schematism connects concepts, which must logically precede the data of cognition if they are to be able to subsume those data in judgements and intuitions, the manifold data of cognition.[11] It is, then, what allows us to 'see something as something', by linking the two separate realms, turning the 'sensuous manifold' into entities which can be identified by concepts:

> This idea of a universal procedure of imagination to provide a concept with its image I call the schema to this concept. Indeed it is not images of the objects which underlie our purely sensuous concepts, but schemata. (*KrV* B pp. 179–80, A pp. 140–1)

If empirical images of objects underlay our concepts, the particularity of the actual image would preclude its being able to be generalised into the concept, no particular empirical image ever being received in a manner which could be proved to be absolutely identical with any other. The schema gives an initial coherence to perceptions, so that they can be identified by general concepts, even though there will be empirical differences between those perceptions.[12] Novalis later says of the schema, in 1795–6, that it 'renders the treatment of a single case more easy, because it teaches me to apply the universal laws of the class (*Gattung*) of these cases and thus spares me the effort of again looking for the laws of this case' (Novalis 1978 p. 160). The importance of this aspect of Kant's philosophy is hard to overestimate, in so far as the very possibility of truth must depend upon it. This is why the implications of schematism become so important to the Romantic connection of art to truth, and thus to literary theory.[13]

It is at this point in the structure of his conception of knowledge that Kant will later, in the *Critique of Judgement*, make explicit the vital link between epistemology and aesthetics. In the Preface to the *Critique of Judgement*, which was written in part as an attempt to find a way of answering questions raised by the use of schematism for avoiding the regress of rules for rules, Kant claims that:

> The difficulty concerning a principle [of judgement] (be it subjective or objective) is located primarily in those judgements (*Beurteilungen*)

which one calls aesthetic. . . . And yet the critical investigation of a
principle of judgement in such judgements is the most important piece
of a critique of this capacity.

(Kant Vol X 1977 *KdU* B pp. VII–VIII, A, pp. VII–VIII)

The ground of aesthetic judgements is the difference between pleasure
and unpleasure experienced by the subject in relation to the object. This
difference is, Kant insists, grounded solely in the subject. Importantly,
Kant does not separate the aesthetic aspect of judgement from judgement
in general:

> Admittedly we do not feel any noticeable pleasure any more in the
> graspability of nature and in its unity of *division* into genera and species
> . . . in its time there must have been some, and only because the most
> common experience would not be possible without it has it gradually
> merged with mere cognition and is no longer particularly noticed.
>
> (*KdU* B p. XL, A p. XXXVIII)

The very possibility of judgement is therefore grounded in the pleasure of
grasping and articulating a world. In these terms truth itself is connected to
the faculty of articulation which enables us to make the world intelligible
at all, a faculty which is intrinsically linked to imaginative as well as to
cognitive activity. The realisation of the impossibility of finally separating
imagination from cognition is the vital Kantian insight for Romanticism,
and thus for the emergence of literary theory.

The connection of Kant's conception of judgement to the questions of
aesthetics and language is what makes literary theory possible. Why this
is so should be apparent from the following example. In the *System of
Transcendental Idealism* of 1800, written while he was in close contact with
Schlegel and Novalis in Jena, Schelling says of Kant's schema: 'The schema
. . . is not an idea (*Vorstellung*) that is determined on all sides, but an intuition of the rule according to which a particular object can be produced'
(Schelling (I/3) p. 508). As *intuition* of a rule, thus as immediate access to
the rule, the schema cannot itself be determined: for that, intuitions need
logically prior concepts. There can, as such, be no further grounding of this
intuition beyond the fact of its own functioning, which is what renders the
world intelligible.[14] Schelling concludes that 'From this necessity of
schematism we can infer that the whole mechanism of language must rest
upon schematism' (ibid. p. 509): for words to have iterable significance –
indeed, for words to *mean* anything at all – they must depend upon some
ground of identity which both makes manifest and, so to speak, 'holds
steady' what is meant, while the actual data of empirical reality continually
change. Similarly, if one is to learn the rules for using language appropriately, one must, in order to be able to understand the same utterance
in differing situations, understand in a manner which cannot be further
grounded by rules: otherwise a regress of rules for rules ensues once again.

This point will, as we shall see in Chapters 4 and 5, become vital when considering the problem of interpreting texts outside the contexts of their emergence.

In Kantian terms, true judgements depend upon the subject connecting the apparently incompatible realms of ever-differing sense-data, and stable concepts: the schema is supposed to perform the function of making the realms compatible. Schelling and, in a more developed manner, Schleier-macher realise that this ability to sustain identities is linked to the ability to use a finite vocabulary to talk about a world which is infinitely differ-entiated. As such, language and the activity of the subject suggested by the notion of schematism must be interdependent. A vital problem raised in relation to the functioning of schematism connects the epistemological issue both to language and to questions of aesthetics. Already existing concepts, Kant claims, are applied by 'determining judgement', which, via schematism, the condition of anything having the status of cognisable entity at all, apprehends something particular as a case of a general concept. 'Reflective judgement', which constitutes Kant's response to the question of induction,[15] goes in the opposite direction: its function is to arrive at a general concept, a rule for identifying, a series of particulars. In order to achieve this one must be able to see the differing cases as in some way identical, and thence to *form* a concept which will cover those differing cases. Because there is no concept to begin with, the concept must be 'imagined', in the 'productive' sense that it is brought into existence by the subject. This capacity for judgement does not, therefore, function 'schemat-ically, but technically' (Kant Vol X 1977 *KdU*, original Introduction p. 26), where the former is regarded as part of the functioning of a stable frame-work and the latter as involving 'art', in a sense somewhere between 'craft' or 'technique', and creative or productive ability. It should be apparent from the preceding discussion that Kant had previously used the notion of '*techne*' to describe the working of *schematism*: his uncertainty about the functioning of the imagination is precisely the point which the Romantics will exploit in their rejection of a final articulable ground of epistemology.

Importantly, Kant stresses the fact that reflective judgement need not arrive at any final determinations and can be allowed to function for its own sake, by making links and analogies between differing aspects of the empirical world. There is therefore the possibility of an interplay between the categorisation performed by the understanding and the image-producing capacity of the imagination, in which neither need become dominant. This interplay generates aesthetic pleasure.[16] The easiest way to understand the interplay in relation to language is to think about meta-phors, which may be true in a literal sense,[17] but need not be, and which suspend us between the identification of what the metaphor may mean and the idea that there is no necessary final meaning to the metaphor.[18] Kant's aim is to suggest that there is a harmony between the way the subject apprehends the world and the way the world of nature is systematically organised, thereby grounding the fact that we see nature as appropriate to the organising capacity of our cognition. He is, however, careful to insist that this is only the way in which we can think of it, not that we could ever warrantably assert that such a harmony has a further ground, as that would lead to the kind of 'dogmatic' metaphysics he has already rejected.

These ramifications of Kant's theory of judgement begin to make it apparent how the subject is involved in what has been termed 'world-making', and how 'world-making' relates to language.[19] Attending to the detail of this particular issue here will make its re-emergence in diverse forms within subsequent literary theory more accessible. The question is whether, as Kant hopes, a framework that would draw the boundaries between the sciences, ethics and aesthetics, and which is itself grounded in powers of the subject to which we have theoretical access, can really be established by philosophy. If the framework cannot be finally established, the world-making aspect of the subject cannot be made transparent to philosophy, which means it must be approached in other ways (see Lacoue-Labarthe and Nancy 1988).

The simple way to bring to light the initial problem with Kant's version of these issues was to argue, as J.G. Hamann did in 1784, that Kant's supposedly universal ways of categorising reality were actually dependent upon particular natural languages. These languages do not divide up the world in the same manner and cannot be made to converge via comparison with or reference to a 'general philosophical language'.[20] The perceived importance of 'literary language' at this time derives from the break with the idea of a language which would be able to represent the ready-made truth of the world. The crucial theoretical point here is illustrated by the link Schelling established between language and schematism. The diversity of natural languages appears to be linked to a schematising capacity which does not function in a uniform manner. Different natural languages in differing cultures thus come to be understood as involving a creative, spontaneous aspect, whereby the language grows from the culture in which it originates, and particular languages are precluded from being circum-scribed by a universal theory. From Hamann and J.G. Herder to Wilhelm von Humboldt and Schleiermacher, this conception of language will form a vital new departure in modern thought. On the other hand, the fact of translation between languages, interest in which also grows in this period,[21] would seem to depend upon a universal schematising capacity. The evidence for such a capacity lies in logical and grammatical functions that can be translated from one language to another. These functions are there-fore not bound to a single language, and they seem to indicate that a general philosophical account of how language works – and thus a general account of the nature of truth – may in fact be possible.

The tension between these positions takes us to the heart of modern literary theory. Foucault's account of the simultaneous rise of linguistics, and of the modern notion of literature – which he terms the 'contestation of philology [in the sense of the academic discipline concerned with explaining language]' – is, for example, bound up with this tension. Indeed, many of the disagreements between the analytical and the European traditions in philosophy that emerge in twentieth-century philosophy are already implicit in the tension. The tension is exemplified by the relationship between hermeneutic accounts of why meaning cannot be reduced to explanation and attempts in analytical philosophy to set up a 'formal semantics' valid for explaining meaning in any natural language. Behind these issues lies the awareness, central to early Romantic philosophy, that language itself presents us with a problem of grounding: when philosophy tries to explain language it must always already be reliant upon what it is trying to explain. If the world is rendered intelligible via systems of relations between linguistic elements, which linguistic elements would themselves be able to circumscribe the *totality* of those relations, without having to make the impossible move of including themselves in the totality they claim to circumscribe? This structure, in which the problems of self-reference that play an important role in modern philosophy from the early Wittgenstein to Derrida and other contemporary thinkers are already apparent, will be one of the crucial issues in Romantic philosophy. First, though, let us briefly consider some further aspects of the changes in the way language is understood in the eighteenth century that are vital for understanding the revolution effected by the Romantics, a revolution whose consequences are still very much with us and which has rarely been adequately understood.

'TO BEGIN WITH ONE ONLY SPOKE IN POETRY'

The widespread concern with the origin of language in the second half of the eighteenth century has seldom been seen in close enough conjunction with the search for the new grounding for knowledge we have considered so far.[22] Texts like those of Hamann, and Herder's *Essay on the Origin of Language* of 1770, shift the focus of philosophy towards analysis of a further condition of possibility of truth which can no longer be assumed to be derived from the divinity.[23] Eighteenth-century debates about the origins of language tend to be located between certain paradigmatic positions. Condillac's reductive 'naturalist' perspective, in which language is a higher form of animal cry and thus amenable to scientific explanation, Rousseau's expressivist claim that language originates in the need to articulate desires, emotions and needs, the rationalist theological attempt – e.g. in Johann Peter Süßmilch – to sustain the idea of the divine origin, and Herder's anthropological grounding of language as part of our 'species being' have been echoed in various forms in the philosophy of language ever since.[24]

Perhaps the most important indicator of the changes in conceptions of language in this period lies in the new relationships, established by Rousseau, Hamann, Herder and the Romantics, between language and music. The idea that the first language was music has a very long history which begins well before the modern period, but the idea takes on new resonances in Europe in the second half of the eighteenth century. This change is, of course, accompanied by a radical transformation of music itself, most strikingly exemplified in the work of Haydn, Mozart, Beethoven and Schubert. Rousseau adopts the idea of language as music in his own manner, when he claims in the 1762 *Essay on the Origin of Languages* that:

> Neither hunger nor thirst, but love, hate, pity, anger tore the first voices [from man] . . . that is why the first languages were sung (*chantantes*) and passionate before being simple and methodical. . . . Figurative language was the first to be born, the literal sense was found last. . . . To begin with one only spoke in poetry; one only thought to reason long after this. (Rousseau 1990 pp. 67–8)

The musician, therefore, 'will not directly represent things, but will excite in the soul the same feelings that one feels on seeing them' (ibid. p. 133). This is, though, clearly questionable as a theory of music's relationship to language. Even making Rousseau's distinction between the literal and the figurative is a problem: one must presumably use the literal to do so, which, unless one already has some other way of establishing when language is literal and when it is figurative, then begs the question as to their primacy. Derrida makes much of such difficulties, and thinkers as different as Charles Taylor and Derrida share the suspicion that the desire to fix the difference between figural and literal is actually the source of many misconceptions concerning the real working of language. Rousseau's contentions do, though, exemplify an awareness at this time of the diverse ways in which the world can be disclosed to and articulated by the subject. The world of things ceases to be thought of as external and as merely mirrored by a mind which also has its own separate internal states, and the internal and the external become interlinked. Music is able to give access to the *world* via the fact that the world brings about feelings in the subject which can also be re-articulated by music. Importantly, Rousseau adds that 'It is one of the great advantages of the musician to be able to depict things one could not hear, whereas it is impossible for the painter to represent things one could not see' (ibid.). The relationship of musical articulation to what is understood via music is not a relationship of representation analogous to the representation of an object by an image, because music can, for example, as Rousseau maintains, evoke *repose* by the nature of its *movement*.[25] If this is the case for music, there are also grounds for suggesting that language may also not function in a merely representational manner.

How, though, is the priority between verbal language and music to be established? If verbal language is thought to emerge historically from pre-semantic forms of articulation, it will be interpreted in a thoroughly different manner from how it is interpreted if it is considered to be already constituted and installed in us by the divinity, as the naming or representation of His world.[26] Furthermore, the decline of the idea of a ready-made language also introduces history into the study of language in new ways: Friedrich Schlegel's ground-breaking work on a developmental history of literature, for example, is unthinkable without this change in the status of language. The growing awareness of the inherent historicity of language, which is also the condition of possibility of the emergence of linguistics, is the vital aspect here. If the semantic level of language emerged via a move beyond merely expressive articulation, something has thereby also been 'repressed' which must be recovered and must find a new outlet. The idea of such a repression is, significantly, connected to the contemporaneous rise of the idea of 'absolute music', music without a text. Music thus comes to be regarded as the highest form of art, because it articulates what verbal language cannot. This change in the status of music is inseparable from the new conception of literature at issue here (see Dahlhaus 1978, Bowie 1990 Chapter 7).

Herder was one of the first to argue that, because the ability to articulate ideas itself *depends* upon language, language cannot be assumed to be a mirror which reflects preceding ideas. The very notion of a word, as opposed to a mere cry, he maintains, becomes impossible to understand if one does not assume a capacity for what he terms 'reflection' (*Besonnenheit*), the ability, as Taylor puts it, 'to grasp something *as* what it is', rather than to just react to it in the manner of pre-linguistic beings (Taylor 1995 p. 103).[27] The idea that language primarily mirrors or represents things depends upon being able to explain how it is that words can designate things in the first place (which is actually a version of the problem of schematism). Herder maintains, therefore, that when Condillac suggests how 'In order to grasp how people agreed among each other on the meaning of the first words that they wished to use, it is enough to notice that they spoke them in circumstances where everyone was bound to connect them with the same ideas' (cited in Herder 1966 p. 18), he has effectively maintained that 'In short, words emerged because words were there before they were there' (ibid.). Language, though, must be the *vehicle* of the awareness which allows the world to be articulated at all as a world in which things can be seen as determinate things. The awareness without the vehicle is inconceivable, and vice versa. The real mystery, which Herder does not explain – though he is clearly aware of it – lies in the fact, as Charles Taylor points out, that 'it seems that we need the whole of language as the background for the introduction of any of its parts, that is, individual words' (Taylor 1985 p. 230; see also Taylor 1995). A 'holistic' understanding of language underlies many of the issues linking Romantic thought to contemporary literary theory and philosophy, as we shall see.

Given the indissoluble link Herder establishes between reason and language, Jacobi's remark in Chapter 1 that 'A reason which does not presuppose the true is an abomination' (Jacobi 1799 p. 27) indicates a major problem. Without the presupposition that the world is always already intelligible, any account of language is faced with insuperable difficulties in explaining what makes a word a word, as opposed to being merely a repeated noise. Indeed, as the notion of schema suggested, even recognising the *repetition* of a noise requires a ground by reference to which identities can be established between differing empirical data. The question is, therefore, how language's intelligibility is to be explained, given language's immanence within that of which it speaks. One answer, as we saw, was proposed by Fichte, who made the activity of the subject the ground of the world's intelligibility. However, in the use of language the activity of each individual subject is channelled by pre-existing forms of articulation which that subject did not create, even though it may render these forms intelligible in its own individual way.[28] The exploration of the tension between the productive capacity of the subject and the constraints on that subject of the systematically constituted medium of articulation is, as I suggested at the end of Chapter 1, germane to the very ideas of literature and of *literary* theory, as opposed to linguistics.

The essential transformation here is from the idea of language as denomination, in which words more or less adequately re-present or name pre-existing things, towards the idea that what things are will also depend both upon their relationship to the activity of the subject, and upon their relations to each other. A further influential aspect of this anti-representationalist conception will lie in the connection of the world's coming to be disclosed in language to the feeling of a lack in the subject which language is somehow to fill. The orientation towards an expressive origin of language, symbolised in the idea that the first language was music or poetry, signals the move away from a conception of language as naming, towards the new conceptions of truth which develop together with the new significance attached to 'literature'. The consequences of this move will concern us in Chapter 3.

3 The philosophy of critique and the critique of philosophy
Romantic literary theory

'THE RIDICULOUS MISTAKE, THAT PEOPLE THINK THEY SPEAK FOR THE SAKE OF THINGS'

The extent to which the understanding of language and truth is transformed in Romantic philosophy can be gauged from Novalis' startling *Monologue* of 1798. *Monologue* is also significant because it offers an enactment of what Romanticism might mean by 'literature' (*Poesie*).[1] By asking the question whether *Monologue* is itself literature or a text about literature one can begin to show both how many of the philosophical issues we have considered so far inform the questions posed by Romantic literary theory and how these questions have returned to the contemporary philosophical agenda. That Novalis and his friend Friedrich Schlegel were thoroughly aware of the philosophical issues is evident from discussions of Kant, Fichte and Jacobi at numerous points in their work. Here is the complete text of *Monologue*:

> It is a strange thing about speaking and writing; a real conversation is just a game of words. One can only be amazed at the ridiculous mistake, that people think they speak for the sake of things. Of the fact that language is peculiar because it only concerns itself with itself, nobody is aware. That is why it is a wonderful and fruitful secret, – that precisely when someone speaks just in order to speak he pronounces the most splendid and original truths. But if he wishes to speak of something determinate, temperamental old language makes him say the most ridiculous and mistaken things. That is also the source of the hatred which so many serious people have for language. They notice its mischief but do not notice that wretched chattering is the infinitely serious side of language. If one could only make people understand that with language it is as with mathematical formulae – They constitute their own world – They only play with themselves, express nothing but their wonderful nature, and this is why they are so expressive – precisely for this reason does the strange game of relations of things reflect itself in them. Only via their freedom are they members of nature and only in their free movements does the world-soul express itself and make them into a gentle measure

and outline of things. Thus it is also with language – whoever has a fine feeling for [language's] application, for its rhythm, for its musical spirit, who hears in himself the gentle effect of its inner nature and moves his tongue or hand accordingly, will be a prophet; on the other hand, whoever knows this well enough but does not have the ears and the feeling for language will write truths like these but will be made fun of by language and will be mocked by people, like Cassandra by the Trojans. If I believe that I have thereby indicated the essence and role (*Amt*) of literature (*Poesie*) in the clearest possible fashion then I yet know that no one can understand it and that I have said something completely stupid, because I wanted to say it, and in this way no literature can come into being. But what if I had to speak? and this drive to speak were the characteristic of the inspiration of language, of the effectiveness of language in me? and if my will as well could only want whatever I *had* to do, then this could in the last analysis indeed be literature without my knowing it and believing it, and could render a secret of language comprehensible? and thus I would be a writer by vocation, for a writer is really only one who is enthused by language [*ein Sprachbegeisterter*, which has the sense of one who is 'in-spirited' by language]?

(Novalis 1978 pp. 438–9)

If *Monologue* is a statement *about* literature, the problem suggested at the end of the text leads to a philosophical aporia; if it *is* literature, what Schlegel means by the 'philology of philosophy' is carried out in the text itself. The tension between these two possibilities opens up the domain of Romantic literary theory, as an examination of a few key points in *Monologue* can suggest.

The most obviously striking aspect of *Monologue* is Novalis' dismissal of the representational model of language: he even points, via the way he uses the phrase 'game of words', to the notion, common to both Wittgenstein and Gadamer, that language is a rule-bound game (or games) whose working does not primarily depend upon the intentional mental acts of its users. Just how far Novalis can go in the rejection of representation is made explicit in the following passage:

All the superstition and error of all times and peoples and individuals rests upon the confusion of the *symbol* with what is symbolised – upon making them identical – upon the belief in true complete representation – and relation of the picture and the original – of appearance and substance – on the inference from external similarity to complete inner correspondence and connection – in short on the confusions of subject and object. (ibid. p. 637)

The essential aspect of language lies, then, not in the identifying of 'things', but in the ways language, like mathematics, can establish new *relations* between things, relations which constitute what a thing is understood to be.

This is symbolised by the association of the 'strange game of relations of things ... reflected' in language, with language's 'musical spirit'. The interplay of the elements in a piece of music is constitutive of it being music at all, nothing beyond this play can be said to make something into music. Music is also, of course, not comprehensible qua music in terms of representation. Vital in this respect is Novalis' adherence to a version of 'holism'. Romantic holism is characterised in Friedrich Schlegel's dictum that 'A real single phenomenon is completely determined and explained via the *context of the whole world* to which it belongs' (Schlegel 1988 1 p. 105).[2] Novalis' linking of the holistic nature of both language and music suggests a vital connection of language to works of art, including non-verbal works, whose elements only acquire significance via their relationships to other elements.

This connection can already help us to make sense of some of the apparently wilder claims in Romanticism, such as the claim that the world itself is a self-producing work of art. The basis for this claim is Kant's notion of reflective judgement: once freed from the task of conceptual determination, the capacity for establishing relationships which renders knowledge possible also allows one to understand something as a work of art, rather than as just an object of cognition. In this sense aesthetic contemplation of the interrelations which constitute the beauty of nature is in fact another form of aesthetic constitution of the object, and, as Schlegel puts it in the *Conversation on Literature*: 'All holy games of art are only distant imitations of the endless play of the world, of the work of art which constantly forms itself' (Schlegel 1988 (2) p. 206). Romantic philosophy's vital addition to the Kantian conception lies in its attention to language, which leads to the correspondences between the world, language and art that are central to Romantic thinking.

For language to be language and music to be music, however, the 'reflective' capacity of the subject to understand something *as* something, upon which Herder insisted in his argument about how words are not merely noises, must come into play. But *how* does the subject play the 'world-making' role implied by the notion of reflection? Clearly Novalis does not think that the subject does so in the manner of the Kantian transcendental subject in the *Critique of Pure Reason*, which grounds necessary ways in which the world is apprehended. The question of the location and exact nature of schematism – the 'hidden art in the depths of the human soul' – has already suggested why this is problematic. Novalis' suspicion, which he shares with Schlegel, is that any conscious intention to arrive at the truth by speaking 'of something determinate' will block essential insights into the nature of truth, because the intention will lead the subject to fix the object via a single determination, thereby inhibiting its own creative capacity and ultimately rendering the world itself lifeless. Schlegel will later claim in the *Notebooks on Philosophy* from 1805 that

there is only one inherited fundamental mistake – the fundamentally wrong concept of the thing – which takes merely relative *finitude* [the particular transient object] as absolute and abstracts the *shadow concept* of BEING from life – *Being* is merely apparent, finitude only relative. Being=life, without life, being=appearance. (Schlegel 1988 (5) p. 108)

Schematism, as the means of fixing things, must therefore be conceived of dynamically and creatively, not as just a substitute for the notion of re-presentation of what is supposedly already there. At this level the Romantics are convinced German Idealists:[3] they regard the world's intelligibility as a product both of the world itself and of the living subject which knows it while being (in one sense) part of it. An analogous more recent conception is evident in Hilary Putnam's assertion against a representationalist conception of truth that 'the mind and the world jointly make up the mind and the world' (Putnam 1981 p. *xi*). As we shall see in this and the following chapters, this convergence extends to other key areas of contemporary philosophy.

In *Monologue* the world of determinate knowledge, as in much Romantic philosophy, is no longer the final locus of truth, because the determinacy of the particular only emerges via its continually being related to other things, which is a process with no necessary conclusion.[4] Language whose propositional aspect is not its most significant attribute therefore takes on a higher status than language which determinately refers to things in the world, because the latter will always fail in its attempt to be definitive. The language in question is, of course, 'literature'. Novalis goes so far as to imagine, thereby explicitly prefiguring later conceptions of non-representational art:

> Poems, just pleasant sounding and full of beautiful words, but also without any meaning or context . . . like fragments of the most diverse things. True poetry can at the most have an allegorical meaning as a whole and an indirect effect, like music etc. (Novalis 1978 p. 769; also cited in Benjamin 1980 (I) 1 p. 363, where the context is illuminating)

Allegory is fundamental to the Romantic conception of language and, as we shall see, to Benjamin's view of the secularised modern world. Schlegel defines allegory as 'the mediating term between unity and multiplicity' (Schlegel 1990 p. 41), which 'results from the impossibility of reaching the Highest by reflection' (Schlegel 1988 (5) p. 105). In trying determinately to state the highest truth the very structure of articulation splits into multiplicity what is meant as unity. Allegory gives us a way of understanding how what we ultimately seek to say may not be able to be stated in propositions, because allegory is manifested in the form of propositions which negate their referential meaning, as well as in entities in the world which do not mean what they appear to be. The Romantics regard the negativity inherent in determinate language as analogous to the world of transient particular things, which appear real and positive but cease eventually to be real by becoming something else. Language is in one sense a means of opposing such finitude, but even language is subject to temporality in its very form, which requires time to be articulated.

The Romantics' wariness of determinate propositions is also what leads them to their particular conception of irony. Normally irony is the determinate negation of what is asserted in a proposition: 'That was good', said ironically, means it wasn't. Romantic irony, on the other hand, requires the negation of the assertion, but not in favour of a determinate contrary assertion. This can be understood via Novalis' link of the poetic sense of language to music: the poet's 'words are not universal signs – they are notes – magic words which move beautiful groups around themselves . . . for the poet language is never too poor but always too universal' (Novalis 1978 p. 322). The crucial factor is the need to combine elements of the world, including the finite elements of language itself, in new ways, which constantly point beyond themselves, thereby employing the finite means to a non-finite purpose.

The problem posed in the later part of *Monologue* – concerning the status of the text itself – should now begin to make the relationship between the concept of literature and the concept of truth which is characteristic of Romantic philosophy more accessible.[5] How can one finally *say* that what one says is true? If one says x is true because of y, one then has to ask why y is true, and so on, which leads to a linguistically formulated version of the problem of grounding seen in Kant and Jacobi. It was Karl Leonhard Reinhold who tried between 1789 and 1794, in his highly influential *Elementarphilosophie*, to solve the problem by establishing, in the light of Descartes and Kant, the absolute '*Grundsatz*'. This was the 'proposition of consciousness', which is the 'grounding proposition' from which all further propositions could be deduced, the proposition that would articulate a relationship in which thought reflects being (see Reinhold 1978; on Reinhold see Beiser 1987). The demonstration of the failure of this sort of programme is the basis of the central insights of Romantic philosophy (see Frank 1994). Language's internal relationships make an articulated world possible, but even if the world of things is also essentially a web of relations one cannot finally articulate a way of mapping, in language, one set of relations on to the other, because that would entail a further web of relations, and so on. The relations in question are anyway not seen as permanent: each shift in one relationship between elements will also alter the relationships between the others. Novalis' claim is that by engaging in the play of the resources within this dynamic web of relationships one can reveal 'truths' that cannot emerge if one wishes to define the relationships or find a grounding proposition. The world thus constituted is not a realm of fixed objects, but rather a world in which 'truths' arise by combining differing *articulations* of what there is. Does this, though, not just render truth merely indeterminate, in so far as there is no absolute point from which these differing articulations could finally be validated?

Novalis' claims about 'truths' might seem almost frivolous, especially to those used to the assumption that truth resides in propositions which adequately correspond to a ready-made world. However, the idea implicit in *Monologue* – that truths can only be understood holistically, because meaning is dependent upon ever-shifting contexts – has now become almost a commonplace in many contemporary accounts of the working of language, from Gadamer to Davidson, or even, in some interpretations, to Derrida. In a recent discussion of holistic accounts of meaning, for example, J. E. Malpas considers the implications for a theory of meaning of what he terms, following W.V.O. Quine, the 'indeterminacy thesis'.[6] The indeterminacy thesis is implied by Quine's assertion that 'manuals for translating one language into another can be set up in divergent ways, all compatible with one another' (Quine, *Word and Object* p. 27, cited in Malpas 1992 p. 14). As such, Quine's argument implies, there is no location from which one can write the final 'absolute' manual – the 'manual' which would correspond to Hamann's impossible 'general philosophical language' – and thus no final ground for adjudication between competing translations (or interpretations), beyond the actual praxis of further use of language.[7]

Malpas looks at this issue in terms of what Jerry Fodor has called, unconsciously echoing Jacobi, 'semantic nihilism'. The indeterminacy thesis, Malpas claims, very much in the spirit of *Monologue*, 'undermines the idea of meaning as a determinate and determinable entity attaching to sentences or terms' (Malpas 1992 p. 63). For Fodor, this position leads to there being no meanings at all, because of the kind of regress seen in Jacobi, the regress of 'semantic nihilism'. In a holist conception terms only gain meaning via their relations to other terms, which means they never gain a final meaning, in the sense of that which could be described independently of context.[8] In order to escape this supposed nihilism Fodor thinks one must ground meaning in terms of reference, 'a causally determined relation holding between mental representations and objects in the world' (ibid. p. 65). This, though, poses the question as to what causes the *intelligibility* of the relationship between representations and objects, the question Fichte had tried to answer without getting into another regress via the 'unconditioned' (uncaused) nature of the subject which is the source of representations, a solution which Fodor's desire for a causal explanation of meaning cannot countenance.[9] Malpas maintains against Fodor, thereby echoing the alternative conception of truth evoked by Novalis, that 'indeterminacy consists, not in the rejection of meaning, but rather in the claim that there is always more than one acceptable way of assigning meanings to utterances' (ibid.) and thus no finally groundable correspondence between representation and object that could define meaning and truth. Such a conception leads to questions of truth in relation to coherence rather than to representation.

Schlegel says in relation to exactly this problem that

> Correspondence with another truth – correspondence with itself [in a coherent system] is a better but *empty* [in the sense that it is not finally positive] characteristic than correspondence with the object, because one only ever has an idea (*Vorstellung*) instead of the object, or there

also is no object [in the sense that many true propositions do not refer to concrete entities in the world]. (Schlegel 1988 (5) p. 108)

The contrast here, between the contention that the move away from a conception of truth grounded in determinacy of meaning and reference leads to nihilism, and the contention that it merely changes the way we theorise and use the truths we always already understand, underlies many of the most controversial debates in literary theory, and suggests how major concerns of literary theory and the contemporary philosophy of language, both analytical and European, have begun to converge in space first opened up by Romantic literary theory.

Novalis' claim about the revelation of truths leads, however, to his paradoxical conclusion, which suggests just how much may be at stake in the contrast just outlined. The paradox emerges because *Monologue* has to *explain* how it is that language discloses the world in *Poesie*, even as it shows that this explanation involves a necessary conflict between two possibly incompatible notions of truth. What status does a discursive explanation of literature have if we must already understand beforehand in a non-discursive manner what 'literature' – as opposed to any other kind of articulation – tells us? As Novalis said in the Introduction: 'Criticism of literature (*Poesie*) is an absurdity. It is already difficult to decide, yet the only possible decision, whether something is literature or not' (Novalis 1978 p. 840). If one could really characterise 'the essence and role of literature' the need for literature itself would, as I suggested in the Introduction, thereby presumably be obviated, because the *theory* of literature would itself be the final truth, and criticism and analysis of the text on the basis of firm foundations for judgement would take precedence over the text itself. This does not, one should add, mean that the text has a status independent of its being read and interpreted, but rather that a *literary* text will always give rise to suspicion of any determinate reading. The Romantics are highly concerned with the issue of interpretation, as we shall see in more detail in the following chapters, but they see it in the creative terms suggested by Novalis' classic formulation: 'The true reader must be the extended author' (ibid. p. 282).

Monologue is, then, either a statement of the highest truth, or it is meaningless, because it refutes its own assertions.[10] Taken literally, *Monologue* must presumably be meaningless, because what it means cannot, in its own terms, be said: but what is meant by taking it literally? 'Literature' and truth are seen as inseparable, but the attempt to *say* this 'in the clearest fashion' refutes content by form: one begins to be 'made fun of by language', because what one means cannot be determinately understood and must instead be concretely experienced in the play of the text, rather than in an articulated analysis of its meaning.

The crucial aspects of language which produce 'truths' are, Novalis alleges, its rhythm and its 'musical spirit', aspects which are not 'truth-functional'.

These aspects cannot themselves be adequately described by another kind of literal language, because their significance will be lost in the process, much as explaining a joke kills the joke qua joke by attempting to replace the effect of the particular *combination* of elements with an account of those elements which does not employ that combination itself. The analogy of describing the real meaning of a piece of music in words, as opposed to listening to a great performance – itself a kind of interpretation – of the music, can also suggest what is meant here. If the significance of a piece of music lies in its articulating a world in ways which nothing else can, our attempts to explain this insight will in one sense miss what it is that the music discloses, even though each statement we make in analysing the piece is, in the sense of 'justifiable assertion', 'true'. This does not mean that a verbal account of music cannot in fact reveal more of that music: the essential fact is that the process can go in *both* directions, so that music can elucidate a verbal account of an aspect of the world, and vice versa. Schlegel summarises what is at issue in this kind of aesthetic apprehension of truth in the following wonderful manner: 'If the chemist thinks a thing is not a whole because he can dissect it, that is just the same as what bad critics do to literature. – Didn't the world emerge from *slime*?' (Schlegel 1988 5 p. 48). Are not the Busch Quartet's recordings of Beethoven's Late Quartets just the articulated – and scientifically describable – scraping of horsehair on catgut or steel, transferred into a material storage medium? We shall encounter another, rather less aesthetically apt, version of Schlegel's position when we later look at Heidegger's conception of 'being' in relation to art in his essay 'The Origin of the Work of Art'. The crucial factor is the suspicion that discursive analysis of any aspect of the world can lose sight of the interplay of that aspect with other aspects which are essential to its determinacy. Literature becomes the reminder of this fact, and therefore only becomes a matter of serious philosophical concern when the analytical method begins to dominate conceptions of truth in the modern period.

A central question with regard to literature is, then, whether we can finally separate the 'musical' aspect of language from its propositional aspect. Gadamer has suggested in line with the Romantic conception that:

> The word which one says or which is said to one is not the grammatical element of a linguistic analysis, which can be shown in concrete phenomena of language acquisition to be secondary in relation, say, to the linguistic melody of a sentence. (Gadamer 1986 p. 196)

In analogous manner, then, by attempting to become theoretically aware of how language renders the world intelligible, the vehicle of that intelligibility may cease to function in the same manner as when one entrusts oneself to its resources for spontaneous creative articulation. These resources appear, for example, in new combinations of linguistic elements in metaphor, or in the use of rhythm, whether in a poem or in everyday usage. Although a writer can work consciously on the development of a new style, in order to articulate a new aspect of the world, the success of this work is not in the final control of the writer.[11] The linguistic resources employed by the writer pre-exist any theoretical attempt on his or her part to understand them, and s/he must also both understand and employ them in order to analyse them.

Language, then, *like nature itself*, of which it forms a part, entails an interplay of necessity and freedom: it is both determinable as a natural phenomenon and beyond such law-bound determination when the resources it offers are recombined to remake our ways of understanding the world. In this vein Walter Benjamin will later say of allegory in the *Trauerspielbuch*, following the Romantics, that 'pulverised language has, in its disintegration, ceased to be at the service of mere communication and places its dignity as new-born object next to that of Gods, rivers, virtues and similar natural figures which shade over into the allegorical' (Benjamin 1980 (I) 1 p. 382). Once language has ceased to be divine nomination it must be seen as another aspect of a nature which can only ever be understood by recombination of its elements.[12] Whether this leads to another version of Jacobi's nihilism is fundamental to contemporary literary theory and to the worries it has provoked. The issue here is the 'materiality of the signifier', the fact that language is, in one sense, manifested like any other thing in the world. Importantly, though, this does not explain how it is that language is meaningful at all, which is why Romantic holism differs from the more nihilistic versions of deconstruction.[13]

The issues just outlined connect *Monologue* to a tension in aesthetic and literary theory which recurs from Hegel's *Aesthetics* to contemporary debates over the relationship of art to truth. The tension is between the need to state what is disclosed by literature and other art, thereby making the translation of art into discursivity the primary goal in the search for the truth it may contain, and the idea that the final success of such a discursive account either renders literature and other art superfluous or fails to understand the truth of art – and, perhaps, the nature of truth – altogether. The result of this latter position is to suggest in a thoroughly consistent and non-mystical manner that the 'truth' revealed most evidently in art is 'unsayable'.

This raises the further question, though, as to whether it is even meaningful for Novalis and Schlegel to *assert* that literature is the privileged location of *truth*, which points to an issue in modern philosophy that has been vital to many versions of literary theory. As is well known, Nietzsche will later, not least via the influence of Romanticism, ask what *value* truth possesses, thereby attempting to undermine the idea that truth qua representation of a ready-made world could ever be grounded. Nietzsche's questioning has had a decisive influence on subsequent discussions of the 'end of metaphysics' in contemporary literary theory. The Romantic understanding of truth both prefigures Nietzsche's question and implies that any determinate answer to it, for example, in terms of power as the ground of truth, fails to understand the real nature of truth. Novalis' fear of writing truths and being 'made fun of by language' already suggests why. The attempt to cash out the doctrine of truth as power (or in terms of 'ideology', construed as the product of power) rapidly leads to absurdities, because only the 'performative' aspect of what one asserts in this context can be taken into account. This means that whether I assert x or not-x becomes a question of my strategic goals, so that my *assertion* that, for example, 'truth is/is not grounded by power' can only be evaluated in terms of whether truth is/is not grounded by power, which leads either into a familiar regress, or to the circular argument that assertion itself is an exercise of power. How, then, given the inherent tendency of such questions to lead to circularity, does Romantic theory defend a non-representational conception of truth?

In the major Western traditions of philosophy since Aristotle, truth has, as we have seen, principally been understood via some version of a correspondence between thought or language and how the world 'really is'. The ultimate form of this correspondence should therefore take the form 'A is A', in the sense that the world is showing itself in one aspect – as being – to be ultimately the same as itself in another aspect – as thought or language. Schlegel explicitly rejects such a conception:

> The criterion of truth . . . is, especially since Leibniz, defined as corres-
> pondence of the representation (*Vorstellung*) with the object; this
> presupposes the half-empiricist separation of object and representation;
> the object would, as such, have to be compared with the represen-
> tation; but that is not at all possible, because one only ever has a
> representation of the object, and thus can only ever compare one
> representation with another. (Schlegel 1964 pp. 316–17)[14]

Novalis remarks in the *Fichte Studies* of 1795–6, while reflecting on the 'statement of identity', 'A is A', which gives the form of the ultimate proposition, that 'The essence of identity can only be established in an apparent proposition (*Scheinsatz*). We leave the identical in order to repre-sent it' (Novalis 1978 p. 8). How, though, can 'the identical' be *known* to have been represented? In order to be determinate in any sense which we can understand, the identical must cease to be present as itself: only that which is in some sense *different* can be *identified* as the same, otherwise one has only stated an empty tautology, thus 'A is A'.[15] The problem is another version of what was revealed by Jacobi when he claimed that 'We can only demonstrate similarities (*agreements, relatively necessary truths*), progressing in statements of identity. Every proof presupposes something which has already been proven, whose principle is *revelation*' (ed. Scholz 1916 p. 178), where revelation cannot itself be based on a further presupposition. The ground of truth thus falls outside 'reflection', the attempt to state the final identity, in which A mirrors A as itself. We shall encounter the move from revelation to literature in various forms, which all share the idea that when literary language reveals truths those truths can never be exhausted by any further description of what is revealed by that particular linguistic articulation. The structure of the basic problem here gives rise to the concern with how one could articulate the structure of what in this period is termed 'the Absolute', or the 'unconditioned', which is crucial to the Romantic conception of literature.

'ALL HIGHEST TRUTHS OF EVERY KIND ARE THOROUGHLY TRIVIAL'

Discussion of 'the Absolute' in the English-speaking world has tended to move in one of two directions, neither of which, to their cost, owes much to the Romantic conception. In the first, because it is beyond anything we can know discursively, and can therefore only be 'known' 'intuitively', the Absolute is regarded as a mystical issue for theologians. In the second, the Absolute is the world uncontaminated by the relative ways the human mind 'sees' it within particular local interpretations: truth here is the final correspondence of 'objective' scientific knowledge to the ready-made world. Bernard Williams, who in this respect (though not in others) is thoroughly in line with the Spinozism we considered in Chapter 2, has approvingly termed this version of truth the 'absolute conception'. In both cases, it would seem, the arguments of Kant have been forgotten. The Romantic approach to the Absolute, on the other hand, *begins* with Kant's own failure adequately to deal with the problem of the 'unconditioned', but does not ignore his demonstration that we cannot claim to know the world 'in itself' through science, preferring to try to understand, in the light of Kant, why it is that we pursue truth at all. The real issue for the Romantics is how one comes to terms with the relativity of particular claims to knowledge without becoming trapped by the paradoxes of relativism and the regresses of nihilism: hence the importance of some notion of the Absolute, and, by extension, of the notion of literature. The continuing significance to contemporary theory of what is involved in the Romantics' reflections derives from the way they attempt to sustain an orientation towards truth, even though the idea that specific truths can be finally epistemologically grounded without falling prey to the regress revealed by Jacobi is abandoned, in favour of an alternative approach which has many echoes in philosophy today.

Manfred Frank has suggested that

> two incompatible demands are contained in the thought of the Absolute: in order really to be absolute it must exist in itself, i.e. without any relation to an other; on the other hand the Absolute as highest principle of philosophy must be thought of as self-conscious (consequently as dependent on consciousness). (Frank 1989b p. 239)

The two demands entailed in the idea of the Absolute set the agenda for philosophy after Kant in ways we have already explored. The first demand points in the direction of Jacobi's 'unconditioned', the unknowable ground which cannot be the same as the relative 'conditions' which it sustains. The second points to Fichte's insistence that subjectivity cannot be generated by anything which we think of as an object and therefore must have a status above that of the determinate object world. The reason why the Absolute must be thought of in terms of self-consciousness is, significantly, evident from Hilary Putnam's 'Fichtean' argument against Bernard Williams' 'Spinozist' absolute conception: 'It cannot be the case that scientific knowledge (future fundamental physics) is absolute and nothing else is; for fundamental physics cannot explain the possibility of referring to or stating anything, including fundamental physics itself' (Putnam 1990 p. 176). Putnam's argument raises the problem of self-reference, which is vital to Romantic arguments about literature, as we shall see in a moment. The problem of self-reference is the problem of how to gain the external perspective – which would allow one to assert that the universe is 'really "x"' (e.g. 'law-bound matter') – without leaving the place from which that assertion is made outside what is described as the grounding reality.

The fact is that it is contradictory to think that a complete account of the world in terms of scientific laws is absolute, unless consciousness could explain *itself* in a completely law-bound manner. The problem is that the explanation must be of the kind used to explain a phenomenon of nature like any other, but the whole point of transcendental philosophy, which Fichte saw more clearly than anyone, is that the condition of possibility of grasping natural phenomena in terms of laws cannot itself be of the same status as those phenomena. If consciousness is to explain itself qua object it must already be unquestionably familiar in a non-objectified manner with what is to be explained; otherwise it would have no criterion for knowing that it had explained *itself*. The prior condition of my seeing myself in a mirror as *myself*, rather than as a random object, is that I must be already familiar with myself in some way which does not require a mirror. This awareness is of a different order from the awareness I have of the 'not-I', the appearing object world. As Novalis puts it, following Kant's arguments discussed in Chapter 2, 'Can I look for a schema [as that which enables one to identify objects] for myself, if I am that which schematises?' (Novalis 1978 p. 162). Furthermore, consciousness' inherent familiarity with itself cannot be equated with the cognitive, objectified account it has of itself once it has questioned its own status in transcendental reflection. Novalis maintains 'What reflection *finds*, *seems* already *to be there*' (Novalis 1978 p. 17). The Kantian categories, established in Kant's 'transcendental deduction', seem to be the a priori conditions of reality, which are revealed in reflection upon what we already know. However, the already existing 'I' must in fact be prior to the ways it attempts to describe itself via the self-reflection demanded by transcendental philosophy, and thus can never be circumscribed by something which depends upon it as its ground.[16]

In the first of Frank's cases, then, the Absolute cannot be articulated, and can be construed either, as it is in Jacobi, in terms of how the 'real' truth is hidden from us and can only be revealed in an act of faith or, as it is for the Romantics, in terms of the truth as a 'regulative idea' of that which we seek but which we could never finally claim to have found. In the second case, the problem of how the subject relates to its ground must be answered without making it into merely another part of deterministically conceived nature, in the manner of Williams' 'absolute conception', or, as Jacobi claims Fichte does, rendering the object merely a function of the subject.[17] Romantic literary theory and its connection to truth result from the tension between these alternatives, alternatives which, as we shall see in subsequent chapters, recur throughout modern philosophy.

The following characteristic remarks by Schlegel, from the essay 'On Incomprehensibility' of 1800, a reply to criticisms of the *Athenäum* journal in which many of his boldest ideas were first made public, can now show how consideration of the Absolute leads to the question of literature:

> All highest truths of every kind are thoroughly trivial and for this reason nothing is more necessary than always to express them anew and if possible ever more paradoxically, so that it is not forgotten that they are still there, and that they can never really be completely expressed.
>
> (Schlegel 1988 (2) p. 237)

The need for constant re-articulation of these truths goes along with the fact that each particular expression is incomplete because it requires its context to be meaningful. The highest truth ought presumably to be a statement of identity, of the form 'A is A', but that is also the ultimate trivial statement, as Novalis suggested. One could, looking at Schlegel's view from a different angle, construe the claims of contemporary physicists about the 'final building blocks of the universe' in a similar way: how different would the world really look if they discovered them? It all depends on where you are standing and what you think is the final reality: there is no philosophical reason, as Putnam makes clear, to suppose that this must be deterministically conceived matter. Schlegel later maintains, thereby raising a vital question about the philosophical enterprise itself: 'In truth you would be distressed if the whole world, as you demand, were for once seriously to become completely comprehensible. And is even this infinite world not formed by understanding out of incomprehensibility or chaos?' (Schlegel 1988 (2) p. 240). In the same vein Novalis suggests 'Now all sciences are connected – therefore philosophy will never be completed. Only in the complete system of all sciences would philosophy be properly visible' (Novalis 1978 p. 827) and 'Philosophy is, so to speak, the substance of science – which is sought everywhere – which is present everywhere and never appears to him who seeks' (Novalis 1978 p. 537).

The very idea that philosophy could *say* how truth is finally to be understood is, then, perhaps itself the real mistake. Novalis claims in this connection that 'If the character of a given problem is its insolubility, then we solve the problem by representing its insolubility' (Novalis 1978 p. 613). The 'true philosophy could never be represented' (ibid. p. 828), whereas 'literature ... represents the unrepresentable' (ibid. p. 840), namely that which cannot be stated in propositions, in the medium of determinate knowledge. The Romantic holist approach, in which truths emerge by continual recontextualisation, rejects approaches to truth in which a unitary origin is supposed to lead to a unitary goal. The most readily accessible medium of understanding this approach to truth is literature. Literature depends on the freedom of the imagination always to move beyond any particular determination, without any obligation to arrive at a conclusion, and its goal, most directly evident in metaphor, is continually to render the world meaningful by connecting its aspects in new constellations. It therefore, Novalis claims, 'heals the wounds struck by the understanding' (ibid. p. 814), which can only synthesise determinate facts.

Schlegel's position with regard to truth is encapsulated in the following classic passage from his *Transcendentalphilosophie* of 1801:

> Truth arises when opposed errors neutralise each other. Absolute truth cannot be admitted; and this is the testimony for the freedom of thought and of spirit. If absolute truth were found then the business of spirit would be completed and it would have to cease to be, since it only exists in activity. (Schlegel 1991 p. 93)

In this sense '*There really is no error*' (ibid. p. 94) because truth and error are identical: determinate truths are the product of error's self-cancellation, and thus cannot exist without error.[18] Only if one had a founding absolute proposition of the kind demanded by Reinhold could any subsequent truth not be seen as merely the refutation of a preceding truth. Schlegel is well aware that his *claim* that all truth is relative is itself open to the objection that the claim is self-refuting: 'If all truth is relative, then the proposition is also relative that all truth is relative' (ibid. p. 95). As such one cannot *assert* in a general proposition that all truth is relative, without making a claim that cannot be meant, given the content of what one has asserted.

This impossibility, it should be apparent, connects in a decisive way to Novalis' claims about literature. For Novalis, the essence of literature could not be discursively represented, and could only be experienced in a continual engagement with language. Novalis claims in the *Fichte Studies* that the 'Absolute which is given to us can only be known negatively, by our acting and finding that no action can reach what we are seeking' (Novalis 1978 p. 181). Crucially, and contrary to so many interpretations of Romanticism, this does not mean that one gives way to an indeterminate longing for the impossible:[19]

> But human beings must never, like a fantasist, seek something indeter-
> minate – a child of fantasy – an ideal – They should only proceed from
> determinate task to determinate task. An unknown beloved admittedly

has a magical charm. Striving for the Unknown – the indeterminate is extremely dangerous and disadvantageous. One cannot produce revelations by force. (Novalis 1978 pp. 793–4)

Manfred Frank has suggested that the Romantic Absolute therefore 'exists as that which, in the divisions and fragmentations of our world of the understanding, yet creates that unity, without which contradiction and difference could not be shown as such' (Frank 1989b p. 340). The Absolute ceases to be what philosophy can describe, and becomes that which renders our knowledge relative. Without the continuing pursuit of *and belief in* truth, generated by our inherent dissatisfaction with any claim to have achieved it, the propositional claim that truth is always merely relative is undemonstrable, or even 'false', given that there is no way of confirming it. Schlegel realises, then, that the relativity of all truth can only ever be continually experienced in the failure of the attempt to get beyond that relativity.[20] He talks in this respect, and in thoroughly *non* 'post-modern' fashion, of 'the higher scepticism of Socrates, which, unlike common scepticism, does not consist in the denial of truth and certainty, but rather in the serious search for them' (Schlegel 1964 p. 202). 'Common scepticism' is famously and evidently self-refuting, but an anti-sceptical position which maintains it is possible to know in an absolute manner is subject to the regress we have been considering all along, which Jacobi countered with his notion of 'the true', and which the Romantics connect to their conception of literature.

The vital point is, then, that for the Romantics *assertion itself* is rendered inherently problematic: one assertion is only an error opposed to another error, but the second assertion will always require the first, even though this cannot, however far back one goes, lead to a grounding assertion. The mistake is to believe that one can assert a truth which would avoid a new kind of nihilism, the nihilism that results from thinking one knows the final answer. The most valuable thing to do is, therefore, to render the truth questionable once more, rather than attempt to dissolve it into final comprehensibility. In Derrida's Nietzsche-inspired remarks in 'Structure, Sign, and Game' cited in Chapter 2, the very idea of truth in traditional metaphysics, which is conceived of as a ground or origin that would 'escape the play and the order of the sign' by being re-presented, falls prey to the regress of signs whose meaning always depends upon other signs. The Romantic view, however, does not conceive of truth as ground or origin in any straightforward sense: 'Every real beginning is a *secondary moment*' (Novalis 1978 p. 380) because it must always be relative to what follows it for it to be a beginning at all. If truth were correspondence to the origin, Schlegel suggests, in striving for a 'completely comprehensible' world, we would arrive at the nihilism of a world where we actually knew everything, or at least knew the systematic form which all knowledge must take. The highest truth can therefore only be approached by realising that there can always be more to be said.

This might sound far from the concerns of a more empirically oriented approach to literature, or from contemporary epistemological concerns, but the position implied by the Romantic contentions is congruent, for example, with the idea of literature's 'defamiliarising' of habitual perceptions we saw in the Introduction, or, as we shall see in later chapters, with some of the philosophical ideas in Heidegger and Adorno that have become central to contemporary debates. Novalis demolishes the received idea of the Romantic position when he asserts in this connection that

> By giving the commonplace a higher sense, the usual a mysterious appearance, the known the dignity of the unknown, the finite an infinite appearance, I romanticise it – The operation is the other way round for the higher, the unknown, the mystical, the infinite – it is logorhythmised by this connection – It gains an everyday expression.
>
> (Novalis 1978 p. 334)[21]

The neologism 'logorhythmised', which combines the sense of rational ordering, verbalisation and mathematical progression with the sense of the music inherent in the use of everyday language, epitomises the Romantic position.

'TRANSCENDENTAL LITERATURE'

In the modern period the world becomes more and more knowable, and more and more meaningless, as Jacobi's assertion that Spinozism is nihilism already implied. Although they do not regressively reject advances in scientific knowledge – Novalis' and Schlegel's Romantic contemporaries like Johann Wilhelm Ritter were themselves successful scientists and Novalis was a mining engineer – the Romantics look for a conception of truth which does not simply equate truth with conceptual determination, at the same time as regarding the natural sciences as a vital part of the new picture of the world. The crucial aim was a new *integration* of the elements of the world: hence the idea that aesthetic forms give a higher kind of meaning than assertions of a determinate nature, whose meaning is anyway dependent upon their contexts. 'Literature', in the Romantic sense, embodies this idea.

This may seem an inflated claim for literature, and some of the relevant formulations by Schlegel and Novalis do tend towards mere hyperbole, though it is a hyperbole which is almost always tempered by self-ironisation. The fact is, though, that most criticisms of the Romantic position presuppose a received conception of 'literature' of the kind which, as I suggested in the Introduction, is no longer defensible. Given the arguments seen so far, one must take into account how the meaning of the term 'literature' only emerges in specific historical contexts, and thus cannot be made intelligible via received assumptions about an 'essence' of literature. The received assumptions require the sort of definition which the whole

Romantic position is concerned to deconstruct. Schlegel maintains in the *Notebooks on Philosophy*, for example: 'Massive mistake, that only *One* definition is possible of every concept. Rather infinitely many, real synthetic [definitions]' (Schlegel 1988 (5) p. 29), i.e. definitions which result from new combinations. This does not mean, though, that pursuit of truth gives way to an uncontrolled relativism, only, as we have seen, that the idea that truth could be grounded via a correspondence to a ready-made world is renounced.

The key to the Romantic position is echoed in Hilary Putnam's contention, with regard to recent debates over the relativity of differing cultural standards of judgement, that 'The very fact that we speak of our different conceptions as different conceptions of *rationality* posits a *Grenz-begriff*, a limit-concept of the ideal truth' (Putnam 1981 p. 216); otherwise we could not even know if we understood anything at all of what someone with a different conception was saying. Schlegel, whose brother, August Wilhelm, was perhaps the greatest literary translator of the modern period, maintains that 'The imperative of translation rests on the postulate of the unity of languages' (Schlegel 1988 (5) p. 77). It is the attempt to show and understand this limit-concept or postulate which motivates the Romantic conception of art and literature. One of the reasons that it must be a limit-concept was already suggested in Putnam's claim that the attempt to arrive at the absolute conception failed to give an account of that which is able to have any conception at all, and by his rejection of the idea of the ready-made world.

The essential problem is suggested in remarks by Novalis on understanding the nature of self-consciousness. In revealingly paradoxical formulations, Novalis terms consciousness 'a being outside being in being', and 'an image (*Bild*) of being within being' (Novalis 1978 p. 10). Consciousness must be directed towards something, which Franz Brentano will later term its 'intentionality': it must be consciousness *of* something, of its object. It is, though, with the exception of the act of thinking about itself, not itself the something of which it is conscious: hence the sense that it is only ever an *image* of a world which is not itself an image, even though images are an aspect of that world. Representing consciousness requires, Novalis maintains, that the 'image is painted in the position that it paints itself' (ibid. p. 15): otherwise the productive aspect of consciousness evident in the imagination would be excluded. What is to be represented cannot, though, *appear* as itself: only objects can appear. The I is itself what renders objects, in Kant's sense of appearances of which true judgements can be predicated, intelligible. Novalis explores this point in relation to the signifier 'I', thereby revealing a vital fact about language. If the I is, as Novalis claims, 'that which schematises', language's 'schematic' relationship to what it designates means that one requires the schema for the schematiser, or the representation of the representer. The impossibility of rendering consciousness objective means, though, that what is most fundamental about ourselves seems inaccessible to representation, especially in determinately true assertions of the kind which apply to the object-world.[22] Because the condition of possibility of knowledge of objects cannot itself be defined as an object, art and literature – in which aspects of the world which transcend what can be determined in cognitive judgements can be revealed and articulated – become the centre of Romantic philosophy.

The link between the epistemological and the literary to which this rather intricate argument has been leading is made fully explicit in Schlegel's conception of 'transcendental literature' (*Transzendentalpoesie*) in the *Athenäum Fragments*. Here, Schlegel, like Novalis, puts paid to the idea that Romanticism is concerned with vague religious and aesthetic feelings, and thereby opens up the space for some of the most significant theories of literature in modernity, from Lukács' *Theory of the Novel*, to Bakhtin's theory of polyphony and Adorno's stringent demands on the truth-content of modern literature and art. The literary source of Schlegel's ideas is predominantly the novel, particularly in the self-ironising forms exemplified by Sterne and Cervantes, in which the novel includes a critique of its own failings and, above all, contains an ironic account of its own production. These novels attempt to encompass their own genesis, via a kind of self-reference which can, as Tristram Shandy realises so wonderfully, never be complete, because writing the story of the whole of one's life requires writing a description of writing that description, so that the temporality entailed by the writing process thwarts the desire for completion: 'Every person', Schlegel maintains, 'is only a piece of themselves' (Schlegel 1988 (5) p. 38). Such novels thereby prefigure the model of the philosophical systems, beginning with Schelling's 1800 *System of Transcendental Idealism* and most famously exemplified in Hegel's 1807 *Phenomenology of Mind*, whose aim is to comprehend within the system itself the history which enabled the philosopher to come to the point of creating the system.[23] At the same time they suggest why such systems must eventually break down, as Schelling himself would later realise (see Bowie 1993).

The vital point for Schlegel is the interplay between the philosophical and the literary, which suggests a further approach to what the Romantics mean by truth:

> But in the same way as one would not greatly value a transcendental philosophy which was not critical, which did not portray the producer along with the product, and whose system of transcendental thoughts did not at the same time contain a characterisation of transcendental thinking, such literature should also unite the transcendental materials and exercises for a poetic (*poetisch*) theory of the poetic capacity (*Dichtungsvermögen*) common in modern poets, with the artistic reflection and beautiful self-mirroring which is found in Pindar, the lyric fragments of the Greeks, and ancient elegy, and, among more recent poets, in

Goethe, and in each of its representations should include a representation of itself, and be always at the same time literature (*Poesie*) and
literature of literature. (Schlegel 1988 (2) p. 127)

The very nature of these formulations seems to point to another regress, in
which the representation of the representation includes the representation
of itself, and so on. What, though, prevents this being merely a return to
Jacobi's problems?

In his wide-ranging 1796 review of Jacobi's own philosophical novel,
Woldemar, Schlegel suggested that Jacobi's relationship to the 'unconditioned' becomes a problem because he thinks philosophy 'begins with a
single proof. But what if a *reciprocal proof* (*Wechselerweis*), which was
not conditioned from outside itself but which was conditioned by and
conditioned itself, were the ground of philosophy?' (Schlegel 1988 (1)
p. 188). Rather than being grounded in a 'fundamental proposition', then,
as Reinhold had suggested, truth now becomes a function of coherence
between propositions in a context, in the manner which has recently re-
emerged in one view of Davidson's and others' semantics.[24] In the
Notebooks on Philosophy Schlegel asserts that 'Philosophy must begin
with infinitely many propositions, according to its genesis (not with One
proposition)' (Schlegel 1988 (5) p. 12), and that 'Philosophy is an επος,
begins in the middle' (ibid. p. 26). This touches on a vital nerve in modern
thought. Hegel will try to obviate the problem of the ground by constructing
a self-supporting philosophical system in which, to use Novalis' image,
which corresponds to one interpretation of what Schlegel might mean by
Wechselerweis: 'The Whole rests rather like people who play the game of
sitting down in a circle, without a chair, with each just sitting on the knee of
the other' (Novalis 1978 p. 152). Schlegel is tempted by an approach to
philosophy like that which Hegel would soon develop – Hegel was almost
certainly influenced by attending Schlegel's 1801 lectures on *Transcendentalphilosophie* – but he is suspicious of the idea that it could be articulated
into a complete system, even though the drive to completion is fundamental
to the way he conceives of truth. The fact is that, instead of the question of
regress being the fundamental problem for the Romantic notion of literature, regress for Schlegel is actually constitutive of literature, as the famous
Athenäum-Fragment 116 on 'Romantic literature' as 'progressive universal
literature' demonstrates.

Romantic literature, Schlegel maintains, aims to 'reunite the separate
genres of literature', and to 'put literature into contact with philosophy and
rhetoric' (Schlegel 1988 (2) p. 114). Schlegel's apparently mystifying formulations, in which Romantic literature 'encompasses anything at all which
is poetic, from the greatest systems of art which contain several systems
within themselves, to the sigh, the kiss which the child who composes (*das
dichtende Kind*) exhales in artless song' (ibid.), make sense when interpreted via the Romantic holist view of truth and the epistemological issues

we have been examining. Romantic art, Schlegel declares, has, 'like the epic', to 'become a mirror of the whole surrounding world' (ibid.). It does so, though, not in a mimetic, 'representational' sense: the potential for regress which prevents the articulation of a final ground becomes positive and revelatory, a source of ever-renewable articulations, rather than being the failure to represent a ready-made truth.[25] Once more the capacity for creating new relationships is the central factor, not the establishing of stable facts. Romantic literature

> can hover, in the middle, between the represented and the representer, free of all real and ideal interest, on the wings of poetic reflection, can continually potentialise this reflection and multiply it as if in an endless row of mirrors. . . . Romantic literature is, among the arts, what wit is to philosophy, and society, sociability, friendship and love are in life. Other forms of literature are finished and can now be completely analysed. The Romantic form of literature is still in a process of becoming; indeed that is its real essence, that it can eternally only become, and never be finished. It cannot be exhausted by any theory.
>
> (Schlegel 1988 (2) pp. 114–15)

If this seems merely hyperbolic, consider another aspect of Malpas' recent account of semantic holism, which he regards as a way of 'seeing epistemology in the mirror of meaning', thereby, without realising it, echoing Schlegel almost verbatim:

> One might think of a holistic system on the model of a system of mirrors, rather than a single mirror, and of the mirrors as mirroring each other in a play of reflections or of meanings . . . the mirror of meaning is not a mirror which re-presents the world. The world is not reflected *in* meaning. Rather . . . the world is the mirror of meaning.
>
> (Malpas 1992 p. 7)

Contemporary approaches to a theory of meaning and truth which have given up the idea that the theory should be an explanation of the kind used for natural phenomena, in favour of an account of how truth works in a context, are therefore interestingly linked to theories devoted to understanding the status of literature and the other arts at the beginning of modernity.

The essential reason for this connection is that both approaches share the anti-representational premise, and realise that the only way to approach the problems involved is holistically. Why, though, does the Romantic theory lay such store by the aesthetic, thereby creating what we now know as literary theory, and how is it that the aesthetic aspect of the argument tended, until very recently, to disappear from so many subsequent approaches to truth in modern philosophy? The answer will lie, as we shall see in later chapters, in the success of the natural sciences, and the concomitant domination of notions of truth as determinate explanation.

The ways in which this conception has been called into question in recent years echo largely forgotten questions first posed by Romantic philosophy.

In his *Philosophical Lectures* of between 1800 and 1807 Schlegel gives a revealing account of 'Platonic philosophy' that echoes the 116th *Athenäum* fragment and which is evidently meant to be applied to philosophy as 'metaphysics', as foundational discipline, in a more general way:

> Philosophy thought of in a completely pure way does not have its own form and language; pure thought and pure knowledge of the *Highest*, of the *Infinite*, can never be adequately represented. But if philosophy is to communicate it must take on form and language, it must employ every means to make the representation and explanation of the Infinite as distinct, clear and comprehensible as is at all possible; it will in this respect wander through the realm of every science and every art, in order to choose any aid which can serve its purpose. To the extent to which philosophy encompasses all kinds of human knowledge in art, it can appropriate the form of every other science and of art. . . . Just as philosophy as science is itself not yet completed, so its language is also not completed. (Schlegel 1964 p. 214)

Seen in this perspective the very idea of philosophy as a foundational enterprise, which is so often associated with Platonism, and which even survives into those versions of modern philosophy which would provide us with a 'logic of science', is regarded as a misunderstanding of the intent of philosophy from its very beginnings. In the sense Schlegel intends, far from condemning art in every respect, Plato's philosophy may in fact itself *be* art, albeit not art in the sense of *mimesis*, of re-presentation. The reason is that its concern is with the pursuit of truth, which Schlegel regards as common to art and philosophy. In the *Critical Fragments* of 1797 Schlegel claims that 'Novels are the Socratic dialogues of our time' (Schlegel 1988 (1) p. 240) and that 'The whole history of modern literature is a continuous commentary on the short text of philosophy: All art should become science and all science should become art; literature and philosophy should be united' (Schlegel 1988 (1) p. 249), where the vital emphasis is on the 'should'. If there is to be final truth it must take in all the new (and old) ways in which the world comes to be meaningful in language, rather than one particular way that is apparent in scientific method.

Even the form of Schlegel's remarks suggests the consequences of this new approach. The fragments which Schlegel uses for many (though not all) of his important works are not necessarily consistent with each other. Non-systematic contradiction is understood as a means of arriving at new insight: the notion of 'literary theory' developed by the Romantics deconstructs the received idea of theory as the creation of systematic coherence by making theory itself literary in its form. The truth is a product of continual re-articulation, and new syntheses, suggested in the fragment: 'The *world*, regarded as music, is an eternal dance of all beings, a universal song of everything living, and a rhythmic stream of spirits' (Schlegel 1988 (5) p. 58). The Romantics understand rhythm as the uniting of difference into forms of identity, and as inseparable from both language and music. Rhythm, though, requires interpretation, and can be fundamentally ambiguous. Each fragment, however much it may make a universal claim (and many do), already subverts itself both via the ironic suspicion of all determinate assertion brought about by a collection of juxtaposed fragments, and via the fact that its connection to other fragments is contingent upon the synthetic ability of the readers of the fragments. Although Schlegel maintains it can and should be trained and developed, that ability is also subject to the individual's freedom to articulate and connect the aspects of the world in new ways. This might seem to lead to a mere randomly 'subjective' plurality of world-articulations, but the orientation towards truth means that the plurality is still predicated upon the regulative idea of unity, without which the conflict between the articulations would simply cease to matter, or even to be recognisable at all. The question which Romantic philosophy bequeaths to the modern world is how this unity can best be understood.

THE AESTHETIC AND THE HERMENEUTIC IMPERATIVES

Many of the ideas outlined here inevitably lead to the sense that irony is the result of the failure of the attempt to understand truth in a definitive philosophical manner, a position which has, of course, been echoed in many aspects of Western culture in the late twentieth century. Irony can be conceived of nihilistically, as both Hegel and Kierkegaard suggest it should be, on the basis of what they see as Schlegel's irresponsible refusal to commit himself.[26] It can also, however, be seen as a liberation from the dangers of dogmatic fixity, the dangers of what is now termed 'fundamentalism'. In line with the Romantics, Richard Rorty has recently associated the ironic stance with the idea that philosophy should give way to literature. He suggests, echoing Novalis' *Monologue*, that 'the problem of how to finitize while exhibiting a knowledge of one's own finitude . . . is *the* problem of ironist theory. It is the problem of how to overcome authority without claiming authority' (Rorty 1989 pp. 104–5), oddly associating the idea with Kierkegaard, while not even mentioning either Schlegel or Novalis, who were the main sources for Kierkegaard anyway. Ironically enough, Schlegel claims that 'Philosophy is the real home of irony, which one would like to define as logical beauty' (Schlegel 1988 (1) p. 242): he can do so because, *pace* Rorty, philosophy is for him no longer a foundational discipline. Irony is beauty in the sense that beauty reveals more than can be determinately stated in relation to that which is beautiful: it thereby embodies the truth which Romanticism never renounces. It is 'logical' beauty because it depends on 'logos', on assertion, the locus of propositional truth, but it is assertion which, as we have seen, negates itself without leading to a final opposed positive position. The final position is, for

Schlegel, only ever pointed to by the failure of attempts to ground a philosophical system. This failure is now, though, also, as the 116th *Athenäum*
Fragment implied, the source of the world being – albeit in a thoroughly
temporalised manner – meaningful at all.[27]

Given the repeated argument that the Absolute could not be represented, and that philosophy should therefore renounce the idea of ever
giving an account of the absolute conception – a view which is in certain
respects common to both the Romantics and Rorty – why not, then, simply
renounce the whole project, as Rorty tends to do, and accept a 'post-
modern' plurality of viewpoints, without the supposedly obsolete demand
for a ground or for a 'regulative idea' of unity beyond the divisions?
Attempted – and often highly problematic – answers to this question will
concern us for the remainder of this book. The main reasons for rejecting
a merely relativist view should already be apparent from some of the
arguments presented so far. There is, though, a vital problem here, which
relates to questions raised at the end of Chapter 1 and which we must briefly
consider in this context, because it will become central in later chapters,
especially when we consider Benjamin and Adorno.

The kind of contemporary position which advocates an unrestricted
plurality of viewpoints is often linked in contemporary Western culture to
the commodity system. This system generates both random plurality,
because commodities, especially in a multinational market, are produced
increasingly for their universalisable exchange value, not for their specific
use value, and systematic determination in terms of form, because the value
of the object is determined in relation to the universal commodity system.
The Romantic conception of art and literature might seem to correspond,
via its insistence on the lack of a final, groundable truth, to the celebration
of diversity for its own sake which links post-modern theory to 'late capitalism' (see e.g. Jameson 1990). The Romantic conception does not, though,
entail accepting merely relational values, even though it no longer admits
the possibility of a grounding which would enable a philosophical account
of truth to be definitively legitimated.

In Schlegel's *Conversation on Literature* of 1800 the exploration of
the interaction between philosophy, science and art leads one of the
participants to ask: 'Is then everything literature [*Poesie*, with the sense
of *poiesis*]?', to which the reply is given that 'Every art and every science
whose effect is achieved by language (*Rede*), if it is practised as an art
for its own sake and achieves the highest peak, appears as literature'
(Schlegel 1988 (2) p. 198). Once the possibility of a final grounding has been
abandoned, what renders life meaningful can no longer be sought in a
transcendent answer. It must, furthermore, involve a value which does not
simply lead back to something instrumental or cognitive, which merely
creates another kind of regress.[28] The power of Kant's view of aesthetics, as
we saw, lay not least in the notion that there are aspects of the world which
are valuable for their own sake. This linked to his notion of 'dignity', the

intrinsic worth of the rational being, who should not be merely the means for the ends of another rational being.[29] In Kant's moral philosophy this sense of intrinsic worth is used to argue for the imperative '*Act in such a way that you always use humankind, both in your own person and in every other person, as an end and never merely as a means*' (Kant *KpV* p. 61, p. BA 67). For Kant, the pleasure and insight generated by the work of art need have no further purpose than the disinterested, non-appropriative fact of that pleasure itself, which connects it to the sense of intrinsic value upon which Kant's moral philosophy relies.[30] The moral imperative, which we aspire to follow for its own sake but may always fail to live up to, is significantly analogous to the Romantic idea that even truth may be such an ideal, which is felt to be of value in itself, rather than that which can be grounded by philosophy or grounded in ulterior motives, such as the desire for power over the object. The further turn in the Romantic position is to make the substantial links between these differing aspects of the new philosophy which are only hinted at by Kant.

One way of understanding the Romantic position is therefore to suggest that it involves two further 'imperatives', which complement Kant's categorical ethical imperative. The first, the 'aesthetic imperative', is a term coined by Novalis; the second I shall term 'the hermeneutic imperative'. Novalis expressly links the aesthetic imperative to Kant's moral philosophy:

> The highest works of art are completely *recalcitrant* (*ungefällig*) – They are ideals, which only could and *should* please us approximando – aesthetic imperatives. In the same way the moral law should approximando become the formula of inclination (will). (Ideal will – infinite will. There is, in terms of its character, no way of conceiving of the attainment of the unattainable – it is, so to speak, only the ideal overall expression of the whole sequence. . . .) (Novalis 1978 pp. 652–3)

Just as the idea of being moral is only ever something at which one can aim, but never claim to have achieved, the particular empirical engagement with a work of art will often be frustrating, and the truth of that work only glimpsed in repeated engagements with it which give rise to the demand to understand more of what it means. Art thereby provides a model for an attitude to the world which goes beyond what is apparently merely aesthetic, because it confronts one with the reality of the need always to try to see another perspective, without any guarantee that it will lead to a truth which is intersubjectively acceptable.

In this sense the 'hermeneutic imperative' follows from the aesthetic imperative. What I mean by the term is evident in Novalis' remarks in the collection of fragments called 'Mixed Remarks' (the first of which is also a part of the collection called 'Pollen'):

> The highest task of *Bildung* is – to gain power over one's transcendental self – to be simultaneously the I of one's I. For this reason the lack of

complete sense and understanding of others is all the less strange. Without complete understanding of oneself one will never truly learn to understand others. (ibid. p. 238)

Given the impossibility of complete self-transparency and the fact of one's ability both to grasp the world cognitively and to re-articulate the world in an individual manner, the hermeneutic imperative becomes perhaps the most vital imperative in the Romantic conception of a modernity which can no longer appeal to absolute foundations. The standard rejection of Kant's attempt to use the categorical imperative – the imperative to make the ground of one's action the maxim that one would wish all rational beings to follow – which suggests that the imperative is useless in real-life situations, fails to take account of the need to integrate the hermeneutic imperative into such an account of morality. Ethical decisions are in this view inseparable from interpretative decisions, which inherently entail the need to understand the Other.[31] As such, ethical decisions make the content of what could be universally legitimate indeterminable, which leaves the need always to interpret. Novalis goes on to maintain, in the next remark, which was also published in the *Athenäum*, that 'Only then do I show I have understood an author if I can act in his spirit, if I can, without reducing his individuality, translate and change him in multiple ways' (ibid.). There can never be a final symmetry of meaning, because all interpretation changes the nature of what is interpreted, but the aim is to do it justice, which can again only be a regulative idea. The model of the difficulties of interpretation, that shows why there is an imperative to interpret, is the work of art, which always poses new interpretative tasks, at the same time as generating new ways of making the world meaningful. It is only at the historical moment when the changes in the understanding of language I have tried to explicate here first emerge that such a conception of art and literature becomes possible and that the hermeneutic imperative begins to play a central role in philosophy and art.

4 Interpretative reasons

THE 'ANARCHY OF CONVICTIONS'

The 'hermeneutic imperative' described in Chapter 3 might seem intrinsic to any culture concerned with the adequate interpretation of texts or other linguistic utterances. Gerald Bruns, for example, who thereby provides a condensed history of many of the concerns that have at times been located under the banner of 'hermeneutics', considers an examination of hermeneutics to be potentially concerned with:

> the interpretation of oracles, the silencing of the muses, the quarrel of philosophy and poetry, the logic of allegory, the extravagance of midrash, mystical hermeneutics, the rise of literalism and the individual interpreter, the relation of self-understanding and the understanding of other people ... the problem of historicality or the finitude of understanding. (Bruns 1992 p. 17)

In the light of such a list one can see what Gadamer means when he talks of the 'universality of the hermeneutic problem'! It is, though, important to see that the hermeneutic imperative as I have tried to characterise it emerges as a response to a series of issues which had not previously been the central concern either of philosophy or of theology. A re-examination, on the basis of issues raised in the preceding chapters, of the aims and development of some of the modern versions of hermeneutics which begin with Romanticism can, I want to show, both indicate new directions for literary theory and contribute to debates over questions of meaning which form a central aspect of contemporary European and analytical philosophy. Why, then, does the hermeneutics initiated by Romanticism now seem so relevant to the contemporary philosophical scene?

Romanticism has quite often been interpreted as replacing universalist Enlightenment assumptions with a relativism in which each culture has a legitimate claim on its own truth, furnished by its own 'organically grown' language. Herder's questionable account of the role of the natural world in the constitution of language already makes the problem with this position clear:

The more alive a language is, the less one thought to grasp it in letters, the more originally it ascends to the full, unarticulated sound of nature, the less it can be written, the less it can be written with twenty letters, indeed becomes unpronounceable for outsiders (*Fremdlinge*).

(Herder 1966 p. 11)

If a culture's experience of nature is wholly divergent from that of other cultures, because of local geographical and biological differences, then the language which emerges in relation to nature will mirror such differences. Furthermore, in this view, the nearer the language is to its particular origin, the more primordially will it be connected to the nature which gave rise to it. When linked to the way in which human identity is inextricably bound up with particular natural languages and environments, such assumptions can too easily lead to the tendency of ethnic groups to regard their own language as inherently superior to that of other groups, with consequences which these days are yet again all too familiar.[1] The underlying issue here is, however, evidently much more complex than it might at first appear. In both Enlightenment scientific universalism and nationalist particularism there is a pattern of exclusion of an 'Other'. On the one hand, the repressions created by a procrustean conception of universalising 'reason' threaten to make humankind wholly alienated from a nature whose truth is only to be seen in terms of the principle of sufficient reason – this consequence, of course, was what Herder sought to avoid by his valorisation of the origins of a language over its development into an abstract means of instrumental control. On the other hand, the Enlightenment universalism exemplified in the American Declaration of Independence or in the at least notional universal openness to scrutiny of modern natural science can all too easily be replaced by an irrationalist particularism which insists upon its own self-legitimating status against all Others. Even in the light of this less than appealing alternative – as Herder already realised – the insistence upon the validity of locally grown forms of communication and expression can play a role in a pluralistic multiculturalism, which forms part of many developments that are, sometimes rightly, regarded as emancipatory. The revelation of how dominant cultures in modern societies repress alternative modes of communication and articulation has become a critical issue in contemporary politics. It is clear from this how interpretative questions which give rise to controversy within literary theory are inextricably bound up with much broader issues, and it is essential to understand the historical and philosophical development of these issues, at the same time as assessing the validity of the theories to which they are linked.

The problem of how particularistic world-articulations can claim a validity beyond the boundaries of the group (or even the individual) which asserts the truth or validity of its form of world-articulation becomes central to modernity. As will become apparent in Chapter 6, the conflict between individual world-disclosure and universal claims to validity lies at the root of the contrast between '*Verstehen*' ('understanding') and 'explanation' thematised by Wilhelm Dilthey in his work on what he termed the '*Geisteswissenschaften*' ('human sciences').[2] Tensions between universalist and particularist assumptions about language and truth are also the condition of possibility of a serious notion of literature. The desire to 'say the unsayable' in literature is best understood as the desire for forms of articulation which would escape the necessarily general nature of the material via which we communicate, in order to get in touch with a new particularity, be it the particularity of my individual world, or of a truth which does not reside in what natural science can tell us, of the kind suggested in Kant's notion of a 'code through which nature talks to us figuratively through its beautiful forms' (Kant *KdU* (1977) B p. 170, A p. 168). Most importantly, of course, this particularity ceases in the process to be merely particular – otherwise it would be radically incomprehensible – and takes on universal potential precisely *because* of its particularity. It is in this sense that questions concerning the 'truth' of literary texts can arise in ways which are central both to Romanticism and to the hermeneutic traditions carried on by Heidegger, Benjamin, Adorno, Gadamer and others. The light shed on questions of truth by the aesthetic reflections upon the nature of literary texts we considered in Chapter 3 is therefore germane to any scrutiny of language in modern philosophy.

In the German tradition at issue here the awareness of the new centrality of language is accompanied by the growing historicisation of questions of truth, which begins in earnest with Romanticism's move away from the idea of the ready-made world. The difference between the following two related observations by Dilthey points to a significant ambivalence: 'The *historical consciousness* of the *finitude* of every historical phenomenon, of every human or social state, of the relativity of every kind of belief, is the last step towards the liberation of humankind' (Dilthey 1981 p. 363). This positive assessment can, though, be easily replaced by the fear of nihilism, of which Dilthey was also capable, in relation to much the same conception:

> The historical view of the world (*Weltanschauung*) is the liberator of the human spirit from the last chain which natural science and philosophy have yet to break – but where are the means to overcome the anarchy of convictions which now threatens to descend upon us?
>
> (Dilthey 1990 p. 9)

The tension in Dilthey's comments, between the need to liberate the human spirit from foundations which can no longer claim absolute validity and the fear of what this might actually entail, will underlie the issues of this chapter and Chapter 5 and concern us for the remainder of this book. The battle over these issues was carried out and is still being carried out in relation to the rise of 'hermeneutics' in its modern forms.

It should already be clear, then, that Derrida's model of the 'two interpretations of interpretation' in modernity, the one seeking the origin and

foundation of meaning, the other delighting in the infinite play of signification, is inadequate to the real tension in question here, because it does
not give sufficient space to other ways in which conceptions of language
and meaning are explored. The 'play' of meaning can, for example, be
understood in terms of the same scepticism as a nihilism which sees the
proliferation of languages as evidence that language has come apart from
the world, rendering language a randomly constituted 'all too human'
order. At the same time it can also be regarded as a liberation from an
imprisoning order of language that opens up space to say what previously
could not be said, which is a necessary condition of the modern conception
of autonomous art.[3]

In order both to articulate the major theoretical positions and to show
the continuing significance of the hermeneutic theories that emerge from
Romanticism, I want in this chapter to prepare the ground for a consideration in Chapter 5 of the hermeneutic theory of F.D.E. Schleiermacher,
which will relate it to key aspects of recent semantic theory. Semantic
theory in certain areas is increasingly converging with many of Schleiermacher's ideas (as it is with the ideas of Schlegel and Novalis). The fact
that theories which lie nearly two hundred years apart should now converge in the ways I shall demonstrate is a vital part of the larger story being
told here. This convergence is the result of a shared suspicion of models
of truth which take truth to be adequacy to a ready-made world. It also
involves an appreciation, in the light of this suspicion, of the centrality of
dimensions in communication which cannot adequately be characterised
in terms of the following of linguistic rules. From this perspective, ideas
based on the Romantic concern with 'literature' become an integral part of
contemporary theories of language. The emergence in Schleiermacher of
a concern with the nature of normativity in language, rather than with the
way language mirrors a pre-existing objective world, has wide-ranging
philosophical consequences that will be explored in subsequent chapters.
My contention will be that hermeneutic positions thereby introduce an
irreducible ethical and normative dimension into communication which
cannot be separated from the concerns of literary theory. First, though, we
need to understand more about the emergence of modern hermeneutics in
order to be able to appreciate Schleiermacher's achievement.[4]

SPIRIT AND LETTER

It is well known that Schleiermacher was a theologian, who played a decisive role in establishing modern Protestant doctrine. The fact that major
developments in modern hermeneutics are the achievement of someone
whose primary concern was theology should not be surprising, however.
Hermeneutic reflection is necessarily part of any religion which relies upon
canonical texts. Given that interpreted reality is in constant movement and
that canonical texts themselves must be understood as remaining in some

way static if they are to be canonical at all, the task of making the two congruent is an enduring necessity. The ways in which this problem is understood shift radically in differing historical constellations up to the present day. Changes in meaning can be located on the side of the word, or of the world, on the side of the language user, or of the recipient of language. Much depends upon how the lines between these possible locations are drawn, in that they affect each other's boundaries. The failure to appreciate the complexity of this issue is the source of the ineptitude of much traditionalist literary interpretation, and one of the strengths of recent literary theory has lain in its re-examination of those boundaries. The important point in this context is to understand the effects of the philosophy of Kant and of the other theoretical positions considered in the preceding chapters on the boundaries in question. Although it will not be the central issue here, the drawing of these boundaries will also be the source of many of the debates over the political and ideological implications of literary theory to be dealt with in later chapters.

Manfred Frank suggests that prior to Schleiermacher the doctrine of correct understanding is defined in two essential ways: either language is the *object* of understanding, for example, when Plato takes poets to be the interpreters of the linguistic utterances of the Gods, or language is the *subject* of explication, when Aristotle regards language itself as the interpreter via which non-linguistic impressions made by reality on the soul can be articulated (Schleiermacher 1977 p. 10). Schleiermacher is not least interesting for his exploration of the ways in which these two opposed positions can be shown to be less mutually exclusive than they might seem. The issues taken up by Schleiermacher and Romanticism are the outcome of changes in received conceptions of interpretation which begin with the Reformation,[5] prior to which the carriers of meanings were, importantly, not only words, but things themselves. This was apparent in the doctrine of similitude, for which the meaningfulness of the natural world was manifested in resemblances between differing aspects of the 'book' of nature itself: flowers that looked like eyes were, for example, good for eye diseases.[6] The dominant strand of mediaeval Christian hermeneutics relied upon the notion that the Scripture had a fourfold sense: the meaning of the Scripture was 'literal or historical', and was approached via 'grammatical interpretation', which aimed to translate linguistic structures of the past into structures comprehensible in the present, but it could also be completed in the 'mystical or spiritual sense' (cited in Birus 1982 p. 19), which involved allegorical, tropological and anagogic meanings, as well as the literal meanings. Allegorical interpretation became particularly necessary, of course, when the apparent literal meaning, for example, of the erotic Song of Solomon, seemed in contradiction with its supposed spiritual import.

These assumptions gave rise to a baroque complexity of possible interpretations, and a concomitant degree of obscurity, as well as to the question why there were so many (often contradictory) meanings to the Scriptures. In order to counter the impression that it was therefore not clear what God was saying, Aquinas and others insisted that it is the word which is stable, as opposed to the vagaries of the world.[7] Martin Luther goes further in insisting upon the fact that the Scripture has only one meaning, its literal meaning, but he does so while making vital new moves with regard to a Christian ontology of interpretation. Bruns cites Luther's contention that

> The Holy Spirit ... is the simplest writer and speaker in heaven and earth. This is why his words can have no more than the one simplest meaning which we call the written one or the literal meaning of the tongue. (Luther, cited in Bruns 1992 pp. 143–4)

The vital issue is how Luther conceived of the relationship between the 'letter' and the 'spirit' of a scriptural text, which provides us with an important model: 'We must recognise that [Scripture] is in itself the most certain, most easily understood, most plain, is its own interpreter, approving, judging and illuminating all statements of all men' (ibid. p. 145). The implicit problem here, which will recur in many guises, is the actual location of the meaning of texts. Gerhard Ebeling sees Lutheran hermeneutics as 'a surrender of the mind of the interpreter to the mind of the Scripture' (ibid. p. 147). Instead of being a subject whose interpretative activity generates textual meaning, the reader is 'subjected' to the text. However, this subjection does not take place in terms of an external authority merely subordinating the reader to itself. If the subject gains its *own* truth by this experience, it cannot be said to be imposed upon by its surrender to the text. Access to the truth is achieved by being a receptive listener who hears the meaning of the text in his or her heart and accepts its authority as a higher truth than he or she alone is capable of, rather than by an objectification of textual meaning in the sort of exegesis characteristic of allegorical interpretation. This last contrast, between receptive listening and active exegesis, plays a role in most approaches to interpretation in literary theory. It is evident, for example, that aspects of Gadamer's hermeneutics derive from something not so different from the Lutheran conception. The fact is that theories of the reader/text relationship involve a historical and theoretical oscillation between notions of the reader as both active subject and as passive object, and the text itself as both object and as subject. The perceived role of the individual author of the text, which only later becomes a primary concern, adds a further unstable dimension to these relationships.

Enlightenment hermeneutics moves in a different direction from Luther, and provides further useful models. On the assumption that all readers have the same potential to partake of the light of reason, correct interpretation now becomes dependent upon the correspondence of the text to the pre-existing ideas of reason, with no necessary reference to the intentions of the author. Spinoza therefore maintains 'To summarise briefly, I say that the method of the explanation of Scripture is in no way distinguished from the method of the explanation of natural science, but is rather in complete agreement with it' (Gadamer and Boehm 1976 p. 53). Given the objections to Spinozism that we have already encountered, the potential for trouble implicit in such a view should be obvious: the authority of the canonical text appears subordinated to a prior authority whose status depends more upon the sciences than upon revealed religion – hence the Pantheist equation of God with the order of nature and Jacobi's ensuing accusation of nihilism. The contradictions for a theological hermeneutics suggested by this dilemma lead us closer to the concerns of literary theory.

The very title of Johann Martin Chladenius' *Introduction to the Correct Explication of Reasonable Sayings and Writings* of 1742 sums up the whole enterprise of an Enlightenment hermeneutics based on the idea of a ready-made world. For Chladenius, the meanings of a text need bear no relation to the 'subjective' meanings intended by its author: interpretation can be either of the 'speech or text looked at in itself' (Chladenius 1969 p. 87), which means things the author might not have been aware of, or of the author himself or herself, which might not depend upon the actual words of the author's text, because the author may have failed to communicate what it was he or she had in mind. In both cases the question is of the truth of an 'object', which is accessible via our participation in reason, not via access to the author as he or she is manifested in the text: 'One understands a speech or a text completely if one takes account in doing so of all the thoughts the words can awake in us according to reason and its rules of the soul' (ibid. p. 86). Essentially, then, one understands without any need to interpret, in that familiarity with these rules will obviate all uncertainty. This is not quite as unconvincing as it might sound: at the level of our intuitive, unquestionable ability to understand any individual word we are familiar with in a language we speak – an ability which we must presuppose even to be able to begin to formulate questions of meaning – something as objective as this might seem to be the case. It is only at the level of a text as a whole, and in terms of our disagreements with others about particular word-meanings and the meaning and intention of whole texts, that we might be said to need to interpret in an emphatic sense.[8]

Much depends here upon how one understands the notion of 'interpreting'. In the *Philosophical Investigations*, for example, Wittgenstein denies that most of our everyday understanding of language within an already familiar language-game can be said to involve the need for any kind of active 'interpretation'. We only need to interpret, he maintains, when the rules of communication are no longer self-evident. However, such a claim leaves the question unanswered as to how, as a child, one arrived at the first understanding of the language-games into which one was socialised. This would seem necessarily to require interpretation in the active sense. As such, given our continuing ability to revise them, our linguistic horizons would seem always already to involve interpretation. This issue will, as we shall see, be central to Schleiermacher, and Wittgenstein does not seriously address it. Schleiermacher thinks that a minimum of interpretative activity is always part of understanding because of the inherent instability of all forms of communication in relation to the real. The simple question for the Enlightenment position is why one needs to interpret at all. Hermeneutics in the modern sense only becomes a central issue in the light of the disintegration of Enlightenment assumptions about the inherent rationality of the world. It does so in two main waves: the one we are about to describe and, much more recently, in the light of growing philosophical suspicions about the ability of explanation in the manner of the natural sciences to explain meaning; hence the link of Schleiermacher and recent semantics.

The lurking tensions in the hermeneutics of the Enlightenment, which provide us with a further useful model, become apparent in Georg Friedrich Meier's *Attempt at a Universal Art of Explication* of 1757. Meier rejects the doctrine of resemblances because it merely leads to the proliferation of ambiguities, via the multiplicity of the ways in which natural objects can be said to resemble each other,[9] and he wishes to control meaning by a 'science of rules, via the observation of which meanings can be recognised by their signs' (cited in Schleiermacher 1977 pp. 14–15: 'meaning' in this sense signifying something like 'referent'). Meier claims 'If one explicates the utterance [*Rede*, which can be both spoken utterance and text] of an author, one says that one is explicating the author himself' (cited in Birus 1982 p. 24). This, though, becomes ambiguous: the meaning of an utterance, he maintains, is 'the sequence of linked ideas (*Vorstellungen*) which the author wishes to designate via the utterance' (ibid.). The sequence is to be determined by the habitual use of the rules of language, in which the schematism inherent in language allows this sequence to be communicated, on the basis of the pre-established harmony of ideas from one rational being to another.

Ultimately, though, the meaning is the 'intention/opinion of the will (*Willensmeinung*) or the desire of the author' (ibid.). There are obvious grounds for thinking that this '*Willensmeinung*' is ontologically irreducible to the general rules of communication: how could *my* individual free will be actually *shown* to be compatible with a general symbolic order, unless one dogmatically presupposes this compatibility as part of language itself? The tension here points to future battles over questions of linguistic meaning. Many analytical philosophers have relied and still do rely upon versions of semantics which see meaning as determined primarily by rules that are wholly independent of speakers' inner intentions and desires, language being presumed to be independent of individual psychology and not subject to the whim of the individual. In Michael Dummett's terms: 'words have meanings in themselves, independently of speakers' (Lepore 1986 p. 473). Attention to regularities of context in particular cases is understood in an Enlightenment view as eventually revealing the underlying meanings by their correspondence to the ideas of reason. What, though, does one make of interpretations of literary and other texts that are not always compatible with what we know about the contexts and material conditions of a text's emergence, which obviously rely on insights gained from the interpreter's experience of subsequent contexts, but which yet seem to reveal more of the text than would be possible by attention just to the knowledge of the period and its semantic possibilities? Clearly this question becomes most pressing in relation to aesthetically significant works, but it can also play a role in any interpretation, once one questions the notion of meaning implied in Dummett's remark.

Despite often being patently anachronistic, 'strong' interpretations can be understood as revealing more of the truth of a text than interpretations based on assumptions which limit interpretation to the contexts of the text's origin. Such interpretations 'understand the text better than the author herself understood it', if one takes the understanding of the author to be determined by the horizon of what we take it she could have known about the assumptions and meanings of her era, or by the rules of Enlightenment hermeneutics. Now, as Chladenius suggests, the Enlightenment conception clearly also involves a sense of understanding a text better than the author herself understood it. The crucial difference is that a Romantic conception will not necessarily assume that 'better understanding', as I shall term it from now on, is based upon an underlying rational pattern not necessarily accessible to the author, but rather that it is based upon 'creative interpretation', which discloses a potential in the work to which the originator of the text may not have had direct access.[10]

Dilthey claims that the 'proposition [of 'better understanding'] is the necessary consequence of the doctrine of unconscious creation' (Dilthey 1990 p. 331). The question as to the actual nature of 'better understanding' and of 'unconscious creation' is germane both to Romantic hermeneutics and to literary theory. Unconscious creation, a term which in the sense intended here probably originates with Schelling's *System of Transcendental Idealism*, can be interpreted in a variety of ways, from the idea that, as Kant maintains, 'nature gives the rule' to art in the genius by giving rise to more than the conscious self could intend with the existing rules of a particular aesthetic praxis, to Lacan's notion that language and the unconscious are structurally connected to each other. The consequences Schleiermacher and others draw from these problems have, as I shall show in Chapter 5, now invaded analytical accounts of meaning. This is a result of the realisation that discovering semantic rules followed by the speakers of a language is not sufficient to account for how a text is actually to be understood.

The obvious problem here, as many traditionalist literary critics fear, is that the decidability of the correct interpretation seems to be deeply threatened by the idea that the truth of an articulation might appear finally to be accessible neither in terms of the possible intentions of its producer, nor even of its historico-linguistic context. As such, the question of interpretation begins to involve dimensions that pose apparently insoluble methodological dilemmas, with the danger of the 'reader's barely disturbed solipsism' (Reed 1990 p. 26) becoming the source of an inherent indeterminacy of textual meaning. The worry is understandable, but it is vital to be clear what is really at issue in these differing assumptions concerning interpretation. The explicit idea that one should 'understand an author better than she has understood herself' is not an irresponsible invention of solipsistic literary theorists, it being at least as old as (and probably older than) Kant's claim to exactly this effect with regard to his interpretation of Plato in the *Critique of Pure Reason* (*KrV* p. B 371, A 314).[11] Both Schlegel and Schleiermacher acknowledge the importance of this dictum, but why is it so important, and how *is* understanding to be realised in a valid manner?

If the essential philosophical task of the modern era is taken to be the search for new foundations, these foundations will presumably be what enable an author's text or utterance to be understood. In the Enlightenment view, as we have seen, it was easy to suggest how the text will make sense if it corresponds to the pre-established ideas of reason, rather than to its utterer's aims. If, though, the structure of the knowable world is, as Kant claimed, now to be understood as located in the subject, the ground of what the subject means would necessarily seem to be a moment of the subject's complete transparency to itself, otherwise the whole transcendental project already begins to unravel. Such transparency is evidently a problem in relation to language, as opposed to the immediate 'Cartesian' certainty that I experience at any particular moment,[12] because language is learned via its manifestation in 'external' material objects in the world (sound waves, marks, etc.), not as something already inherent in subjectivity. Now it is clear for many utterances that our meaning-intentions are largely transparent to us, and can to all intents and purposes remain so, but in other instances this is patently not the case, as when we come to realise we meant something completely different from what we thought we were saying at the time. Lacan and others term this difference the difference between the 'subject of enunciation' and the 'subject of the enunciated'. The possibility of reflexive self-correction is, of course, already a kind of 'understanding the author better than she has understood herself', this time via 'self-reflection'. The question is how this kind of understanding can itself be understood: *which* self is the source of the truth of the utterance, and why?[13] This returns us again to the Kantian transformation of the role of the subject in the Copernican turn.

KNOWING WHAT WE MEAN: THE SEMANTIC AND HERMENEUTIC ALTERNATIVES

Kant's claim was that by revealing the necessary rules of synthesis through which cognition became possible he could give an account of what the rational subject must do if it is to speak truly. These rules must evidently transcend the contingent cognitive failures of individual empirical subjects, who are often mistaken in their judgements. We have already considered aspects of Kant's realisation that judgement has to be thought of as an 'art' if the potential regress entailed by the application of rules is to be avoided. The further problem for the Kantian position was that the functioning of cognitive rules also depended upon natural languages. As Hamann argued, though, there can be no 'general philosophical language', of the kind presupposed by the Enlightenment position, to mediate between these differing languages. One could not even begin to understand such a language, let alone construct it, without the presupposition of the particular natural language or languages via which one learned what a language is.[14] The Kantian a priori was therefore confronted with semantic problems, because an adequate fulfilment of the Kantian project would seem to require a workable theory of meaning for it to make cognition in differing languages commensurable. But how do we establish that the way the world is given to others 'in intuition' corresponds to the way it is given to ourselves, except via linguistic communication?[15] The scientific success of what Husserl will term the 'mathematisation of the cosmos' gave rise to the need for an explanation of that success, as Kant had shown, but Kant's explanation seemed to be lacking in essential ways.

The fact is that the origins of the 'continental'/'analytical' divide in philosophy can already be traced to differing responses in the first half of the nineteenth century to questions concerning the Kantian a priori and the role of judgement.[16] Filling the gaps in the Kantian project with regard to language is, to take one of the most important responses, the major explicit and implicit source of the 'semantic tradition' which initiates modern analytical philosophy. Investigation of language in the semantic tradition does not, as it often does for the Romantics, lead to doubts about the very viability of a foundational philosophical project: in fact the semantic position is arguably a sophisticated example of the foundationalist Enlightenment version of the topos of 'better understanding'. Richard Rorty has claimed in this context that

> 'Analytic' philosophy is one more variant of Kantian philosophy, a variant marked principally by thinking of representation as linguistic rather than mental, and of philosophy of language rather than 'transcendental critique', or psychology, as the discipline which exhibits the 'foundations of knowledge'. (Rorty 1980 p. 8)

In one of a growing number of books tracing the historical origins of analytical philosophy,[17] J. Alberto Coffa argues that the central Kantian problem was the appeal to 'pure intuition'. Pure intuition is Kant's device for explaining 'synthetic a priori' knowledge, such as the irrefutable propositions of arithmetic or geometry, to which nothing available in the world of empirical intuitions could be said directly to correspond. The semantic tradition's problem, Coffa claims, 'was the a priori; its enemy, Kant's pure intuition; its purpose, to develop a conception of the a priori in which pure intuition played no role; its strategy to base that theory on a development of semantics' (Coffa 1991 p. 22). If Kant's founding of cognition in the subject foundered on the problem of 'pure intuition', then it might be possible to reform transcendental philosophy by grounding it in semantics, replacing the obscurity of intuition with the clarity of meanings. Versions of the move to replace 'intuition' by analysis of language as the source of the conditions of knowledge still, of course, dominate analytical philosophy.

The basis of the semantic project was, Coffa shows, first established by Bernard Bolzano, at almost exactly the same time as Schleiermacher establishes modern hermeneutics, in the first half of the nineteenth century. The basis of the project is 'the separation of meaning from psychological processes', whereby 'the objective representation associated with the word "table" (i.e. the meaning of "table") should not be confused with tables, the objects of that representation' (ibid. p. 30). It is significant that this view is not so far either from Saussure's later differentiation between signifier (corresponding to 'word'), signified (corresponding to 'objective representation'), and world-object, or from Frege's distinction between '*Sinn*' and '*Bedeutung*' (usually – but questionably – translated as 'sense' and 'reference', where the 'sense' of 'the morning star' and of 'the evening star' is different, but the 'reference' eventually turns out to be the same, namely the object we have come to call 'Venus'). Saussure's distinction is itself already prefigured by Schlegel, who maintains that the idea still adhered to by Kant of the correspondence of 'idea' (*Vorstellung*) and 'object' (*Gegenstand*) actually 'says no more . . . than what a sign says of what is to be signified' (Schlegel 1991 p. 4).[18] The initial moves in this area are therefore evidently made on *both* sides of what will become the hermeneutic/analytical divide. In Bolzano's view there were three crucial elements in a 'grammatical unit', which should not be conflated: 'meaning' qua 'objective representation', the entity in the world referred to, and the psychological process involved in a particular case of thinking about that entity. Vital as these distinctions turn out to be, the semantic tradition they help establish is now, qua foundational project, as Rorty suggests, beginning to look almost as precarious as the more emphatic versions of Kantianism it attacks.

The coming rift between the semantic and the hermeneutic traditions is already apparent in the focus of the respective attention to language of their earliest representatives. Bolzano is oriented primarily towards mathematics and the natural sciences, and the validation of 'objective knowledge'; the Romantic locus of reflection upon language is primarily 'literature', in the senses we have examined above. Tensions between the traditions are in many ways still the tensions between these initial foci. This is evident in the fact that the analytical tradition has rarely seen the literary as a major philosophical issue, and that parts of the hermeneutic tradition have tended to regard the natural sciences with suspicion, because of their perceived failure to deal with meanings which were not reducible to externally verifiable explanation. The divergence of such approaches to language and understanding depends upon metaphysical assumptions about the nature of being – most notably assumptions concerning the relationship between a deterministically conceived nature and a non-deterministically conceived human world – of the kind that will underlie most of the positions to be considered in the remaining chapters of this book.

The chief reason why post-Kantian hermeneutic positions and those contemporary theories of semantics which have renounced a foundationalist project now intersect in quite striking ways is that attempts to establish a theory of meaning in the semanticist manner have repeatedly come up against problems of regress analogous to those we encountered in preceding chapters. The status of the first of Bolzano's elements – 'meaning' – causes most of the trouble: how and where is one to locate such meanings? Indeed, just what are they? The fact is that, if one is not simply to repeat the Kantian problem of the relationship between the empirical and the transcendental subject implicit in the notion of 'pure intuition', one has to have a watertight answer to this question. If they are to be amenable to any kind of law-like analysis, meanings *must* in some sense be separate from the psychological processes that accompany them in an individual speaker. In that case, though, how does the psychological subject have access to them as *meanings*, rather than as materially instantiated recurrent events of the kind a machine could record, except by the kind of mental act supposedly characteristic of a transcendental subject? Frege, for example, later tried to posit an essentially Platonic 'third realm' or 'realm of sense', where such objective meanings as those exemplified in statements of scientific laws must be located. This realm was supposed to be a semantic ground of truth independent of individual subjects, because it did not matter whether any subject contingently gains access to the truths for which the 'senses' stand.[19] Appealing as this sounds in terms of *prima facie* persuasive assumptions about the independence of scientific and other truth from individual interpretation, it completely fails to answer most of the major modern questions about the relationship of world, word, meaning and language-user which have been the concern of analytic philosophy of language and which in other ways form the object of hermeneutics.

A crucial later development in the semantic tradition, which brings it closer to the hermeneutic tradition, is the notion that meaning is able to function as an objective quantity because it depends upon intersubjectively constituted rules of praxis governing the intelligibility of utterances, so that knowing the meaning of an expression is knowing when it is correctly used. Such conceptions were, though, and still are often contrasted with the idea that hermeneutic or phenomenological approaches to meaning rely upon somehow getting empathetically in touch with the psychologically conceived meaning-intentions of the individual.[20] As Herbert Schnädelbach puts it, suggesting the links between the semantic tradition and the neo-Kantianism that develops later in the nineteenth century:

The hermeneutic turn to language [he is referring in particular to Schleiermacher] is ... under the conditions of the later 19th century, experienced as the invasion of psychologism and historicism into the realm of reason [he is mainly referring to Dilthey], which one thought had to be contained by neo-Kantian 'purity'. (Schnädelbach 1987 p. 95)

The hermeneutic view therefore supposedly failed to account for Bolzano's 'objective representations', the meanings which must exist independently of the representations of individual speakers of a language, a view of hermeneutics also shared by many structuralist accounts of language and interpretation. It will, though, become clear in Chapter 5 that many of the directions explored by Schleiermacher do not actually fit into a model of wholly 'subjectivised' or psychologised meaning, though they do involve the need to relate meaning to the real speakers of a language in ways which many versions of semantics must avoid. The relationship between the semantic and hermeneutic traditions must therefore be rethought if we are to gain an adequate picture of the issues confronting interpretation in contemporary literary theory. Too much of the argument within literary theory has, for example, effectively tried to excise the subject from the question of textual meaning, because of its 'subversion' by the language into which it is 'inserted'. It is this kind of reification on the side of both language and the subject that Schleiermacher's theory can help one avoid, with consequences that can change the focus of literary theory and the philosophy of language.

5 The ethics of interpretation
Schleiermacher

BEGINNING IN THE MIDDLE

The common factor between many of the most significant developments in contemporary philosophy and literary theory, from semantics to deconstruction, is the revaluation of the nature of interpretation which ensues from a mistrust of both epistemological and semantic foundationalism. Schleiermacher's work can still play a significant role in this revaluation, as I shall now try to show.[1] Before moving to an account of Schleiermacher's contemporary significance, it is important first briefly to establish historical links to the theories considered in previous chapters, which will make the direction of my alternative story of modern literary theory clearer.

Here the neglected figure of Jacobi once again plays an important role.[2] Schleiermacher's extensive but unsystematic notes and commentaries, probably from the years 1793–4, on texts published by Jacobi, including the *Spinoza Letters* (in Schleiermacher 1984 pp. 513–97), demonstrate that he was thoroughly conversant with the Pantheism controversy. The notes take up two related problems concerning Spinoza that we examined in Chapter 1: the regress of 'conditioned conditions' and the relationship between the ground and the world of finite things. In addition Schleiermacher asks, in precisely the same way as did Jacobi, with regard to Kant's account of the relationship of 'intuitions' to the world of things in themselves, whether 'the category of causality is applicable to noumena' (Schleiermacher 1984 p. 570), thereby putting into question any attempt at epistemological grounding.[3] Prefiguring his later reflections upon the part/whole relationship in interpretation, he also ponders the necessarily holistic consequences of Spinoza's way of thinking about the relationship of the ground to the world of particulars, in which each thing's identity can only be gained via its relations to other things (ibid. p. 576). This is the model which began to be transposed into the area of language by Novalis and Schlegel, and will be further developed by Schleiermacher himself, in such dicta from the hermeneutics as 'in its single appearance the word is isolated; its determinacy does not result from itself but from its surroundings' (Schleiermacher 1977 p. 106). It is evident from the notes that he understands the problems of Kant's new foundations in a way which was very soon to become germane to Romantic philosophy, of which he can in certain ways be considered a part. The move from these issues to the hermeneutics he begins to formulate in 1805 was not least occasioned by the work of his friend Friedrich Schlegel, as well as by their joint project of translating and editing Plato.[4] For both thinkers a concern with the implications of Kant's, Fichte's, Schelling's and Jacobi's views of philosophy, and a growing suspicion of philosophies which claim to be able to articulate their own foundations, increasingly determine the direction of their thought.[5]

The hermeneutics initiated by Schlegel and Schleiermacher can, then, be understood precisely as a response to the new dilemmas of regress and circularity that emerge with Kant and which are taken up by Jacobi and the Romantics. Schlegel, prefiguring aspects of the 'hermeneutic circle', questions philosophical foundationalism in a brilliant formulation in the *Athenäum*:

> Demonstrations in philosophy are just demonstrations in the sense of the language of the art of military strategy (*im Sinne der militärischen Kunstsprache*). It is no better with [philosophical] deductions than with political ones; in the sciences as well one first of all occupies a terrain and then proves one's right to it afterwards. (Schlegel 1988 (2) p. 111)

Another fragment, also from the *Athenäum*, suggests that after Kant – hence the 'subjectively' – one cannot hope to establish absolute philosophical foundations, because the subject is not its own ground: 'Looked at subjectively philosophy always begins in the middle, like an epic poem' (Schlegel 1988 (2) p. 112), which is another way of stating Novalis' dictum that 'What reflection *finds*, *seems* already *to be there*' (Novalis 1978 p. 17) already considered in Chapter 3, this volume. Elsewhere in the *Athenäum* Schlegel famously maintains: 'In order to understand someone who only half understands himself, one must first understand him completely and better than he does himself, but then only half as, and just as well as he understands himself' (Schlegel 1988 (2) p. 147). Schlegel's paradoxical comment can be interpreted on the one hand as an ironic critique of Enlightenment hermeneutics' repression of individuality via its dogmatic foreclosure of interpretation in terms of the underlying ideas of reason, and on the other as an acknowledgement of the problems of identifying just what it is to which 'better understanding' is applicable – what *does* the second half of the fragment actually mean? Schleiermacher's own primary, ethically motivated concern was the irreducible individuality, most manifest in *Poesie*, with which interpretation of another person confronts us. What makes his work so significant is that he at the same time never loses sight of the fact that our understanding must take account of the inherent universality of language and of the demands this imposes.[6] At the end of this chapter I will suggest, by linking it to a key aspect of Davidson's semantics, that Schleiermacher's version of the interplay between freedom and constraint is still important for the question of literature and ideology.

Schleiermacher's hermeneutics, unlike the already existing 'special hermeneutics' for particular theological, legal and other purposes, aims at giving the rules for the 'art' of interpreting *any* linguistic utterance.[7] The crucial presupposition about language for Schleiermacher – a presupposition which he shares with analytical philosophy – is that it consists of a finite number of relatively fixed elements, which can be used for an infinite number of semantic and other purposes.[8] It is therefore possible to identify lexical, pragmatic, syntactical and grammatical constraints in language which can be disregarded only at the risk of wholesale unintelligibility. Schleiermacher insists, though, that these aspects of language 'are not positive means of explanation, but negative ones, because what contradicts them cannot be understood at all' (Schleiermacher 1977 pp. 171–2). Much of the divergence between the semantic and hermeneutic traditions depends upon the status attributed to these constraints, and upon how a particular theory deals with those aspects of language which cannot be understood just by attempting to define such constraints.[9]

PLAYING BY THE RULES

The source of significant divisions between the traditions can here once again be traced to paradigmatically differing responses to Kantian questions of cognitive validation: these can be crudely divided between what Robert Brandom has termed the 'regulist', and what should be termed the 'hermeneutic' responses. Brandom terms the latter the 'pragmatic' response, claiming that the decisive argument is derived from Wittgenstein. However, the fact is, as we shall see, that Schleiermacher is the first to make the argument explicit, following Kant's insight into judgement which we examined in Chapter 2, and Kant's own attempt to come to terms with that insight in the *Critique of Judgement*. The regulist approach to meaning works on the more than questionable assumption that, as Wilfrid Sellars puts it: 'learning to use a language is learning to obey the rules for the use of its expressions' (cited in Brandom 1994 p. 24). This is a linguistic formulation of the Kantian assumption that what determines 'the propriety or impropriety of some judgement or performance' (ibid. p. 19) is a 'rule' or 'law' which underlies the performance. The problem, as Sellars himself showed, is the status of this rule: is it something which can be made explicit and be shown to exist independently of the praxis in relation to which we take it to exist, or is it just a norm which is implicit in such a praxis but not explicitly analysable apart from the praxis? The contrast is between a kind of 'Platonism' concerning the existence of rules (of the kind implied by Frege's 'third realm') and an 'Aristotelian' insistence upon the ontological primacy of what we do before the ways in which we try to explain what we do. By insisting that 'if one considers language as emerging from each act of speaking, it cannot . . . be subjected to calculation' (Schleiermacher 1977 p. 80) – 'calculation' in the sense that it could be assumed to be systematically constituted in the manner of mathematical rules – Schleiermacher places himself firmly on the 'Aristotelian' side of this division. The 'Platonist' version is essentially the result of thinking that 'meanings' are abstract entities, like Bolzano's 'objective representations', concerning which philosophy can give a definitive theory.

The impetus behind the Platonist theories lies in the presupposition that words and sentences must have a meaning which is independent of context if the theory is to make any sense of facts about the regularised use of finite linguistic means for an infinite number of possible utterances, a thought made more persuasive by the assumption that statements about scientific laws must in some way be true beyond local linguistic praxes. Partly as a result of taking mathematically based natural science as the model, so that language is regarded as a system analogous to deterministically conceived nature, much of the tradition of analytical philosophy – at least until Quine, who essentially decided there were no such things – was stuck with the probably insoluble problem of 'meanings', for reasons we shall discuss below. The point of the post-Enlightenment hermeneutic tradition we are considering here is precisely that it does not need to rely on the assumption that a theory of meaning, qua definable sense attached to a word, is essential to account for the fact of understanding, and this brings it close to certain recent influential views of semantics.

Schlegel claims in the *Notes on Philosophy*: 'That one person understands the other is philosophically incomprehensible, but certainly magical' (Schlegel 1988 (5) p. 71). Understanding would be philosophically comprehensible if there were a systematically grounded account of what it is to understand an utterance. This is the aim of what Michael Dummett, continuing the semantic tradition initiated by Bolzano, calls a 'full-blooded theory of meaning', a theory which 'must give an explicit account, not only of what anyone must know in order to know the meaning of any given expression, but of what constitutes having such knowledge' (Dummett 1993 p. 22). What constitutes having it is, for Dummett as in many ways for the later Wittgenstein, thought of in terms of behaviour which exhibits understanding: the aim here is to avoid any reference to epistemological issues in relation to semantics. It is, however, already anything but clear whether this approach is adequate to allow one to assert that we could know if someone has *understood*: it all depends where and how understanding is located. There is, in fact, an obvious circularity in assuming that behaving in a certain way is an index of having understood: what counts as behaving in that way – indeed, what makes it behaviour rather than involuntary random bodily movements? – except responding to that which is to be understood in the 'correct' way?[10] This would seem to imply that only the interpreter was really acquainted with whatever meaning is and that only the interpreter was able to judge that others had understood it, via their behaving in the 'correct' way. But exactly who is this interpreter, and what makes this way correct? For behaviour to be understood as exhibiting understanding, the interpreter must interpret the behaviour as fulfilling a criterion not included a priori in the notion of behaviour itself (unless one is prepared to accept another circular argument, in which behaviour is defined a priori in such a way as to obviate the problem). At some point in the construction of the theory one is forced to introduce the fallible activity of interpretation, which rests, as both Schleiermacher and Davidson (who does, though, have his behaviourist moments and is in some ways an externalist)[11] will suggest, upon the presupposition that we both understand what it means for something to be true. This presupposition cannot just be derived from observation of regularised behaviour, because even to see behaviour as a regularised response to a repeated stimulus requires interpretation, based on the structure of 'seeing as' associated with schematism.[12]

Dummett maintains that one need not carry out his kind of analysis for a whole language, but can assume that what works for a particular expression will in principle work for all others. This, though, raises further difficulties. In an excellent account of Dummett in relation to Schleiermacher, Beate Rössler claims that Dummett 'is only interested in the context-free determination of the meaning of sentences, in a general criterion which explains the meaning of sentences for every situation of utterance' (Rössler 1990 p. 221). Using aspects of Schleiermacher's hermeneutics she questions whether meaning can really be grasped by the systematic analysis of language entailed by this approach:

> for Schleiermacher every understanding of a sentence becomes the understanding of a text to the extent that for him a single sentence has no (determinate) meaning 'in itself', is completely 'indeterminate' (Schleiermacher 1977 p. 101) and can only be understood in the context of its particular situation of utterance, as only in this way can the specific meaning of the utterance be differentiated from possible other meanings which it can also have, and be determined. (ibid.)

Dummett contends that the theory he requires cannot make any presuppositions, such as the presupposition of our understanding of truth, on pain of circularity or regress. Rössler shows, however, that such a theory must meet the following demand:

> This condition of the systematic presuppositionlessness of the theory is linked to that of the thorough systematisability, to the extent that the demand for presuppositionlessness implies at least prima facie that all the relevant data for the understanding of language must be systematisable.
> (ibid. p. 98)

This demand, which also requires one to be able to show exactly what belongs to language and what does not, helps to establish perhaps the core philosophical difference between a Romantic hermeneutic approach to language and truth that is explicitly holistic, and a piecemeal analytical approach which holds to the idea of philosophical grounding, a difference which occurs in varying forms across modern philosophy and is at the root of many of the controversies over literary theory's approach to meaning.[13]

The essential divide lies between those like Dummett who think that a theory of meaning must also give us an account of the notion of truth without presupposing an understanding of truth, and those like Heidegger and Davidson who think truth must be presupposed, for the sort of reasons shown by the hermeneutic tradition.[14] Rössler maintains that, in terms of Dummett's theory:

> even for the understanding of a relatively uncomplicated sentence one could put together an indefinite list of necessary preconditions of understanding . . . on the other hand such a list, even if it could be brought to a conclusion, would lead into an infinite regress. (ibid. p. 140)

The regress, which relates to those we have been considering all along, results because the specification of the conditions for understanding one sentence must themselves be formulated as propositions and therefore have their own conditions of understanding, and so on. Rössler is happier, against Schleiermacher, with Dummett's idea that knowledge of the meaning of a sentence is also linked to the rules for verifying its truth conditions: but this actually repeats another version of the same problem. How do we *decide* which rules are the right rules for the verification of a particular utterance without again falling into a regress of judgements? The fact is that, as Davidson will argue, one can get any word to mean anything if one finds a way of getting others to understand it: there can be no generalisable verification procedure for this. None of this denies the evident role of rules in language use, but it does mean that Dummett's approach to rules could not give us the theory it promises.

The structure of the central argument for the hermeneutic positions has already been revealed in Jacobi's arguments about truth considered in Chapter 1: if a regress is to be avoided one cannot begin with something of the same status as what is to be analysed. This is what lies behind the objection to the behavioural account of meaning: how, as we saw, does an interpreter's behaviour show that she has really *understood*? We may in general assume it to be the case, but an analysis of understanding requires the presupposition of understanding, which must be logically prior to its supposed manifestation in behaviour. Taking another brief look at an issue we considered in relation to Jacobi can elucidate what is at stake here. The demand for presuppositionlessness as the necessary condition of a complete systematic theory was the basis of Hegel's *Logic*. Certain aspects of Schleiermacher's hermeneutic theory can be linked to his rejection of Hegel's attempt at a self-bounded system of philosophy.[15] Everything in Hegel's system must be justified within the system, because otherwise what founds it is left outside it, rendering the system incomplete. Hegel's way of avoiding a founding presupposition is to reveal that every aspect of the system depends upon something else, without which it would entail a contradiction (the analogy to a structuralist conception of language as a system of differences with no positive terms can help make the idea clearer, assuming the system is regarded as at least synchronically complete).[16] Completion of the system is therefore achieved at the end of the system, where the point is reached at which there are no further interdependencies beyond those already articulated in the system. The critique of Hegel by the later Schelling, which is very closely related to the Romantic ideas seen in the preceding chapters, and which was also influenced by Jacobi, contends that this kind of presuppositionlessness leads to insoluble dilemmas with regard to our real dealings with the facticity of how the world is given to us, which cannot be reduced to the system that attempts *post factum* to transcend that facticity (see Bowie 1993, 1994a, Schelling 1994).

Applied to language, the idea of a presuppositionless system entails, as it does in some structuralist conceptions, that the infinity of possible 'meanings' should be assumed a priori to be potentially graspable, given the systematic constitution of language apparent in the rules governing our correct use of it or in its structurally identifiable attributes. For Schleiermacher, though, this infinity can only be a regulative idea, which gives one no grounds for assuming that language is in fact systematically constituted in a manner amenable to finite analysis. Whether there can be complete 'understanding of understanding' is not something a theory could ever claim to guarantee, even though we may be ethically bound always to acknowledge the potential meaningfulness of any articulations we take, on the basis of the *presupposition* of understanding, to be linguistic. Grounding that presupposition is what Schleiermacher regards as impossible. The essential point lies in the status of the rules of language: in Dummett's approach, and its 'Hegelian' equivalent,[17] one must take a regulist approach to those rules, so as to make the area of investigation rule-bound in a stable manner. Schleiermacher is the first to spell out the new hermeneutic approach implicit in much that we saw in Schlegel and Novalis, which can be understood as the alternative to failed attempts at philosophical grounding. He is also perhaps the first to appreciate fully the general import of hermeneutics for modern philosophy, in ways which are still echoed in many current philosophical debates.

The wider paradigmatic significance of the divergence between the demand for a system without presuppositions and the assumption that one must always 'begin in the middle' will concern us at various points later. Underlying this issue are, once more, problems of circularity and regress. Dummett makes his difference from the hermeneutic tradition very clear when he claims in relation to Davidson's equation of truth and meaning:

> if we want to maintain that what we learn, as we learn the language, is, primarily, what it is for each of the sentences that we understand to be

true, then we must be able, for any given sentence, to give an account of what it is to know this which does not depend upon a presumed prior understanding of the sentence; otherwise our theory of meaning is circular and explains nothing. (Dummett 1993 p. 43)

The hermeneutic tradition can, in contrast, actually be defined by its *acceptance* of an inherent circularity in understanding, because there is in its terms no way of escaping the need to have already understood something before attempting to explain understanding: this is precisely the point of the 'hermeneutic circle'. Hermeneutics can also be defined by its concomitant rejection of the idea that meaning can be encompassed by theoretical explanation, a rejection based on its presupposition of a holism in which linguistic rules cannot be said to exist independently of the shifting contexts and praxes in which they are instantiated. It is an interesting coincidence – and probably more than this – that the first explicit formulation of the hermeneutic circle, by Friedrich Ast, a pupil of Schelling's, in 1808, is made around the group of philosophers who were very concerned with the problems of regress suggested by Jacobi.[18]

The main source of the hermeneutic rejection of regulist explanations is Schleiermacher's response to the regress of judgements. Brandom summarises the vital aspect of 'Wittgenstein's Regress Argument' by saying that in relation to interpretation 'The rule [of language] says how to do one thing correctly only on the assumption that one can do something else correctly, namely apply the rule' (Brandom 1994 p. 21). When Schleiermacher, while arguing exactly this point, claims understanding is an 'art' he is not therefore making a 'Romantic' appeal to 'intuition', in the sense of a mysterious faculty, but naming the same philosophical insight which Brandom sees in Wittgenstein's 'master argument for the appropriateness of the pragmatist, rather than the regulist-intellectualist, order of explanation' (ibid. p. 23):[19]

> The complete understanding of speech or writing is an artistic achievement and demands a doctrine (*Kunstlehre*) or technique to which we give the name hermeneutics. We call art . . . every compound product in which we are aware of general rules, whose application cannot in the particular case be again brought under rules.
>
> (Schleiermacher, cited in Rössler 1990 pp. 232–3, from
> *Short Account of Theological Study*)

Interpretation 'only bears the *character* of art because the application is not also given with the rules' (Schleiermacher 1977 p. 81). The initial difference between the pragmatic and the hermeneutic formulations of the response to this issue lies in hermeneutics' linking it to questions of literature and aesthetics. This has important effects on how questions of language and interpretation are approached, on the assumption that, as we saw in Chapter 4, the difference of focus between the Romantic and the semantic perspectives can best be explored with regard to the question of 'literature'.

Schleiermacher's crucial insights have, then, a dual source: they are derived both from his experience of the Romantic revelation of the linguistic possibilities opened up by the new non-representationalist conceptions of *Poesie*, and from philosophical reflection in the wake of Kant, of the kind usually associated with the semantic tradition. This dual perspective was already implicit in Kant's own conception of judgement: the distinction in the *Critique of Judgement* between 'determining judgement', judgement of particulars based on a pre-existing general rule, and 'reflective' judgement, establishing a rule in relation to particulars, was an attempt to respond to the problem of regress of which Kant was aware in the *Critique of Pure Reason*.[20] Reflective judgement involved the same capacity of the subject as was required for aesthetic apprehension, because it could not rely on prior rules and could itself give rise to new rules by generating new forms of synthesis. It is also, crucially, the faculty which enables understanding of the genesis and interpretation of metaphors and of non-standard linguistic usage.

The division of the types of judgement is mapped by Schleiermacher on to central aspects of his theory of interpretation. However, even more importantly, he realises that the division cannot be finally sustained, because even a determining judgement requires interpretation for the appropriate rule to be applied. Dummett's approach to a theory of meaning can in these terms (albeit somewhat crudely and unfairly) be seen as the attempt to use determining judgement to explain meaning, whereas the hermeneutic tradition regards reflective judgement as the core of our understanding.[21] In the following characterisation of hermeneutics from the *Ethics*[22] Schleiermacher suggests vital reasons why determining judgement is inadequate as a basis for interpretation; at the same time, however, he also shows that he does not psychologise language and understanding:

> Looked at from the side of language the technical discipline of hermeneutics arises from the fact that every utterance can only be counted as an objective representation (*Darstellung*)[23] to the extent to which it is taken from language and is to be grasped via language, but that on the other side the utterance can only arise as the action of an individual, and, as such, even if it is analytical in terms of its content, it still, in terms of its less essential elements, bears free synthesis [in the sense of individual judgement] within itself. The reconciliation (*Ausgleichung*) of both moments makes understanding and explication into an art [again in the sense of that whose 'application is not also given with the rules']. (Schleiermacher 1990 p. 116)

In these terms there can be no understanding of an utterance solely in terms of its standing for an 'objective representation', because this would ignore the fact that all utterances are to varying degrees context-dependent, relying for one aspect of what they mean upon what an individual could have meant, given who that individual is.

This aspect of meaning need not be thought of as an exclusively internal psychological process, or in terms of naïve intentionalism, because the writer/speaker himself or herself, as Schleiermacher emphasises, also depends upon external influences and contexts for their identity (a fact which also applies to the interpreter). Certain obvious objections here, concerning specific kinds of text, of the kind often cited in structural textual theories, might appear to invalidate Schleiermacher's position, but this is not the case. In the example of a computer generated text – to take an extreme case of a text whose author is 'unknown' qua possessor of meaning intentions – this theory would, given the lack of meaning intentions on the part of the text's producer, concentrate upon the actual linguistic praxes of the context of its genesis, doing so initially in terms of what Schleiermacher calls the 'grammatical', which these days appears, initially at least, as the programmable aspect of language. All the evidence shows, though, that such texts are tied to the meaning-horizons of those who programme their possibility, so that what we can understand is a combination of those horizons.

Try the following sub-Beckettian accidental collaborative product of myself and the Mac while writing this chapter. MacLucky speaks:

> Without the work, no properties, without the interpretroperties, without the interpreter, no properties either.roperties;pretes, as Schleiermacher makes clear in the arguments cited belowarticulatedcan here usefully be brought in such different waysdifferentunlikes of human autonomy-universal couldin ian traditions of human autonomy, in the name of a sman autonomy. (Author? 1995)

Interpretation of 'intentionless' texts depends upon the activity of individual interpreters with some kind of intentions: any decent literary critic should, for example, be able to make quite interesting sense of the way this text recombines the elements of everyday language and creates new rhythmic echoes with parts of words. The fact is that the very question as to the meaningfulness of any piece of language depends upon already understanding what it is for anything to be meaningful at all, which is not a question of the programmable aspect of language, but, as Heidegger will show, of location within a world of already 'disclosed' meanings. The alternative to this is another version of Jacobi's regress, which would render all understanding impossible, because one would have only rules, and no means of applying them, or, for that matter, reason to apply them.

Schleiermacher is rightly insistent that all interpretation involves some degree of creativity on the part of the interpreter. However, as we have just seen, we can now generate texts without there being any meaning-intentions. This might seem to create deep problems for a conception of interpretation like Schleiermacher's, which requires the free activity of the subject. However, the idea that we could mechanically generate *interpretations* of whole texts again leads into problems of regress: is the above passage in fact an interpretation of what I was writing at the time, and is any interpretation of the computer text of the same order as that text itself? Do we therefore just keep generating new texts, rather than actually understand something? It is obvious that there is an important asymmetry here between the generation of a textual object and the interpretation of such an object. Computers can do only the former, even when it may appear like the latter. Schleiermacher's theory is not least valuable for the ways in which it distinguishes between the *degrees* to which creative initiatives by interpreters play a role in the interpretation of differing kinds of utterance, from a bare minimum in conversations about the weather, or in passing on information which may be dealt with algorithmically, to a great deal in literary contexts. Only if language is reified into a pre-existing regulist entity, as opposed to it being that which must, as Schleiermacher maintained, be considered 'as emerging from each act of speaking' – including the acts of the interpreter – can the extreme example of a textual object just cited be taken as theoretically decisive.[24]

The assumption of the contextuality of all interpretation actually renders these extreme cases relatively uninteresting, as compared, for example, with the attempt to grasp the meanings of a major modern poet, where the degree and nature of deviation from the standard usages of the poet's context opens up an endless field for interpretation. Clearly one can produce endless interpretations of any text, but here the question of normativity intervenes once more: there is, once the undeniable fact of endless interpretations is accepted, no obvious reason to think this *matters* in relation to a computer-generated novel in the ways it does for Hölderlin's late poetry. It is only when one accepts the reality of such evaluative facts that one can begin to see how the notion of the truth of literary works becomes significant. As we shall see later in this chapter, the sort of approach that wishes in the name of a theory of ideology to level such evaluations into mere subjective preference or power-motivated interest involves bad faith on the part of the critic: as though the acknowledgement of aesthetic value were merely laying oneself open to the – always possible – seductions of the text, rather than also realising its truth-content.

Texts where intentions do play a part in interpretation open up a whole series of methodological questions, of which Schleiermacher was fully aware. Relevant influences on any individual include the collective development of the linguistic praxes of their particular context, praxes which also affect the unintended 'external' – and thus in one sense 'unconscious' – performative effects of a speaker's utterances. Performative effects also influence future interpreters, interpreters who can, of course, include the writer/speaker himself or herself:

> If we now assume that the utterance is a moment of a life, then I must seek out the whole context and ask how the individual is moved to make the utterance (occasion) and to what following moment the utterance was directed (purpose). (Schleiermacher 1977 p. 89)

Such classic hermeneutic formulations are now increasingly part of analytical approaches to meaning. Malpas maintains in his account of Davidson and discussed in Chapter 3, this volume:

> Any theory which purported to provide an account of a speaker's overall psychology would need to make explicit the entire set of intentional-horizonal structures which went to make up that speaker's psychological network. But of course these horizons do not merely belong to the individual speaker, and the very attempt to interpret involves the artic-ulation of a horizon shared by both interpreter and interpretee.
>
> (Malpas 1992 p. 124)

Some interpretations are – to counter a further standard objection, this time from the intentionalists – therefore demonstrably incorrect, if they claim the producer of the text meant something which all the evidence shows was not part of the context of production (Malpas' 'intentional-horizonal structure') or could not have had the performative effect claimed. In Malpas' terms, which are congruent with Schleiermacher's: 'The horizon within which interpretation operates, and with respect to which the inter-pretative project is constituted, will place constraints on the number of acceptable theories' (ibid. p. 125). This does not, then, necessarily mean that 'better understanding' may not reveal sides to a text of which the author was not conscious or even that one cannot interpret in a deliberately anachronistic manner from one's own horizon. The fact is that there is nothing in such theories to preclude the possibility of future creative inter-pretations of a text by others being understood as part of the aims of the writer herself, and thus as apt to the text in question. Even if this is not the case the assessment of such an interpretation is always open to critical debate in terms either of its revelatory effects, or of its aptness to the text from a contemporary perspective. The same questions, it is worth noting, play an essential role in the realm of music: Furtwängler's Beethoven cannot sound the way Beethoven intended, but it has claims to truth which transcend the local horizon of Beethoven's concerns.

The point about interpretation in this view is that interpretative decisions are inescapably normative decisions, depending upon the goals of the activity of interpretation in an already meaning-imbued world. These are goals about which one can argue, on the assumption that there is no final court of appeal. Such argument must depend, however, as we shall see in a moment, upon an – always revisable – consensual foundation. Schleiermacher's underlying maxim is that one must avoid inconsistent or reductionist bases for interpretative praxis: this is itself, of course, a normative demand to seek the truth of an utterance, a truth which is in no way exhausted by its notional 'propositional content', but includes perfor-mative, expressive, musical and other possibilities implicit in utterances. Looked at in this way the hoary old question of authorial intentionality must give way to a whole series of differing and equally possible ways of understanding an utterance, which can include expressive intention: Kafka may have unconsciously written to 'get his father off his back', as his Sancho Panza tells stories to do the same with Don Quixote; performative intention: Kafka may have meant us to laugh (but to whom does it matter if he did not, and we still do?); the intention to generate interpretations: the discussion of the story 'Before the Law' in *The Trial* reads like a splendid parody of a bad literary seminar, in which the text patently begins to get lost beneath its interpretations; literary intention: writers often just write, including, like E.T.A. Hoffmann, when they are too drunk to be sure what they intend.

The real non-starter in interpretation is the exclusive idea that the goal of the process is to establish 'what the author intended': in these terms there are so many such possible intentions that one has to reformulate the nature of the activity of interpretation itself if another regress or a circular approach is to be avoided. None of these approaches is possible without the activity of interpreters – and to that extent there is no extra-interpretative place from which to validate interpretations – but the necessity for validation demands attention to context and the acknowledgement of revisable interpretative constraints. The most important complicating factor here will arise if one works with certain assumptions about the difference of literary texts from others, a difference which, as we shall see in the final section of this chapter, demands a place for the freedom of the interpreter to realise the aesthetic potential of the text, a freedom which might seem incompatible with interpretative constraint. Schleiermacher has important resources to offer here, but they can only be properly assessed after seeing more of the major assumptions behind his hermeneutics.

'THOUGHT' AND 'FEELING'

So far I have been considering these issues at a predominantly analytical level, and it will not be until later that their wider-ranging implications become fully apparent. An important reminder, though, that these interpretative issues do have a political dimension, which is sometimes obscured by the assumption that a semantic approach to meaning can dispense with the normative, is apparent in the fact that the passage quoted above from Schleiermacher's *Ethics* comes, not from a discussion of literary interpretation, but from a discussion of the formation of a nation state. Schleiermacher later adds a footnote which maintains that 'The awakening of consciousness of language corresponds to the forming of a state' (Schleiermacher 1990 p. 111). This is because subjects must legitimate actions by reference to what he calls 'universal schematism' (ibid. p. 26), which is the basis of intersubjective truths that result from the inherently normative obligations of communication. In a later draft he claims, prefiguring Davidson's insistence on the 'principle of charity', the principle that in interpreting another person's utterances one must assume that most of what they say is true: 'In the thoughts of every person there is only truth to the extent to which truth is in language, and it is only in language to the extent that word and thought of each individual are the same' (ibid. p. 263). Schleiermacher insists, much as Habermas later will, upon an orientation towards consensus based on the necessarily intersubjective aspect of language; he does so, though, not because he thinks consensus is entailed a priori by the ready-made nature of language and logic, but because it must be *presupposed* as a *goal* if interpretation is to begin at all.

Davidson makes the same point as Schleiermacher when he says of his approach to interpretation: 'The method is not designed to eliminate disagreement, nor can it; its purpose is to make meaningful disagreement possible, and this depends entirely on a foundation – *some* foundation – in agreement' (Davidson 1984 pp. 196–7). Truth for both Schleiermacher and Davidson is necessarily intersubjective, as otherwise communication becomes inexplicable:

> What we in general call thinking is an activity of which everyone is conscious that it is not particular to them, but the same in all people. . . . Thus it makes no difference whether the same thought is carried out by one individual or another individual, and every thought which is determined by its content is the same in and for every person.
>
> (Schleiermacher 1990 p. 256)

In this way Schleiermacher is initially in agreement with the semantic tradition – the remark quoted here is strikingly reminiscent of both Bolzano and Frege, for example – to the extent that understanding cannot possibly be built on the basis of the irreducible psychological differences between speakers. In the light of these differences, for 'thought' to be possible at all we must postulate a semantic symmetry between what you mean and what I mean by a word. Without such a postulate we would actually have no reason to assume the utterances of the other were linguistic at all, because we would, on the assumption that language and the *postulate* (but emphatically not the *fact*) of identity of thought between self and other are inseparable, not know what language is: 'Speaking in this general sense is so essentially attached to thinking that no thought is complete until it has become word' (ibid.). Novalis claims in this respect that 'The whole of language is a *postulate*. . . . One must agree to think certain things in relation to certain signs' (Novalis 1978 p. 347). Human social existence consists in striving for the identity present in understanding, which Schleiermacher regards as being demanded by the act of thinking itself, and there is 'no limit to how far [individuals] can get in the mutual taking up of their thinking' (ibid. p. 257), and thus no a priori theory which could map out such limits.

Schleiermacher's theory might now appear to repress the ways in which power is an inextricable aspect of all communication and interpretation, be this in terms of ideology, a Nietzschean linking of truth and power, or psychoanalytical links between desire and language. Surely much of communication is predicated upon the need consciously or unconsciously to sustain oneself against the other, either directly or by subterfuge? This may well be empirically the case, but it does not make the position more defensible if it is taken as a universal basis for understanding, nor are particular empirical cases incompatible with Schleiermacher's theory. The problem is, as was already suggested in Chapter 3, that any claim that 'truth is power' must at least be capable of being validated, on the assumption that the very stating of the position is either itself a subterfuge, which must potentially be recognisable as such, or a truth claim, or a piece of random performativity. Theories that can be classed under the heading of the 'hermeneutics of suspicion' tend to share a reductionism, in much the way Jacobi suggested must be the case for any foundational theory.

The most convincing versions of the hermeneutic circle can be seen as attempting to avoid the reduction which results from a grand theory of how truth is to be understood, because of the need to 'begin in the middle' already revealed by Schlegel. The advantage of the Romantic positions we have been considering lies in their realisation of the *diversity* of possible modes and purposes of understanding which cannot be reduced to a common denominator, even to the idea that language is always meant to communicate or achieve something determinate, be it power over, or even ethical acknowledgement of, the other. Novalis suggested in his idea of 'Poems, just pleasant sounding and full of beautiful words, but also without any meaning or context . . . like fragments of the most diverse things' (Novalis 1978 p. 769) that there are times when the refusal to mean determinately is the source of philosophical insight. In the light of the very different history which Benjamin and Adorno will confront, this refusal to 'mean' will take on a thoroughly transformed significance, as I shall demonstrate in the following chapters, when determinate meaning comes in certain contexts to be regarded as a surrender to the language of the administered world of the 'culture industry'.

Schleiermacher may also appear to offend against virtually every recent assumption about the undecidability in the last analysis of all interpretation, thus against *différance*, the 'slipping of the signified under the signifier', and any other candidate for undecidability from recent literary theory which denies the full transparency of enunciated to enunciator or insists upon the irreducibility of one kind of discourse – be it of race, gender, or ideology – to another. Take Lyotard's characteristic claim: 'All the researches of scientific, literary, artistic avant-gardes are directed at revealing the mutual incommensurability of languages' (quoted in Welsch 1993 p. 165), an incommensurability he regards as characterising the 'post modern' renunciation of 'grand narratives', thus of ultimately consensual stories of legitimation. These researches do so in order not to repress the resources uniquely particular to a specific discourse. But can we even understand such a position? The difficulties it entails are suggested in Schleiermacher's

alternative approach and are already apparent in the performative contradiction involved in stating it: how does Lyotard know what he claims is the
case, and how is he able to claim in a language that all these researches are
directed towards the incommensurability of languages? From what position
can such a claim be asserted, and what identifies an avant- rather than,
say, an arrière-garde? Presumably for such a universal claim to be valid,
Lyotard's own language cannot itself be considered as part of the avant-
garde, because it is trying to make all the objects of this judgement
commensurable as avant-garde researches. If the incommensurability of the
language to other languages is of a different kind in each case – if that
makes any sense anyway: in what sense could they be said to be languages
at all? – how do we identify the way in which a language is different without
again slipping back into a language of commensurability?

The fact is, as Schleiermacher contends, that the possibility of difference
always already presupposes some version of identity and understanding
for difference to be intelligible at all. The only alternative to this is to give
up the idea of theory altogether, in favour of mere performativity, so
that stating such a position is just done to see what happens. The initial
objection to this is not theoretical, but ethical: it is an abdication of responsibility, on the specious grounds that one cannot anyway control the effects
of one's utterances. However, the fact that one cannot control all the
effects is no reason to ignore the ways that one can control some of them,
or to ignore the fact that in many circumstances we have no choice as moral
agents but to try. For Schleiermacher, pure performativity would be the far
end of a continuum which moved from the minimally performative level of
the merely 'mechanical' to the irreducibly aesthetic and individual whose
performative effects cannot be controlled. In his terms, though, the ends of
this continuum can never be finally separated from each other, and only
the fallible art of interpretation can judge how much of each is in play in
any real instance. Lyotard's and others' antagonism towards theories of
meaning which rely on some version of consensus relies on the assumption
that an orientation towards consensus blocks the possibility of what can
happen via utterances which escape the attempts to understand them,
so that understanding becomes a way of repressing the potential for the as
yet unsaid. An aestheticised conception of language is thereby extended
to all communication while largely disregarding the ways in which we can
make pragmatic discriminations concerning the goals of differing kinds of
articulation.[25]

Despite his refusal to move in such a direction, Schleiermacher's orientation towards consensus emphatically does *not* imply that because language
is the realm of the universal the process of interpretation can reach any kind
of end-point. The reasons for Schleiermacher's rejection of finality in interpretation are, though, not the ones usually adduced these days, of the kind
evident in Lyotard's concentration in *Le différend* on the 'rules' of a 'regime
of discourse'. These rules supposedly prevent the subject of one discourse

moving between incommensurable 'regimes', so that Nazis and liberals could never communicate about, let alone agree on, certain contested issues. The fact is that it is precisely because Lyotard formulates the whole issue of validity in terms of the incommensurability of 'regimes' of rules that he generates so many aporias: the assumption that the rules of a discourse or a language game finally determine the actual interpretative praxes of those 'located' within it (which is itself a questionable metaphor) is pure Platonism. Attention to the central role of the 'regress of rules' arguments at issue here might have spared Lyotard a lot of trouble. If we cannot claim that there is a final foundation for the employment of rules the obvious conclusion, given the fact of continuing, sometimes successful, communication, is that there is no reason to see rules as the final criterion of meaning. In this sense there is no reason to accept the necessity of ontologically irreconcilable regimes of discourse, as opposed to the ever-present fact of conflicting but potentially revisable beliefs held by real individuals: Nazis, after all, do sometimes become good liberals. The conflicting regimes of the *différend* are therefore the regulist's, not the hermeneuticist's theoretical problem (see Frank 1988).[26] This does not entail, though, that one has to presuppose a metaphysically guaranteed, rule-governed basis for consensus, just that without some *orientation* towards consensus one cannot even understand language at all. In this perspective many of the more extreme conceptions of language in the post-structuralist tradition can be seen to rely on assumptions that had already been convincingly undermined in the early part of the nineteenth century.[27]

Against the tendency to see language as functioning independently of subjects that is common both to Lyotard and objectivist semantics, Schleiermacher thinks the location of misunderstanding depends on the fact that 'self-consciousness is the most particular and untranslatable aspect of the symbolising activity' (Schleiermacher 1990 p. 259). He terms the aspect of self-consciousness which inherently individualises us and prevents interpretative closure 'feeling' or 'immediate self-consciousness' (see Bowie 1990 Chapter 6). For all the Romantics, and for Fichte, the term 'feeling' designates the aspect of the structure of self-consciousness which must be presupposed if another regress associated with Kant is to be avoided. The potential for this regress is suggested in Novalis' contention in the *Fichte Studies* that 'feeling cannot feel itself': feeling is immediate, the truth of feeling cannot be articulated in a concept or proposition. This is most immediately obvious in the proposition 'I know that I know'. Unless the first and the second 'know' have a different status, so that the first I is immediate and the other the result of reflection, a regress results which makes the undeniable fact of consciousness unintelligible (see Bowie 1990 Chapter 3). Feeling is therefore the ground of reflection, but cannot explicate itself, because it is immediate and unitary, not dual: it 'cannot feel itself'. Many misunderstandings of Romantic philosophy have resulted from taking the reference to 'feeling' as the sign of conceptual laxity, rather than as a *logical* condition for an account of the structure of self-consciousness. Such misunderstandings also affect all those accounts of interpretation, from behaviourism to Lyotard, which wish to exclude consideration of the subject from the understanding of utterances.

Human thought is located, for Schleiermacher, between the poles of linguistically instantiated – 'schematised' – 'objective representations', and the irreducibility of 'feeling'. Feeling can only be made empirically manifest in non-verbal 'gestures', which are not truth-determinate. What is meant here can be approached by the analogy of the interpretation of music and it will also form part of Schleiermacher's conception of literature. Given a musical score, contemporary technology can now produce a realisation of its instructions. This will, though, only be an adequate *interpretation* of the score if the score is predicated solely upon mechanical reproduction of the differential marks that constitute the score: this kind of 'interpretation' is straightforwardly circular, within a closed system of rule-bound articulation.[28] A technologically based realisation of the score constitutes an analogy to part (but only part) of what Schleiermacher means by the 'grammatical' side of interpretation. Without that side there could be no interpretation of written music in an aesthetic sense, even though, because it does not involve 'feeling', the grammatical in no way instantiates anything aesthetic. Although the forms and rules of types of music at any particular moment in history are generally quite rigidly defined, the actual employment of those forms always involves what is meant by feeling. Feeling is manifested in the aspects of the performance which are non-semantic, in the sense that they cannot be notated as 'objective representations' (which correspond in this analogy to the pitches and the durations of the notes) but are essential to what is conveyed in the performance.

Schleiermacher's conception of language – where the 'musical' plays an ineliminable role 'Even in the most strict form (*Gattung*) of utterance the musical influence will not be absent' (Schleiermacher 1977 p. 160) – incorporates dimensions of interpretation which these days have been too one-sidedly theorised in terms of semantic undecidability, into a kind of *understanding* of what an utterance may say which we cannot convert into discursivity. Instead of orienting himself towards the aporetic sense of coming up against what cannot be articulated often encountered in Lyotard, Schleiermacher's aim is to find ways of keeping in touch with other ways in which articulations are significant. His key demand, then, is to mediate between thought and feeling, but not so that the former, as it does in Hegel, merely swallows the latter. He later maintains, linking this to the need for a state to allow individual development, that 'A language is incomplete to the extent to which it does not admit individual treatment' (Schleiermacher 1990 p. 309), which in essence means that a language cannot be complete, and thus, as Davidson will claim, that 'there is no such thing as a language' in the sense of a theorisable entity. The route from these ideas to the pivotal role of the literary in such theories should already be discernible.

Similar polarities to that between thought and feeling play a major role in the methodological divisions of Schleiermacher's hermeneutics. Underlying his conception is the refusal to reify language: although he has no doubt that the conditions of possibility of our analysis of language are its objectifiable, rule-bound aspects, he does not think this gives an adequate account of understanding:

> A simple appropriation of thoughts which have already been laid down in language is not an activity of reason, and if we assume someone whose whole thinking is nothing more than those thoughts, then that person is hardly a person at all. (ibid. p. 264)

Such a person fails to reach the ethical level, which combines the universal demands inherent in language with the imperative to think for oneself. On the one hand, then, 'nobody can get out of language', but on the other 'the individual (*das Individuelle*) must remain within language, in the form of combination' (ibid. p. 323). The latter appears as 'style', the individual combination of the pre-given elements of language that cannot be prescribed in advance in terms of rules. This means that 'there can be no concept of a style' (Schleiermacher 1977 p. 172; see also Frank 1977, 1992). Feeling cannot be rendered objective, because the individual must employ the same signifying elements as others in order for it to be manifest, even though it is inherently particular to the individual. Access to the feeling of another can therefore only be achieved by awareness of the individual *differences* of combination and articulation of the *same* notional finite number of elements which are employed to communicate thought: 'in lyric poetry, where it is a question of expressing the movement of immediate self-consciousness [= feeling], the thought is itself really only a means of presentation [and thus not the aim of the utterance]' (Schleiermacher 1977 p. 138). The analogy to one kind of musical interpretation can again make the idea clearer: feeling will become accessible differentially, by comparing performances (or even ideas of performances with actual performances) in order to grasp what is different in each individual's performance of the same piece, not by empathy, as is often claimed in relation to Schleiermacher. It may be, of course, that we never really get in touch with the aspect of feeling in an utterance, but the demand that one should attempt to do so is once again an ethical, rather than an epistemological matter.

Schleiermacher distinguishes between 'grammatical' interpretation, in which 'the person ... disappears and only appears as organ of language', which largely corresponds to semantics, and 'technical interpretation', in which 'language with its determining power disappears and only appears as the organ of the person, in the service of their individuality' (Schleiermacher 1977 p. 171). One becomes aware of individuality, then, because what grammatical interpretation tells us is not all there is to be understood: 'to carry out grammatical explication on its own is a mere fiction' (Schleiermacher 1977 p. 164). What 'technical interpretation' attempts to interpret is therefore 'unsayable': it cannot just consist in a mechanical repetition of the utterance or text, and any other verbal response to the utterance will inevitably exclude some of what is articulated by the particular combination of words to be interpreted. The recurrent misunderstandings concerning Schleiermacher's supposed subjectivism derive from his increased attention in later versions of the theory to 'technical' interpretation (in the sense of '*techne*' seen in Kant), which he also terms 'psychological' interpretation, before 'grammatical' interpretation. Late in his work he then makes the following distinction between psychological and technical: 'the former is related more to the emergence of thoughts from the totality of the moments of life of the individual, the latter is more a leading-back to a determinate wish to think and present' (Schleiermacher 1977 p. 181). The psychological links the freedom of the author to the circumstances of his life as 'the principles of his self-determination' (ibid. p. 184); the technical concerns the 'core decision' ('*Keimentschluß*'), the individual's approach to the form in which they work, such as the novel or lyric poetry, a form which has already established historical constraints with – and against – which the author decides to work. In the case of the psychological there is no sense in which this side of interpretation will provide a final explanation of an author's meaning, because the totality is a regulative idea which one can never be sure one has adequately grasped.

The circular structure of interpretation makes it evident why this uncertainty is inherent in interpretation. One must always begin with some projection of what one thinks is meant by a text, which can then be tested and confirmed, or altered, by engagement with the text, but this can only be done on the basis of establishing further projections of meaning, not all of which are directly connected to the text.[29] What refutes the idea of Schleiermacher the psychologiser is that in both technical and psychological interpretation the evidence must be open to scrutiny, which means it must be 'schematised', rather than available as 'feeling'. As such, even first-person utterances are not necessarily wholly subjected to the authority of the writer/speaker, which therefore already prevents any kind of 'empathy':

> The task can also be put like this: 'to understand the utterance at first just as well as and then better than its author'. For because we have no immediate knowledge of what is in him, we must seek to bring much to consciousness which can remain unconscious to him, except to the extent to which he reflexively becomes his own reader. On the objective side he as well has no other data here than we do.
>
> (Schleiermacher 1977 p. 94)

The topos of 'better understanding' is not located exclusively on the side of the interpreter or the interpretee, because both could be the source of better understanding of an utterance. Decisions on this procedure are

pragmatic ones, precisely because the task is 'endless': 'Complete knowledge is always in this apparent circle, that every particular can only be
understood via the universal of which it is a part and vice versa' (ibid. p. 95).
The need to avoid misunderstanding is, as such, always present. This does
not mean, as is sometimes suggested, for example, by Gadamer, that
Schleiermacher fails to see the need for presupposing a consensus inherent
in language if understanding of any kind is to be possible. In relation to the
'stricter praxis' of hermeneutics:

> It is a basic experience that one does not notice any difference between
> the artless [= rule-following in what Wittgenstein will term a language-
> game] and the artistic [which requires non-rule-bound judgement, or
> what Wittgenstein means by 'interpretation'] in understanding until the
> occurrence of a misunderstanding. . . . It [the 'stricter praxis'] begins
> with the difference of language and the manner of combination, *which,
> though, must of course rest upon identity*. (ibid. p. 92, my emphasis)

It is only if one underestimates the weight attached to his arguments about
schematism that Schleiermacher could be said to psychologise or subjectify
meaning and interpretation.

Schematism plays a vital connecting role in Schleiermacher's approaches
to these questions, in ways which will again be important to discussion in
subsequent chapters. In a section of the *Ethics* on 'Identity of Schematism'
he states:

> Every person is a completed/closed-off (*abgeschlossen*) unity of
> consciousness. As far as reason produces cognition in a person it is,
> qua consciousness, only produced for this person. What is produced with
> the character of schematism is, though, posited as valid for everyone,
> and therefore being in one ['*Sein in Einem*' – by which he means indi-
> vidualised self-consciousness] does not correspond to its character [as
> schematism]. (Schleiermacher 1990 p. 64)

Language, then, is a 'system of movements of the organism which are simultaneously expression [on the side of 'feeling'] and sign [on the side of
'thought'] of the acts of consciousness as the cognising faculty, under the
character of the identity of schematism' (ibid. p. 65). The 'identity of
schematism' is the locus of truth. When I talk or write about x in order to
articulate what is true of x, I have to presuppose that x is as I say it is for
both myself and the other person,[30] but at the same time my relationship to
x cannot be *shown* to be that of the recipient of my utterances concerning x:
'all communication about external objects is a constant continuation of the
test as to whether all people construct identically' (Schleiermacher 1976
p. 373). Schleiermacher describes the schema as an 'intuition which can be
shifted within certain limits' (quoted in Frank 1989a p. 28), and Gadamer,
in a later essay which partially corrects his misleading presentation of
Schleiermacher in *Truth and Method*, explains its function as follows:

the doctrine of the schema makes it possible to keep away all rationalistic distortions from the problem of meaning. The meaning of a word itself has the character of schema. That means that the meaning is not unambiguously fixed to a particular realm of application or an objective sphere. It is precisely mobility (*Verschiebbarkeit*) which is the essence of schema. (Gadamer 1987 p. 367)

Interpretation thus becomes a constant play between identity and difference, the schematic aspect and the side of what is designated by feeling remaining in continual interplay. If language were essentially constituted in terms of rules and conventions, then the discovery of these rules, in the manner of regulism, would establish the conditions of truth. However, the point is that language cannot be said to possess a finally stable structure, precisely because this structure would have to be constituted in terms of rules, which, for the reasons we have seen, cannot account for the actual functioning of understanding. Given the constant shifts in the real working of language for both interpreter and interpreted, one is faced with an 'endless task' (Schleiermacher 1974a p. 131). The interplay between identity and difference also gives a vital clue as to the nature of the literary in this theory: the 'purely literary' would function at the level of feeling alone, but this is not possible, as the very nature of language always requires the interplay of the two sides, the schematic and feeling, in varying degrees.

Instead, then, of the ultimate undecidability of interpretation leading to nihilism, understanding is for Schleiermacher primarily ethical: it does not derive final foundations from already existing rules, but rather imposes a continuing obligation upon free actors to attempt to see the world from the viewpoint of the other, and to articulate the potential created by the other, *including oneself as other* in self-reflexive interpretation. The optimistic view of this conception – in subsequent chapters we will consider how these kinds of Romantic theory change their significance in the light of the demise of the optimistic side of the Romantic vision that results from historical catastrophe – regards literature as the meeting place of the ethical and the aesthetic. Literature both obliges us to interpret and renders the failure to reach final determinacy of understanding potentially pleasurable, thereby manifesting a reconciliation of necessity and freedom. The very idea of such reconciliation *is*, though, as I suggested in the Introduction, highly controversial. Is reconciliation of contradictions in the realm of appearance not definitive of ideology? What, then, of the critiques of the notion of literature I began to examine in the Introduction, which regard it as a form of ideology: do these invalidate the Romantic conceptions by showing that they involve a naïve failure to see their own rootedness in the power relations of a bourgeoisie which falsely universalises its own economic emancipation? This topic will repeatedly concern us from now on. The important point here is to see these historical critiques in relation to the broader philosophical problems of interpretation, rather than let the critiques set the agenda before one has adequately dealt with certain inescapable methodological issues.

'THERE IS NO SUCH THING AS A LANGUAGE'/'THERE IS NO SUCH THING AS LITERATURE'

The title of this section is a juxtaposition of two controversial claims that are central to the contemporary theoretical scene, whose interconnections need to be understood if the question of literature and ideology is to be adequately assessed. The consequences of this assessment are vital for the future direction of literary theory. In pragmatic terms there is actually a way in which one might say 'there is no such thing as anything', in the sense that pragmatism, like Romantic philosophy, renounces essentialist characterisations of both concrete and abstract entities, in favour of a world whose furniture is always open to re-description.[31] A thoroughgoing anti-essentialism may seem to abolish any kind of controversy here, but the questions involved do not go away just because we give up one version of Platonism. What matters are the effects of the arguments for these claims upon how we deal with real problems of language and understanding.

Davidson's claim that 'there is no such thing as a language' (Lepore 1986 p. 446) is a way of arguing for the pragmatist/hermeneutic suspicion of regulism that has concerned us in this chapter. The title of his essay 'A Nice Derangement of Epitaphs', in which the claim appears, is a malapropism which becomes intelligible when one realises that the essay is about how we are able to understand deviant utterances via their contexts, without relying on a rule-based description of how we do so. Davidson's title enacts what Schleiermacher referred to when he claimed that in lyric poetry 'the thought [which Davidson sees as 'first meaning' – see below] is itself really only a means of presentation' of the nature of a particular process of self-consciousness, in that the concepts actually employed are not what is meant. In this case the intended meaning of 'a nice arrangement of epithets' is less the issue than is the unconsciously inventive nature of the repeated linguistic misapprehensions of the person who makes the utterance. To be able to understand the deviant utterance, Davidson suggests we require what he terms (rather problematically)[32] a 'passing theory' – which plays the same role as does Kantian reflective judgement – and, like Schleiermacher, he thinks semantics in real communication inherently relies on reflective rather than determining judgement: 'For there are no rules for arriving at passing theories, no rules in any strict sense, as opposed to rough maxims and methodological generalities' (Lepore 1986 p. 446). This can, I want to contend, lead us to the claim that, *because* there is no such thing as a language, literary texts can reveal ineliminable aspects of the nature of language that cannot be accommodated by a theory of ideology. While this may not give us a 'thing called literature' it does have important effects on how we deal with Eagleton's proposition that 'there is no such thing as literature', 'in the sense of a set of works of assured and unalterable value' (Eagleton 1983 p. 11, cf. discussion in the Introduction). Much here depends, as I have repeatedly suggested, upon how evaluation is conceived and upon the status of judgement in such theories.

Eagleton's claim about literature clearly has a different status to Davidson's about language, given the presumed nature of the entity whose existence is being denied. My concern in this section is with whether a sense of the literary can be established that is theoretically productive in the light of the issues raised in this chapter. Eagleton's description does, one should note, assume that the notion of literature is normatively constituted. I want to claim that the normative aspect should lead one in different directions from Eagleton, as the following can suggest. The fact that the very willingness (for example, in a wholly alien context) to treat an utterance as potentially linguistic, rather than as a mere natural occurrence, already introduces normative decisions concerning how to respond to the assumed capacity of the other to 'make sense'. Those norms will be different again if the premise is that the utterance in question is a piece of literature. In both cases there is, crucially, no meta-rule to govern the initial interpretative decision. However, the assertion that literature is ideology, because it is a product of socially and historically situated evaluation – a fact which is anyway in one sense a priori undeniable – denies the possibility of special status to any kind of text or utterance, on the assumption that the significance of all texts must be understood in terms of their possible effects within the power relations and cultural praxes of a particular historical context.

There is already a potential regress here: the interpreter who identifies the value horizon of these possible effects is herself working within a value horizon, and therefore must presuppose valid self-interpretation if her own role in the functioning of ideology is to be understood in relation to her interpretation. What worries me about the ideology-based view is that any sense that literature has to do with the freedom of individuals to re-articulate aspects of the world in ways which are not exhausted by theory-led interpretation gives way to the incorporation of the literary into society and history as just another determinate 'signifying praxis'. In such theories the Romantic valorisation of *Poesie*, of the ability of an individual to re-articulate the world through their spontaneity, is understood predominantly in genetic terms. Art becomes a response to the process of secularisation and the rise of commodity-based societies, for which nothing has intrinsic value: art is therefore elevated, as it is in Kant's notion of disinterested pleasure, to being the illusory repository of intrinsic value, via the 'ideology of the aesthetic', with the autonomous artist taking the place of the creator-God. Literature in this view is consequently to be understood via a critical examination of its conditions of production. This reveals, for example, the patriarchal assumptions which inform essential aspects of the text, such as the different fates of Faust and Gretchen at the end of Goethe's *Faust* Part 2, and shows how those assumptions informed the social groupings within which the text was written. The interplay between text as part and context as whole is thereby decisively weighted towards the determining aspect of the latter, be it understood as 'history', 'class-society', 'gender relations' or whatever. There are, one should add, very convincing arguments to suggest the aptness of such analyses for many purposes. At the same time, there are other crucial arguments ignored by these approaches.

Views based on the critique of ideology have tended to derive from certain versions of Marxist theory and it is therefore not surprising that they are also congruent with a Hegelian conception of art. For Hegel, the truth of art is articulated by philosophy, art itself remaining at the level of 'immediacy', the pre-conceptual level of the image, as opposed to the level on which the general truth of the image is theoretically cashed out.[33] Language here becomes analogous to Hegelian *Geist* – Hegel himself, as we have seen, refers to language as the 'existence of *Geist*' – because truth is the universal embodied in the capacity of finite but generally shared linguistic means to articulate all that can be meant.[34] Moving from the already questionable idea that the totality of the signifying means in any society are determinately constituted as an interlocking system prior to the individuals who employ them, to the idea that those means are fundamentally expressions of ruling power relations, is highly problematic, given the diversity of the real contextual functioning of language, including what I wish to refer to as literature.[35] A theory of ideology that does not wish to invoke a grounding conception of truth as the criterion for the identification of ideology must, though, try to suggest how it can legitimate itself without laying claim to the kinds of metaphysical foundationalism it is itself intended to oppose, on the grounds that foundations are historically generated. The awareness of this issue will be central in Adorno.

Within the Marxist tradition the *locus classicus* in this century of the attempt to ground such a theory is Lukács' *History and Class Consciousness*, which explicitly tries to replace the transcendental subject of the Kantian metaphysical tradition with the really existing proletariat – and the party which articulates its practically generated insights – as the ground of truth which can unmask the system-generated social and cultural effects of the commodity structure and the reified labour process. Lukács thereby develops the implicit link discussed at the end of Chapter 1 between structures of language and of political economy, in which the system dominates the individual: this issue will become vital in subsequent chapters. In the terms we have established in this chapter the essential relationship is between the general, systematically constituted signifying material and individual subjects, thus between Lacan's 'symbolic order', which Althusser, among others, links to the notion of ideology, and whatever theoretical candidate one places in the location of the subject who uses language. If there is no such thing as a language, though, the very notion of the symbolic *order* already begins to look shaky. This suggests, given the links often made between language and ideology, that the notion of ideology itself may, in some contexts at least, be subject to much the same problem as the regulist notion of a language. The further reason to question such positions is that they must presumably always already know what the artwork is telling us, thus leaving no space for the truth-content of art beyond what can be stated within the theory at a particular historical moment. The vital point I wish to make here with the help of Schleiermacher is that the truth-content which transcends the context of production of a literary text can only be made accessible via a presupposition of *freedom* on the part both of the producer and the receivers of the work.

It should already be apparent that reducing the understanding of aesthetically significant texts to the establishment of their place within an ideological formation, such as 'bourgeois literature', or the 'closed work of art' risks landing one in the sort of circularity or regress we have been considering all along. If one looks at a text as a piece of ideology one will inevitably see ways it can be construed as ideology: this much is already obvious from the hermeneutic circle. The same applies in terms of looking at it as literature, but this just means that it is vital to work out a notion of literature adequate to the issues to be raised below. Obviously it would be mistaken to deny the importance of ideological analysis in many contexts for many purposes, and there is nothing from a hermeneutic perspective to exclude such approaches: people can and do come to reflect upon ways in which they were objects of an ideology, and there may be no determinate end to such reflection. The annexation of literature into ideology can, though, as I argued in the Introduction, too readily subordinate the literary to instrumental goals or use it as just another resource for sociological and other analyses: if that is all there is to 'literary' texts for us there really could be no such thing as literature. However, if the point of unmasking ideology has to do with the wish for emancipation, this already poses the question as to the symbolic resources which could make an *understanding* of that emancipation available at all: otherwise one begins to wonder what the notion of emancipation is there for anyway. The utopian aspect of the literary and aesthetic which I pointed to in the Introduction here becomes central. It should already be apparent that this is now actually not just a question about the evaluation of the literary but also a question about the very nature of everyday language and understanding, which is not confined to the area of aesthetics and politics, and is even, as we saw in Davidson, germane to semantics.

Considering an example from music can again most obviously suggest what is being repressed by, to take the most prominent contemporary instance of a theory founded on the notion of ideology, cultural materialism. Do cultural materialists really think they *understand* Beethoven's Ninth Symphony just by looking at its contextual functions, for Beethoven's world and in subsequent ideological contexts? These latter contexts are often illustrated (for example, by John Berger) by the notorious bit of film of Furtwängler conducting the Ninth during the Second World War with Hitler in the audience. The film awakens a series of highly troubling sedimented associations, along with the wholly justifiable sense that there is no guarantee that great art will not be ideologically misused: the Nazis in the audience may well have had Nazi thoughts, as *A Clockwork Orange* implied in a different context. Try, though, listening to a justly famous performance of the Ninth by Furtwängler, from 1942 in Berlin, and find any trace of Nazi ideological influence in the actual performance, as opposed to the sense of an extreme tension between preserving the humanist heritage expressly invoked in the work and performing the work in those historical circumstances. The result of this tension is a revelation of expressive resources in the work perhaps never heard before, or since. The same applies to Furtwängler's recorded performances of other major 'bourgeois' works from during the Nazi period. One cannot but listen to these performances with ambivalence, but they enact that ambivalence themselves: denying their aesthetic import now may be a valid option for some purposes (and more than understandable for those who suffered but survived), but reducing their significance in this respect to mere ideology is the mark of theoretical abdication. If one knew nothing of the context of the performance, it would still be possible to make similar aesthetic judgements by comparison with other performances. The fact that there will be no consensus over such judgements is not a central problem: any judgement can be contended by someone, which is why fallibilism and the demand for public accountability is so important.

What are in question, then, are dimensions of symbolic articulation and understanding which cannot be even *understood* in a perspective defined exclusively in terms of ideology, unless the concept is used, in a circular manner, to refer to all kinds of evaluation. It is precisely when one takes the example of media like music which are not immediately translatable into discursivity that the reductiveness of cultural materialism most obviously begins to emerge. Remarks like Antony Easthope's, in opposition to a formalist account of 'aesthetic properties' in a literary text, that 'all texts have formal properties ... all texts are dense, precise and vigorous in certain ways' (Easthope 1995 p. 31), would be unexceptional if he did not thereby render all modes of apprehension of texts equivalent in the last analysis. Given that this levelling of differentiation is precisely what is most characteristic of the worst aspects of modern commodity-based societies and of the cultural impoverishment to which they lead, there are serious grounds for thinking that such a theory is actually colluding with the *status quo* rather than providing a new critical perspective. The same levelling presumably applies to pieces of music, all of which are 'dense, precise and vigorous in certain ways', but does that mean, to ask a familiar question, that Beethoven is no more significant than Roger Whittaker? Clearly the next question, as Easthope suggests, is 'to whom?', 'where?', but any position which fails to give room for qualitative distinctions beyond the contingencies of merely individual (Nazi?) reception is pretending to give up on any normative sense at all. At the same time, of course, such views reintroduce other norms by the back door, such as a misplaced blanket suspicion of formally integrated works of art, whose signifying potential anyway far transcends the fact of their formal integration. It is for these reasons that the need to sustain the truth-claims of aesthetic products becomes imperative: a Nazi interpretation of Beethoven may be socio-logically significant, but it is demonstrably unable to be validated in relation to its object if that object is to be understood in aesthetic terms that can claim universal validity.[36] This does not mean that aesthetic judgements do achieve universal validity, but that they must strive to do so if they are to be aesthetic judgements in the sense intended here; otherwise, as Kant already suggested, one has no grounds for claiming to make aesthetic judgements as opposed to mere judgements about what one likes.

Easthope's fear is that by taking account of the aesthetic one must be invoking intrinsic properties of the work in the Platonist manner character-istic of the ideology of the aesthetic, but this cannot be the case in terms of the hermeneutic anti-essentialism being advanced here. If such works as Beethoven's are important it is because they keep on transcending contexts via their *renewed* reception, *not* because we can claim they always will, which would be mere Platonism again. As so often in certain areas of literary theory, the fear of one particular kind of repression leads to the elision of crucial evaluative distinctions: the concealed basis of this elision is nearly always the same, namely a positivism which thinks that – as opposed to the supposedly hard facts of science, history and politics – aesthetic value decisions are merely local and ideological. A thoroughgoing normativity of the kind I am proposing here on the basis of Schleiermacher's insights renders this stance otiose: there *is* no location we can definitively establish in which there are no normative conflicts, so interpretation and evaluation are universal, even in the cognitive realm. As such, the fear of asserting aesthetic value as having normative potential in the same way as any other kind of articulation ceases to be an issue. The fear of seeing the aesthetic as an intrinsic property also goes out of the window if one gives up on intrinsic properties in general, as the hermeneutic position advanced here does. The answer to the traditionalist protest from the other direction, that 'surely you must accept works of art have *some* intrinsic properties?' is simply to become engaged in a debate about the properties an inter-preter wishes to attribute to the work. Without the work, no properties; without the interpreters, no properties either, as Schleiermacher makes clear in arguments to be cited below. Intrinsic properties in this sense are those which seem to be able to command universal assent: but this still leaves open the possibility that these properties may turn out to be mistakenly attributed and that judgements on them will later be revised. The crucial point is whether the work sustains the need to keep revising its interpretations.

The problem with the notion of ideology is that if one defines it too widely anything ever articulated belongs in it and the term becomes empty. If everything is x, nothing is x: a theory of ideology presumably cannot be itself ideological, otherwise, as we saw, one has the regress and circularity problem all over again. Narrowing the definition necessarily leads to complex reflections upon truth and values that ought to form the core of any interpretative enterprise. The notion of ideology works best against false universalism, as suggested in Adorno's notion of 'immanent critique', where, in order to avoid making claims that entail an extra-mundane position free of ideology, one tries in a manner exactly congruent with what Schleiermacher insists on as the complement of hermeneutics – critique – to show how a piece of articulation fails to live up to its own immanent logic and demands. The revealing tensions generated by Adorno's approach derive from the difficulty of establishing a theoretical location from which the truth of the work might be articulated, and from finding a mode of communication which would not either just replace the work with its analysis, in the manner of theories based on a reductive conception of ideology, or surrender critical responsibility to unquestioning enjoyment.

The resources offered by Schleiermacher can profitably be brought into play here. If one has said goodbye to regulism and the dilemmas considered above in the example of Lyotard's 'regimes of discourse', many of which are repeated in cultural materialism, certain notions of language and their connections to ideology cease to be viable options. As has just been suggested, the insistence on contextualism characteristic of theories of ideology is in no way a priori incompatible with the hermeneutic position advanced here. It all depends upon how 'context' is conceived. The revelation of ideological functions in a putatively literary text within its own period is not, for example, necessarily incompatible with seeing the same text as having an emancipatory function in a later period, or vice versa. It can equally have very different functions in the same period. The question is, therefore, whether the fact that such a text signifies in such different ways makes it in some way unlike other kinds of utterance, *any* of which can potentially signify in an infinity of ways by being re-contextualised, which is a question about the nature of normativity in interpretation.

In the Romantic tradition engagement with the work of art becomes the model of all philosophically serious understanding, which is why Romanticism is often the target of those who think that the understanding of art as vitally significant for philosophy masks the lack of real freedom in modern societies by appealing to a sphere in which freedom is mere appearance. The real issue is whether one wishes to invoke freedom at all in this connection. Very often positions like that of Eagleton – and even Adorno at times holds to such a view – seem to imply that freedom is so utopian (in the strict sense) that we could only use the notion in a world in which the dominance of the exchange principle would already have been overcome. However much we are aware of living in a commodified and administered world, this basically Hegelian concentration on freedom as solely constituted by social relations seems to me to be mistaken. It derives from a renunciation of all the resources of the post-Kantian traditions for thinking about human autonomy, in the name of the assumption that only a transformed totality could enable us to recognise what freedom really is. This conception is, though, philosophically indefensible: unless we *already* have some sense of what freedom can be, of the kind manifested in aesthetic experience, we would not even *recognise* its instantiation in transformed socio-economic structures. As Schnädelbach puts it in relation to Sartre, whose thought converges in many ways with that of Schleiermacher: 'only a being with the existential structure of being-for-itself and being-beyond-itself can have the experience of alienation' (Schnädelbach 1992 p. 271). Any claim on behalf of a theory of ideology which refuses to accept this must offer an alternative reason for wanting to criticise an existing society in the first place. Freedom is therefore not an option in this debate: without it there *can be* no debate about ideology.

The more fundamental fact here is that some notion of freedom is inescapable even in terms of interpretation itself, let alone in terms of 'literature' or art. Schleiermacher terms art 'free production', but, crucially, it is 'production on the part of the same functions which also occur in the bound activity of mankind' (Schleiermacher 1974a p. 375): 'bound activity' is activity that takes place in accordance with pre-existing rules. Schleiermacher's claim can now provide us with the crucial link between the two propositions at issue in this section. The fact is that Schleiermacher's approach to the literary and aesthetic intersects with Davidson's ideas about the misapprehensions of regulist theories of language in ways which demand an approach to the problem of 'literature' that does not merely rely on the concept of ideology. Davidson initially maintains that, in order to understand a literary image: 'unless we know the literal, or first, meaning of the words we do not grasp and cannot explain the image', but then he asserts: 'But "the order of interpretation" is not at all clear. For there are cases where we may first guess at the image and so puzzle out the first meaning' (Lepore 1986 p. 435). Forms of aesthetic apprehension thus begin potentially to appear in relation to any unfamiliar linguistic usage. Schleiermacher claims 'in all areas, including outside the real realm of art there is a certain tendency towards art' (Schleiermacher 1977 p. 192), which is significantly ambiguous between the sense of art we have seen associated with hermeneutics and the sense of art as 'free production'.

The fact is that art must be formed out of non-art. At the same time – and this is the critical point – the possibility of the transition from what is not art to art, or, in the more specific case, from what is not literature to literature, must always *already* be present, unless one wishes to discard any conception of the aesthetic or the literary at all. The emergence of aesthetic and literary experience becomes inexplicable if what makes aesthetic experience possible is not always already potentially present

within non-aesthetic experience. Without the *possibility* of 'free production' – even in the most 'bound' (or ideologically circumscribed) activities
– there can be no art and no experience of art. Schleiermacher sees the
difference between the free and the bound as manifested in language, in
relation to what Davidson terms 'the infinitely difficult problem of how a
first language is learned' (Lepore 1986 p. 441):

> the bound and the free are always next to each other, even in childhood,
> only that in childhood, where subject and object have not yet separated
> to such a degree, it has only emphasised and differentiated itself to
> a small extent. However, as soon as children grasp language – for it is
> the first beginning point where objective consciousness fixes itself – this
> difference between free and bound activity emerges.
>
> (Schleiermacher 1974a, p. 108)

The emergence of the awareness of the difference of freedom from 'bound-
ness' (*Gebundenheit*) can, though, *only* be understood via a prior freedom,
the spontaneity of the interpreting subject, otherwise we would have no way
of understanding it at all. This prior freedom is only available to 'feeling',
because it would otherwise be just the conceptually determinable opposite
of *Gebundenheit*. Because it is indeterminable this freedom cannot finally
be understood conceptually or theoretically, which leads to the need for
other, non-conceptual – metaphorical or aesthetic – ways of understanding
it. These alternative ways rely, of course, upon what is 'bound' if they are to
be intelligible at all, but they do so only in order to break up the inherent
generality of what is bound in order to render new articulation possible.
The abandonment of the possibility that such articulation could help make
freedom intelligible would indeed mean there is no such thing as literature,
but is this really a convincing option?

In an account of Adorno's aesthetics which raises questions we shall consider further in Chapter 9, Christoph Menke suggests that the 'constitution
of aesthetic signifiers' lies 'in the de-automatised repetition of automatic
acts of understanding' (Menke 1991 p. 75), thus in that which is opposed
to regulism, but which still, as we just saw, must rely upon the identities
required in any attempt to understand. As opposed to Schleiermacher,
though, Menke makes an over-radical separation between determining
– 'automatic' – and reflective – 'de-automatised' – judgement, between
regulist semantics and hermeneutics. This can most obviously be questioned via Schleiermacher's example of the linguistic creativity of children:
the prior aspect in a child must be non-automatic understanding as otherwise there would be no way of grasping how such creativity was possible.
The lack of fixed linguistic rules is the norm, of course, for the child in the
initial process of language acquisition. Schleiermacher sees this in terms
of 'divination', his term for the art of interpreting when there can be no
rule for the application of rules.[37] Automatic acts of understanding must by
definition be learned as rule-bound acts, and can also be thought of in terms

of ideology, on the assumption that the speaker is understood to have only limited reflexive ability to criticise the content of such acts. The capacity to de-automatise must, though, already be present *before* the automatic processes of understanding, otherwise such phenomena as those cited by Davidson in relation to 'deviant' utterances would become incomprehensible.

Importantly, the *same* difference in types of judgement suggested by Menke is the basis of an aesthetics of reception and an aesthetics of production, which Schleiermacher rejects, by claiming that the 'pathematic' and the 'productive' viewpoint are only relatively different forms of the same activity (Schleiermacher 1974a p. 30) – there is no *aesthetic* reception which does not require free activity of the same kind as aesthetic production, and therefore no literature without free subjects who render it possible, both as writers and readers. The same polarities can, as Davidson implies, be mapped on to a semantics which is not grounded in rules but which assumes instead that 'we have erased the boundary between knowing a language and knowing our way around in the world generally' (Lepore 1986 p. 446). On the one hand, then, literature cannot be separated by a definitive line from other forms of language, because what constitutes the literary may come into play in any piece of language; on the other hand, the conception of language at issue here cannot be understood in terms of ideology, because it inherently requires freedom, freedom which is most obviously manifest in precisely those works that have a claim to literary status. The argument against the theory of literature as ideology is not, then, a sentimental appeal to the creativity of the bourgeois subject, but a methodological objection to the implicit conceptions of the subject and understanding in that theory. No one is claiming that the functioning, particularly of modern societies, does not involve too much that is in Schleiermacher's sense 'bound' activity, with often devastating effects, but this cannot provide a convincing account of the also ever-present potential for new semantic and ethical resources that can be understood via the theory I am suggesting here, in which the aesthetic and the literary play an ineliminable role. The ideology theory actually risks becoming part of what it wishes to criticise: if it can offer no methodologically defensible resources for escaping the prison house of ideology, it is reduced merely to describing the supposed given rather than trying to change it on the basis of already existing possibilities.

The major issue now becomes how to connect this conception of literature to questions concerning the functioning of truth in modern societies. Although such an approach does not lay claim to an essentialist conception of literature, it does claim that the reduction of literature to ideology or to notions of the symbolic order renders the very nature of real understanding obscure, thereby hiding resources of meaning which are always already in play in all forms of articulation. Furthermore, by re-connecting the literary to ethical issues – without reducing it to the ethical – this approach leaves space for the argumentative defence of aesthetic evaluations in a way that ideology-based theories do not. By admitting the inescapability of evaluation *and* the freedom it necessarily involves, this hermeneutic approach allows both the kind of analysis upon which the critique of ideology relies *and* appreciation of why such analyses cannot be adequate to the most aesthetically significant texts. In these terms, the literary may well only be the far end of a postulated linguistic continuum, that becomes significant at a particular point in the development of modern secularised society, but its importance lies in how it reveals to us why we should wish to keep on trying to understand beyond what can determinately be said – and analysed – at a particular moment. The ways in which the questions of literature and aesthetics raised here inform philosophical investigations in the wake of the demise of Romantic philosophy will, then, form the basis of the following chapters.

In Chapter 6 the historical continuity of the story which has taken us in a fairly direct line from the Pantheism controversy and Kant to Romantic hermeneutics will be broken. Much of Schleiermacher's best work was produced in the 1820s, and we have now to move on a hundred years, via a consideration of Dilthey, to the work of Heidegger, if the main questions established in previous chapters are to be taken up in a manner which reaches the theoretical level we have encountered so far. The reasons for this leap are themselves also germane to what is at issue here. It is clear, not least in the light of the wholesale misinterpretation of his actual texts on interpretation which is still prevalent even today, that the questions raised by Schleiermacher's work did not become fully integrated into the mainstream of the philosophy that followed him. Although his work was influential, more dominant tendencies within the thought of the post-Romantic era – which include the demise of Hegelianism, the spectacular practical success of the industrialisation and institutionalisation of the scientific method and the rise of neo-Kantian attempts to ground that success philosophically, the growing process of secularisation and the accompanying development of materialist philosophy – drew attention away from many of the ideas we have been considering.[38] There were those who carried on Schleiermacher's heritage within academic philosophy, such as August Böckh, and Schleiermacher's influence on theology was considerable, but the very fact that hermeneutics needed to be revived as part of academic philosophy later in the century by Dilthey's work on *The Life of Schleiermacher* and in his other work on the *Geisteswissenschaften* makes it evident that something crucial had changed. Furthermore, the fact that it was the work of Nietzsche, a philosophical outsider, which most obviously carried on some of the Romantic themes examined here suggests how removed from the mainstream of academic philosophy in the second half of the nineteenth century many of the ideas about hermeneutics we have been concerned with here had become.[39] This distance from academic philosophy has been continued in the Anglo-Saxon realm almost until the present day, as I have already suggested. The underlying factor in the vagaries of the reception of hermeneutics after Schleiermacher is a scientism which believes philosophy's main job is to underpin the results of research in the natural sciences, and which therefore puts the status of art and literature in question as a subject of serious truth-oriented analysis. In Chapter 6 I will look at a few issues in the work of Dilthey and Husserl in the context of an introductory examination of central aspects of the work of Heidegger. The overarching theme shared by Dilthey, Nietzsche (who, as I suggested in the Introduction, will only be considered *en passant*) and Heidegger – and even, to a certain extent, by the later Husserl – is an awareness that the undeniable success of the newly developed natural sciences, which came to dominate philosophical conceptions of truth in the second half of the nineteenth century, failed to answer many of the major philosophical questions posed by modernity. Their response to this failure led them to new evaluations of aesthetic questions which have decisive effects upon modern conceptions of truth.

6 Being true
Dilthey, Husserl and Heidegger (1)

HEIDEGGERIAN QUESTIONS

Like other controversial figures in the intellectual history of modernity, such as Nietzsche and Freud, Heidegger is too frequently credited, particularly by literary theorists, with fundamental innovations that had actually already been initiated by others.[1] The fact is that Heidegger, far from carrying out a final break with the past, actually follows many of the paths we have already investigated, although he radicalises some of the ways of exploring them. We shall see later that the continuities between Heidegger and the figures we have considered so far belie the temporal distance between them. Indeed it is clear that, because of its refusal to give the natural sciences a privileged role in philosophy, some of Heidegger's best work is closer in certain ways to that of the Romantics than to much of the intervening philosophy. The Romantic approaches to the problems of grounding the truth which ensue from Kantian philosophy and Jacobi are once again the key issue here, and Heidegger's work is thoroughly continuous with much that we have investigated in this respect. That this continuity now connects to the dark side of 'Romanticism' which follows from the perversion of supposedly 'Romantic' ideas in Nazi and other right-wing ideology will be a crucial topic, especially when we move in Chapter 7 to an examination of Heidegger's conception of art and truth, and in the following chapters to Walter Benjamin's and Adorno's contributions to Frankfurt School critical theory.[2] Heidegger, Benjamin and Adorno all owe much to the Romantic heritage in sometimes remarkably similar ways, which means that the reasons for their *political* divergences will become as important as their common attachment to philosophical conceptions that emerge from Romanticism. It should already be clear from the preceding chapters that I think it is impossible to convert the cosmopolitan anti-foundationalism of Schlegel, Novalis and Schleiermacher into Nazi ideology, and the Nazis themselves thought the same, having no time at all for the early Romantics. Given the convergence of some of Heidegger's ideas with those of the Romantics, one way of understanding aspects of his politics will be to consider how he *departs* from Romantic ideas, rather than seeing *both* the Romantics and Heidegger as potential or real contributors to Nazi ideology.

The complexities here have, of course, been added to by the re-examinations of Heidegger's political life which began with the publication of Victor Farias' book on Heidegger and Nazism. In order to preclude any possible doubts on the matter I should state at the outset that I think Heidegger behaved disgracefully from 1933 onwards, and that there were few, if any, mitigating factors in his behaviour.[3] The most cursory perusal of Hugo Ott's biography of Heidegger, which tries to be as understanding as it can, will make the reasons for this judgement clear. At the same time it should already be apparent from the hermeneutic ideas outlined in Chapter 5 that reducing the work to the failings of the man is a mistake. Although the intentions of certain of Heidegger's texts were clearly disreputable – what else could one think, for example, of his Rectorship Speech at Freiburg University in 1934 that linked his philosophy to the vocabulary and ideas of Nazism, or of his refusal to make any public acknowledgement after the war that his support for the Nazis was wrong? – there is also a philosophical impetus in some of his work which one directly assimilates to his politics and his moral failures only at the risk of jettisoning work that is an enduring challenge to any modern philosophy. Heidegger wrote some really frightful rubbish, some of which explicitly links his philosophy to the most abominable political movement of the modern period, but he wrote much that was anything but rubbish, and it is mainly on some of the latter material that I shall focus here. Given the obvious limits of the present context I shall adopt a deliberately selective approach to Heidegger's work, concentrating on his contributions to questions of philosophy, literature and truth raised in the preceding chapters. In Chapter 7 I shall try at least to begin to take account of the political issues that must accompany these questions.

Now it is almost axiomatic that, along with the historical, political and ethical problems associated with his thought, Heidegger also poses formidable problems of comprehension for his readers – though one should add that this is much more the case in his later work than in his work until the early 1930s, much of which, given Heidegger's reputation, is a great deal more lucid than one might expect.[4] The best way of finding an accessible approach to his work here is to locate him in relation to already familiar issues, which is not at all difficult. Take, for instance, the following historical echo, which will link Heidegger to both Jacobi and Davidson. In Chapter 1 we considered Jacobi's contentions that 'all our knowledge is nothing but a consciousness of linked determinations of our own self, on the basis of which one cannot infer to anything else' (Jacobi 1787 p. 225), and that 'We can only demonstrate similarities (*agreements, relatively necessary truths*), progressing in statements of identity. Every proof presupposes something which has already been proven, whose principle is *revelation*' (Scholz 1916 p. 178). Compare that with the following assertion by Davidson, nearly two hundred years later, on the necessity of holism in knowledge claims: 'our only evidence for a belief is other beliefs; this is not merely the logical situation, but also the pragmatic situation. And since no belief is self-certifying, none can supply a certain basis for the rest' (Lepore 1986 p. 331). In both cases the concern is with a ground which would prevent the regress of 'beliefs about beliefs': eventually one reaches a level which could not, unless we were to make an absolute metaphysical presupposition, of the kind Reinhold and Fichte proposed, give a definitive ground for how we are to understand truth claims. Some kind of presupposition is nevertheless required to prevent a regress into meaninglessness or into a sceptical inability to validate anything, an inability which would also render unintelligible our undoubted ability to cope with the world in many ways. Understanding what prevents such a regress means understanding something vital about the nature of truth, and Heidegger will be concerned with such questions of grounding and truth throughout his career. For Jacobi, the crucial fact was that revelation itself is of a different order from the interlinked chains of judgements whose possibility is grounded by revelation. As I have already suggested in Chapter 1, the structural role of 'revelation' in Jacobi, that haunts subsequent philosophy, relates both to Davidson's sense of truth as something of which we have an 'intuitive grasp' and in certain ways to Heidegger's notion of truth as a 'disclosure' prior to determinate propositional assertions, which he comes to link to questions of literature and art. It will also, as we shall see, relate to Dilthey's notion of *Erlebnis*. In this sense, then, we have, despite the very different historical context, not yet moved to any essentially new philosophical territory.

Given the link just outlined, it is hardly surprising also to find substantial links between Heidegger and the arguments of Schleiermacher.[5] These are apparent, to take one of many examples, in the following passage from his 1928 lectures on *Metaphysical Foundations of Logic*, where Schleiermacher's regress-of-rules argument appears in another guise, in relation to the status of logical rules in thought:

> Thinking and the use of rules might be unavoidable for the carrying out of all thought, thus also for the foundation of metaphysics itself, but from this it does not follow that this foundation lies in the use of rules itself. On the contrary, from this it only follows that this use of rules itself requires grounding, and it further follows from this that this apparently plausible argumentation is not at all capable of carrying out a foundation. (Heidegger 1990 p. 130)

What led Schleiermacher to the idea of the non-rule-bound 'art' for the application of rules of interpretation, and thus to a ground which involves the freedom inherent in reflective judgement, will lead Heidegger to his central questions for philosophy, which he explores via the question of 'being'.[6] At the risk of gross over-simplification it can be argued that much of modern philosophy between Romanticism and the present has been an ongoing attempt to escape the consequence seen by Schleiermacher and the Romantics, namely that philosophy cannot articulate an absolute presupposition which would ground the truth, of the kind philosophy had sought in varying ways since Plato. The conclusion that Schleiermacher, and more recently Habermas, Putnam and others draw from this is that we are therefore ethically obliged to come to terms with the fallibility of all understanding. Other alternatives are to seek, like Nietzsche, to circumvent this consequence in the direction of a new 'transvaluation of all values', or to explore some of the directions opened up by Heidegger. It will only become clearer why Heidegger moves in the directions he does in relation to the Romantic tradition once we understand what he was reacting against in his own period. At the same time it will also become clear in Chapter 7 that Heidegger can only tell his story in the way he does by dint of almost completely neglecting all the thinkers, with the exception of Kant, with whom we have so far been concerned.

Let us now take another introductory example of a parallel which can reveal something of the nature of Heidegger's enterprise. We will eventually be confronted with his judgements on the whole of 'the history of the West', so it is as well to make it clear that Heidegger is always at the same time concerned with the implications of more everyday matters. In the essay 'A Nice Derangement of Epitaphs', cited in Chapter 5, Davidson illustrates his approach to the philosophical understanding of language by the following example:

> Jonathan Bennett writes, 'I doubt if I have ever been present when a speaker did something like shouting "Water!" as a warning of fire, knowing what "Water!" means and knowing that his hearers also knew, but thinking that they would expect him to give to "Water!" the normal meaning of "Fire!"' Bennett adds that 'Although such things could happen, they seldom do.' I think such things happen all the time; in fact, if the conditions are generalized in a natural way, the phenomenon is ubiquitous. (Lepore 1986 pp. 433–4)

Davidson's point is that if we can understand a malapropism, even though the wrong rule for the use of a word is being followed in that malapropism – or though no rule can be said to be followed at all – we are eventually led to the realisation that much real understanding is not explained by the rules we can formulate about the use of particular words and utterances in a language, because this would lead us once again to the regress of rules. That this is almost continually the case in any text which we would consider to be a literary text should almost go without saying. Now consider the following instructive coincidence. Gadamer has pointed out that at the beginning of his career Heidegger wrote a dissertation on the logic of impersonal judgements:

> The result of the dissertation, that the cry of 'Fire!' resisted logical transformation into a predicative judgement and could only be subordinated

to the logical schema by force could seem to the later Heidegger like a confirmation of first suspicions that logic was subject to an ontological deficiency. (Gadamer 1987 p. 273)

For both Davidson and Heidegger it is not something inherent in an utterance (such as the 'objective representation') which determines how language works in the world, but rather how the world itself is understood. The semiotic or semantic levels of language, which depend upon the discovery of rules, therefore depend upon a prior understanding within a world which is infinitely more diverse than the linguistic material via which we articulate that world. This understanding cannot be finally analysed via the content of a determinate utterance, such as 'Fire!'. As Davidson suggests, the utterance could just as easily be 'Water!': the person might be calling for water to extinguish the fire as a way of signalling the presence of fire (though they might just as easily not) and would often be correctly understood. He or she would not be concerned with the semantics of the word but with the revelation of what mattered in the world. They could also be just plain confused and still be understood in the way they wanted, despite what they actually say, given other things people knew about them or about such situations.

The connection of language to the world is no longer thought of here as the relation between a proposition and a state of affairs, in which the former re-presents the latter, or in which the speaker can be shown to know the rules for the correct use of the piece of language. These approaches do not explain Davidson's example, because he is concerned with cases where the rules patently cannot determine whether there is understanding. As we shall see, Heidegger also insists that the propositional aspect of language cannot be the ground of our understanding, even if it has been the focus of so many of the attempts to explain truth in Western philosophy. Language in both Davidson and Heidegger is in this sense constituted via our very involvement with a world, rather than being a medium through which we 'see' a 'ready-made' world.[7] As Malpas' unconscious reminiscence of Schlegel quoted in Chapter 3 suggested: 'The world is not reflected *in* meaning. Rather . . . the world is the mirror of meaning' (Malpas 1992 p. 7). Understanding therefore results from the fact that the world always already *is* in certain ways, but not in ways which can be thought of as separate from the fact that we ourselves are already in it. Once again this is thoroughly in line with Romantic conceptions: Schlegel explicitly rejected the idea of truth as 'agreement of subjective and objective' in 1800 because 'reality . . . cannot be called either subject or object' (Schlegel 1991 p. 92). It will be his development of the Romantic rejection of a subject–object dualism which leads Heidegger to many of his major insights, but also to some of his most questionable positions.

The example of 'Fire!' helps to suggest what Heidegger is concerned with when he begins to explore what is meant by 'being'. Crudely, 'being' is the always prior fact that the world is intelligible at all: this can be explained neither in terms of semantic analysis of a language, because the explanation already requires language itself for the analysis – thus threatening a regress already suggested by Novalis in *Monologue* – nor in terms of a conception of the subject's representation of the object, because this poses Schlegel's question as to what kind of subjective representation could validate the objectivity of the representation. For the early Heidegger at least, the meaningfulness of 'Fire!' rests upon being in a world in which fire concerns us, not upon the relationship between the utterance and a fact, or between a subject and an object, such that the philosophical task would be to explain the connection between the two: in Davidson's phrase, then: 'we have erased the boundary between knowing a language and knowing our way around in the world generally' (Lepore 1986 p. 446).[8] That there is an entity 'fire' is, for Heidegger, not grounded in there being a word for it – that still leaves the problem of how the word is to be connected to that which it is supposed to represent – but in there being a 'disclosed' aspect of a world, a 'meaning', though not in the rule-determined, semantic sense, to which the word or a whole series of words 'accrue' via our 'being in the world'. It is therefore 'not that word-things are provided with meanings' (Heidegger 1979 p. 161), because meanings are always already part of 'being', the fact that the world is always already meaningful. In his early philosophy Heidegger tries to understand the nature of 'disclosure' – which is inextricably linked to what he means by truth – in pragmatic terms, by giving an essentially transcendental account of the human practical relations with the world that necessarily precede the theoretical attempts to characterise those relations. In the later philosophy he will try to formulate a new approach to language as the 'house of being' (Heidegger 1978 p. 357), as the 'clearing' in which we encounter the truth of being that transcends what both natural science and previous philosophy can say about truth. Literature plays an increasingly important role in the later work, though the reasons for this are already apparent, as we shall see in Chapter 7, at least as early as the essay 'The Origin of the Work of Art' of 1935–6.

Understanding what makes Heidegger's approaches so vital to questions of philosophy, literature and truth requires us first to take a look at some of the ideas which inform his investigations. Many of these ideas have already been examined in our tracing of the responses to Kant. Gadamer summarises the crucial new aspects in terms of

> the attempt of Heidegger to modify the systematic transcendental conception of philosophy of his admired teacher Husserl, the founder of phenomenology, via the historical work of reflection of Diltheyan thought, and to bring about a sort of synthesis between the problematic of historicity in Dilthey and the problematic of science of the transcendental fundamental orientation of Husserl. (Gadamer 1987 p. 298)

144 *Being true: Dilthey, Husserl and Heidegger (1)*

Later in Heidegger's career Schelling and Nietzsche will be added to his main points of reference. In the next section I will outline some aspects of the work of Dilthey. Dilthey's work bridges some of the historical gap between this and the preceding chapters, plays a vital role in the development of philosophically informed modern conceptions of literature and literary theory, and highlights perhaps the central philosophical division that Heidegger's work will attempt to overcome.

UNDERSTANDING AND EXPLAINING

Despite fundamental differences, the work of both Dilthey and Husserl can be linked by their shared concern to find new ways of *philosophically* grounding truth in the face both of the positivist conviction that philosophy is increasingly redundant in relation to the results of the natural sciences and of neo-Kantian attempts to use philosophy to articulate the ground of the successes of the natural sciences. The occlusion from the 1840s onwards of much of the Romantic and hermeneutic tradition we have considered so far has much to do with the perceived failures of the systematic approach to philosophy epitomised by Hegel. This approach manifested itself after Hegel's death in ever more scholastic attempts to do philosophy by writing another system that unified increasingly divergent areas of scientific and cultural investigation in a putatively Hegelian manner. How inappropriate to actual Romantic philosophy the perception of philosophy which leads to the neglect of Romantic ideas really is can be suggested, though, by Schlegel's characteristic *Athenäum* fragment, which is often echoed by Novalis: 'It is just as fatal for the mind to have a system and not to have a system. It will therefore have to decide to connect the two' (Schlegel 1988 (2) p. 109). Without the coherence necessary for a system, intelligibility begins to dissolve, but grounding the system leads to the aporias and regresses we have been considering all along. The fact is, of course, that the anti-foundational insights of Romantic philosophy had not been that widely disseminated or understood, and enormous scientific, political, social and economic shifts were taking place which pushed the insights of Romantic philosophy into the background, in the name of an anti-Idealist materialism (which was, of course, often just as obsessively system-oriented as the Idealist systems it opposed) and a reliance on scientific progress.[9] Dilthey, probably rightly, maintains that the diminution of attention to hermeneutics after the middle of the century, which he was, via his work on Schleiermacher, the first seriously to counter, derives precisely from the failure of the hermeneutics of his time adequately to confront the new developments in natural science (Dilthey 1990 p. 333).[10]

Later in the nineteenth century, however, the division in Germany between conceptions of philosophy oriented towards the natural sciences, and those oriented to areas such as history, art and the understanding of society, which cannot be adequately accounted for in terms of natural science, becomes the crucial framework for the most important theoretical debates, as well as for the understanding of the massive politico-cultural changes taking place at this time. Dilthey's attempts to differentiate '*Verstehen*', which he regarded as the basis of the '*Geisteswissenschaften*',[11] and 'explanation', the basis of the natural sciences, are the most obvious sign of the challenge of the natural sciences for philosophy, and Husserl's desire to make philosophy a 'strict science' with its own grounding criteria of validity that are not subordinate to the truths of the natural sciences is a manifestation of similar concerns. The Nietzsche of *The Birth of Tragedy* (1872) in particular regarded modern science, like Jacobi, as leading to 'nihilism', and Nietzsche's philosophy is unthinkable without his attention, initially derived from Schopenhauer, to the effects of the rise of scientific materialism upon optimistic conceptions of metaphysics.

For all these thinkers a tension becomes increasingly apparent between, on the one hand, the apparently inexhaustible capacity of modern natural science to solve practical and technical problems and to explain the laws governing phenomena, and, on the other, the ways the modern world is actually understood and experienced by those who live in it, ways which are, for example, manifested in modernist literary texts that break with the constitutive forms of pre-modernist literature.[12] In certain ways this tension exemplifies what underlay Jacobi's fear of nihilism. The principle of sufficient reason connects more and more aspects of the world of nature at the same time as rendering our place within nature more and more meaningless. Added to this is the social dislocation accompanying the new division of labour and the rapid growth of modern cities. If the truth of natural science lies in what can be established about the world which is in some essential way separate from anything we may experience by actually living in the world, what is left of the convictions, evaluations and forms of articulation in religion and culture through which individuals and societies orient their lives? Furthermore, philosophy which exhausts itself in attempting to ground the truth provided by the sciences can be seen to be rapidly putting itself out of a job, by pursuing metaphysical worries about the connection of explanations to facts when the actual process of scientific discovery can and clearly does largely ignore most such concerns.[13] The recognition, which already begins earlier in the century, of the need for philosophy to become more connected to what people really do and to how they experience their own existence comes to be shared by directions as diverse as Feuerbach's and Marx's materialism, Kierkegaard's refusal of Hegelian abstraction in the name of inescapable individual deci- sion, Husserl's phenomenological insistence upon getting 'to the things' ('*zu den Sachen*'), and Dilthey's desire to get in touch with the actual lived experience of historically situated individuals in what he already termed in 1867 a 'science of the experience of the human mind' (Dilthey 1990 p. 27) – not, it is important to note, given his attention to psychology that we shall consider in a moment, a science of the human mind. These positions also echo concerns which had fuelled the beginnings of German Idealism and Romanticism, which were the result of the conviction that the separation between abstract scientific knowledge and concrete human experience would lead to profound social and political crises that could only be overcome by an aesthetic 'mythology of reason' (see Bowie 1990 Chapter 2). Heidegger will take up elements related directly and indirectly to all these positions.

The implicit contrast between Dilthey's 'science of the experience of the human mind' and the idea of a 'science of the human mind' suggests one major reason for the attention of his philosophy to the literary and the aesthetic. A lot depends, of course, upon how the word 'science' is understood, and it is here that the division between *Verstehen* and explanation plays such an influential role in Dilthey's work, and in its effects upon subsequent philosophy, including upon Heidegger. The experience of the human mind must in one sense be the experience of every single individual, none of whose experiences can be shown to be finally identical: you cannot have my experiences, simply because you are not me. In this way 'experience' initially seems to exclude the possibility of truth or scientific legitimation, for the reasons suggested in Schleiermacher's distinction between 'feeling', as that which is radically individual, and universalisable 'thought'. Getting beyond the notion of experience as mere 'opinion' was, of course, a basic concern of philosophy from the very beginning, including when philosophy was not seen as separate from natural science. The new complicating factors in Dilthey's period are the increasing awareness, which we saw already exemplified in Herder's work on language, of just how fundamentally different experience can be in differing cultures and at different times, and the increasing divergence between what science tells us and what experience in the 'life-world' tells us.[14] Dilthey regarded his enterprise as the establishing of a 'Critique of Historical Reason', which would – and this is vital for Heidegger – do justice to the contingency of the ways human reason has actually appeared in history.[15] The enterprise has obvious historical roots in Kant and Romanticism, but it also constitutes a vital break with the tradition which it cites in its title. Let us briefly outline another version of the moves in this tradition, concentrating this time on a perhaps more familiar version of its development than the one I have presented so far. This will bring together some central questions that lead from Dilthey to Heidegger and beyond.

In the *Critique of Pure Reason* Kant had set out to provide what Fichte then tried to develop into a 'science of knowledge' (the usual English translation of '*Wissenschaftslehre*', which literally means 'doctrine of science'). This was to be a science of the human mind as the universal condition of all truth, the constitutive operations of the transcendental rather than the empirical subject being what grounds the truth of judgements. Hegel took up this enterprise via its critical elaboration in Schelling's *System of Transcendental Idealism* and other work and via aspects of Schlegel's

Trascendentalphilosophie, and attempted in the *Phenomenology of Mind* to write what he termed a 'science of the experience of consciousness', which would really establish the possibility of grounding philosophy in self-consciousness that he regarded Kant, Fichte and Schelling as having failed to achieve in a convincing manner. The new kind of grounding which Hegel proposed was meant to overcome Kant's dualism of subject and object by giving a genetic historical and transcendental account of what Fichte had merely presupposed when he made the activity of the subject the source of the world's intelligibility (cf. the discussion of Fichte and Jacobi in Chapter 1, and the discussion in Chapter 8). In line with the trans- cendental tradition Hegel attempts to show that truth, as the intrinsically universal, is rendered unintelligible if the immediate experience of each individual is considered to be the primary 'truth': 'absolute knowledge' can therefore only be arrived at by describing how it is that all truth is inherent in the universal rather than in individual self-conscious experience. The *Phenomenology* accordingly describes the historical development of the kind of structures Kant required to ground knowledge whose *origins* Kant's, in this sense, rationalist philosophy had no reason to trace. Hegel does so by endeavouring to prove that self-consciousness can only be determinate because it is always already engaged in interacting with the world, so that a philosophical account of consciousness' development is only possible by seeing that the supposedly internal aspect of consciousness and the external world are in fact inseparable. Much of both Dilthey's and Heidegger's work relates closely to Hegel's approach, and some of Dilthey's major problems derive from his frequent failures adequately to theorise how internal and external must be interlinked.[16]

Hegel's approach to the historical truth of human consciousness already points to the sort of tension which underlies Dilthey's division between the natural sciences and the *Geisteswissenchaften*. Schleiermacher, for example, insisted that Hegel's philosophy invalidly excluded individuality in the name of an overarching philosophical truth.[17] The differences between the conceptions of art in Schleiermacher and in Hegel follow from the ways each deals with the conflict between the need to value the individual, and the desire to reveal that which must transcend individual consciousness if the notion of truth is to be meaningful at all. In many ways Dilthey's enterprise oscillates between aspects of Kant, Schleiermacher and Hegel, between the need for a truth concerning the activity of the human mind which could claim objective validity, of the kind demanded by the increasingly scientistic climate in which he worked, and the sense that individual experience in history may come to be repressed by the demand for 'objectivity'. Dilthey mistrusts the division between transcendental and empirical subjectivity, at the same time as wishing to sustain some kind of 'scientific' status for the actual lived experience of human beings. His response to this dilemma is to try to develop a method for the *Geisteswissenchaften* which is as valid for its own domain as what he regards as the method of the successful natural sciences. He thereby highlights issues that are still manifest in the perceived tensions between the 'humanities' and the natural sciences today, tensions which were not necessarily entailed in the most convincing aspects of Romantic philosophy. Once again we are confronted with an issue which is essentially to do with the understanding of truth, and it will be here that Heidegger offers some of his most revealing insights.

Perhaps the main problem in Dilthey's approach – a problem of which he became aware not least via the influence of Husserl – is the danger of 'psychologism', the idea that problems concerning logic and the validation of truth can be given answers derived from empirical investigations of the functioning of the mind. This is not a merely theoretical issue: implicit versions of psychologism are still rife, for example, within traditional biographically based literary criticism, when inferences are made from evidence about the author's life directly to the meanings of the text being interpreted. Dilthey on occasion did fall prey in his approaches to literature to the idea that the interpreter had when interpreting somehow to reproduce or 'feel their way into' the experience and intentions of the interpretee if the text is really to be understood (see Makkreel 1992 p. 9). In a German context at least some of the blame for the failings of such criticism can therefore be laid at Dilthey's door, even though his theory at its best offers far more than such crass psychologism. For Dilthey, the really significant aspect of psychology was implicit in Kant's distinction between pure and practical reason. In his day this distinction came generally to be manifested in the relationship between what can be found out experimentally about 'the mind',[18] in the form of law-bound explanations of the kind encountered in the rest of the natural sciences, and what can only be accounted for by being interpreted on the basis of a shared capacity for understanding which is not finally explicable in terms of rules. Psychology, then, is at this time the classic locus of the difference between explanation and understanding. The underlying issue is still present in the very divergent nature of what is studied, from behaviourism to psychoanalysis, under the heading of psychology today, in ongoing metaphysical debates concerning the status of the mental in relation to the physical, and in controversies over the notion of meaning of the kind we saw in Chapter 5.

One of the main reasons why Dilthey's work was largely ignored with the rise of the analytical tradition, and has never played a serious role in structuralism or post-structuralism, is that in his reflections on these matters language plays a relatively subordinate role. Language has, of course, increasingly come to be seen both in the hermeneutic tradition – not least via the influence of Heidegger – and in the analytical tradition as the source of possible answers to the apparent irreconcilability of explanation and understanding. The problem which the semantic notion of 'objective representation' was concerned to overcome lay precisely in the need to separate truth and meaning with regard to any truth-determinate issue from the contingencies of what goes on in the mind of the speaker writing or talking about that issue. It is, as we have seen, more than arguable that in interpreting we never have access to a speaker's mind anyway, because the access can only be via other spoken or written utterances, which therefore involve the same interpretative problems as the initial utterance (as well as the threat of another regress). Some theories, such as psychoanalysis, particularly in its Lacanian version, would suggest that such access may not in one sense even be available to individuals reflecting upon their own meanings, language always being the 'discourse of the Other'.[19] The opposed worry for Dilthey, though, which was occasioned in part by his study of Schleiermacher, lay in the fact that the result of the semantic separation of objective representations from mental processes, or of related attempts to objectify meaning, gave no serious way of taking account of the particular historical location and motivation of any individual's articulations. At the same time, approaches to meaning relying solely upon investigation of the individual's life lead precisely to the problems of psychologism which the semantic tradition (and most serious literary theory) rightly opposes, on the grounds that meaning becomes simply incomprehensible in its terms.

We are faced here with a series of familiar dilemmas. In essence they again depend upon how the subject–object relationship is conceived. Language, qua object that is instantiated in the world in the form of differential marks, precedes the subjects who employ it, but the meanings conveyed by a language would not be *meanings* were there not a sense in which the subject moves beyond the fixity of the linguistic means towards that which she alone intends at the moment of utterance in a concrete situation. Dilthey is sometimes, with a degree of justification, seen as giving too much scope to the experience of the individual subject as a criterion of textual meaning: it is therefore instructive that, as a way of avoiding the dangers of psychologism, in his later work Dilthey moved closer to Hegel's notion of 'objective spirit'. In the notion of objective spirit the essential conceptions and attitudes to life in a period are always already constituted in ways which transcend the capacity of individual subjects decisively to determine those ideas (a notion which comes, of course, close to one sense of 'ideology'). The move from 'objective spirit' to language forms the basis of quite divergent kinds of literary theory, including those aspects of the later Heidegger suggested by the dictum 'Language speaks. Man speaks to the extent to which he corresponds to language' (Heidegger 1959 pp. 32–3). If one conceives of language as a 'symbolic order' prior to its users, then it is clear, as we saw in the last chapter, that aspects of what is to be interpreted always already exist at a level beyond the final control of those users. Derrida's assertion that the subject is merely an 'effect of the general text' is another obvious example of such a conception. The key problem is the relationship between the 'general' aspect of the text and what Schleiermacher and Dilthey see as the inherently individual aspect of 'literature', which

Schleiermacher tried to approach in non-psychologistic terms via his notion of style. Dilthey maintains in 1900 that 'the immeasurable significance of literature for our understanding of mental/spiritual (*geistig*) life and for history lies in the fact that in language alone the internal aspect of human beings (*das menschliche Innere*) finds its own complete, exhaustive and objectively comprehensible expression' (Dilthey 1990 p. 319). However, this later formulation still suggests that Dilthey has not adequately realised the implications of language for the issues he is dealing with: he resolves the problem in a Hegelian (or for that matter proto-semantic or structuralist) manner by now suggesting that language, qua external manifestation, simply dissolves the subject–object dilemma. As we saw in the last chapter, though, Schleiermacher has a much more sophisticated view of the issue, refusing to accept that the universality of language's schematisation obviates consideration of the individual subject in interpretation.

The question of literature is evidently germane to the major philosophical questions here. In his earlier work Dilthey had often claimed that the difference between the natural sciences and the *Geisteswissenchaften* lay in the fact that the former deal with the objects of 'external experience', whereas the latter deal with 'inner experience' (Dilthey 1990 p. 254). 'Inner experience', the 'psychic act' which 'is because I experience it' (Dilthey 1983 p. 98) may be 'carried over onto external objects by a kind of transposition' (Dilthey 1990 p. 250). He is referring here to 'feelings, affects, passions, processes of thought, and acts of will' (ibid. p. 245), and he assumes that we have access to them, for example, in 'lyric poetry . . . which in its most complete forms, as in Goethe, always represents the poet's own life in a situation, thus surrounded with circumstances which present themselves in ideas of objects (*von in Objektvorstellungen sich darstellenden Umständen umgeben*)' (ibid.). How one establishes the priority for the interpreter between the objects which give access to the internal experience and the experience itself is, though, already less than clear. What counts, Dilthey claims, is understanding the 'living nexus (*Zusammenhang*)' (ibid. p. 143) of these inner experiences, not their isolation as separate facts that could be subsumed under psychological laws: 'We explain nature, we understand the life of the soul' (ibid. p. 144), because 'only what the mind has created does it understand' (Dilthey 1981 p. 180). The simple fact, though, which repeats the basic dilemma of psychologism, is that if this experience really is wholly 'inner', wholly on the side of the subject, it becomes incomprehensible how anyone else can talk about it, given that all our experience of others is, in the terms Dilthey employs here, outer experience. The problem of solipsism beckons.[20] Dilthey is forced by his tendency merely to oppose the inner and the outer to have recourse at times to such terms as '*Nacherleben*', literally 'after-experience' (Dilthey 1981 p. 184), in order to suggest that we have access to the meanings to be understood by a kind of intuitive re-creation. This issue now begins to reveal itself as another instance of the problem of grounding, and raises, not always in a manner favourable to Dilthey, some of the questions we have already encountered in Schleiermacher's hermeneutics.

Dilthey's ground is precisely 'experience' (*Erlebnis*) (Dilthey 1990 p. 151), which, given that it is generally conceived of in pre-propositional terms, puts him in the camp of those whom Derrida regards as seeking 'to decipher ... a truth or an origin that escapes the play and the order of the sign' (Derrida 1967b p. 427). The distinction between *Erlebnis* and *Erfahrung*, both of which can be translated as 'experience', lies in the former being an immediate given, an 'origin' in Derrida's sense, and the latter, as it generally is in Kant, being the result of a judgement in which a concept is applied to an intuition. A science like psychology belongs for Dilthey to the *Geisteswissenchaften* 'only if its object becomes accessible to us in behaviour which is founded in the nexus of life, expression and understanding' (Dilthey 1981 p. 99): the trio of '*Erlebnis*, expression and understanding' (ibid.) therefore becomes the foundation of the *Geisteswissenchaften*. Manfred Riedel (in Dilthey 1981 p. 9) suggests that part of what is meant by *Erlebnis* will also play a role in logical positivism's recourse to supposedly pure 'observation sentences' as the ground of scientific theories. In both cases the desire is, in different ways, to get to what is independent of the vagaries of judgement because of its inescapable presence to the subject prior to its – therefore fallible – subsumption under a pre-existing concept in what Dilthey terms 'reflection'. As such: '*Erlebnis* does not stand opposite the person who grasps it, but rather its existence for me is different from *what* in it is there for me' (Dilthey 1981 p. 168). Kant tries to abstract the operations of the transcendental subject from the empirical subject and make those operations themselves the ground of truth claims. Dilthey, on the other hand, tries to show, in a manner which leads towards Heidegger's early attempts at a theory that founds the abstract operations of the Kantian transcendental subject in immediate practical activity in the world, how the 'mental nexus (*der seelische Zusammenhang*) forms the ground beneath (*Untergrund*) the process of cognition' (Dilthey 1990 p. 151) of the Kantian subject: 'The foundation of epistemology is contained in living consciousness and in the universally valid description of this mental nexus' (ibid.). The nexus is to be understood via the interrelation of the parts with the whole in the manner of the hermeneutic circle, such that 'all constitution of unity and all single contexts are grasped by [the *structural nexus of the life of the mind*]. We cannot go back behind this nexus' (ibid. p. 237). The 'life of the mind' therefore plays the structural role of Jacobi's 'revelation'. Despite all the problems his version of the theory involves, Dilthey's approach here brings us close to Heidegger's insistence upon finding a ground for truth which is prior to theoretical judgements. Crucially, both Dilthey and Heidegger at times regard literature as an essential source for understanding this ground.

In an important echo of a theme we have repeatedly encountered, and shall encounter again, Dilthey claims that a decisive aspect of the

Geisteswissenchaften is the 'continuous refutation of Spinoza's proposition *"omnis determinatio est negatio"'* (Dilthey 1983 p. 55), thus the refutation of what led to Jacobi's notion of the world of 'conditioned conditions'. Like Jacobi, he is therefore looking for a ground of a different order from what can be explained in a determinist explanatory theory, in order to sustain the role of individual world-disclosure. At the same time, however, Dilthey's whole theory of a 'Critique of Historical Reason', qua truth-determinate enterprise, depends upon the ways in which systematic, generalisable connections can be established between the material constituted by 'inner experience'. He insists that these connections actually involve the same mental processes of association, inference, etc. as are involved in scientific judgements of outer experience. Later, therefore, contrary to a common assumption about Dilthey, and more in line with Heidegger's hermeneutics, this leads him to the realisation that there can be no ultimate separation between explaining and understanding. He suggests as much when considering a concrete case of how one would explain a piece of aggressive behaviour:

> the milieu is indispensable for understanding. At the highest point understanding is therefore not in this way different from explaining, to the extent to which explanation is possible in this area. And explaining for its part has the completion of understanding as its presupposition.
>
> (Dilthey 1990 p. 334)

Dilthey's notion of a 'Critique of Historical Reason' is, then, primarily intended to link the insights of hermeneutics to a new version of epistemology, in order to ground those aspects of human knowledge which rely upon understanding. Whether such a combination is possible in the terms within which he was working is, though, more than questionable. It is no coincidence that one of the central aspects of Heidegger's enterprise will be to try to dissolve epistemology into an all-encompassing hermeneutics which results from a farewell, of the kind we have already encountered in aspects of Romantic thought, to ultimate epistemological foundations.

Karl-Otto Apel suggests that the enduring value of Dilthey's distinction between understanding and explanation lies in its highlighting differing kinds of reference to objects of study, such as the world of nature and the social world, as well as in its separating out of the various knowledge constitutive interests within differing branches of the sciences. Apel's contention, which itself derives from Heidegger's radicalisation of the questions raised by Dilthey, is that Dilthey moves philosophy towards the realisation that *both* natural sciences and *Geisteswissenschaften* depend upon 'the unity of the claim to truth and the possibility of its realisation in *argumentative discourse*', and not, therefore, upon one particular kind of assumption about the objects of science (for example, that they are law-bound physical phenomena), or one kind of method (for example, that the method is necessarily hypothetico-deductive) (Orth 1985 p. 344). This conception is, yet again, close to the view presented by the Romantics, including Schleiermacher. It is increasingly clear that the scientism which has dominated so much Western philosophy from the time of Dilthey onwards, and which led Dilthey into some of his dilemmas, has had its day. One of the first to see why will, of course, be Heidegger.

Heidegger will undercut Dilthey's attempt to link hermeneutics and epistemology via a radicalisation of aspects of what Dilthey himself initiated. In 1883 Dilthey saw the 'main problem of all epistemology' as 'the nature of immediate knowledge of the facts of consciousness and their relationship to cognition which progresses according to the principle of sufficient reason' (Dilthey 1983 p. 86). It is clear, though, even from the arguments seen so far, that Dilthey himself never really reaches a satisfactory account of this relationship.[21] On the one hand, he moves in the direction of a proto-structuralist sense that the *Geisteswissenschaften* 'are directed towards objective cognition of their object' (Dilthey 1981 p. 379):

> universal movements go through the individual as their point of transit
> ... we must seek new foundations for understanding universal move-
> ments. . . . The individual is only the crossing point for cultural systems,
> organisations, into which the individual's existence is woven: how could
> they be understood via the individual? (ibid. p. 310)[22]

On the other hand, he often sustains the sense that all objectivity of this kind is thoroughly at the mercy of the historical contingency of individual *Erlebnis*, the value of which is most apparent in the uniqueness of artistic production. In some ways the failure to resolve these tensions is to Dilthey's credit: they still form the material of many subsequent, ongoing debates in philosophy, social theory and literary theory. Heidegger, though, comes to regard these tensions as a Gordian knot to be sundered by a thinking which will perhaps eventually move altogether beyond philosophy qua foundational discipline.

UNDERSTANDING BEING

Let us take two further aspects of Dilthey's approach, which lead to the issues that will concern us in the rest of this chapter and in Chapters 7, 8 and 9. If the originary notion of *Erlebnis* is so central, and *Erlebnis* is inherently individual in important respects, how does one articulate valid truths about history, especially in the light of conscious deceptions on the part of the major historical figures who would seem in other senses to offer the most insight into 'objective spirit'? In 'The Origin of Hermeneutics' of 1900 Dilthey claims in this connection that

> We can be mistaken about the motivations of the actors in history,
> the actors themselves can spread a deceptive light over them. But the
> work of the great poet or discoverer, of a religious genius or of a real

philosopher can only ever be the true expression of the life of his mind; in this society which is full of lies such a work is always true, and it is, in contrast to every other utterance in fixed signs, capable of a complete and objective interpretation. (Dilthey 1990 pp. 319–20)

Getting to a truth which is beyond the vagaries and deceptive motivations of subjective intention is therefore possible for Dilthey in two main ways: one is via scientific explanation, the other via the fact that artists in particular can render their individual *Erlebnis* in a manner that reveals a truth which is inarticulable in any other way, and which therefore sheds a universal light on the truth of the artist's world. This position should not be dismissed too hastily. Take the following example: whereas Napoleon may be regarded qua empirical subject as a megalomaniac deceiver, the impetus of the Napoleonic era's transformation of the direction of modern society is undoubtedly in some important way an aspect of Beethoven's *Eroica* Symphony, or of Balzac's best novels. The symphony's and the novels' continuing power cannot be regarded as merely the result of internal processes in Beethoven or Balzac, because their potential for what Heidegger terms world-disclosure persists even today, not least in the way they affect our very sense of the history in which they were written. Very different versions of the view that art conveys a truth unavailable to determinate cognition, and that it can thereby reveal more about the nature of truth than such cognition, will become a vital part of the thought of Heidegger, Benjamin and Adorno. In Heidegger's case the reasons for this linking of art with truth have much to do with his transformation of ideas from Husserl's phenomenology.

The wide variety of philosophical approaches explored at various times by Husserl, coupled with the diversity of the thinkers who are seen as coming under the general heading of 'phenomenology', make it difficult to say exactly what it is that has made phenomenology such a major aspect of twentieth-century philosophy and literary theory. Gadamer offers the helpful suggestion that

The fundamental insight [of phenomenology] is that consciousness is not at all a sphere enclosed within itself, within which its representations are closed off as in its own inner world, but that, on the contrary, in its own essential structure consciousness is always already among things (*bei den Sachen*). (Gadamer 1987 p. 106)

As such, 'The image that we have of things is . . . generally the manner in which the things themselves are conscious to us [*sic*: Gadamer deliberately blurs the priority of subject and object in his formulation]' (ibid.) – what he is referring to was, of course, implicit in the example of 'Fire!' cited earlier. In phenomenology the concept, derived principally from Franz Brentano, of 'intentionality' – the fact that consciousness is inherently 'directed' to things – is employed to establish, for example, why it is that asking if my perception of the computer on which I am writing this sentence is *really* a perception of the computer on which I am writing this sentence involves a fundamental misrecognition of the nature of consciousness.[23] There is no point in asking how the internal subject adequately mirrors or makes its representations correspond to the external object, because the very nature of subjectivity inherently always already entails consciousness as consciousness *of* something, otherwise subjectivity is an empty notion.[24] Gadamer says of Husserl's notion of 'life' that 'What Husserl wants to say is . . . that one may not think of subjectivity as the opposite to objectivity, because such a concept of subjectivity would itself be objectivistic' (Gadamer 1975 p. 235): it would deal with subjectivity in terms of determination by negation like any other world-object. Riedel suggests an informative link when he claims that Dilthey's *Erlebnis*, which Riedel also saw in connection with positivist 'observation sentences', 'has roughly the same structure as Brentano's concept of intentionality' (in Dilthey 1981 p. 38). Around the beginning of the twentieth century moves against seeing philosophy in terms of the task of establishing the relationship between the inner and the outer world, subject and object, led to a revaluation of notions of 'intuition' or 'life'. Intuition here stands for a ground of truth which is 'immediate' and therefore not susceptible to further explanatory analysis of the kind which is applicable to determinate objects in the world – to what Jacobi meant by the world of 'conditioned conditions' – or, for that matter, analysable in terms of the internal workings of a transcendental subject.[25]

The investigation of the ways in which phenomenology deals with intuition are a vital part of the genesis of recent literary theory, and it is worth briefly seeing here why this is so. It was, of course, Derrida's critical engagement with Husserl which led him, via his engagement with Heidegger and via a rethinking of the nature of language's relationship to consciousness, to the deconstruction of the idea of meaning as 'presence' (itself a form of 'intuition'), for which he uses the term '*différance*'. Because each element of language only gains its identity via its relations to preceding and succeeding elements in a temporal sequence, the 'meaning' of a word can never, in Derrida's terms, be said to be definitively present to the subject, because it is 'deferred' via its dependence upon chains of other signifiers. This may be apt as an attack on Platonist 'representational' conceptions of meaning of the kind we considered in preceding chapters, but it is not necessarily applicable to the hermeneutic or the Davidsonian sense that knowing language and knowing our way round the world are not finally distinguishable kinds of knowledge. Derrida's approach in fact fails to give any plausible account of why we hold things true at all. Charles Taylor (Taylor 1995 p. viii) argues, for example, that the very notion of 'presence' may actually be unintelligible: what criterion for *understanding* the failure of thought to achieve presence do we possess if presence is supposedly unattainable anyway? The Romantic conception of truth as an idealised goal which is accessible only via the inherent potential for dissatisfaction with what we hold true at any particular time here seems a better alternative.

The assumption that, because what we intend is always already linguistically mediated, we never finally reach 'self-presence', gets things the wrong way round, as important aspects of the work of both Heidegger and Davidson can suggest. It does so because it reifies the notion of meaning by beginning with the assumption that previous philosophy thought that meanings qua 'presences' or 'representations' must be mediated by something called a language. As we saw in Chapter 3, Malpas suggested with regard to Davidson (and in line with Novalis) that the 'indeterminacy thesis', 'the claim that there is always more than one acceptable way of assigning meanings to utterances', leads to a rejection of 'the idea of meaning as a determinate and determinable entity attaching to sentences or terms' (Malpas 1992 p. 65), and this was backed up by Schleiermacher's approach to regulism in Chapter 5. Derrida actually looks at meaning in the terms he does, of course, only to show that the Platonist notion of meaning is not convincing anyway. However, he demonstrates the failure of models of meaning which understand meanings as ideal entities defined by their place in a language without offering any account of how it is that we understand at all, which both Heidegger and Davidson think has to do with the relationship between truth and meaning within a world which *is* in one sense at least always immediately present to us. It is only if one insists that meanings fulfil the demands of complete transparency in the manner of Platonist theories, while at the same time showing the impossibility of such transparency via the differential constitution of language, that one ends up with the 'Derridean' sense that we never 'really' have access to meaning and truth. Both Heidegger and Davidson can be regarded as assuming that we have access to both truth and meaning all the time, because the Platonist notion of meaning is the wrong place to begin thinking about the issue of meaning anyway. How this relates to the more complex question of truths which transcend what can be communicated in semantically determinate uses of language will later concern us in relation to Heidegger's views of art, and in the theories of Benjamin and Adorno. The crucial fact for the moment is that without an initial sense of meaning and truth of the kind it is hard to find in Derrida the concern with a truth only available in art, and particularly in literature, cannot even be discussed.

The undermining of the notion of presence, in the reflexive form of 'reason listening only to itself', was already germane to the emergence of Romantic philosophy, where it led to an ironic sense of the limits of determinate cognition and of the importance of art as a medium which tries to 'say the unsayable' by inherently undermining determinacy. At the same time, as we saw, Jacobi insisted on the irreducibility of truth via his notion of 'the true', the necessarily immediate ground of all mediated cognitive claims to knowledge. Now the primary issue in phenomenology is the status of the immediacy of what is given to us in the world, which leads phenomenology to vital questions about the status of what is held to be true. In line with his semiotically inspired conception Derrida concentrates on Husserl's attempt to salvage the concept of a pure transcendental ego as the ground of truth, which Derrida sees, in ways which are convincing for Husserl's more purist attempts at characterising a transcendental subject, as being subverted by the fact that language always already precedes the subject's ability to *articulate* self-presence. For the subject to 'hear itself speak' its self-presence must have already been divided into a 'before' and an 'after' by the incursion of language, the condition of possibility of the subject's self-articulation, into the subject.[26] Valid as this critique may be, Derrida tends to underplay the extent to which the real importance and influence of Husserl, especially upon Heidegger, lay in his new approaches to the world of lived experience which we have suggested in the link between *Erlebnis* and intentionality.

The most fundamental problem here, as Husserl realised, is how to account for our indubitable ability to distinguish between true and false. The very fact that we often encounter the experience of realising that we are mistaken means that we must have a prior awareness of truth, which cannot be said to come about because our thought failed to apprehend what is 'really out there independently of our knowledge of it'. The position from which this claim could be made was, since Kant, no longer available in that form: judgements of what there is are constituted for Kant in terms of rule-bound syntheses of representations. The question is what renders such judgements true, which had, as we saw in Chapter 2, to do with the question of schematism, the 'hidden art in the depths of the human soul', which itself can be seen as a kind of 'intuition'. Husserl's lifelong, and ultimately unsuccessful, struggle with these issues clearly cannot concern us here, so I want to take just one aspect that was determining for Heidegger, which will lead us to Heidegger's linking of truth with art via the question of schematism. This requires us now to gain a more articulated sense of what is at issue in the notorious 'question of being'.

As Gadamer, Mark Okrent and Heidegger himself point out (Heidegger 1969 p. 86), Heidegger was particularly influenced by Husserl's discussion of 'being' in his sixth *Logical Investigation* of 1920. The vital aspect of that discussion is the link between 'being' and 'truth'. The basic sense of truth in Husserl's phenomenology lies in the 'fulfilment' of an 'intention': I think – 'intend', in the sense of directing my thoughts – that the piece of paper I saw yesterday is white, look at it today and the paper is 'in truth' white, so the intention is 'fulfilled'. The point is, though, Husserl maintains, that I see the whiteness of the paper, not its *being*-white. Things and attributes of things can be perceived as objects, *that* the things are, and *that* they truly have those attributes cannot be seen:

> Being is not anything *in* the object, not a part of it, not an inherent moment of it; no quality or intensity, but also no figure, no inner form

of any kind, no constitutive characteristic which could be grasped in some way or other . . . *being is quite simply nothing perceptible.*

(Husserl 1992 p. 666)

As opposed to 'sensuous intuitions' of what is 'real', which are the 'correlates' of intentions directed to concrete things in the world, that can be 'fulfilled' or not, 'categorial intuition' is concerned with things like 'The *one*, and the *the*, the *and* and the *no* (*Kein*), the *something* and *nothing*'; these are 'all significant elements of sentences, but we would seek their objective correlates in vain . . . in the sphere of *real* objects' (ibid. p. 667).[27] Given the prior logical necessity of the existence of these aspects of the way the world is rendered intelligible before specific cognitions, how do we have access to them, given that they do not manifest themselves qua objects?

Husserl's answer is as follows:

*Not in **reflection** upon judgements or rather upon the fulfilment of judgements, but instead in the **fulfilments of judgements themselves** does the origin of the concepts state of affairs and being* (in the sense of the copula [the linking 'is' in a predicative judgement such as 'this piece of paper is white']) *lie*; not in these *acts as objects*, but in the *objects of these acts* do we find the foundation of abstraction for the realisation of the said concepts . . . the concept of being can only arise if *some being or other, real or imagined, is put before our eyes.* If being is *predicative* being for us, then some *state of affairs* must be given, and this via an *act* which *gives* it – *the analogy of common sensuous intuition.*

(ibid. pp. 669–70)

For Husserl, then, if the predicate 'white' truly applies to the paper, the 'categorial act' that founds 'predicative being' comes into play along with the sensuous intuition of the real – perceived – white piece of paper, even though, as Kant had already claimed, being itself 'is not a real predicate'. In Husserl's terms this categorial act is available to us via a reflective intention directed at any apprehension of something as what it was 'intended' as. Even this, though, seems to threaten a regress: if one can intend the intending of the object, by reflecting upon what it is to see the paper as white, what status does the intending of the intending of the intending have? The problem of the ground we have been considering all along begins once again to emerge in ways that Heidegger himself only gradually comes to appreciate. Okrent claims that for Husserl 'The fulfilment of the meaning "being" is in the fulfilment of any intention insofar as it is fulfilled' (Okrent 1988 p. 121), but this leaves one with the problem of the grounding intention, which Husserl wishes, in order to establish firm cognitive foundations for truth, to keep as a pure intuitive act in which the subject grasps what it is for something to be the case.

What this means in Heidegger's terms, which already distances him from

Husserl's conception, is that as soon as we intend something *as* something – say, the piece of paper as a possibility of writing a letter – we have an 'understanding of being': 'being is understood ... whenever we intend anything as anything (intend anything) at all' (ibid. p. 122). Husserl, then, regards truth as being founded in the pure structures of categorial intuition, whereas Heidegger thinks such intuition cannot be pure, because it is always in play in a world whose *practical*, rather than cognitive horizons, are the prior condition of any truth. We are always already involved with practical horizons in ways no theory can exhaust, because the theory itself depends for its existence upon these horizons. This can be summed up rather crudely in the idea that, in Heidegger, 'knowing how' comes before 'knowing that'. Heidegger's crucial difference from Husserl becomes apparent, then, when he claims that the notion of intentionality, a notion inherently connected to consideration of consciousness, is not sufficient to account for the nature of truth. He does so most illuminatingly in an important section of *Metaphysical Foundations of Logic* dealing with 'Intentionality and Transcendence', which comes in § 9 on 'The Essence of Truth and Its Essential Relationship to the "Ground"'. Heidegger's gravitation towards questions of art and truth, and to the main questions of the rest of the book are latent in the issues raised here. It is worth already stating that the direction of Heidegger's thought parallels the way in which Kantian philosophy begins by attempting to map out a transcendental account of truth, before the *Critique of Judgement* helps initiate the Romantic awareness that many of the most important philosophical questions lead inevitably to issues connected to art.

Metaphysical Foundations of Logic is concerned with the problem of grounding, which it approaches via Leibniz's 'principle of sufficient reason' – 'nothing is without a ground/reason' – a topic to which Heidegger will later, in 1957, devote a whole book. The basic issue is, of course – and this further confirms the underlying structure I have been trying to establish – the one which we considered in Chapter 1 in relation to Jacobi. Jacobi's awareness of the issue was formed via the assumptions of the rationalist followers of Leibniz and Spinoza, who were themselves one of Kant's main influences (and targets). The question for both Heidegger and Jacobi is 'What is the ground of truth?'. Heidegger claims: 'The holding-true [he uses the same word as Jacobi] of a true proposition (*Aussage*), the appropriation of truth must, in order to be certain of itself, hold in the last analysis to the ground of truth' (Heidegger 1990 p. 149). In the Western philosophical tradition the location of truth is generally, since Aristotle, assumed to be the proposition or judgement. Judgement is the synthesis of differing elements, in which truth is understood as the adequacy of idea to object, a notion which Schlegel, as we saw, already put into question. Heidegger does not reject the idea that truth is something to do with propositions, but wants a phenomenologically convincing characterisation of how truth and propositions relate. This takes us back to what was suggested in the example of 'Fire!', as well as eventually opening up a path which will lead to Heidegger's concern with forms of language in art whose truth does not reside in their propositional content or reference to real objects in the world. In 'The Origin of the Work of Art' he will cite, for example, the case of a poem called 'Roman Well', which is neither about a specific well nor about the 'essence' of Roman wells.

Heidegger takes the example of the person in the lecture hall who says 'The blackboard is black'. The truth of the utterance, he suggests, does not have to do with our orientation to the utterance itself, or to our mental 'representation' of the state of affairs, but rather 'to the black board itself, here on the wall' (ibid. p. 157):

> it is not the utterance which produces the relationship, but the other way round: the utterance is only possible on the basis of the always already latent relationship to entities (*zum Seienden*). The I which speaks, Dasein, is always already 'among' ('*bei*') the entities of which it speaks. (ibid. p. 158)[28]

'Dasein' is famously defined in *Being and Time* as being 'ontically distinguished [i. e. differentiated from other things in the world, which includes mountains, flowers, animals etc.] by the fact that this entity [Dasein] is concerned in its being *with* this being itself' (Heidegger 1979 p. 12), thus by the fact that it interprets itself via its relation to its world. The development of the point concerning the basis upon which a true utterance can be made is the crux of the question of being as it presents itself to Heidegger in the earlier work. True propositions about an entity are only possible, he maintains, 'because this entity is already revealed (*enthüllt*) in some way, i.e. an utterance about . . . is only true because the involvement with . . . already has a certain truth' (ibid. p. 158. NB: the dots are in the text, not an indication of an omitted piece of text).

This difference between the primary 'disclosedness' of things in the world, and propositions about entities, defines what Heidegger means by 'ontological difference'. In *The Basic Problems of Phenomenology* he explains this difference as follows:

> To the entity which is perceived in perception belongs not only that it is discovered (*entdeckt*), the discoveredness of the entity, but also that the kind of being of the discovered entity is understood, i.e. disclosed (*erschlossen*). . . . Entities can only be discovered, be it via perception or some other kind of access if the being of the entity is already disclosed, – if I understand it. (Heidegger 1989 pp. 101–2)

In the terms used by Dilthey this means that understanding must always precede propositionally articulated explanation, and that there cannot therefore be a final explanation of understanding. 'Ontological difference' has important consequences for a variety of philosophical problems from differing traditions. These problems play an often neglected role in literary theory, whose concern with truth has, regrettably, rarely been more than cursory.[29]

Ernst Tugendhat makes a vital aspect of 'ontological difference' clear when he uses Heidegger's basic idea to show how a familiar problem in Western philosophy is a result of ignoring ontological difference. How does one say that something does not exist, without becoming involved in the paradox that by asserting its non-existence one is also asserting its existence? If I say 'There are no unicorns', how do you understand me without positing the existence of things called unicorns? Parmenides' problem of non-being, which denies the possibility of saying something does not exist, results, Tugendhat maintains, because 'the complex structure of "something as something" is compressed into a simple "something"': as such 'it can no longer be said of the "something" that it "is not" because the "is" has, so to speak, become one with the "something" ("being" is "mistaken for", as Heidegger says, "entities")' (Tugendhat 1992 p. 46). Heidegger attributes this mistake to the lack of a distinction in the tradition of Western metaphysics between categorial statements of the kind we saw in relation to Husserl's 'categorial intuition', and statements about entities in the world (Heidegger 1976 p. 410). Being-true and being-false are therefore not polar opposites that could be understood in analogy to perceptions, where one either perceives the unicorn or perceives nothing at all. In Tugendhat's terms:

> In order to establish whether the proposition 'Unicorns exist' is true, we do not examine the (possible) unicorns to see whether the predicate existence is applicable to them, but we instead look at the animals in the real world to see if some of them are unicorns.
>
> (Tugendhat and Wolf 1986 p. 189)

The core difference is that between not-saying or not-thinking 'This is a unicorn', in which case there is nothing at issue at all, thereby generating Parmenides' problem, and predicatively saying or thinking p is not, such that 'This x (which exists) is/is not a unicorn', which is, of course, still fallible. The structure of being is, then, always already present, in that there is no doubt *that* there are things disclosed in the world: *what* things are disclosed as is, therefore, the realm of possible error, which is always secondary to being itself.[30] Exploration of the prior dimension of being is, despite Tugendhat's attempt to reduce it to merely a semantic issue concerning the meaning of the word 'being', the source of a whole series of philosophical investigations of the kind inaugurated by the Romantics.[31] The fact that what things are seen as can be radically altered by new forms of metaphorical description or by other semantically undecidable forms of aesthetically oriented articulation, such as music, will be the vital issue here, which connects being, truth and art. Heidegger will only come to this realisation in an explicit manner at the beginning of the 1930s.

Heidegger's description of how it is that things are, and thus are true, in many ways follows that of Husserl, but his primary interest is in a level which, he claims, Husserl's version of intentionality fails to articulate. Intentionality is a kind of 'transcendence', in the phenomenological sense that, because the subject's consciousness is always consciousness of something, it takes the subject beyond itself: 'An entity (Dasein) climbs over to another entity' (Heidegger 1990 p. 169). In its most fundamental version, therefore:

> The problem of transcendence . . . is not identical with the problem of intentionality. The latter is as ontic transcendence [thus as intention cognitively directed at entities] only possible on the basis of primary transcendence: of *being in the world*. This primary transcendence makes possible all intentional relationships to entities. (ibid. 170)

The primary transcendence of 'being in the world', which Heidegger characterises in pragmatic terms of 'caring' and being involved with the things of everyday life, is prior to any cognitive theory of what there is that is part of a specific science. As such, 'the proposition does not have a primary function of cognition, but only a secondary function. Entities must already be revealed [*as* something] for a proposition about them to be possible' (Heidegger 1989 p. 299). The horizon within which this is possible is *time* – hence the title of his most famous work – which Heidegger approaches in all his earlier work via Kant's account of 'schematism' that we began to examine in Chapter 2 and which, as we have seen, played a vital role in the thought of nearly all the Romantics.[32]

The ability to see things as things, which grounds the structure of propositions, depends upon a unity that renders sensuous multiplicity determinate, rather than merely indeterminately multiple in a way which cannot even be apprehended or stated. The connection between the changing sensuous manifold and the identifying categories of the understanding takes place for Kant on the basis of time. Without the dual aspect of the endlessly different temporal nature of what is given to us in the sensuous world and the sameness that renders difference identical which is present in schematism there could be no meaning and no truth. This means for Heidegger that time, whose very nature is a relationship between identity and difference, is the '*Sinn*', the 'meaning' of being, because without the interplay of identity and difference nothing could be disclosed as anything determinate at all. The ground of truth therefore ceases to be assumed, as it was in the main since Plato,[33] to be something which transcends temporality, and instead becomes the interplay of identity and difference which takes place via the intrinsically temporal nature of our 'being in the world'. Kant sees this ground as inherent in the nature of the transcendental subject, but admitted that it is a 'hidden art'. Heidegger therefore suggests that this admission leads Kant to an '*Abgrund*' (Heidegger 1976 p. 378), which usually means 'abyss', but which also has the sense from Schelling onwards of the 'ground-from-which', the '*Ab-grund*'.

Heidegger sees his task as, in effect, exploring the '*Ab-grund*' from which Kant steps back. The ground is time as the meaning of being, as that which is 'the condition of possibility for the fact that there is something like being (not entities)' (ibid. p. 410).

At this stage of his work this ground is still somehow connected for Heidegger to the nature of subjectivity. He observes that in Kant the definition of the I as '"the correlate of all our representations" is . . . almost literally the definition of time' (ibid. p. 406).[34] His objection to the Kantian view is that it attempts to begin in Cartesian manner with the 'empty I' (ibid. p. 407) in order to get to the world, so that instead of time being the 'structure of Dasein itself', it seems to come in a 'mysterious way from outside' the subject (ibid. p. 408). For Heidegger, the basic temporal structures of Dasein lie in its always already being in a world in which those structures are Dasein's possibilities of being, its possibilities of engaging in future projects that will constitute what it is. This possibility becomes linked to freedom, which Heidegger sees as '*the ground of the ground*. . . . As this ground, though, freedom is the *ground-from-which* (*Ab-grund*) of Dasein' (Heidegger 1978 p. 171). Heidegger will come to suspect, as we shall see, that this ties truth too closely to a conception not ultimately different from that of a transcendental subject, of the kind made most explicit in Fichte's conception of the absolute spontaneity of the I. This suspicion is suggested by his remark in 'On the Essence of Truth' of 1930, during the phase of the transition to the later philosophy: 'Man does not "possess" freedom as an attribute, instead at the most the opposite is true: freedom, ex-sisting (*ek-sistente*), revealing *Da-sein* possesses man (ibid. p. 187). It should already be apparent, then, even from this brief analysis, that Heidegger's concerns, which are often presented as a total novum, map on to the dominant concerns of Romantic philosophy and the history of Kantian and post-Kantian philosophy from which those concerns emerge. In Chapter 7 I want to show how these issues become central in the cultural politics of the twentieth century, by looking at Heidegger's move towards questions of art and truth, before moving in Chapter 8 to Benjamin's explorations of these questions, which are connected to his work on the early Romantics, and in Chapter 9 to Adorno.

7 The truth of art
Heidegger (2)

THE TURN TO ART

The arguments considered in Chapter 6 were not least intended to make it clear why Heidegger's approaches to philosophy are now becoming an inescapable part even of debates in the analytical philosophy of language. Gadamer's perhaps rather too sympathetic characterisation cited below can help us to move now from a primarily analytical demonstration of the inescapability of Heidegger's questions for any consideration of truth in modern philosophy, to a consideration of the Heidegger whose effects on the self-understanding of the modern world are evident in the most diverse debates, and whose reflections on truth and art are still germane to any serious literary theory. Gadamer claims that what motivated Heidegger was the

> question how this finite, irrelevant human existence, which is certain of its death, could understand itself in its being despite its own evanescence, and indeed understand itself as a being which is not a privation, a lack, a merely passing pilgrimage of the citizen of the earth through this life to a participation in the eternity of the divine.
>
> (Gadamer 1987 p. 182)

The crucial aspect of self-understanding for the later Heidegger can be suggested by the following. In the modern world, where the speed of generation of testable facts and theories about both human and non-human nature increases at an exponential rate, the philosophical question of truth can either become reduced to the attempt to give an adequate explanation of how it is that we can generate valid evidence for ever more such theories – a project which is in certain ways still compatible with the project of the early Heidegger but which also leads in the direction of Jacobi's arguments about nihilism – or it becomes a location of ways of thinking which have no obvious place in a world where calculability and pragmatic success increasingly dominate public discourse about truth. Taking the latter position seriously is no mere 'Romantic' or mystical attempt to escape the nature of the modern world, because it is this kind of challenge which confronts us with the deepest questions about our self-understanding. This becomes evident if one again considers the attempts to ground truth that we have been considering all along.

Heidegger's development beyond Dilthey lay, as we saw, in his deconstruction of the difference between explaining and understanding, in which the defensive sense that the natural sciences provide more reliable forms of truth than those available in philology or history is put into focus by a consideration of the implications of ontological difference. Very simply, the point of the question of being in this respect is to reveal that all understanding is understanding of being, which means that any particular kind of understanding has no right to arrogate to itself a grounding explanatory role for other kinds. I cited Heidegger's formulation against the philosophical primacy of scientific explanation in Chapter 1, in relation to Jacobi's insight into the circular structure of interpretation. Even in the terms of the earlier Heidegger scientific explanation is only intelligible on the basis of the fact that 'All explication which is to provide understanding must already have understood what is to be explicated' (Heidegger 1979 p. 152). His contention is therefore that

> It is not a question of accommodating understanding and explication to a particular ideal of cognition [such as that of the natural sciences], which is itself only a derivate of understanding. . . . This circle of understanding is not a circle in which a random kind of cognition moves, but is rather the expression of the existential *fore-structure* of Dasein itself.
>
> (ibid. p. 153)

Most challengingly he goes on to claim, in a manner which will be paralleled by Benjamin in *The Origins of German Trauerspiel*,[1] that 'mathematics is not stricter than history, but only more narrow with regard to the extent of the existential foundations which are relevant for it' (ibid.). Understanding something as something in the pragmatic manner that is the core of *Being and Time* and the other work of the 1920s is always prior to the propositional articulation of 'x as something': 'The proposition is not the primary "location" of truth, but rather *the other way round*: the proposition as the mode of appropriation of discoveredness and as the manner of being-in-the-world is grounded in discovering, or in the *disclosedness* of Dasein' (ibid. p. 226). Explaining the world in mathematical terms depends upon the world already being disclosed as that which can be made determinate in such terms, which means one has no right in Platonic manner to suppose that the world is inherently mathematically ordered, because there is no location from which this judgement could be validated without either presupposing it, or landing in another regress. One cannot use mathematics or logic to ground mathematics or logic, as Schelling demonstrated in the 1820s (see Bowie 1993 Chapter 6). The idea that, in the last analysis, truth can be reduced to what the mathematically based sciences can tell us therefore begins at the wrong end, in a manner which Heidegger regards as characteristic of most, if not all, of the Western philosophical tradition.

The Romantic farewell to the ready-made world here receives one of its most developed phenomenological articulations, but not one which, as Nietzsche does, tries to unmask truth itself as grounded in something else such as the 'will to power'. Instead, truth and being are inherently bound together. Truth, though, is not something we cognitively presuppose:

> for to the extent to which we exist, we are in the truth, we are revealed to ourselves and innerworldly entities which we are not are at the same time revealed to us in some way . . . being true, revealedness is the basic condition for the fact that we can be in such a way that we exist as Dasein. (Heidegger 1989 p. 315)

Any attempt to presuppose a cognitive ground must face the prior fact that the ability to presuppose is itself dependent upon always already being in a disclosed world. At this stage Heidegger claims, in line with the arguments of *Metaphysical Foundations of Logic*, that the 'transcendence of Dasein' means that 'truth . . . only exists to the extent to which Dasein itself exists' (ibid. p. 316). However, this now raises a whole series of vital problems associated with the attempt to ground truth in the subject.

The most immediate problem arises if one asks about the location from which this foundational propositional claim could be validated: is it a claim by Dasein on its own behalf? If so, is Dasein not laying claim to the sort of 'self-presence' that Fichte termed 'intellectual intuition' – 'that through which I know something because I do it' (Fichte 1971 p. 463) – in order to validate a truth which must surely transcend itself qua individual subjectivity? To *know* that truth only exists to the extent that I exist – on the assumption that I exist as Dasein – means that I must have an intuitive access to truth which is wholly transparent to myself, precisely because I am the source of that truth. However, this raises the problem of grounding all over again, in that it gives primacy to the reflexive, the knowing I, over the existential I, in a manner which Jacobi and the Romantics already suggested could not be sustained, because my knowledge of myself does not even make me fully transparent to myself. This, of course, is one of the key sources for the growth in philosophical interest in non-cognitive modes of self-understanding of the kind exemplified by music, and in the aspects of language which do not make propositional claims: I shall return to these points later. The questioning of the subject as ground can also, though, go in the other direction, as the later Schelling already showed (see Bowie 1993), and Heidegger makes this point essential to his new orientation. Mark Okrent, who gives an excellent account of the problem, suggests that 'early Heidegger always speaks of Dasein's transcendence, rather than the transcendence of beings over the intentions directed towards them' (Okrent 1988 p. 202). This concentration on the subject's transcendence, Heidegger himself now comes to realise, brings him, despite the pragmatic revisions, too close to a kind of transcendental idealism, which seeks to map out the conditions of possibility of how things are truly apprehended. Such a position involves problems which formed the basis of many of the Romantic ideas we have already examined. Heidegger himself, with the exception of his concern with the Schelling of the essay 'On the Essence of Human Freedom', to which he owes more than he admits, never seriously, to my knowledge, pays any attention to the Romantic ideas.[2]

The missing third part of *Being and Time*, which was never written, was precisely intended to show how one can move from the understanding of Dasein to the understanding of being. Okrent suggests that the conclusion of *Being and Time* is that '"Being", as such and in general, means presence' (ibid. p. 213), and that presence is defined phenomenologically and by a kind of verificationism in terms of Dasein's essentially pragmatic relation to entities. At the level of how we make discriminations in the world and arrive at truths that enable us to manipulate our environment this is in one sense unquestionable. Within a perspective oriented towards the natural sciences there really are few serious reasons to question such a view and the philosophical task (if it is worth carrying out at all, which is by no means self-evident) would simply be to characterise in a more effective manner how the relations to entities are constituted.

It is here that the parting of the ways already suggested by the division between semantics and hermeneutics and by Dilthey's separation of explanation and understanding occurs in many areas of modern philosophy. Given the success of the scientific method in generating more and more truths on the basis of the presence of entities, what reason is there to ask further questions about this presence, which seems only to lead to an unnecessary obscuring of what is in one sense self-evident? We may make mistakes about what is actually evident, but this is corrected in the further process of research, whose pragmatic assumptions are increasingly universally shared by a world-wide scientific community.[3] The question which divides positivistically oriented philosophy from philosophy still (albeit often unconsciously) informed by Romanticism is the question of the ground of presence itself, which from Kant onwards always involved the problem of the relationship of subject to object and of the ground of that relationship. Okrent maintains: 'the making-present of an entity in perception . . . directly gives us evidence only for the perceivability of the entity, not for its existence in the sense of the ground for its perceivability' (ibid. p. 217). This means that Heidegger now must seek an answer to 'the question of how there can be an intention directed toward the being-identical of intended and intuited' (ibid. p. 207), which I suggested in Chapter 6 was a problem in a different way for Husserl because it led either to another regress or to the need for an absolute ground. What is at stake in this question is the very point of philosophy which understands itself in epistemological or ontological terms in relation to the natural sciences. Okrent maintains of the later Heidegger:

Instead of asking about the meaning of being in the sense of what it is for a being to be, he came to focus exclusively on the meaning of being in the sense of the horizon in terms of which there can be presenting and, hence, being. (ibid. p. 218)

As Gadamer puts it: 'In the turn ['*Kehre*', the term later used by Heidegger for the move just described] one begins with being instead of with consciousness which thinks being' (Gadamer 1987 p. 191). In certain ways Heidegger therefore pursues a similar path to that proposed by Jacobi against Fichte's subjectivism, which led Jacobi to his *Unphilosophie*.

Heidegger now also says farewell to philosophy as an epistemologically grounding enterprise, in order to escape a notion of 'metaphysics' which he characterises in a way analogous to Jacobi's characterisation of the 'independent philosophy of intelligence' of Fichte and Spinoza. It is, then, hardly surprising that Heidegger should also take some similar paths to the Romantics in their consideration of art in relation to the problem of grounding. Novalis' question in Chapter 3, 'Can I look for a schema for myself, if I am that which schematises?' (Novalis 1978 p. 162), which implied that 'What reflection *finds*, *seems* already *to be there*' (ibid. p. 17), points to the structure of Heidegger's problems from now on. It does so by suggesting that what is disclosed to the subject precedes the subject in a manner which is not cognitively, or even, given the direction of *Being and Time*, pragmatically available to the subject.[4] What does thought look like, though, which renounces the enterprise of grounding the truth that constitutes most of the tradition of philosophy since Parmenides? We have already considered aspects of such thinking with regard to the Romantics, where the consideration of *Poesie* was precisely intended to explore the consequences of giving up philosophical grounding. The issues now begin, though, to take on aspects which lead us into disturbing territory, territory that is on the one hand firmly connected to questions of aesthetics and literary theory, but which on the other reveals dimensions of these questions which were, for obvious historical reasons, only hinted at in Romantic philosophy. It is here that we shall encounter the issue of whether Heidegger's politics and his philosophy are essentially, or merely contingently related.

The Romantic understanding of *Poesie* derived in key respects from the realisation, germane both to Kant's ethics and his aesthetics, of the modern need for a sphere of value which was not dominated by the exchange principle. This need is, of course, yet another version of the problem of grounding in a post-theological world, and I shall return to the responses to this need later, particularly in relation to Adorno. In 1800 Schelling claimed that the demand that art should be useful was 'only possible in an age which locates the highest efforts of the human spirit in economic discoveries' (Schelling (I/3) p. 622). The question is how this situation is to be confronted, and this will be where Heidegger and the critical theorists will part company. The implicit link between what Heidegger terms 'Western metaphysics', and worries about the nature of truth in the modern

world which are explored via philosophical reflection upon art and literature are apparent in structures which we have already investigated. At the
end of Chapter 1 I suggested that there is a crucial homology in modern
European philosophy between the constitution of metaphysical systems
in 'Spinozist' terms via the principle of determination as negation, the
structuralist idea of language as a system of differences without positive
terms, and the commodity-based economy of negatively related exchange
values. In all these cases the question arises as to the ground upon which
the differentially constituted system relies: the system of 'conditioned
conditions' leads in Jacobi's terms to the question of being; meaning cannot
be explained in differential terms because mere differentiality requires
a ground of identity (semiotics cannot generate semantics); and the notion
of value itself makes no sense in purely relational terms because exchange
values are grounded in use values.[5] This link of these at first sight disparate
theoretical problems becomes crucial both for Heidegger, and for Benjamin
and the Frankfurt School, which is why exploring the political differences
between them will now become inescapable.

Lest there be any doubt about the underlying continuity of the methodological issues in question here, consider Gianni Vattimo's reference to
what is in fact another version of Jacobi's nihilism. The conception, as we
saw, was based on the Spinozist idea of a system based on determination as
negation, and it is this conception which provides the abstract framework
for the link of philosophy, language and political economy:

> according to Nietzsche and Heidegger nihilism is the dissolution of use
> value in exchange value. Nihilism does not consist in the fact that being
> is in the power of the subject, but rather in the fact that being has
> completely dissolved itself in the circulation of value, in the unlimited
> transformations of universal equivalence. (Vattimo 1990 p. 26)

The 'unlimited transformations of universal equivalence' also play a role in
the other systems, as is evident in their correspondence to Jacobi's notion
of the chain of 'conditioned conditions': in the same way as each condition
is only what it is in relation to the others, one exchange value appears
wholly determined by its relation to other exchange values.

The later Heidegger becomes concerned, through his exploration of
these issues, that a purely pragmatic approach to the understanding of
being leads to the positive sciences becoming the replacement for what
philosophy had been since the Greeks.[6] This is because 'metaphysics'
increasingly reveals itself as the description carried out in the history
of philosophy of a real process of transformation in the human world, one
which becomes most visible for Heidegger in the wake of the Cartesian
grounding of certainty in the subject. In that process, truth becomes
reduced to the theoretical expression of how the world is objectified in real
terms into what can be manipulated for the subject's instrumental purposes.
This can be manifested in the form both of the technical application of

systematic theories in the natural sciences and of systematic relationships between commodities qua exchange values in capitalism. However, the growing success of that manipulation often goes hand in hand with the idea that the reduction of the world to that which can be manipulated may actually be a route to disaster. The crucial problem with this idea lies in establishing the perspective from which it can be stated, and this problem will, despite their political differences, link the theories of Heidegger, Benjamin, Adorno, Habermas (and many others, including the Lukács of *History and Class Consciousness*). The significant fact is that the claim very often involves reflection on the significance of art for philosophy.[7]

PUTTING THE TRUTH INTO THE WORK

Kant's move to questions of aesthetics had itself been motivated by a concern with non-instrumental approaches to the objects of the world, and Heidegger now takes a related path because of worries about the implications of his essentially pragmatist attempt in the earlier philosophy to ground the truth. Let us now, therefore, consider a few aspects of the essay 'The Origin of the Work of Art' in the light of the change in Heidegger's philosophy that later comes to be known as the 'turn'. From now on things get more difficult. While the Heidegger of *Being and Time* is increasingly, in particular via his links to American pragmatism, regarded as part of mainstream developments in modern philosophy, the later Heidegger is often seen as retreating both into philosophical irrationalism and into, for want of a better word, irrationalist politics, as well as into incomprehensible prose.[8] The initial reason for the philosophical suspicions is in one sense obvious: if what Heidegger is now interested in is immune to explanation in the terms we use for entities in the world, and if it is also not accessible via what was implied in his pragmatist revision of Husserl's notion of categorial intuition, it falls outside the main ways in which philosophy has approached rationality. Does this, though, mean that 'The core of the turn consists in the fact that Heidegger equips in a misleading manner the meta-historical instance of a temporally liquidified power of origin with the attribute of the happening of truth' (Habermas 1985 p. 183)? In order to answer this question we need both to make more sense of Habermas' compressed remark, behind which lie some of the differences between Heidegger and the tradition of Benjamin and Adorno, and, in order to be able to do that, to outline an accessible account of what Heidegger seems to be trying to achieve. One should keep in mind that he is trying to achieve it for all the time between 1933 and 1945 as a member of the NSDAP.

If metaphysics turns out to be the consideration of being as presence, with the consequences suggested above, escaping from metaphysics must in some way have to do with absence or, as Heidegger terms it, 'hiddenness'. But how does hiddenness relate to the question of truth? In the transitional essay 'On the Essence of Truth' Heidegger talks of 'The hiddenness of being as a whole' ('*Seiendes im Ganzen*') which he elsewhere says 'never coincides with the sum of what happens to be known'. What he means has to do with how we live in a disclosed world which is yet never fully transparent to us. Such a world is, especially in a traditional myth-based society, still meaningful despite (or even because of) the limited theoretical knowledge of entities in that society. The hiddenness of being as a whole, he claims, 'never results after the fact as a consequence of the always piece-meal cognition of entities. The hiddenness of being as a whole, the real un-truth, is older than every openness of this and that entity' (Heidegger 1978 p. 191). This might sound merely like an appeal to an origin, but the arguments Heidegger develops in relation to this theme do not necessarily entail an origin, in the regressive sense of something from the past which alone can confer truth on the present, such – in the worst scenario – as the rediscovery of Germanic myths. Furthermore, his arguments certainly do not entail our ability, in the manner of the tradition beginning with Descartes, philosophically to ground our access to whatever is meant. In the Heidegger we have considered so far, Dasein was the location of the disclosure of being as true being, which left the problem of grounding we encountered above. He now moves towards a position which no longer attempts to establish a ground for the truth of being, but which instead seeks other ways of thinking about that truth, by trying to think about what cannot be determined as an entity – hence the notion of hiddenness that always already precedes the disclosure of entities[9] – and the attention to art.

The simple way to approach this is to ponder the fact that every way of determining an entity as what it is leads to other determinations, in the manner of the chain of conditioned conditions. Access to the notional totality of these conditions, which Hegel sought to articulate in his version of 'absolute knowledge', would, in principle at least, be equivalent to the ability to manipulate the whole of the world in which we live. This world, though, is itself in fact more and more constituted as that which is already open to manipulation, which is summed up in Descartes' idea that we can be 'lord and master of nature'. Heidegger's claim is that this openness increasingly makes philosophy forget the fact that the real truth of being is that being is also hidden: each new disclosure both reveals an entity in a way that was previously hidden and, precisely by doing so, again makes the hiddenness at the heart of being forgotten. The task is now to find ways of approaching this hiddenness.

There is, however, no point in attempting to ground a *philosophical* position from which a critique of this philosophico-historical situation would be possible: this would just repeat the basic moves in metaphysics by forgetting ontological difference, now in the sense of the difference between entities and the truth of being. Indeed, as Okrent stresses, intro-ducing two key terms in the later thought, Heidegger 'is unequivocal in holding that only through the domination of technological, pragmatic metaphysics does it first become possible to think specifically about *Ereignis* or *aletheia*' (Okrent 1988 p. 221). As such, it is only through the process of philosophical reflection itself, not via some irrational intuitive access, that what is at issue emerges.[10] The attempt to think about *Ereignis* ('event' or – given the root of the word, which involves the notion of '*eignen*', as in '*aneignen*', 'to appropriate' – 'appropriation') and *aletheia* ('unforgetting' or 'disclosure', which Heidegger substitutes for the usual translation of the word as the Greek word for 'truth') emerges most graphically in the essay 'The Origin of the Work of Art'.

Heidegger here begins to develop the questions which dominate his later philosophy. This is apparent when he asserts, in the light of the issues discussed above, that

> science is not an original happening of truth but in each case the extension of a realm of truth which is already open. . . . If and to the extent that a science goes beyond rightness to a truth, and that means that it comes to the essential revelation of entities as such, it is philosophy.
>
> (Heidegger 1960 p. 62)

It is now in the work of art that 'truth', rather than the 'truths' about entities in a science, is rendered accessible: 'The installation of truth into the work is the bringing forth of an entity which previously did not yet exist and afterwards will never become again' (ibid.). Obscure though these assertions may sound, they do point to the sense that truth is now for Heidegger something which 'happens', and which happens most essentially in art, rather than in the natural sciences. Instead of being based on the principle of sufficient reason, thus upon an epistemological or ontological ground,[11] the truth in art is more fundamental and also not universal to a whole series of entities of the same kind. The basic point will eventually be that the truth of being, as Okrent puts it: 'has no ground at all, admits of no explanation, and is an ungrounded gift of "appropriation"' (Okrent 1988 p. 277). The real question, then, is whether this position entails the kind of irrationalism that Habermas claims it does.

Looked at in the terms of the natural sciences, the essential point about a work of art is that it is an object which presents itself like any other object: a sculpture is in these terms primarily a piece of stone like any other stone of the same kind. Heidegger insists, though, that the work is not an object:

> the work in no way affects what there is up to now ['*das bisherige Seiende*' in the sense of the cognitively disclosed world] via causal contexts of interaction (*kausale Wirkungszusammenhänge*). The effect of the work does not consist in an effecting (*in einem Wirken*). It resides in a transformation, which happens from out of the work, of the unhiddenness of beings ['*des Seienden*', i.e. the world of entities] and that means: of being. (Heidegger 1960 p. 74)

How, then, can art be said to transform being? The stakes here are obviously very high. Given the development of important aspects of modern art in the direction of the destruction of the very notion of a 'work' of art, as well as the theories of literature and other arts as ideology that we have considered, a theory which wishes to claim that the truth made available by art is philosophically more significant than that of the sciences will need to put up a case strong enough to overcome the obvious objection that some people 'just can't see it' – whether it be Beethoven, Leonardo, Hölderlin or, for that matter, Joseph Beuys – let alone the objection that, as Hegel argues in the *Aesthetics*, 'art is no longer for us the highest manner in which truth makes existence for itself' (cited in ibid. p. 84). Furthermore, attributing such enormous significance to 'art' runs the danger of linking it to issues which, especially given the time of the writing of the essay, may turn out to be anything but linked to the 'truth' in any defensible sense of the word at all. Heidegger's essay is, on the one hand, deeply important as a response to a key issue and, on the other, contains signs of a malaise that must make one at the same time question the very nature of his later philosophical enterprise.

'The Origin of the Work of Art' wants to discredit the idea that a work of art is a truth-determinate entity like any other, which is only subsequently transformed into something special, both by being produced out of other things by a creating subject and by its reception as an aesthetic object by a subject. Were it constituted in terms of the latter, of course, the objection suggested above looms.[12] Heidegger's question is, then, 'whether the work is basically something else and never a thing' (ibid. p. 11). With his usual thoroughness he therefore undertakes one of his investigations as to just what a 'thing' is. The Western philosophical tradition has three dominant accounts of a thing, associated, in turn, with Aristotle, Kant and Aquinas: as the 'bearer of its attributes' (ibid. p. 16); as 'the unity of a multiplicity of what is given in the senses' (ibid. p. 17), and as 'the synthesis of matter and form' (ibid. p. 19). The 'thingness' (*das Dinghafte*) of the work would seem most obviously to be 'the matter of which it consists' (ibid. p. 19). But, Heidegger claims, 'Form and matter are not at all original determinations of the thingness (*das Dingliche*) of the simple thing' (ibid. p. 21): the temptation to use form/matter as the most general determination derives not least from the biblical notion of 'the whole of being as created' (ibid. p. 22). In a way which he does not really explain,[13] the form/matter distinction becomes the dominant conception in the Western metaphysics that he is now trying to overcome. This distinction is also, of course, fundamental to those kinds of literary criticism that presuppose a conception of literature as the re-presentation, involving formal characteristics that can be analysed in terms of 'style', etc., of a ready-made world. Heidegger goes on to investigate the difference between a thing and 'material' – '*Zeug*', in the sense of that which can be made into something by adding attributes to the original material – using the now notorious example of the painting of a pair of boots by van Gogh, which he interprets, probably wrongly,[14] as being those of a woman peasant. The suggestion is that the painting 'is the opening up of that which the material, the pair of peasant shoes is in truth. This entity steps out into the unhiddenness of its being' so that there is a 'happening of truth at work' in the painting (ibid. p. 30), because the world of which the 'material' is an integral part emerges via the existence of the painting. Given the fact that the truth which happens in the painting is now rather contentious there are already grounds for suspicion, but the deeper argument is actually not as evidently vulnerable to criticism as the example used to propose it.

The vital distinctions turn here around the relationships between 'thing', 'material' and 'work':

> What we . . . wanted to grasp as the most proximate reality of the work, the thingly base (*Unterbau*), does not belong in this way to the work.
>
> As soon as we attend to the work in this respect we have unintentionally taken the work as material, to which we also grant a superstructure which is supposed to contain that which is artistic. But the work is not a piece of material which is equipped besides with an aesthetic value that is attached to it. The work is as little this as the simple thing is a piece of material which just lacks the real character of material, its disposability ['*Dienlichkeit*' in the sense of that which can serve for a purpose] and being-manufactured (*Anfertigung*). (ibid. p. 33)

The point is that it is the work which actually reveals the truth of things in the world, on the assumption that entities are always also hidden, because their truth, in the sense now being explored, is precisely not apparent via their being determined in a chain of conditions. Such chains can also include, for example, the chain of art objects in some versions of literary or art history, where the main aim is to see the work as an example, say, of the category '*Novelle*' or 'mannerist painting'. Determination of the object in the terms of a science, now in a very wide 'German' sense of '*Wissenschaft*', is precisely what makes it equivalent to other objects, as merely an example of a particular concept defined by its relation to other concepts. In these terms the objects are all explained on the basis of the disclosure which is initiated in the foundational link of Western metaphysics to natural science. This kind of disclosure happens in a related way in the modern rendering of the world of objects into a world of equivalent exchange values. The sheer tediousness of so much work in literary and art history would derive in this perspective from the fact that it ignores the one thing which matters about its object, namely the way in which it can disclose a world in ways nothing else can. Given the development of the market for works of art as commodities this conception is clearly apt to vital aspects of what Heidegger is trying to understand in terms of the role of art in modernity. How apt the connection of natural science and the development of the commodity form really is has now become strikingly apparent in the sometimes successful attempts in some countries to patent the products of genetic manipulation as commodities belonging to their – 'creator'?, 'discoverer'?, 'manufacturer'? There is, then, something powerful going on in this theory. If all the world 'really is' is the concatenations of the elements discovered by science, and every other approach to existence is always secondary to the prior scientific possibility of giving an account of any thing at all, this still does not explain why the scientific account should be the prior account, unless this is presupposed.[15] In this respect Heidegger is right to ask whether there may not be forms of access to truth that cannot be explained by beginning one's investigation with the world of determinable objects.

Heidegger's other main example in this context, the Greek temple, is used to introduce the core distinction of the essay as a whole, that between 'world' and 'earth', which frames the question of 'hiddenness' in a new way. This example, significantly, works much better. Unlike a building, a painting can be investigated in certain cases as to the entities it may in fact also represent, thereby putting into question the sense that it is self-evidently revealing the truth about a world – especially, given Nazi ideology, a world in which peasants put their shoes away in a (oh dear) 'hard but healthy tiredness' (ibid. p. 28). The role of a building qua art work, in the sense of that which reveals truth, does not necessarily entail the same problems. This is most immediately apparent in the fact that attention to Heidegger on the part of architects has in recent years opened up vital new perspectives on the nature of the relationship between buildings and public space.[16] It is worth already suggesting here – the issue will be vital in Adorno – that something similar to what can be said about buildings applies to the non-representational form of music, which can also disclose a world in ways that have nothing to do with what the music is qua analysable entity. Heidegger stresses the religious connotations of the temple for a community in a manner which is, given his historical context, open to question, but parts of his description do give a masterly sense of the revelatory possibilities of what he means by 'art'. The location of a temple in a landscape is not the addition of a manufactured object to the landscape:

> In standing there the building ['*Bauwerk*', which contains the sense of 'work' as in 'art work'] stands up to the storm which rages over it and in this way first shows the storm in its power. The splendour and the glowing of the stone, apparently itself dependent on the blessing of the sun, first renders the lightness of the day, the breadth of the sky, the darkness of the night manifest. (ibid. p. 38)

The point is that these aspects cannot be said already to 'be there' as what they subsequently reveal themselves to be,[17] even though the objects themselves in some sense must already exist. 'Being there' is still inextricably connected to truth, and the idea that the brute existence of things in a wholly indeterminate manner (which can anyway only be expressed via a questionable abstraction) is the best way to talk about their being is precisely what Heidegger – who, of course, knows his Kant – will not accept: 'The temple first gives things their visibility ['*Gesicht*', via the derivation of what is now the word for 'face' from the verb 'to see'] and first gives people the view of themselves' (ibid. p. 39). It is also, therefore, not the case that the formal beauty of the temple is, in Platonic fashion, its link to truth. Without the tension and conflict which the work brings into being – which Heidegger describes in terms of the relationship of 'world' and 'earth' – things cannot truly be manifest.

He then suggests, this time in again less convincing fashion, that the same applies to the 'language-work' ['*Sprachwerk*', in analogy to '*Bauwerk*'] of Greek tragedy as to the temple. Heidegger sees tragedy merely in terms of the battle of the old and the new Gods. The argument actually works better, though, in terms of tragedy's revelation of the nature of law, which emerges in the move from the order of a predominantly rural community to the order of the *polis*. Seen in this way, an Athenian tragedy like the *Oresteia* is not just a symbolic re-enactment of a past conflict, but the revelation of the truth that constitutes the forming of the state in which it is performed, the truth that the institution of law inherently entails conflict and suffering in ways which cannot be rationalistically explained away. There is, though, a missing dimension here. The fact that such a form of art is connected to a particular historical kind of community is, despite his references to 'history' and '*Volk*', not seriously considered by Heidegger, with consequences we shall see in a moment. It does in many ways make sense to see Athenian tragedy, not as a symbolic expression of what that society already was, but as an event in which it revealed to itself what it was and constituted itself as a public sphere. The really important question is, though, whether this model makes any sense for, say, the drama of Weimar classicism, Viennese classical music, or Kafka's 'literature'. Furthermore, Heidegger does not seriously discuss how it is that Greek tragedy today still has a claim to truth in the sense at issue here; indeed, he seems to think that outside of their original context the works no longer have a claim to disclose truth in the same way. Let us, though, further elucidate the key terms in which Heidegger maps out his conception, where some of the same problems will be apparent.

The notion of 'world' means much the same as it does in his earlier work, namely the horizon within which things are always already intelligible. The 'earth', on the other hand, is the resistance of things against which the emergence of the world becomes possible, which was implicit in the example of the temple and its environment. How the two relate can best be explained by considering a version of a closely related idea. The new conceptual pair almost certainly has its origin in Schelling's middle philosophy, which is usually known as the philosophy of the 'Ages of the World', on which Heidegger works during the 1930s and to which he also returned in the 1940s. In the essay 'On the Essence of Human Freedom' of 1809, upon which Heidegger writes a whole book (Heidegger 1971), Schelling talks of the 'real', which is the patent source of Heidegger's 'earth', as the 'ungraspable basis of reality in things, the remainder that never comes out, that which can never, even with the greatest exertion, be dissolved into understanding, but remains eternally in the ground' (Schelling (I/7) p. 360). Heidegger sees the earth via the example of a stone, whose weight (Schelling uses the notion of 'gravity', which he contrasts with 'light') 'rejects ... any penetration into it. If we try to do this by breaking up the cliff, then it never shows an inside, something revealed, in its pieces' (Heidegger 1960 p. 43). All attempts to dissolve the stone into its calculable attributes via the understanding merely lead to its destruction as a stone and to the realisation of the hiddenness of the earth.

Schelling's target in his work of the middle period is precisely a Spinozism which would reduce the world to the world of conditions, of the kind which we have already linked to Heidegger's moves away from the metaphysical tradition. In the light of his reading of Jacobi, Schelling suggests:[18]

> If the world were, as some so-called sages have thought, a chain of causes and effects which runs forwards and backwards into infinity, then there would be neither past nor future in the true sense of the word. But this incoherent thought ought rightly to disappear along with the mechanical system to which it alone belongs. (Schelling 1946 (I) p. 11)

Schelling therefore questions the idea of a ground from which things follow, in the manner of traditional metaphysical grounding, and talks of the 'unground (*Ungrund*) of eternity' (ibid. p. 93) which he, like the Heidegger of 'On the Essence of Truth', sees in terms of 'freedom', the world having, with respect to the principle of sufficient reason, no reason to exist as a manifest world. Schelling is attempting to build a theology of the world as God's free deed, which he connects to the human freedom to do good and evil, but the structure of his account of how the world is manifest does not require the theological support. He later, thereby prefiguring the distinction of earth and world, distinguishes between two aspects of the same being, which he terms 'quodditative' and 'quidditative' being, and which Wolfram Hogrebe has usefully re-titled 'pronominal' and 'predicative' being (see Hogrebe 1989, Bowie 1993 Chapter 5). The former is a force of contraction and hiddenness, the latter a force of expansion and manifestation: the forces cannot, though, be finally separated, standing in a relationship to each other which is analogous to the fundamental structure of utterances, where 'argument' and 'function', 'name' and 'description' only make sense together. The conflict of the kinds of being is what makes the manifest world a world of temporality, in which what is manifested is also hidden again by what becomes its ground by negating it, so that it 'goes to ground', which in German means that it is destroyed.[19] The relationship of the forces is, for Schelling, also the source of the nature of language itself, which on the one hand is contracted into a limited number of fixed signifiers or names, and on the other is able to open up the infinite possibilities of meaning precisely via the capacity of these fixed means to reveal by predication while yet also concealing. As such the truth must be kept alive precisely by striving against the tendency of language to be reduced to its existing forms, a notion which relates to some of the Romantic ideas we considered in earlier chapters. Heidegger, in certain ways, does little more than repeat some of Schelling's ideas: world and earth are 'essentially different and yet never separated. . . . The opposition of world and earth is a conflict' (Heidegger 1960 p. 46) via which the truth of being arises in a temporalised happening which is both revealing and concealing. For Schelling, primary being is precisely 'in contradiction with itself/contradicted by itself (*von sich selbst im Widerspruch*)' (Schelling (I/8) p. 219) in much the same way as earth and world. One could go on: there are plenty more parallels, and one wonders why Heidegger does not bother to mention them.[20] We have here, once more, of course, a further example of the subterranean influence of Romantic philosophy.[21]

Schelling's version of the conflict is a story about the tragic difficulty of attaining rational understanding of our place in a finite, conflict-ridden world, where 'error, crime and deception', as Habermas approvingly says of Schelling's conception, are not 'lacking in reason, but forms of appearance of *perverted* reason' (Habermas 1985 p. 377). In contrast, Heidegger's version of the conflict now becomes, on the basis of the totalising critique of metaphysics outlined above, more and more questionable: 'In the essential conflict . . . the sides mutually raise each other into the self-assertion of their essence',[22] which is a 'giving oneself up into the hidden primordiality of the source of one's own being' (Heidegger 1960 p. 46). The echoes of Heidegger's 1934 pro-Nazi Rectorship Speech in the term 'self-assertion', in the valorisation of 'the source of one's own being' and in the notion of 'conflict', leave the way open for a regressive sense in which the truth of art is bound exclusively to particular communities, and thus, in a modern context, to ethnically defined nations, to the '*Volk*'. At such points Habermas' objection that Heidegger is offering a philosophy of origins, in which rationality is surrendered to an original ground that is supposed to be more true than anything which rational discourse can communicate, is clearly valid.[23]

What, though, of the rest of the argument linking art to truth: does it necessarily lead to the irrationalism that emerges in passages like the one just cited?[24] The next stage for Heidegger is to ask 'to what extent does truth happen in the carrying out of the conflict of world and earth?' (ibid. p. 47). Here the central term is the 'clearing' (*Lichtung*), the 'open place' in the middle of beings where things appear (ibid. p. 51): the clearing is, though, 'in itself at the same time concealment' (ibid.). The 'essence of truth' is, then, the conflict between openness and concealment, in which truth 'happens' as the tension between the revealing of a presence and the sense that this revelation means that something else is concealed. Although Heidegger does not see it in these terms, Novalis' account of *Poesie* in *Monologue* which we examined in Chapter 3 is congruent with the defensible side of this notion of truth, in which the truth of anything particular is only ever relative to the context in which it is able to be determinate. This means that the attempt to state the absolute truth about anything must always fail, even as one may feel obliged to try to do so. In this respect it is hard to square Heidegger's position with an account of art in terms of a primordial and irrational source: the crucial aspect of art here is that, in a world of the increasingly 'ever-same', it makes something new happen by bringing things to unconcealment. A more accessible version of this view is, as I suggested in the Introduction, developed in the Russian formalist notion of *ostranenie*. The only meaning the truth of being can now have must therefore be the meaning that is to come. This truth happens in an exemplary manner in art, precisely because art, unlike natural science, does not follow in the path of already established truths. At this level Heidegger cannot be accused of being a philosopher of origins, but his later work does seem constantly to vacillate between regression and the attempt to overcome the metaphysics of the ready-made world by developing new paths for our self-understanding.

In the light of the idea that metaphysics is inextricably linked to domination of the object by the subject, the concern with the dual aspect of 'clearing' and 'concealment' leads Heidegger to a vital question with regard to art and truth. The scientific analysis of any entity in the world, like the stone used as an example above, leads both to the destruction of the particular entity as that entity and to a process of disintegration of the entity which may or may not end with the revelation of the fundamental components of that entity. Having supposedly reached that point, what would necessarily have changed in the world of our self-understanding, apart from the fact that the entity is no more as the entity it was, and the fact that we have another theory of another entity which may or not be important for its possible applications?[25] Schlegel's wonderful dictum we cited in Chapter 3, 'If the chemist thinks a thing is not a whole because he can dissect it, that is just the same as what bad critics do to literature. – Didn't the world emerge from *slime*?' (Schlegel 1988 5 p. 48), underlines what is meant here. This situation is, of course, part of what Jacobi meant by nihilism, and is the core reason for the attention to the philosophy of art of those who are, like the Romantics, Nietzsche, Heidegger, Benjamin and Adorno, most aware of the questions posed by nihilism.

Now the 'creation of the work' *also* involves the need to use an entity and to destroy some aspect of its being: 'But this use does not use up and abuse the earth as a material (*Stoff*) but rather first frees it to itself', by 'constituting the truth in the form (*Gestalt*)' (Heidegger 1960 pp. 64–5). The work, be it the temple, the sculpture, the poem, the symphony or whatever – the generality of the thesis, as Adorno suggests (Adorno 1967

p. 184), already begins to point to problems – is what enables us again to be astonished that things are: 'But what is more usual than the fact that there are entities? In the work, in contrast, it is the fact that it *is* as a work that is unusual' (Heidegger 1960 p. 66). Its being a work is not constituted by being subsumed under the concept 'work of art' but by what happens in our relationship to it. Crucial to this conception is that this relationship should not be simply the *Erlebnis* – Heidegger uses Dilthey's term because of its psychologistic connotations – of the private individual who enjoys the work, but should instead be the '*Bewahrung*' ('testing', in the sense of both encountering and preserving the truth, the '*Wahrheit*', of the work). The 'manner of the right *Bewahrung* of the work is co-created and sketched out ['*vorgezeichnet*', in the sense of 'pre-drawn'] first and only through the work itself' (ibid. p. 69). The work, of whatever genre of art, is 'in essence *Dichtung* ['poetry', or 'literature' almost in analogy to the Romantic notion of *Poesie*, with the sense of 'constituting' by giving a *Gestalt* to entities in the world]' (ibid. p. 74). Unlike Pater, in his famous dictum that 'all art constantly aspires to the condition of music', Heidegger regards verbal art, the 'language work', as having a 'special place among all the arts' (ibid. p. 75). At this point Heidegger outlines the whole direction of his later philosophy, by pointing to the need for the 'right concept of language' (ibid.) for his assertion to be understood.

The Romantic move away from the idea that language is primarily an instrument which re-presents things in the world did not entail an 'other-worldly' relationship to natural science and to the pragmatic necessities of life. It was in fact meant to keep open the diversity of ways in which we make sense, including of our lack of ultimate control of meaning and truth. Heidegger now maintains that

> language first brings the entity as an entity into the open (*ins Offene*).[26] Where there is ['*west*' in the temporalised sense of '*Wesen*' noted above] no language, as in the being of stone, plant and animal, there is also no openness of entities and correspondingly also no openness of non-being (*des Nichtseienden*) and of emptiness. (ibid.)

In *Being and Time* words 'accrue' to meanings generated by practical concern with a world, a concern which, in the transitional texts such as the *Basic Concepts of Metaphysics* of 1930, led Heidegger to see animals as merely 'poor in world', rather than devoid of it, on the assumption that in certain respects animals share attributes with Dasein which stones do not. Even though animals do not have words they seem to have meaning in one of the senses of the word in *Being and Time* (which, though, actually grants animals no world at all).[27] Now, however, although the conception of language at issue is again not based upon propositionality, something vital has changed. Rorty rightly maintains, with regard to the move from *Being and Time* to the later philosophy, that 'The stock of language rises as that of Dasein falls' (Rorty 1991a p. 62). The genesis of meaning is now no longer predominantly a function of social praxis, in the way which leads Apel, Rorty and others to link the early Heidegger to the later Wittgenstein's related notion of language, but happens instead via the 'event' of language, which is where the real trouble starts.

In 'The Origin of the Work of Art' the trouble is more than obvious, because Heidegger makes another of his dreadful links between what is, despite all, a challenging philosophical position concerning how to understand art, truth and language, and his need to be part of the happening of history. On the one hand, the concern cited above for art to 'free things to themselves' suggests a sense in which art is to be a source of a non-instrumental relationship to the world of the kind we will also find in Benjamin and Adorno, and which is still vital, for example, in relation to questions of ecology, or in aspects of education. On the other hand, '*Dichtung*' now becomes a 'saying' ('*Sage*', with the implications of 'saga', and all the rest), such that

> In such a saying the concepts of the essence of a historical ['*geschichtlich*', which Heidegger wants now to mean something to do with 'being sent', and 'destiny' (*Schicksal*), thus to do with that which is beyond the control of the individuals involved] *Volk* are pre-formed for it, i.e. its belonging to world-history ['*Welt-Geschichte*', which takes up the sense of history as 'being sent']. (Heidegger 1960 p. 76)

The tortuousness of any translation of the sentence already suggests that something is going seriously wrong: the refusal to speak the language of the dominant forces of a repressive and instrumentalised society is, as Adorno and others insist, a vital factor in the truth of modern art, and this position will be central to my further argument. Heidegger, though, is here suggesting that the dominant forces of his society, in the form of the historical mission which is in fact that of the *Führer*, are precisely evident *in* the language which he wishes to develop *against* everyday language. He will come to term everyday language, in one of his most questionable philosophical moves, 'the language of metaphysics', a move even Gadamer, who makes important attempts to salvage something from Heidegger's position, finds thoroughly beyond the pale. Well before there was any immediate personal need (which Habermas suggests was a motivation for Heidegger's 'turn') to suggest that Nazism was something beyond the control of real people, and especially of Martin Heidegger, he already maps out, via his own modification of language, a conception which claims to look beyond the mere surface phenomena to a deeper 'event', which is now linked to the primacy of a national symbolic order based on the happening of being which transcends individual subjects.[28] Rorty refers to Heidegger's 'reification of language', and here the effects of such a reification become very evident. We have already seen ways in which the best theories of understanding, including aspects of the work of the earlier Heidegger, assume that 'there is no such thing as language', in order to escape another version of the regress of grounding that is based on the attempt to give a theory of entities called meanings. The most pernicious aspects of such statements as Heidegger's cited above now begin to fulfil the potential for danger suggested in Herder's idea that really living language 'becomes unpronounceable for outsiders (*Fremdlinge*)' (Herder 1966 p. 11). What, then, is left of Heidegger's conception, once these aspects come to the fore?

The main text of 'The Origin of the Work of Art' concludes with a quotation from Hölderlin, which is introduced with a bizarre (and unintentionally comic) reference to Hölderlin as 'the poet the Germans still have to *bestehen*' (Heidegger 1960 p. 81): the word '*bestehen*' is most frequently used in German as the word for passing a test or an exam. Now it is well known that the discovery and the academic exploration of Hölderlin's work only really began in this century and that much is still very open in our understanding of Hölderlin. It is also true that Hölderlin is one of the poets whose poetic power does not seem to diminish with time: Heidegger himself devotes much attention – of varying degrees of interest and quality – to why this is the case. The trouble is, though, that this is not what Heidegger means here: he seems to think that the poet's challenge is something which is to be put on the same level as the admittedly pretty earth-shaking (though not in the sense Heidegger thinks) events that were going on around him. The importance of art as the 'putting into the work of the truth' is at this level merely a gross inflation of the significance of particular art works in modernity, perhaps on the model of the possible constitutive force for the *polis* of Greek tragedy that we observed above. This was the way Hegel also tended to see tragedy and was part of what led him to the thesis of the 'end of art' as a form of the highest truth. Without detailed discriminations concerning the context and the actual material possibilities for the reception of major art, of the kind the Romantics and Hegel began to introduce into philosophy, however, the idea that art can be so immediately connected to politics is simply absurd. Is there, though, no way in which the Romantic aspects of Heidegger's approach to art and truth may not still be significant, or does one, in the light of these pretty damning failures, have to take on all of Habermas' position concerning Heidegger? In the last section of the chapter I shall use the relationship of Habermas to Heidegger as a way of highlighting issues that will lead into the investigation of Benjamin and Adorno, and to the Conclusion.

THE SUBJECT OF ART

Habermas thinks that Heidegger correctly identifies the impossibility of grounding modern philosophy in subjectivity, tries unsuccessfully to overcome that problem with his still subject-oriented version of pragmatism in *Being and Time*, and makes the problem worse in the work from the Nazi period onwards by seeking a new kind of foundation in the conception of being as a 'power of origin' (Habermas) whose history can only be understood by listening to a truth which is wholly divorced from the totalising effects of the dominance of subjectivity in Western metaphysics. Heidegger later calls this dominance the '*Ge-stell*', the 'enframing', which renders being merely an object for the manipulating subject, in the form of the application of modern technology.[29] By making the story one of total domination, Habermas maintains, the perceived way out of the situation takes Heidegger 'beyond' truth, in the sense of 'a validity claim which transcends space and time' (Habermas 1985 p. 182), towards a mystical need to try to hear the 'words of being' in the poetry of Hölderlin, Trakl and Rilke. It also, more recently, leads towards the excesses of some French literary theory. Despite their differences, however, Habermas shares with Heidegger the conviction that the question of subjectivity is secondary to the question of language, because, crudely, language precedes the subject which employs it.

It should be obvious from preceding chapters that a great deal turns on exactly what language itself is understood to be, which is yet another problem of grounding. The explication of what language is must be undertaken by language itself: this was already an issue for Novalis, and is one point of Derrida's use of the notion of *différance* to deconstruct the idea of a 'transcendental signified' which would stop the regress of signifiers that results from trying to get to a philosophical truth, for example, about language, which is free of context. Given the refusal, characteristic also of the semantic tradition, to locate meaning and truth in the subject, the circularity built into philosophical investigation of language is, as we have seen in relation to the emergence of hermeneutics, inescapable. It may also, as Rorty proposes, be an issue which we should simply circumvent in the manner of the later Wittgenstein 'turning his spade' to avoid destroying it on rock which may actually obviate the need for further foundation-building. However, this view risks obscuring questions which are still of importance to Rorty himself: if philosophy, in the sense of 'metaphysics' at issue here, is to be replaced by 'literature', it is as well to take attempts to rethink their relationship seriously. In general Rorty sees philosophy anyway as a kind of literature, but even if the distinction is at best heuristic, it is still necessary to see how it is worked out in differing historical contexts, as the investigation of Heidegger's account of truth and art should already have made clear. Heidegger, who is, like Habermas, aware that a *philosophical* grounding of language, in the sense of an articulated account of the relationship of language and being, cannot be carried out for lack of a location from which this would be possible, still tries to find ways of making language 'of being' in the 'subjective genitive'. This is in many ways the basic project of his later philosophy. Because the relationship cannot be explained in purely theoretical terms one has to try to arrive somewhere that philosophy cannot go – namely at direct contact with being. Poetry may be able to achieve this, Heidegger thinks, because of its 'revealing-concealing' nature which we considered above. Habermas, on the other hand, tries to use a theory of language as social praxis as a way of replacing the grounding role of the transcendental subject. The very incompatibility of the aims in question already makes the matter tricky, but Habermas and Heidegger do share the conviction that 'subject philosophy' is the main obstacle to new insight and that the real source of insight must now be language.

The alternative to Heidegger's approach is, then, for Habermas, an *inter*subjective theory of communicative action, which regards language as the realm of criticisable cognitive, ethical and aesthetic validity claims (see Habermas 1985 p. 366 for a useful condensed summary). He thinks this theory can lead one out of the aporias of subject philosophy into a consensus theory of truth based upon the *counterfactual* notion of the 'ideal speech situation'.[30] For Habermas, only communication which orients itself towards the acceptance that the ideas and expressions of the other have the same right as my own to be tested as to their validity can keep open the process of critical inquiry without making knowledge into merely the exercise of the power of the subject over the object, in the manner of the version of Western metaphysics which both he and Heidegger associate in particular with Nietzsche. In many ways, Habermas' position is a version of the hermeneutic imperative suggested by the Romantics and Schleiermacher, which makes truth inherently normative. Its main normative objectives cannot, from within the positions I am trying to elaborate here, be gainsaid. There are, though, two vital problems in Habermas' position, one of which – the tendency, despite all claims to the contrary, to reify language – he shares with Heidegger (albeit not always for the same reasons), the other of which – the failure to see that questions to do with art cannot be finally separated from questions of truth – he evidently does not. These problems cannot be adequately explored here, but it is helpful at least to indicate these weaknesses, so as to establish a perspective from which we can both underline once again the importance of the best of the Romantic ideas and salvage something of Heidegger's conception. This will lead us to a consideration of Benjamin and Adorno in terms not dictated in advance by Habermas' influential critiques.

Both Heidegger and Habermas agree that 'Because self-reflection must make something into an object which, as the spontaneous source of all subjectivity, withdraws itself altogether from the form of objectivity' (Habermas 1985 p. 433), a philosophy in the tradition of Kant cannot finally succeed in articulating the ground of truth. The only way of definitively trying to do so would, they think, end up with something like Hegel's 'absolute reflection'. Hegel tries to overcome the finitude of subjectivity by articulating its intrinsically infinite nature, which emerges at the end of the system when apparently finite thought can find no more contradictions in its attempt to objectify itself. At the end, though, the subject can 'listen only to itself', with all the problems we have already suggested this entailed, which, as Derrida also maintains against both Hegel and Husserl, are (in this view) a result of the priority of language before the subject. The move to language, either as the condition of possibility of intersubjectivity or as a happening beyond the individual subject, decentres a subject which cannot claim to be ground of itself because its very nature is a result of always already requiring language to be itself. How, then, in the light of these questions concerning language, does the question of art and truth relate to the similarities and differences between Heidegger and Habermas?

There are, remember, very divergent ways of taking seriously the idea that art – particularly literature – is connected to truth, as should already be evident from the differences between Heidegger and the Romantics. Habermas has warned against 'an abdication of problem-solving philosophical thinking before the poetic power of language, literature and art' (Habermas 1991 p. 90), but the warning itself relies, as we shall see in a moment, upon the validity of its strict separation of philosophy and art. His targets in this warning are Heidegger and his successors, including Derrida.[31] Let us, then, first try to see some of what is worth keeping, and what is not, in Heidegger's later view. Heidegger's conception of truth in the later work, particularly after he has forsworn his direct 'activist' links to the Nazis, was implicit in the Lutheran model of interpretation we discussed in Chapter 4, connecting it to Gadamer. In this model truth is received, so that the subject is transformed by its encounter with the text. For the later Heidegger this is part of a happening, evident in the 'essential' thinkers and poets, like Hölderlin, in which 'Thinking is at the same time thinking of being, to the extent that thinking, in belonging ['*gehörend*', which hints at the verb '*hören*', to listen or hear, that is echoed at the end of the sentence] to being, listens to being' (Heidegger 1949 p. 8).

Heidegger understands the ever more important role of language for his conception in historical terms, talking of a 'process' in which 'language under the domination of the modern metaphysics of subjectivity almost continuously falls out of its element. Language still refuses us its essence: that it is the house of the truth of being' (ibid. p. 10). Instead of granting us this essence language has become 'an instrument of domination over entities' (ibid.), which means the only alternative is to wait to be 'spoken to by being again' (ibid.), thus by language which is the 'clearing-concealing arrival of being itself' (ibid. p. 18), rather than another articulation of entities. This language is the language of *Dichtung*. Heidegger maintains, therefore, that 'Being is still waiting for It itself to become worthy of thinking by man' (ibid. p. 14). At this point the cynic rightly asks: 'How does he know this is the case?', to which the only answer would seem to be that, unlike the cynic, Heidegger has been listening attentively enough. But what gives anyone the right to say that? This is exactly the problem of grounding language that we described above. The claim relies upon an intuition whose compelling force would remove the need for any kind of articulated validation, because a validation in this sense requires a grounded metaphysics of the kind Heidegger is seeking to avoid. In

Heidegger's terms, the language of *Dichtung* happens to be 'of being' in the subjective genitive, but we are offered no serious way of engaging with this notion beyond engaging with the *Dichtung* itself.

To the extent to which Heidegger's concern remains the idea that by listening appropriately one will begin to think being, and that language is being's 'house', we can fairly safely part company with him.[32] Citing Wittgenstein's *Tractatus*, Herbert Schnädelbach makes the vital point, which will also be relevant for Benjamin and Adorno, that '"A sentence can only say how a thing is, not what it is." There can be no predication which says (*ausspricht*) the thing itself', so the 'hope for a final *identity* of word and thing' implied in notions like the 'words of being' must be renounced (Schnädelbach 1992 p. 327).[33] Although this seems to me in many ways the decisive point to make in this context, I shall try to suggest a possible way of defending conceptions which invoke the idea of the unity of word and thing in relation to Adorno in Chapter 9. With regard to the notion of language advanced in the 'Letter on Humanism' and other, later, work Heidegger is his own worst enemy: vital aspects of his thought have already made it clear that what he later proposes is not necessarily the only way to think about the question of language and being. The version of ontological difference which we saw Tugendhat derive from the early Heidegger in Chapter 6, for example, makes much the same point as Schnädelbach does here, and the point is anyway implicit in some of Husserl's phenomenology and Heidegger's development of it in terms of the claim that understanding is always of a thing *as* something, and not a direct intuition of an object.

At the same time, the growing sense in Heidegger's later work that silence is the only real answer to the attempt not to slip back into a 'metaphysical' language of entities should not be dismissed out of hand.[34] The idea of renouncing philosophy as foundational discipline in the name of 'literature' was, as we have seen, already an important aspect of Romantic thinking and has often been associated with the modern revaluation of the importance of music for philosophy. In both language and music the very possibility of articulation is dependent, as Derrida has reminded us, upon the – silent – gaps between the moments of articulation, so that the sayable, as Frank puts it, depends upon the unsayable (see Frank 1989a). This makes some sense of what Heidegger mistakenly inflates into his view of language and being.[35] The idea that the most important things cannot be said but can only be shown or made available in 'allegorical' form may have religious roots, for example, in negative theology, but its modern manifestations cannot be reduced to their being a repetition of these roots. Instead the idea evidently relates to how the positive sciences, by bringing more and more of the world into the realm of causal explanation, leave less and less space in which people can make individual sense of their lives. The important issue here is to try to separate what is still a philosophical matter of importance for reflection upon truth in any area of articulation from those aspects of

articulation which are random performative or expressive events of importance only to those immediately engaged in them. The problem, especially
given the nature of avant-garde questions about the very status 'work of art'
and the nature of radical art itself in the later twentieth century, is that the
criteria for such distinctions are anything but obvious.

How, then, do these questions look in the light of Habermas' enterprise?
Habermas asserts that, within his conception, the 'potential for the creation
of meaning (*Sinn*) which today has largely withdrawn into aesthetic realms,
retains the contingency of truly innovatory powers' (Habermas 1985
p. 373). The question is exactly how this possibility of innovation relates
to the rest of his theory. Habermas' model of a new approach to 'post-
metaphysical' thinking depends, rather like Schleiermacher's *Dialectic*,
upon the ungroundable 'telos of agreement' which is always already present
in the 'concrete Apriori of world-disclosing language systems' (ibid.)
– hence the notion of the 'ideal speech situation'. He tries, therefore, to
give a methodological account of the kinds of validity entailed in differing
forms of 'communicative action', which would provide criteria, based on
what we always already do, for what can and cannot legitimately be asserted
or done. There are serious problems with this position, but it is first of all
informative to see why the problems cannot be revealed by using the later
Heidegger's position.

In the later Heidegger's terms *any* account of language qua communication necessarily makes language into an entity, because it, for the
reasons we have repeatedly observed, requires a ground and therefore
leads to the problem he sees as common to all versions of metaphysics. This
fundamental assumption, which *can* be made into an arguable position, leads
Heidegger, though, to a justly notorious piece of absurdity, on the basis
of his later almost paranoid conviction about the link between metaphysics
and technology-driven modern societies. He – really – claims: 'Meta-
language and Sputnik, metalinguistics and rocket technology are all the
same' (Heidegger 1959 p. 160). This can only be because a theory of language
needs to be language about language and therefore falls prey to the traps of
subject-based thinking we have been considering since Chapter 1, which
Heidegger thinks are inherent in all accounts of entities within a science.
That this judgement is not a one-off mistake is confirmed by his probably
even more grotesque equations of the Soviet Union with the United States,
or, effectively, anything in the modern world with anything else except
Dichtung, on the basis that this is a world constituted in terms of 'Western
metaphysics' which therefore does not listen to being. Although there
are very serious grounds for questioning the ways in which the modern world
is systematically constituted, what we need are ways of theorising both
the interrelationships and the differences between the consequences of a
commodity system, the reification of language, and the effects of increasingly
dominant natural science, not a verdict on modernity which blurs everything
into the Same.

Habermas is in many ways the ideal point of reference here: one of his major concerns is precisely the analysis of the relations between the world of modern systems and the 'life-world' in which people make sense of their lives. His attention to the ways in which we, as real embodied, feeling, worried and concerned subjects actually talk to each other and carry on political struggles is a breath of fresh air after the paranoid obsessiveness of some of the later Heidegger.[36] The assumption of the telos of agreement in everyday communication about the nature of what there is and what is to be done in the world must surely be unobjectionable for many kinds of communicative action: as we saw in relation to Schleiermacher, without some notion of agreement even the very idea of a dispute makes no sense. What makes Habermas' position problematic, though, are the ways in which he tries to distribute types of validity between the cognitive, the ethical and the aesthetic spheres. He regards the separation of the spheres as definitive of the liberation of modern philosophy from pre-modern conflations of myth and rationality, and thinks conflating them is characteristic of precisely the sort of politics for which Heidegger was in part responsible. The place from which such a separation could be undertaken is, however, precisely the kind of location which his theory needs to avoid: this will point to the moment of truth in Heidegger's absurdly hyperbolic approach to such theories.

The empirical fact that 'subjects capable of language and action' make fallible discriminations between the illocutionary intentions of their own and others' communicative actions, with respect to whether what is at issue is cognitive, ethical or expressive, is no basis for saying in a theory that there are in fact clearly definable lines of demarcation between the differing spheres of validation – if, of course, they are really spheres at all. To which sphere does the theory of communicative action itself belong? Here the choice would seem once again to be between a regress or an absolute presupposition.[37] Rorty refers to 'unfortunate residues of scientism in [Habermas'] thought' (Rorty 1991a p. 24), and this is one place where these residues are apparent. At this level there seems little alternative but to say that Habermas' theory takes the place of Kant's epistemological conditions of possibility, which are now seen in terms of a theory of communicative action that tries to ground the truth in what we always already do in the life-world. Even this is basically Kantian: Schnädelbach maintains, for example, that one can understand 'the transcendental as a whole as the *competence* of empirical human beings to *follow* certain rules and principles in thinking, cognition and action' (Schnädelbach 1992 p. 289). Given that Habermas admits the contingency of his starting point in the 'always already' present aspects of communication, this might again seem all there is to say about the matter, because there *is* no obvious alternative from this perspective. Two related questions arise here. One concerns the strict division, upon which we saw Habermas insisting above, between truth as a 'validity claim which we connect to statements when we assert them' (Habermas 1984 p. 129), and truth as the world-disclosure evident in the experience of the work of art; the other concerns the very notion of 'subject philosophy' itself.

From the hermeneutic point of view, which in many ways Habermas shares, the fact is that there can be no prior specific form of truth, because all kinds of truth are dependent on what Manfred Frank, in line with the Heidegger of *Being and Time*, terms 'truth-qua-comprehensibility', which is the ground of propositional truth (Frank 1992 p. 73 – my argument from now on will owe much to Frank's).[38] Habermas himself seemed to suggest something similar when he talked above of the 'concrete Apriori of world-disclosing language systems'. The assumption of truth-qua-comprehensibility/disclosure is what is required to avoid the regress of rules for rules which we considered in Chapter 5. It is therefore necessarily prior to any attempt to divide understanding into cognitive, ethical and aesthetic: this division requires a meta-rule for making the initial distinction between the kinds of understanding, and therefore threatens another regress. In this sense, as we saw, all truth relies upon a disclosure which cannot itself be grounded by giving primacy to the determinate truths arrived at in a particular 'ontic' science. The relativity of all such forms of disclosure is what concerned Novalis in *Monologue* and was one of Schlegel's key ideas. Now, as we have seen, Habermas, like Heidegger, presupposes the validity of the idea that modern philosophy has been dominated by the notion of the subject as the self-transparent ground of truth. What happens, though, when this assumption is itself put into question?

Heidegger's concern after *Being and Time* was to avoid the Cartesian idea that the ground of truth lay in the self-certainty of a subject. This notion has, though, been in question here all along, because, especially since Jacobi, none of the thinkers in Romantic philosophy we have looked at held to such a notion anyway. In Frank's terms:

> early Romanticism is convinced that being oneself owes itself to a transcendent ground which *cannot* be dissolved into the immanence of consciousness. In this way the ground of being oneself becomes a puzzle which cannot be finally interpreted. This puzzle can no longer be dealt with (alone) by reflection. For this reason philosophy ends in and as art.
> (Frank 1992 p. 62)

Rorty suggests some of the consequences one can draw from the notion that philosophy and art may be inseparable when he maintains that 'Important, revolutionary physics, and metaphysics, has always been "literary" in the sense that it has faced the problem of introducing new jargon and nudging aside the language-games currently in place' (Rorty 1991a p. 99).[39] This is a thoroughly Romantic conception, of course, and it suggests that art may indeed tell us something significant about the nature of truth. If it is true that those works which we term 'art' reveal what cannot be explained in other terms – one obvious model here is music, but something similar applies to the question of paraphrasing or translating a poem or describing what a painting shows, as well as to paradigm-shifting science – then these forms of articulation, by their very meaninglessness in the terms of established rule-based apprehension, and meaningfulness in terms of what happens when we engage with them, perhaps come closer to questions of truth in the life-world than the self-transparency of any philosophical theory. This position is reinforced by the fact that the results of 'art' can lead to propositionally formulated theories (but, importantly, not vice versa), as is evident in the example of metaphor discussed below.

If the idea that the subject is the transparent ground of truth has been renounced as a result of the failed paradigm of subject philosophy, how does truth relate to subjectivity at all in Habermas' account? Habermas suggests that the sole alternative for philosophy which does not make the move to intersubjectivity is between understanding subjects as 'either lords or [Heideggerian] shepherds of their language system' (Habermas 1985 p. 369). This is, though, a false alternative, based upon a reification of the notion of a thing called language, of the kind we questioned in earlier chapters. A better alternative is the following: either the elements of which literature 'consists' are from the outset the ready-made signifying material of language, whose meaning is guaranteed because that material is based on rules generated in social practices that can be reconstructed in a theory of communicative action or a formal semantics, or the process which becomes visible in a 'literary' text is actually the prior key to the way in which language and truth are to be understood.

The most immediately available location for examining these issues at the empirical level is metaphor. Davidson claims that metaphor 'makes us notice things', which is another way of suggesting that it is a form of 'world-disclosure'. Paul Ricoeur has suggested in this respect that:

> We certainly know of no other manner of functioning of language than the one in which an order is already constituted; metaphor constitutes a new order only by creating deviations within a given order; can we not, despite this, begin with the idea that the order itself emerges in the same way as it changes? Is not, in Gadamer's phrase, a 'metaphorics' at work in the origin of logical thinking, at the root of every classification?
>
> (Ricoeur 1986 pp. 28–9)

Frank's contention, against the dominant ways of seeing this issue from Heidegger to Gadamer, as well as in most analytical philosophy which works with the idea of 'objective representation' (see Chapters 4 and 5), is that the only defensible location of this metaphorics is the subject. The basis for his contention is the Romantic conception recalled in the quotation from Frank cited above.

The Romantic subject is clearly not the lord of its language, because, in one important sense, there is nothing to be lord of: without the ungroundable assumption of the existence of a final meta-linguistic description, of the kind required by most versions of semantics or semiotics, the very ability to make the claim that one is lord of a symbolic order, of a 'thing called language', becomes incoherent.[40] One would in these terms have to be lord of something that, qua total system, one has no guarantee even exists. The order in question cannot, in Romantic terms, be a pre-existing structure or just a series of rule-bound praxes. It is, rather, a series of socially established virtual discriminations which continually have to be interpreted and negotiated anew in changing contexts. The prior aspect is therefore that which interprets: as we saw Novalis saying in Chapter 6: 'The whole of language is a *postulate*. . . . One must agree to think certain things in relation to certain signs' (Novalis 1978 p. 347). By the same token, it is equally invalid to see the subject merely as the object of the symbolic order or as the 'shepherd' who guards the integrity of a language: the rules of language only give rise to *meaning* via what Schleiermacher termed the 'art' of interpretation. 'Meaning' (remembering the doubts about substantivising the term) is constituted in the inherently individual interpretative acts of a subject in a context: that was the point of the regress-of-rules argument. This means the rules can – but need not – be altered by the influence of the subject, a fact which is most immediately apparent in the genesis of new metaphors and in 'style' in Schleiermacher's sense. Evidently such alterations also come about because the world itself changes, but these changes have to be *interpreted* as changes and cannot themselves provide an explanation of the new ways of 'seeing as' to which they are – non-causally – linked. There are, then, in these terms, serious reasons for retaining the sort of connection between art and truth which Heidegger attempted to develop, albeit from a different vantage point.

The challenge is to arrive at a theory which is philosophically serious, because it can cater for the kind of propositional truth which Heidegger was too ready to condemn as merely instrumental – and to this extent the work of Habermas still offers plenty of vitally important arguments – at the same time as understanding the nature of the resources available for the development of new truths evident in art. If it is right that semantic and semiotic conceptions, which both rely on the 'subversion' of the subject by language, do not adequately theorise what is at issue here, then the wider sense of truth as disclosure, in which the articulation of the truth of our being in the world also entails an exploration of the non-propositional aspects of self-consciousness, becomes a central philosophical issue. The aim must be, then, to develop a theory which, while taking into account approaches to truth developed in the semantic tradition, no longer occludes those dimensions of our self-understanding and understanding of the world which cannot be reduced to what can be said about them. Such a theory would result from the change in priority between truth as comprehensibility and truth as propositional truth which seems to me the salvageable core of what Heidegger revealed in the best parts of 'The Origin of the Work of

Art'. The dangers we saw in that essay and elsewhere in Heidegger's work
clearly derive from the problematic relationship to political rationality of
any theory which gives art a central role in our understanding of truth. It is
in the light of these dangers that the theories of Benjamin and Adorno will
now be examined.

8 Understanding Walter Benjamin

LANGUAGE AND ORIGINS

The work of Walter Benjamin has now begun to play a major role in many investigations into the nature of modernity. It is understood, to take just a few examples, as offering resources for understanding how technology affects the status of the work of art, for rethinking the very nature of historical time, for opening up new possibilities of reading literary texts, and for re-defining how the relationships between culture and politics are to be understood. Benjamin's work remains, though, in many ways a mystery. This is not least because many of its contexts are still too rarely explored in sufficient depth. The importance for the understanding of his work of Benjamin's Ph.D. dissertation on the German Romantics,[1] for example, still tends to be underestimated.[2] Given that, as I hope to have established, Romantic philosophy is still significant for the contemporary philosophical scene, a reassessment of Benjamin which gives initial priority to his work on the Romantics seems overdue. The fact that the focus of Benjamin's work, from the beginning to the desperately bitter end,[3] can be characterised in terms of the relationships between language, art and truth will allow us to suggest how some of his work poses questions that are of interest to contemporary philosophy, both analytical and hermeneutic (see also Bowie 1995a).

The reception of Benjamin's work has, though, made these matters rather problematic: his explicit and implicit connections to traditions of thought, like Jewish mysticism, which not uncommonly regard clarity as a positive obstacle to truth, have sometimes led his commentators either to a rejection of his work as impenetrably esoteric or to a dutiful dependence on the terms which Benjamin himself establishes. The reactions of commentators to his work too rarely show the independence of mind characteristic of Benjamin himself. The fact should also not be ignored that some of what Benjamin wrote has turned out to offer little which can be said to stand up to methodological scrutiny. Although it is a mistake to try simply to reduce Benjamin to other, perhaps more familiar or accessible terms, without the attempt to translate him out of his own idioms his work risks becoming merely the esoteric preserve of the growing Benjamin industry.

Take, then, one example of a possibility for a more critical interrogation of Benjamin. It is clear that at times Benjamin comes philosophically very close to Heidegger's accounts of the relationship between the idea that truth is expressed most reliably in the propositions of natural science and the idea that such 'truth' in fact obscures the real truth of being. If this parallel is not taken seriously we will fail to see how Benjamin relates to a whole series of issues we have already investigated. The obvious justification for taking it seriously is, of course, that one source of the parallel is the common links of both Heidegger and Benjamin to Kant and Romanticism. A further reason for pondering this question is that, despite their proximity in this respect, Benjamin went in almost exactly the opposite political direction to Heidegger.[4] Now there is clearly no space here for a detailed investigation of Benjamin's labyrinthine oeuvre, so I shall concentrate on some aspects which can illuminate – and be illuminated by – the major issues we have considered so far. This will entail concentrating on his earlier texts: his Marxist work, which has been the object of most of the attention to Benjamin, will be only briefly considered in relation to issues in the early work and at the end of the chapter.[5] This necessary limitation can be balanced by the fact that some of the most important issues the Marxist work raises will be dealt with in Chapter 9 when I look at Adorno. It can also be balanced, as I shall show at the end, by the fact that the core of Benjamin's work is already developed in the *Trauerspielbuch*. After appearing to reject some of that book's ideas in essays like 'The Work of Art in the Age of Its Mechanical Reproducibility', his last work demonstrably returns to those ideas.

One of the biggest problems here is whether, in the face of the enormous apparent divergence of Benjamin's theoretical positions – from theologically influenced reflections on language to analyses of the effects of the commodity structure on perception in modern societies – to treat his various approaches to his major themes as separate from each other, or to try to show an underlying continuity. In interpreting many thinkers the attempt to show hidden continuities can become counter-productive, because it levels vital distinctions between different phases of their work. This would seem to be the case for Nietzsche and Wittgenstein, for example. Benjamin is different in this respect, because the hidden continuities beneath the manifest differences can help us understand better the often oblique nature of his theoretical enterprise. At the same time there is no point in pretending that this interpretative approach is unproblematic: the sources of Benjamin's work are so diverse, and so many of them are never made explicit, that the task of philological interpretation becomes thoroughly intractable if one aims to be comprehensive even for a small part of the work. Benjamin himself offers some help here: one of his central theoretical ideas is that the truth about an object of study can emerge via the establishing of a new 'constellation', or context for that object. This involves wrenching it out of the kinds of context which dominant philological assumptions deem apposite. My contention will be that the constellation already established here sheds vital light on Benjamin's work.[6]

Rather than beginning immediately with the dissertation on the Romantics I want first to consider aspects of some earlier work that reveal a continuity in the main themes at issue in the present book. In an essay on 'Two Poems of Friedrich Hölderlin', of 1914–15, Benjamin takes us *in medias res* by citing Novalis' dictum that 'Every work of art has an ideal a priori, a necessity in itself to be there' in relation to the claim that his approach to the poems is meant to

> disclose that particular area which contains the truth of the poetry (*Dichtung*). This 'truth', which precisely the most serious artists assert so emphatically of their creations, is to be understood as the objectivity of their creation, as the fulfilment of the particular artistic task.
>
> (GS II 1 p. 105)[7]

The truth in question is, though, to be arrived at independently of considerations to do with the author of the work, having rather to do with a 'certain context of life determined by art' (ibid. p. 107). Artistic production can lead the poet to a truth which everyday life would never have offered, had the need both to render aspects of the world intelligible and to live up to the formal demands of a genre imposed by art not intervened. In the dissertation on the Romantics, Benjamin will, in line with the contentions of the present book, cite Novalis' dictum as signalling

> the overcoming in principle of dogmatic rationalism in aesthetics. For this is a viewpoint to which the evaluation of the work according to rules could never lead, as little as could a theory which understood the work as the product of a mind of genius. (GS I 1 p. 76)

Benjamin's concern is with what he terms – in a manner which prefigures the etymologies of the later Heidegger in relation to '*Dichtung*', 'poetry' – the '*Gedichtete*'.[8] This is defined as the unity of the 'inner form of the particular creation', which is not identical with the work, the '*Dichtung*' or the '*Gedicht*', itself. The type of analysis proposed in the Hölderlin essay aims to reveal the 'task' of the poem, which may not actually be fully solved by the poem itself. The structure suggested by this is crucial: the gap between the aesthetic object as empirical object of analysis – what Heidegger terms an 'entity' – and the ways in which the object discloses truth will remain constitutive for Benjamin's work throughout his life, from the understanding of the 'Idea' of German baroque *Trauerspiel* considered below, to the interpretation of film and mass media as possible means of political transformation. There is, though, also a danger here, of which Benjamin only sometimes seems aware, namely that the 'truth' revealed in such an approach can be simply imposed from outside the work. The opposing danger is, of course, that in trying to sustain the work's integrity as a self-contained work of art its truth-content cannot emerge at all.

The vital aspect of engagement with the literary work, Benjamin maintains, using ideas with which we are already familiar from Romantic theory, is not the analysis of 'elements' of the poem, in the sense of the final constituents which philology can analyse or locate via other related contexts. Instead:

> all unities in the poem already appear in an intensive interpenetration, the elements are never purely graspable, rather only the web (*Gefüge*) of the relationships [is graspable] in which the identity of the individual being (*Wesen*) is a function of an endless chain of rows in which the *Gedichtete* unfolds itself. (GS II 1 p. 112)

The 'task' of the work is not the subjective intention of the author, nor is it to be derived merely from knowledge of the poet's world. It is, rather, the 'limit concept' of the analysis, what the analysis would reach were it to be complete. This would, in line with Novalis' dictum, be the truth about why the poem is there, the truth about that in the world to which the poem is a 'solution'. What is meant has to do with the Romantic ideas, both that the world is a world of changing relationships, not of determinate things, and that, at the same time, truth remains a normative obligation, as well as with the notion of the 'completion of the work' which Benjamin discusses in the dissertation. In this case the obligation that derives from engagement with the work is to find an appropriate way of responding to the *Gedicht* by revealing the *Gedichtete*. Benjamin's essay does, then, begin to open up some interesting perspectives which were anything but common at the time he wrote it, and which Adorno will develop right up to the end of his life (for example, in his essay on Hölderlin). The sense that the elements of the poem are always already inseparable from the other elements in the context of a world which cannot be made finally determinable is, as we have seen, common both to aspects of Romantic literary theory and to the assumptions of deconstruction. However, despite moments of insight which point to important questions, Benjamin's essay is written in a self-consciously oblique manner which does little to add to the basic argument.

In the two essays '*Trauerspiel* and Tragedy' and 'The Meaning of Language in *Trauerspiel* and Tragedy' of 1916, Benjamin's allusiveness ceases to be just a mannerism, and more successfully becomes part of the attempt to condense essential thoughts into a constellation, in which the manner of their presentation affects how the thoughts in that constellation can be understood. Here we begin to encounter themes that recur as major issues in his later works, themes which are derived from the philosophical questions we have considered so far. One example will have to suffice here. The core of his conception of tragedy is the understanding of time: the tragic hero's very nature, Benjamin claims, is a result of the incompatibility of individual heroism, which is constituted in terms of the 'fulfilled time' of that individual at the height of their career, with an objective order of ineluctable necessity that transcends all individuals and inherently leads to their demise. Tragedy *is* precisely the clash between this order and the individual hero's sense of fulfilled time.

Time, as Heidegger claimed, is a vital key to the questions of 'metaphysics', in the sense of the word we have seen emerge via Jacobi. Benjamin suggests what is at issue in the relationship of this version of metaphysics to time when he asserts that 'The time of history is infinite in every direction and unfulfilled at every moment. This means that no single empirical event is thinkable which would have an essential relationship to the specific time in which it occurs' (ibid. p. 134). Unfulfilled time is, therefore, an aspect of 'nihilism' in Jacobi's sense: the identity of a moment of unfulfilled time depends exclusively upon its relationships to other moments. In order to make the overall argument of this chapter clearer, it is worth already mentioning here that the structure in question will allow Benjamin later to move from these essentially theological questions to questions about the way commodity structure affects modern culture. The basis of this move should already be apparent from the discussion in Chapter 7 of the links between forms of differentially constituted system in modernity. 'Fulfilled time', the time of what Benjamin throughout most of his work terms 'messianism', has to do with 'truth', which, as in Jacobi's 'the true' (and Heidegger's 'being'), is linked to revelation, to the ground of relational truths which can render merely relational 'knowledge' meaningful.[9] The crucial point is that '*Trauerspiel*', which is for Benjamin the artistic form that exemplifies the changes in language characteristic of modernity, breaks with the idea of fulfilled time. *Trauerspiel* does so because its concern is with transience without the possibility of redemption. Tragedy is constituted in a world where the horrors imposed by necessity at least make sense because they are part of an order manifest in the language of that world. *Trauerspiel*, on the other hand, is the form of art which can no longer make the destructiveness of time meaningful by containing it in a form, in the manner Greek tragedy did for the *polis*.[10] The concern with temporality evident here will turn out to be perhaps the dominant underlying concern in all Benjamin's work.

Because the form of *Trauerspiel* is 'unclosed in itself' it can no longer be part of the 'area' of drama, so that 'the remainder (*Rest*) of *Trauerspiel* is music' (ibid. p. 137).[11] What exactly does this last remark mean? The answer lies in Benjamin's theory of language and is vital for his overall conception. I have already told various versions of the story of how the perception of language in modernity changes in the wake of the process of secularisation, thereby giving rise both to hermeneutics in the forms described in preceding chapters and to the related changes in the understanding of music. Benjamin's version of this story is characteristically oblique, not least because of its strange relationship to theological conceptions of language, and of its link to a rather obscure form of drama. Let us, then, try to elucidate a few aspects of the conception of language in the second essay on tragedy and *Trauerspiel*, and in the essay 'On Language and on Human Language', which is also from 1916.[12]

The decisive contrast in the second essay is between the idea of tragedy as based upon a cosmic order manifested in the language of tragedy itself, and the idea of *Trauerspiel*, in which such an order no longer obtains. This lack of an intrinsic order changes the very nature of language. Whereas tragedy is constituted in language in which 'the word as pure carrier of its meaning is the pure word' (ibid. p. 138), 'the linguistic principle of *Trauerspiel* is the word in transformation' (ibid.). The point about *Trauerspiel* is that it relies on a 'feeling' – '*Trauer*', 'mourning' – rather than upon a necessary prior order of the world:

> What metaphysical relationship does this feeling have to the word, to spoken language (*Rede*)? That is the puzzle of *Trauerspiel*. What inner relationship in the essence of mourning makes it step out of the existence of pure feelings and into the order of art? (ibid.)

For there to be a link between these works and truth, art must be more than subjective expression, but if the works depend on 'feeling' they would seem to be irredeemably subjective. The crucial thing to notice is that Benjamin's notion of language is not restricted to the spoken or written word. What he tries to do, once again in a manner close to the Romantics, is to see language as inseparable from being. Language in these terms exists as a continuum of forms of articulation which begins in nature and ends in art. 'Natural languages' emerge in a manner to which we have no direct theoretical access: this means that any attempt to understand the very essence of language via consideration of its origins is forced to consider all forms of articulation as possible clues to that understanding. Recourse to metaphor is therefore inevitable, because the semantic level of language cannot be regarded as the starting point of such an investigation: what is at issue begins before anything which can be characterised in purely semantic terms. This is the reason for the connection of language to music, though Benjamin's story about this connection is anything but straightforward.

Benjamin claims that

> *Trauerspiel* . . . describes the route from the sound of nature, via lament, to music. In *Trauerspiel* the sound explicates itself ['*legt sich auseinander*' in the sense of to 'laying itself out'] symphonically and this is at once the musical principle of its language and the dramatic principle of its division and splitting into characters. It is nature which, only for the sake of the purity of its feelings, climbs into the purifying fire of language, and the essence of *Trauerspiel* is already contained in the old lore, that all nature would begin to lament if it were given language. (ibid.)

However, instead of the move of nature to language being a liberation of feeling, 'nature sees itself betrayed by language' because it is 'inhibited': the result of this inhibition is 'meaning', in the sense of that which is governed by rules. 'Meaning' and 'history' accompany each other in 'human language', because human language 'rigidifies in meaning' (ibid. p. 139). The link of the establishment of human law, as a condition of the ability to write history,[13] to the emergence of codified forms of language has a long tradition. The establishment of law is often understood as a form of the repression that Lacan refers to as the 'insertion into the symbolic order', which separates the subject from the self-transparency of the pre-linguistic 'imaginary'. Benjamin's story can be made some sense of as a metaphysical (and metaphorical) story about the nature of language, even if its historical status is unclear. This is already evident from the way in which the basic structures of the story can be mapped on to Derrida's critique of Husserl which we considered in Chapter 6, where the notional purity of the transcendental subject is subverted by its need for language, or on to Lacan's reflections about language 'defiling' the subject.

The idea of an inhibition of 'creation' which 'wished to pour itself out in purity' (ibid.) also has antecedents in Romantic thought (and in aspects of mystical thinking with which the Romantics were familiar). In much the same way as Heidegger contrasted 'earth' and 'world' by taking up aspects of Schelling's vision of the interaction of contractive and expansive forces, Benjamin's view of the 'inhibition' of nature which 'spreads mourning over nature' (ibid. p. 139) almost exactly echoes Schelling's idea of the 'veil of melancholy which is spread over the whole of nature, the deep indestructible melancholy of all life' (Schelling (I/7) p. 399) in the essay 'On the Essence of Human Freedom'.[14] For Schelling, in much the same way as for Benjamin, this 'melancholy' results from the situation in which, for the world to be determinate, to have forms at all, the expansive force must be inhibited by the contractive force if it is not just to dissipate itself. The result is that when the expansive force succeeds in manifesting itself as something determinate, the 'something' must again 'go to ground' if the condition of possibility of determinacy is not to contradict its own essence as expansion by itself becoming determinate. In the *Ages of the World* Schelling links this idea to music: 'For because sound and note only seem to arise in that battle between spirituality and corporeality [which can also be 'expansive' and 'contractive', or 'predicative' and 'pronominal'], music (*Tonkunst*) alone can be an image of that primeval nature and its movement' (Schelling 1946 p. 43: on this see Bowie 1990 Chapter 8, Bowie 1993 Chapter 5).[15] In *Trauerspiel*, Benjamin claims, the 'redeeming mystery is music; the rebirth of feelings in a supersensuous nature': music is 'the language of pure feeling', and 'Where in tragedy the eternal rigidity of the spoken word asserts itself (*sich erhebt*), *Trauerspiel* gathers the endless resonance of its sound' (GS II 1 p. 140). This resonance is the 'play' – the '*Spiel*' – of 'tension and resolution of feeling' (ibid. p. 139) manifest in 'mourning', '*Trauer*'. Whatever doubts one may have about this extravagantly speculative conception, it does suggest ways of understanding why it is that in the modern period so much attention is paid in art to what everyday language seems to prevent us being able to articulate. Semantic stability grounded in learnable rules can become a repression of the need for language which can release fundamental tensions in our very being, as some forms of psychoanalysis also maintain. What this means in relation to truth will concern us later. Benjamin's early interpretation of *Trauerspiel*, which he claims in 1926 to be the 'primal cell' (GS II 3 p. 930) of the *Trauerspielbuch* – and thereby of dominant ideas in his work as a whole – does, then, take us to the heart of his concern with language.

The essay 'On Language and on Human Language' develops some of the issues just discussed and at the same time introduces a series of problems that will recur in all Benjamin's pre-Marxist work (and, albeit less obviously, in some of the Marxist work). Language here is again by no means restricted to verbal language: 'the existence of language . . . extends to absolutely everything' (GS II 1 p. 140), 'there is nothing in which we can imagine the complete absence of language' (ibid. p. 141). Language is that *in* – Benjamin insists that it is not 'through' – which things 'communicate their spiritual essence' (ibid.): this 'essence' is not the same as the 'linguistic essence'. Benjamin gives the example of a lamp:

> The language of this lamp, e.g., does not communicate the lamp (for the spiritual essence of the lamp, to the extent to which it is *communicable*, is certainly not the lamp itself), but: the language-lamp, the lamp in the communication, the lamp in the expression . . . what is communicable in a spiritual being *is* its language. On this 'is' (which is the same as 'is immediately') everything depends. (ibid. p. 142)

The only way that this might make sense is if one equates being with 'being true' in the manner of Heidegger: the lamp is only the lamp in that it is 'disclosed' as such. True is only true in a language – albeit now in the sense that both language and 'being' are forms of intelligible articulation which are at least analogous, and possibly identical – hence the importance of finding a true way of understanding '*Sprache überhaupt*', 'language in general/as a whole'. Language now has to explain language if the 'is' is to be understood. The circularity involved here should be familiar: it is one source of Heidegger's 'ontological difference', the difference between 'being', in the sense of something being *as* something, the lamp *as* the lamp, which is the condition of possibility of propositional truth, and the untenable idea that the 'entity' the lamp could itself be intuited. The latter idea led, as we saw in Chapter 6, to the Parmenidean problem of non-being: how could we say the lamp did not exist without positing its existence in some form which is then thoroughly inexplicable? Like the later Heidegger, though, Benjamin begins to move in questionable directions because of the ways in which he sees language as coming to conceal the truth of being.

Schnädelbach made the key point in Chapter 7, when he maintained via Wittgenstein that '"A sentence can only say how a thing is, not what it is". There can be no predication which says (*ausspricht*) the thing itself'

(Schnädelbach 1992 p. 327). Benjamin's approach relies, as we have seen, upon extending the notion of 'language' so that it means something like 'being' in Heidegger's sense. He wishes thereby to reject the 'bourgeois conception' of language, in which 'The means of communication is the word, its object the thing (*Sache*), its addressee a person' (GS II. 1 p. 144). At this point, however, things begin to go awry, and will recurrently do so in other work concerned with this issue. Benjamin is aware that what things can be 'seen as' – the structure which underlies, as Heidegger shows, what can be predicated of any entity – is unlimited. Is there, though – and this seems to be what Benjamin wants – a way in which language 'really' designates the truth in a manner which does not lead into the endless possibilities inherent in the 'as structure'? In Heidegger, the notion of such a language came to involve the notion of 'listening' and of a non-instrumental relationship to things, of the kind manifest in *Dichtung* that speaks the 'words of being'. Benjamin now makes a distinction between the languages of nature and the 'naming' language of humankind, such that '*The linguistic essence of humankind is, therefore, that it names things*' (ibid. p. 143). His alternative to the – indeed indefensible – 'bourgeois conception', he maintains, 'has no means, no object and no addressee of the communication. It claims that, *in the name, the spiritual essence of man communicates itself to God*' (ibid.). The fact that 'names', not what is predicated of names, let alone the whole structure of the proposition, are the essential aspect of language points to the problem Schnädelbach indicated above: the true being of the object must here be assumed already to exist, and is what would be expressed by its 'name'. The argument, as one would expect of an argument about a 'ready-made world', becomes thoroughly theological, in that 'God's creation completes itself when things receive their names from humankind' (ibid. p. 144). The fact that creation requires such completion is, again in analogy to Schelling's 'Freedom' essay, the essence of human freedom, and thus the source of possible untruth, which occurs when the name given to the thing distances it from what Benjamin terms 'the Word'.

We need here to be clear about two things: first the reasons for the theological position, and second the philosophical consequences which ensue from that position. The underlying issue in both cases is the question of truth. Benjamin himself says, soon after writing the essay, that 'for me the questions concerning the essence of cognition, law, art are connected to the question of the origin of all human spiritual expressions from the essence of language' (GS II 3 p. 932). If one wishes to understand 'being', in the sense of the world's being disclosed, then the evident theological route which allows one to connect theology and philosophy is one which links language to God and the creation. Benjamin was familiar with Judaic and Christian traditions which see creation in terms of 'the Word', as in the opening of John I in the Bible: 'In the beginning was the Word, and the Word was with God, and the Word was God.' Benjamin's close friend and perhaps the most important Judaist of the century, Gershom Scholem, will later assert that in the tradition of the Kabbala 'the movement in which creation takes place is . . . interpretable as a movement of language' (Scholem 1970 p. 33), and that the 'essence of the world is language' (ibid. p. 10). Similar reflections are also present in Schelling's *Ages of the World*, which was also influenced by the Kabbala (see Bowie 1993 Chapter 5).

In line with such conceptions Benjamin now distinguishes between the fact that 'In God the name is creative because it is Word' and the fact that 'All human language is only a reflex of the Word in the name. The name as little reaches the Word as cognition reaches creation' (GS II 1 p. 149). In this sense 'cognition' is always based on the lack of the final identity of Word and name: 'Humankind is the knower of the same language in which God is creator' (ibid.). Schelling, in a text which one assumes Benjamin did not know, but whose essential idea can also be found in early Romantic thinking with which Benjamin was familiar, maintains in the same vein that 'in man . . . there is no objective bringing forth, but rather just ideal imitation (*ideales Nachbilden*) . . . in him there is only knowledge' (Schelling 1969 p. 27). The question here is how to theorise truth in a manner which does not fall into the traps we have already seen in the later Heidegger. In one sense, what Benjamin offers is an anti-representational conception of truth, because the name and the Word structurally cannot coincide, but the conception seems, at the same time, to rely ultimately on the 'representational' idea that cognition and creation could or should mirror each other.[16]

Benjamin develops this conception of language in the essay for a vital reason, which is where the most serious problems emerge. He wants to oppose the 'bourgeois' conception, for which 'the word relates to the thing contingently', as a 'sign of the things (or of their cognition) posited by some convention or other' (GS II 1 p. 150). The conception of the arbitrariness of the sign he wishes to oppose is these days familiar from literary theory, in its appropriation of Saussure's linguistics. Benjamin does not, however, simply invert the 'bourgeois' position: even though 'language never gives *mere* signs' the mystical conception in which 'the Word is absolutely the essence of the thing' is rejected because the thing has to be communicated via the name, and is therefore never fully 'present', as it would be in the Word. Instead there is a constant process of 'translation', '*Übersetzung*' – in both English and German the term is connected to the notion of 'metaphor' – 'of the language of things into that of humankind'. In a manner close to Hamann, whom he cites in this connection, Benjamin claims that 'every higher language (with the exception of the Word of God) can be regarded as a translation of all others' (GS II 1 pp. 151–2).

Odd as Benjamin's approach may be, it does address an issue central to nearly any area of contemporary philosophy. The initial question for Benjamin himself is not so much the fact of translatability, which is ultimately catered for by theology, as how one thinks about the plurality of languages itself. At this point he talks about the Fall, the tower of Babel and the like, as ways of suggesting why there is a plurality of natural languages.[17] Other aspects of the philosophical view implied here are, however, more interesting than the questionable theology. In analytical philosophy, translation is important because the same proposition seems expressible both by different sentences in the same language and different sentences in differing languages,[18] which means the proposition can be true beyond a particular language, even though there is no agreement as to how this is possible. The problem arises for this view if one thinks translatability is a reason for accepting an essentially Platonic conception of truth, of the kind suggested by the idea of the Word. The *locus classicus* of the question of translation in analytical philosophy is Quine's *Word and Object*, which looks at how the 'field linguist' can learn to translate from a position of initial total ignorance of a culture and a language. The 'indeterminacy of translation' that results from the possibility of having differing 'translation manuals' for the same utterances in an object language leads, though, not to the 'impossibility of translation', but to the need to think, as we saw in relation to Malpas' account of indeterminacy in Chapter 3 (and in Chapter 5), in a different way about the notion of meaning. What does Benjamin have to offer here?

The consequences Benjamin draws that matter for the rest of our investigation are that, after 'the Fall',

> The word is supposed to communicate something (outside/except [*außer*] itself). . . . As humankind steps out of the pure language of the name it makes language into a means (namely of a cognition which is inappropriate to it), thereby in one part at least into a *mere* sign . . . the origin of abstraction as a capacity of the spirit of language may also be sought in the Fall. (ibid. pp. 152–4)

Human language has, then, lost touch with the Word, and therefore 'over-names' (in the sense of 'overdetermines') things, rather in the way Quine's 'indeterminacy of translation' results because of the lack of any determinable Platonic entities called 'meanings'. Now Benjamin regards this situation as a deep metaphysical problem, rather than as something which, as the early Heidegger, Davidson and Rorty suggest, is pragmatically dealt with all the time by real language users. Seeing the very nature of cognition itself as a problem in the manner Benjamin suggests will, however, only become a serious theoretical option when the 'origin of abstraction' is located historically as part of the specific constellation which links language, political economy and metaphysical systems. Benjamin's view here threatens to generalise what ought to be a specific conception of abstraction into an ontological claim. Lurking in his view at this time is the notion of an origin of truth that we have supposedly lost, which has led to the post-Babel confusion of languages. But the simple fact is that nothing that we know from anthropology, linguistics, history or any other empirically-based discipline can salvage this conception. The only question that still offers the hope of any significant philosophical insight into truth in this sense is whether the languages of art offer something which the analysis of languages and the world in determinate sciences does not. This will also be the case for some key aspects of the work of Adorno.

Towards the end of Benjamin's essay, art makes an appearance: 'For the cognition of the forms of art it is a matter of trying to grasp them all as languages and to seek their connections with the languages of nature' (ibid. p. 156). The claim is reminiscent of Novalis' remark that 'art belongs to nature and is, so to speak, nature which looks at itself, imitates itself, forms itself' (Novalis 1978 p. 766), an idea Novalis also connects to language. The problematic aspect of Benjamin's conception lies in the way he wishes to link such a conception of art to the idea that art can restore something like the integrity of the 'name', and thus keep the hope for the 'Word' alive. One aspect of his account prefigures the later Heidegger's sense of the interplay of revelation and concealment, on the basis of the Romantic 'topos of unsayability': 'language in every case is not just the communication of what can be communicated, but at the same time symbol of what cannot be communicated' (GS II 1 p. 156). His overall conception is, though, little different from the hope of hearing the 'words of being', and something like it will also recur in the weakest parts of Adorno's work. Now it does seem to me possible to try to think of truth, in Romantic fashion, as a goal which we can never say we have reached, but which we understand via our very sense that anything we determinately assert is open to potential revision. Something like this view has, for example, recently been advanced in Hilary Putnam's notion of truth as idealised consensus. This, however, does not mean we can *assert* that the ideal of consensus is even potentially realisable: all we can assert is that our experience of truth is of an ongoing insufficiency which yet sustains the continuing demand for a better account. As I have tried to suggest, this can be turned into an account of the intrinsically normative nature of truth, which can be importantly connected to questions of art. Benjamin, though, does not see it this way.

Benjamin wants to keep alive the idea of a theological promise that is inherent in the very fact of language, which would require a truth that really *is* the identity of language and world suggested by the Word. This might appear to be a Romantic idea, of the kind implied in Novalis' remark that 'The so-called arbitrary signs may in the last analysis not be so arbitrary as they appear – but yet stand in a certain real connection with what they designate' (Novalis 1978 p. 540). The Romantics, though, do not always fall into the trap which is inherent in the relationship Benjamin wants to sustain between name and Word.[19] Novalis' remark is in the subjunctive and serves, in the context of many of his other anti-foundational remarks, to suggest that, although language cannot in one evident sense be separate from the nature which it designates, and is itself also manifested in the form of natural objects, the manner in which signs are not necessarily arbitrary can only be articulated as a conjecture. Kant suggested that nature may speak to us via its beautiful forms, even though we can make no cognitive claim to this effect.[20] If we are to take Benjamin's early theological convictions seriously, as I think we must, much of his early work does not actually reach the level of the best work of the Romantics that we have examined. What, then, of his own Ph.D. dissertation on the Romantics of 1919, *The Concept of Art-Critique in German Romanticism*, and its relationship to his more well-known theories? Many of the structures that have concerned us in preceding chapters also play a role in Benjamin's work, but how does his development of their implications compare with the positions we have already investigated?

'THE CONCEPT OF ART-CRITIQUE IN GERMAN ROMANTICISM'

Benjamin's dissertation on the Romantics has not just been neglected by English-language literary theorists and philosophers. The lack of serious theoretical, rather than merely historical attention by English-language Germanists, not only to Benjamin's account of Romantic theory but even to Romantic theory itself, helps explain deep-rooted differences in the assumptions concerning the nature and object of the study of literature on the part of those who want to 'get on with the job' of literary criticism and literary history and of those who think this job too often involves a complacent ignoring of vital philosophical problems. The contemporary literary scholar's aversion to 'talking epistemology' (see Chapter 1 note 7) is evidently nothing new. Benjamin, who manages to get his Ph.D. past the traditionalists but soon afterwards suffers at their hands by being warned to withdraw his *Habilitation* (the *Trauerspielbuch*), insists in his Ph.D. – clearly against the grain of the literary study of the time – that Schlegel's theory of art, let alone his theory of the 'critique of art', is 'most decisively based on epistemological presuppositions, without knowledge of which it remains incomprehensible' (GS I 1 p. 15). What, then, are these presuppositions, which until recently most Germanists seemed to think they could ignore? The journey we have already made through the icy wastes of epistemological reflection should make Benjamin's famously difficult dissertation more accessible. His starting point is in fact the already familiar question of grounding modern philosophy, in exactly the form in which we have considered it so far.

Let us therefore first look briefly again at these issues, as a prelude to outlining the main argument of the dissertation. This will demonstrate the substantial degree of continuity that is present in the story I am trying to establish. Taking us into familiar territory, Benjamin cites Schlegel's observation that 'Jacobi has got caught between absolute and systematic philosophy, and there his spirit has been crushed' (ibid. p. 46, see also

Schlegel 1963 p. 115, and cf. Schlegel 1988 Vol 2 p. 140), remarking that 'Schlegel not infrequently turned against Jacobi in order to castigate his own defects in public' (GS I 1 p. 46). By 'absolute' philosophy, as the related *Athenäum* fragment shows, Schlegel means Leibniz, because Leibniz bases his thought on the absolute individuality of the monads, the irreducible elements of his universe that are co-ordinated by pre-established harmony. The monads are therefore supposedly not just 'conditioned conditions', despite their relating to each other via the principle of sufficient reason in much the same manner as Spinoza's 'conditions'. By 'systematic' philosophy Schlegel means Spinoza, for the reasons concerning the notion of system we have repeatedly seen.[21] The dilemma to which Schlegel's work is a response is, Benjamin claims, how to 'grasp the system in an absolute manner' (ibid. p. 45): this enterprise was 'the essence of [Schlegel's] mysticism' and the enterprise was 'fateful' (*verhängnisvoll*) (ibid.) in what it revealed. What it revealed relates to the problems articulated by Jacobi. However, it is important for the version of the story I wish to tell that Schlegel need not be read quite in the way Benjamin suggests. Given that a lot of discussion of Benjamin is concerned with his relationship to mysticism, it is important to get this straight. Schlegel was indeed very concerned with the nature of philosophical systems, and never produced one that could satisfy either himself or anyone else. The failure to articulate a system is, though, in the best of Schlegel's work, probably the source of some of his most significant insights. His insistence, both upon the fact that articulating the ground of truth in philosophy leads to insoluble dilemmas, and upon the simultaneous inescapability of questions of truth, leads him to his reflections on *Poesie*. The reflections are, as I have shown, proving to be of importance to contemporary philosophy.

What is at issue here will inform many of Benjamin's subsequent views on language, art and truth. It also provides an elucidatory link between the Kantian tradition and Jewish theology in his work. How, then, are we to understand 'mysticism' in this context? The ninth of Gershom Scholem's 'Ten Unhistorical Propositions about Kabbala' of 1938 states:

> Totalities are only transmittable in an occult fashion. The name of God can be addressed but cannot be said. For it is only what is fragmentary in language that makes language sayable. The 'true' language cannot be spoken, just as little as what is absolutely concrete can be understood (*vollzogen*). (Scholem 1970 pp. 270–1)

It is not clear how much Benjamin knew about the Kabbala at this time: he certainly could not read Hebrew, for example (see GS I 3 p. 885). David Biale argues that 'Benjamin developed his views on language before Scholem . . . and he may be considered one of Scholem's predominant sources' (Biale 1982 p. 136): in this sense the '"true" language' is Benjamin's 'Word'. It would seem, then, to be the Romantic influence which is prior for Benjamin: the Romantics were, of course, aware of the

Jewish traditions via Hamann, Baader and others. In this context Benjamin cites Schlegel's observation – which is congruent with Scholem's remark – that 'The communicability of the true system can be only limited' (GS I 1 p. 46) as evidence of his 'mysticism'. Much depends, though, upon how one interprets Schlegel's comment.

If communicability and knowledge are internally connected, what – communicable – form of philosophy could validate knowledge, without the recurrence of the regresses and circles we have considered in earlier chapters? In Schlegel's terms in 1796, echoing Jacobi: 'Cognition already designates a *conditioned* knowledge. The non-cognisability of the Absolute is therefore an identical triviality' (Schlegel 1963 p. 511). Schlegel means by this that knowledge is of differentiated entities, of 'conditioned conditions', that can be expressed in relational propositions. The Absolute or 'Unconditioned' cannot be 'known' in this sense because it cannot be expressed in the dual structure of the proposition: that would introduce relativity and difference into the subject of a proposition about the Absolute. He therefore claims that 'The Absolute itself is undemonstrable, but the philosophical assumption of the Absolute must be analytically justified and proven. This is nothing absolute. – *Mysticism stands and falls* with this *misunderstanding*' (ibid. p. 512). The 'misunderstanding' derives from the assumption that both the presupposition of the necessity of the Absolute for understanding the relativity of knowledge, and the Absolute itself have the same status. In Chapter 3 I cited Novalis' remark that 'The essence of identity can only be established in an apparent proposition (*Scheinsatz*). We leave the identical in order to represent it' (Novalis 1978 p. 8). The problem is that the philosophical demonstration divides what must ultimately be undivided. This was the reason for Schlegel's move, in his search for ways of talking about the Absolute, to forms associated with literature, like allegory and irony (and music), which do not necessarily mean what they state propositionally. The outcome of the problems that result from consideration of the Absolute is that 'mediation', the dependence of intelligibility upon relationships between differing elements, becomes the central issue in consideration of truth. 'Mediation' can, though, take many different forms, which are central to understanding Benjamin's work. Allegory will, for example, be one of the keys both to the *Trauerspielbuch*, and to Benjamin's analyses of the effects of the commodity structure on culture in his Marxist work. This context therefore provides vital clues for understanding Benjamin's later project.

Schlegel's attempts to understand the Absolute in 1796, which accompany his philosophical (rather than philological) insight into the importance of *Poesie*, lead him to the alternatives between what he terms 'scepticism', 'eclecticism' and 'mysticism'. These alternatives provide a fruitful model for a whole series of issues in modern philosophy. Schlegel characterises the terms as follows: 'scepticism = permanent insurrection. Eclecticism = *chaos*. Mysticism = philosophical abyss of all unphilosophy' (Schlegel 1963 p. 12).

There can be no system of scepticism, he maintains, because scepticism cannot *claim* to be true, it can only consist in the constant attack on the idea of a system – hence 'insurrection' – carried out by undermining any system's claims to establish absolute truth. As he puts it in the wonderful *Athenäum* fragment: 'Sceptical method would therefore be something like insurgent government' (Schlegel 1988 Vol 2 p. 113). If, for example, one takes Derrida to be a sceptic, it is clear from this why he insists that deconstruction is not a method: that would indeed be 'insurgent government'. As Rorty suggests, it is therefore when people like Rodolphe Gasché try to formalise a method of deconstruction as a kind of transcendental philosophy that the trouble starts (see Rorty 1991a). The 'eclectic', on the other hand, who wishes to claim possession of truth via the very fact of all those differing things he thinks he can say are true, has to presuppose that what he claims is in fact the truth. This means that the eclectic must then give an explanation of *why* it is the truth, which leads to the need for a system in which one truth justifies others and is justified in its turn by those other truths. Such a system, though, means that the eclectic must contradict himself. The system leads, as Jacobi suggested of Fichte, to the demand for an absolute ground if a chaos of merely arbitrarily connected propositions is not to be the result. This characterisation might aptly be applied at times to Rorty, whose slipperiness over how to legitimate his pragmatism is a result of his wishing to circumvent the problem of Schlegel's eclectic by refusing to be drawn into this kind of discussion at all (a strategy which also brings him close to Romantic irony). The mystic, on the other hand – who would seem to be Jacobi, given the term 'unphilosophy'[22] – 'begins with the arbitrary proposition: there should be knowledge (*Wissenschaft*). But nothing contradicts knowledge so much as an arbitrary proposition' (Schlegel 1963 p. 506). The rejection of these alternatives leads Schlegel to some of the startling assertions which Benjamin's dissertation will explore.

In the definitive Schlegel edition one of the comments Benjamin cites from 1796 on the question of the communicability of knowledge is put in an extended form. The complexity of what is meant by Schlegel's 'mysticism' here becomes apparent:

> The consistent mystic must not only leave to one side the *communicability* of ALL!!! *knowledge*: but indeed actually deny that communicability. The eclectic must affirm it, if he wishes to have some appearance of being right against the mystic and if his criterion is to have *philosophical* validity; he must precisely thereby admit his absolute knowledge, and contradict himself. *Affirmation and denial* ALREADY *in philosophy* presupposes a positive and synthetic concept of knowledge; which only [Fichte's] *Wissenschaftslehre* can give. (ibid. p. 505)

The point of the last sentence is that for philosophy to be able to give an account of truth and falsity it must already in some way 'know' what truth is. Schlegel, then, initially thinks that Fichte may offer a way of avoiding the issues we saw raised by Jacobi. The essential fact is that Schlegel is quite clear that trying to ground knowledge within philosophy leads to aporias. Fichte's answer to the problem of grounding was, as we saw, to base the system on the absolute status of the spontaneity of the I as the ground of truth, rather than on Reinhold's 'founding proposition'. As such, Schlegel maintains: 'if one postulates knowledge and only seeks the condition of its possibility, one gets into mysticism and the most consistent and, from this view-point, only possible resolution of the task is – the positing of an absolute I' (ibid. p. 7). Schlegel will, though, as we saw in Chapter 3, reject this position.

The main philosophical aim of Benjamin's dissertation is, then, an investigation, on the basis of the questions just discussed, of the results of the Romantics' questioning of Fichte's attempt to ground philosophy. Benjamin maintains that the core difference between the Romantics and Fichte lies in the relationship between 'reflection' and 'intuition', thus between that which is dual or 'mediated', which is exemplified in self-consciousness' reflecting upon itself, and that which is 'immediate', which must also play a role in the nature of self-consciousness. Fichte's concern is with the 'mutual givenness-via-each-other of reflexive thought and immediate cognition' (GS I 1 p. 19), which, as we saw in Chapter 7, he terms 'intellectual intuition'. The problem which Schlegel identifies is in fact again the problem of grounding, in a form derived from Kant's difficulties in the transcendental deduction.[23] The attempt of consciousness to grasp itself as the source of knowledge leads to a regress of reflections, in which what I think is true needs to be grounded in the fact that I think it, which means that the fact that I think it must itself become the object of investigation, an investigation which can only be carried out by my own reflection upon myself, and so on. To stop the regress I must therefore in some sense be immediately present to myself in 'intuition', otherwise the ground of knowledge becomes merely reflections of reflections and thus no ground at all.[24] Benjamin carries out a series of penetrating explorations of this issue which have only been superseded by work initiated in the 1960s by Dieter Henrich in relation to Fichte and carried on by Manfred Frank in relation to the Romantics. I have dealt with the basic issues in Bowie 1990 Chapter 3, and at various points in preceding chapters, and there is no space to go into them in detail here. The vital issues at this point are Benjamin's conclusions and his development of the issue with regard to the Romantic view of *Poesie*.

Fichte's difference from the Romantics is that he

> thinks he can shift reflection into the primal-positing [the 'act' via which a world opposed to the subject can emerge at all], into the primal-being, for the Romantics that particular ontological determination which lies in positing ceases to apply. Romantic thought negates (*hebt auf*) being and positing in reflection. (GS I 1 p. 29)

The only reflection in Fichte is the primary reflection in 'intellectual intuition', 'that through which I know something because I do it' (Fichte 1971 p. 463). The rest of Fichte's world ensues from this ground: what ensues is a system where differences are made identical in judgements via the prior synthetic activity of the I. The I grasps itself at the very beginning in a form of 'self-presence' and therefore makes everything subordinate to itself.[25] In the Romantic case the doubts concerning Fichte's position are best seen via one of Schlegel's 1796 fragments, which Benjamin may not even have known, but which underlines the aptness of his interpretative model: '*Philosophy* in the real sense has neither a founding proposition, nor an object, nor a determinate task. The *Wissenschaftslehre* has a determinate object (I and Not I and their relationships) a determinate reciprocal ground [the I and the not I] and thus also a determinate task [the bringing of the not I into line with the dictates of practical reason]' (Schlegel 1963 p. 7). Whereas Fichte assumes that the availability of the I as ground is established by 'intuition', Schlegel speaks, as he puts it in later lectures, of the 'difficulty, indeed ... impossibility of an assured grasping [of the I] in intuition' (cited GS I 1 p. 32). In Chapter 3 we considered Novalis' discussion of the problem of being the 'I of one's I' (Novalis 1978 p. 238) and Schlegel's remark that 'Every person is only a piece of themselves' (Schlegel 1988 (5) p. 38), which both imply that I and world cannot be separated in the manner required by Fichte. The crucial fact for Benjamin is that, whereas Fichte wishes to 'deduce the world-picture of the positive sciences' (GS I 1 pp. 33–4) from the activity of the I, the Romantics give up this conception of philosophy and turn to the implications of these problems that can be explored via *Poesie*. The nature of this difference is also, of course, echoed in Heidegger's relationship to neo-Kantian approaches to science and philosophy.

Instead, then, of an absolute beginning that is required to make the world intelligible, which leads to the danger of 'an eternal reflection of oneself, to an endless row of mirror images which always only contain the same thing and nothing new' (Schlegel cited ibid. p. 35), reflection itself is regarded by the Romantics as always already 'fulfilled'. Each interrelation of I and world is part of an 'infinity of connection/context (*Zusammenhang*)' (ibid. p. 26), where there is no grounding priority, only the 'self-penetration of mind, which never ends' (Novalis cited ibid. p. 38, Novalis 1978 p. 316). In the terms we saw in Chapter 3: 'Philosophy is an εποσ, begins in the middle' (Schlegel 1988 (5) p. 26), and 'Every real beginning is a *2nd moment*' (Novalis 1978 p. 380). Benjamin claims, then, that 'In the early Romantic sense the centre of reflection is art, not the I' (GS I 1 p. 39): the I requires intuition, art is constituted in reflection.

A crucial reason for Benjamin's emphasising this view of Romantic philosophy is that he wishes to counter the notion of Romanticism as a form of vague 'intuitionism', which tends to dominate the perception of Romanticism even today. The reasons for his opposition to this perception are already implicitly political and are directed against right-wing obscurantism, in the name of his desire always to articulate the deepest problems, not merely to invoke them.[26] Because Fichte retains a moment of prior 'intuition' which must be 'unconscious', because consciousness can only emerge via the separation of I and not I, he leaves open space for irrational speculations concerning the origins of the world of knowledge.[27] In one sense Benjamin therefore sees the Romantics as presupposing a 'primary difference', which cannot be understood as a prior origin. This brings him close to Derrida's anti-foundational claims about interpretation: whereas Fichte can be said to require a 'truth or an origin that escapes the play and the order of the sign' (Derrida 1967b p. 427), Schlegel 'seeks . . . a non-intuitive (*unanschaulich*) intuition (*Intuition*) of the system, and he finds it in language' (GS I 1 p. 47).[28]

Language is, as we have repeatedly seen, 'reflexively' constituted, because 'every sign is in its place only what it is via the other signs' (Novalis 1978 p. 14). This means that there cannot be an original 'word' which would ground language: it is only through the movement of articulation that truth is possible at all. Novalis says strikingly insightful things about language in this respect, because he (like Schleiermacher) does not regard the essential linguistic unit as the word: 'To a word a sentence/proposition (*Satz*) corresponds. (A sentence/proposition is the potential of the word. Every word can be raised to a sentence/proposition, to a definition)' (Novalis 1978 p. 534). The Romantic holism of context prevents final determinability of meaning because each determinate proposition is then also 'raised' beyond itself. This elevation is enacted most evidently in art, which creates an endless potential for further articulation. In this context Benjamin cites Novalis on the process of observation in natural science: 'If the observed object is already a sentence/proposition and the process is really in thought, then the result . . . will be the same sentence/proposition, only in a higher degree' (Novalis, cited in GS I 1 p. 61). Once again this is a version of the question of being: the observed object is a proposition because of its manifestation 'as' something determinate, hence it is not 'x', but 'x as something'. Benjamin claims that 'The "sentence/proposition" in [Novalis'] sense can be a work of art' (ibid.), because it discloses the truth. The dissertation's central contention about Romantic theory is therefore that

> Critique is, in relation to the work of art, the same as what observation is in relation to the natural object. . . . Critique is, so to speak, an experiment on the work of art, via which its reflection is awakened, through which it is brought to consciousness and knowledge (*Erkenntnis*) of itself. (ibid. p. 65)

As in Heidegger's 'The Origin of the Work of Art', the work of art is therefore not an object which can be conceptually determined like any other.[29] Benjamin maintains in a manner later to be echoed by Gadamer that the truth of the work is to be talked of in the subjective genitive: 'To the extent that critique is knowledge of the work of art, it is [the work's] own self-knowledge' (ibid. p. 66). At this point, rather than trace the rest of Benjamin's complex argument in detail, I want to give a brief interpretation of its most striking point, which suggests the kind of challenge it still poses both to philology and philosophy.

Benjamin's insight into the core of the Romantic position is wonderfully simple and relies on what ought to be an obvious question for all those engaged in interpretation and criticism, particularly of literary texts. If one reads a literary text and then either makes criticisms of its stylistic, formal and other features, or tries to explicate its meaning, what exactly is one trying to do? The subjective intentions that lie behind such activity can range from the desire for revenge of critics on what they in fact envy, to the desire to communicate one's own joy at the experience of engaging with the aesthetic text. Whatever way one looks at it, there is an undeniable sense in which one is trying to 'complete' the text: the very fact of writing about it means that the text cannot be assumed to be complete 'in itself'.[30] If one wants to say the work is bad, one must be able to invoke what would make a work good; if one needs to say it is good, this fact is therefore in one sense not manifest. In order to do these things at all one necessarily invokes other works. The validation of what is written in relation to the text can thus be said to be an extension of the truth-content of the text: without interpret-ation the text is merely inert, and, without a text to interpret, the I which interprets cannot be engaged with the truth. This interdependence is the real point of Benjamin's interpretation of the notion of 'reflection'.[31]

The Romantic idea upon which Benjamin insists most emphatically is that critique 'negates the difference between critique and *Poesie*' (ibid. p. 69). If there is any point to the activity of literary criticism it can in these terms only reside in the fact that a true interpretation is actually part of the work interpreted: if it is not, what exactly is it for, assuming the work really is a work of art? This truth need not be final or fixed for all time, precisely because the work is not an 'entity', but rather what Benjamin terms a 'medium of reflection'. The individual work of art is inherently incomplete, because its truth emerges only via its being related in 'reflection' to other works within the medium of language. The truth of a work may actually only appear in relation to the incompleteness of other texts that do not reach its level of articulation. The relationships that can be established between the work and other texts cannot be foreclosed, because the writing of another text which can be related to the work may again change our understanding of that work itself. As such, the notional goal of interpret-ation would be the 'making absolute' (ibid.) of the work, which would be the final truth. However, this is what reveals the 'moment of contingency' (ibid. p. 73) of the individual work: it always needs to be related beyond itself for it to transcend its contingency, but this process itself cannot be completed. At the same time, though, the Romantics demand an 'immanent critique' of the work, thereby introducing a familiar critical paradox:

For it is not clear how a work could be criticised via its own tendencies, because these tendencies, to the extent to which they can be firmly established, are fulfilled, and to the extent to which they are not fulfilled, are not firmly establishable. (ibid. p. 77)

This is, of course, a version of the argument about the 'intentional fallacy' in 'new criticism'. The attempt to measure the work against what the author intended would appear to ignore the fact that the intention is presumably manifested as the actual work itself. Benjamin's answer to the Romantic paradox applies equally to the new critical argument, because it refuses to accept the idea of a self-contained 'verbal icon', even though it does not rely on the idea of authorial intentionality. The resolution of the paradox is that the work can only ever be understood in its 'relations to all other works and finally to the idea of art' (ibid. pp. 77–8). Benjamin here cites Novalis' contention that 'Criticism of literature (*Poesie*) is an absurdity. It is already difficult to decide, yet the only possible decision, whether something is literature or not' (Novalis 1978 p. 840, cited in GS I 1 p. 79). Critique is therefore only possible if a text is in fact art and can give rise to a process of reflection 'in the medium of art' (GS I 1 p. 79) because there is an 'immanent seed of reflection' (ibid. p. 78) in the work.

This might seem to make criteria for art simply unavailable. Benjamin argues, however, citing the continuing validity for twentieth-century literary study of the Romantics' choice of major works, that what is at issue is the real historical process of reflection, in which certain works do indeed continue to provoke further reflection, and not a rule-based aesthetic. In this way art, as it will later be for Heidegger, is something which 'happens' in the ongoing disclosure of the world occasioned by 'reflection'. Benjamin goes on to make the even more provocative claim that 'critique . . . is occasioned in its emergence by the work, but its continued existence (*Bestehen*) is independent of the work. As such it cannot in principle be distinguished from the work of art' (ibid. p. 108). Rather, then, than being concerned with the great 'closed' works of art from the canon of art, the theory maintains that without 'critique' the truth of those works is not manifest at all. The activity of critique is therefore potentially more important that the work itself: hence the Romantic 'paradox of a higher valuation of the critique than of the work' (ibid. p. 119). The possibilities of moving from this position to the critique of traditional aesthetics presented in Benjamin's 'The Work of Art in the Age of Its Mechanical Reproducibility' and other later texts should now be apparent. His dissertation suggests an approach to art which depends upon placing the work in contexts that can reveal its truth, thereby undermining conceptions which wish to see the work as wholly autonomous. Benjamin's assumptions will soon lead him to issues in aesthetics and politics that form the material of debate in critical theory. The next stage on Benjamin's way to such issues will be the *Trauerspielbuch* of 1924–5, his withdrawn *Habilitation* thesis on seventeenth-century baroque drama, published in 1928.

214 *Understanding Walter Benjamin*

SALVAGING THE TRUTH

At this point we should take stock. Benjamin's concerns thus far do not
necessarily add up to a clear overall project of the kind so obviously present
in Heidegger. Although much that Benjamin says prefigures Heidegger's
concern with conceptions of truth which can be made accessible in art
rather than in the natural sciences, his work seems more like a series of
localised critical interventions than a unified project. What, then, *is* the
early Benjamin's larger project? In a later text, concerning his 1924 essay on
Goethe's novel *Elective Affinities*, Benjamin says of his work that

> my attempts up to now are concerned to open a route to the work of art
> by destroying the doctrine of the character of art as a specific area. The
> common programmatic intention of my attempts is to encourage the
> process of integration of science, which more and more demolishes
> the rigid separating walls between the disciplines that characterised the
> concept of science of the previous century, by an analysis of the work
> of art that recognises in it an integral expression of the tendencies of
> an epoch which is not to be limited from any side by concern with a
> circumscribed area. (GS I 3 p. 811)

Statements of intent of this degree of clarity rarely surface elsewhere in
Benjamin's work at this time (they are more common in the later work).
The nearest thing to another overt statement of a project is the essay
of 1917, 'On the Programme of the Coming Philosophy'. Here the main
concern is with Kant and the notion of 'experience' in relation to language.
Kant's relationship to the Enlightenment meant, Benjamin claims, that
his work was 'undertaken via an experience which was, so to speak, reduced
to the nil-point, to the minimum of meaning' (GS II 1 p. 159). Even
though Kant's intention is not 'the reduction of all experience to scientific
experience' (ibid. p. 164), in Kant 'the fact that all philosophical cognition
(*Erkenntnis*) has its expression solely in language and not in formulae and
figures recedes into the background' (ibid. p. 168) when confronted with the
certainties of mathematics. As Benjamin himself admits, what he says here
is really just a repetition of Hamann's linguistic critique of Kant from
1784, which played an important role in Romanticism (see Bowie 1990
Chapter 6). The new task he sees is to work out a theory of cognition which
'finds the sphere of total neutrality in relation to the concepts object and
subject', and which thereby escapes the problem of how to move from
'empirical consciousness' to a concept of 'objective experience' (ibid.
p. 162). It is this task, which is essentially the task of grounding truth, that
the Preface to the *Trauerspielbuch* will try to address.

Language is the location of the most diverse attempts in both hermeneutic and analytical twentieth-century philosophy to escape a subject–object
metaphysics, sometimes with problematic consequences of the kind we
saw at the end of the last chapter. Benjamin's attempt to develop a new

conception of language will remain in many ways the centre of his enterprise, but what he means by language can only be understood via his differing conceptions of experience. Even in 'On the Programme of the Coming Philosophy', where he still talks as though a system of philosophy which involves theology were really possible, Benjamin is working towards the idea that a language is a repository of historical 'experience' which transcends the immediate awareness of the individuals who speak that language. The philosopher's task is therefore to reveal the 'experience' to which those individuals have no articulated access.[32] Implicit in this is the link between language and mythology explored by Schlegel and Schelling:[33] both language and mythology arise in ways which cannot be said to be in the power of the subjects who live by or within them. Language and mythology are, as Schelling suggests in 1842, also never finally separable from each other: 'One is almost tempted to say: language itself is only faded mythology, in it is preserved in only abstract and formal differences what mythology preserves in still living and concrete differences' (Schelling II/1 p. 52). Such a link will later, via the further connection of language and mythology to ideology, become vital in Benjamin's attempts to understand what it is about the links to regressive mythology of modern forms of communication and exchange that leads technologically developed societies to the regression to barbarism characteristic of Nazism. A major theme in these attempts, for example, in the essay 'The Storyteller', will be how individual experience is less and less of a reliable guide to what happens in modern history (see Bowie 1979, 1982). The interpretations which Benjamin develops are devoted to seeking new ways of interpreting history that attend to the forms and media of articulation through which the 'objective experience' of those within history is constituted: hence both his desire to get rid of restrictions on approaches to art and, later, his desire to open aesthetic questions to political scrutiny.

Benjamin's growing importance for cultural theory is in this respect a result of his realisation that the apparent material 'objects' in such interpretations, the concrete media in which language (in his broad sense, which essentially includes all resources for articulation) is both stored and manifested, are in some sense always already part of the apparently subjective experience of people.[34] A world which lives via written communication will therefore involve a fundamentally different kind of 'experience' to one which relies on print, film or, to extend Benjamin's argument, digital technologies: 'The Renaissance explores the space of the world, the Baroque explores libraries. Its pondering takes book-form' (GS I 1 p. 319). Notions from the dissertation, such as the work of art as 'medium of reflection' whose truth depends upon a process of contextualisation, will come to be transformed in the later work into tools for analysing the functioning of modes of communication in modern societies. These analyses will eventually put the very idea of the work of art as a medium of truth into question. The essential transitional text in this respect is the *Trauerspielbuch*.

The notoriously difficult Preface[35] to the *Trauerspielbuch* reaches a peak of esotericism which Benjamin's subsequent political involvement will help keep more in check.[36] In the space available here I want to render access to this text, which Adorno rightly regarded as Benjamin's 'theoretically most developed work' (cited in GS I 3 p. 868), somewhat easier, by showing how it takes up the main issues with which we have been concerned so far. I shall also suggest how it relates to his later work. During the planning of the *Trauerspielbuch* Benjamin suggests to Scholem in 1920 that his theme is 'an investigation that falls into the large circle of problems of word and concept (language and logos)' which will need to consider 'the ground of logic' (ibid. p. 869). Scholem suggests that Benjamin should read Heidegger's 1916 dissertation on 'The Doctrine of Categories and of Meaning of Duns Scotus', which Benjamin initially dismisses as merely 'a piece of good translator's work', where 'the unworthy crawling of the author before Rickert and Husserl does not make reading any more pleasant' (ibid.). Soon afterwards, though, he admits Heidegger may have dealt with the topic, at least with regard to scholastic philosophy, in an adequate manner. There is, then, already some kind of common ground in their approaches, as the concern with 'the ground of logic' suggests.

In 1924 Benjamin says of his projected book that 'the beginning and the end will . . . bring methodological remarks on literary study (*Literaturwissenschaft*) in which I want to present myself . . . via a Romantic concept of philology' (ibid. p. 875). This concept derives from the approaches to language that we have already encountered. Benjamin's continuing attempts, in order to avoid the 'bourgeois' idea of language as a collection of merely arbitrary conventions, to see language and nature as inherently related, means that the visual appearance of language in its written form plays a central role in this approach. Benjamin approvingly cites Novalis' friend J.W. Ritter,[37] for whom the 'image-like, hieroglyphic aspect of writing' is not crucial to the revelatory capacity of language. What counts instead for Ritter is the fact that the 'script-image ['*Schriftbild*', which is normally used for 'type', in the sense of the visible image of the letter or word on the page] is an image of the *note* ['*Ton*' in the musical sense, referring to language's acoustic manifestations] and not immediately an image of the things designated [by the words]' (ibid. p. 876). Ritter, then, suggests to Benjamin another way of showing why a conception of language adequate to what actually happens in language cannot be exclusively grounded in the idea that words re-present or 'picture' things. The relations and affinities between linguistic elements, which also play a role in how meaning is constituted in real situations, involve dimensions, such as rhythm and 'music', that most approaches to semantics do not regard as playing a role in the happening of truth. These dimensions are, of course, both crucial to literary texts, and, for Benjamin, central to what he means by language. In a letter concerning the *Trauerspielbuch* Benjamin points to the need for a 'doctrine of the differing kinds of texts', because 'all human knowledge which can be legitimated must take the form of interpretation' (ibid. p. 890). It must take this form because what is at issue are not historical facts, but what he now terms 'Ideas'. The anything but self-evident meaning of 'Ideas' – which does relate to what Plato meant by 'Ideas' or 'forms' – can only be approached by considering the argument of the Preface as a whole. As we shall see, Benjamin is in fact looking for an answer to the problem of induction, which we already encountered in the form of Kant's 'reflective judgement'. Kant attempted to show by the notion how one could arrive, without being led to a regress of judgements, at a universal which subsumed diverse particulars under a single concept, even though there could be no rule for such a procedure. As we have seen, this led to the question of the ground of truth, with all the attendant difficulties we have considered from the Romantics to Heidegger.

Benjamin's argument begins in a very different domain. It is initially directed against the kind of literary history which sees works of art as being best understood by locating them in a linear history of their contexts. Balzac's work, for example, thereby appears as a function of the rise of modern capitalism and the Restoration period in France and is compared to that of other contemporaries who write novels. In opposition to this kind of history Benjamin suggests that 'in interpretation connections of works of art with each other emerge which are timeless and yet not historically insignificant' (ibid. p. 889). The connection of Balzac to Proust, or Balzac to Kafka can reveal more in some contexts than the more immediate connection of Balzac and Eugène Sue. As in the 1940 'On the Concept of History', the key to this conception are the ways in which linear temporality – the temporality of nihilism – obscures the truth about history by failing to see that 'truth' arises via the emergence of non-linear connections of cultural artefacts and images in what Benjamin in the *Trauerspielbuch* will term 'configurations'.[38] Works can come to illuminate each other despite their disparate origins: hence the 'timelessness' of their interconnection and Benjamin's striking claim that 'there is no history of art' (ibid. p. 888). There is no such history because the truth of art, as the dissertation already suggested, is not available via historical or scientific explanation. Explanation reduces art to external forms of understanding that can be generally applied, rather than involving forms of understanding adequate to the particularity of the object. The truth is therefore available only via what he terms the 'representation (*Darstellung*) of an Idea' (ibid. p. 889). The notions of '*Darstellung*' and 'Idea' are the opening themes of the Preface.[39]

One of the reasons the Preface is so difficult to understand is that when he revised the original version Benjamin excluded some of the explanatory material. These exclusions also have to do with his concern in the Preface with esoteric forms of writing, but they are in many ways merely unhelpful. By considering certain bits of the earlier version of the text (GS I 3 pp. 925–48) along with the text published in 1928 (GS I 1 pp. 207–37) we can gain a rather clearer conception of what the text might mean.[40] The basic argument is quite simple, and is close to ideas in the later Heidegger, as well as to forerunners of some of those ideas in Jacobi, the Romantics and Schelling. Benjamin's claim is that the truth provided by the mathematically-based natural sciences, which he terms 'cognition', is not the truth which concerns philosophy. He does not want to maintain that what the sciences do is 'false', but to sustain a position from which philosophical questions can be asked about the nature of science that do not themselves rely on a scientific ground. The 'elimination of the problem of representation' which is characteristic of mathematically-based disciplines and is the 'signum of real cognition' entails a 'renunciation of the realm of truth which is meant by languages' (GS I 1 p. 208). Benjamin contrasts philosophy based on the 'concept of system of the 19th century' (ibid.) – or on 'the Western concept of system' (GS I 3 p. 925) – with what is offered by 'the concepts of doctrine and esoteric essay' (GS I 1 p. 208) which derive from theological traditions. The latter avoid the mathematically derived idea, which is linked to what I have termed 'Spinozism', of trying to 'catch truth in a spider's web drawn between cognitions, as if it flew in from outside' (ibid.). Instead the 'esoteric character of the tractatus' is an index of the fact that 'the main concern is representation' (GS I 3 p. 926). Whereas 'cognition is a possessing' by a 'consciousness – transcendental or not' (GS I 1 p. 209), the crucial aspect in 'representation' is 'contemplation': 'for [contemplation] the object itself is always nearer than everything that it could think of saying about the object' (GS I 3 p. 926). As such the 'essence of the thing is in each case that which is part of it independently of all the relations in which it could be thought' (ibid. p. 928). Rather than being grasped via an analysis which breaks up the object into 'arbitrary forms', in the manner of what Heidegger termed 'ontic' sciences, 'the truth-content of the object can only be grasped via the most exact immersion in the details of the objective content (*Sachgehalt*)' (ibid. p. 927). The immersion is not something mystical, but rather an aesthetic concern with the manner of 'representation' in relation to the object.

It is the *form* of the essay in which the Idea is revealed that is vital to its ability to reveal the truth of the work: 'truth is not unveiling which destroys the secret, but revelation which does justice to it' (GS I 1 p. 211).[41] This is in fact another way of putting the Romantic idea that critique 'completes' the work, rather than giving an objectifying account of it. Whatever else changes in Benjamin's thought, the demand to make the formal construction of his own texts appropriate to what they are to reveal never disappears. This demand is the source of his texts' literary fascination and of their related capacity to generate new insight in different contexts, even when subsequent research invalidates some of their philological and methodological claims. The demand is also the source of his experiments with montages of quotations from diverse sources as mutually illuminating constellations of historical material which allow Benjamin the 'intending' author to recede into the background. Can one, though, make clearer sense of why Benjamin sees truth in the way he does?

One obvious point of reference, given the metaphor of truth as the veiled secret, is Nietzsche's *The Birth of Tragedy*, which Benjamin discusses in other contexts in the main text of the *Trauerspielbuch*. Nietzsche rejects what he considers to be the Platonic idea of truth by suggesting that Socrates, as the 'theoretical man', is in fact the representative of what Benjamin terms 'cognition'. The artist, on the other hand, is always interested in the remaining veils hiding the secret, not, as is the theoretical man, in the results of the scientific process of unveiling which leads 'via the connecting thread of causality' to the tightening 'of a common net of thought over the whole globe' (Nietzsche 1980 (Vol. 1) pp. 99–100). In the last analysis, though, such scientific unveiling via the principle of sufficient reason leads to 'what cannot be enlightened' (ibid. p. 101), and thus to art (or, far more questionably, to the attempt to revive mythology through art in Wagner). The structure of Nietzsche's argument is very closely analogous to Jacobi's arguments about the ground in relation to the 'conditioned conditions', albeit minus the theological let-out.[42] Nietzsche also draws something resembling a Romantic consequence with regard to art in relation to this argument. Benjamin's conception of truth is, to the extent to which it refuses to equate philosophical truth with the results of the natural sciences, related to the argument of *The Birth of Tragedy*. What differentiates Benjamin from Nietzsche all along will be his attempt to arrive at a conception of truth which avoids both nihilism and irrationalism. He will, as we shall see, be followed in this aim by Adorno. In both cases the extent to which theology has to play a decisive role in the concept of truth will be a major problem.

Benjamin's concern, then, is with the uniqueness of the work of art and with an approach which would do justice to the truth of the work that derives from this uniqueness. The methodological problems involved here are evident in two paradigmatic but equally problematic alternatives, the first of which Benjamin evidently rejects, the second of which is the source both of many of his philosophical difficulties and of the complexity of his attempted solutions, in such notions as the 'representation of the Idea'. In the first alternative one reduces the work to its relations, by classifying it as an example of a genre. The relations of the work to other works or to its historical context must therefore be seen as part of a system of classification which it is the task of philosophy to construct. In the second alternative one tries, as Benjamin does, to escape a systematic model. Here the uniqueness of works of art would seem, however, to lead to the situation where each work is monadically enclosed in itself, because the work is not to be systematically related to other things, on pain of it becoming an object of 'cognition'. The work's uniqueness would, though, seem to render it uninterpretable and apparently only true via the very fact of its uniqueness. How does Benjamin respond to this problem? In his esoteric terms, truth is 'made present in the round ['*Reigen*', meaning the dance-form] of represented Ideas' (GS I 1 p. 209), thus in a configuration. What, then, after all this, *are* Ideas? So far it is only clear what they are not. The difference between conceptual analysis and revelation via the Idea depends on the fact that 'While the concept results from the spontaneity of thought, the Idea is given to contemplation' (GS I 3 p. 928).[43] The concept is always mediated, with all the dangers of regress that this implies; the Idea is immediate.

This structure should be familiar, even though the context is new. We are now, in fact, again back with Jacobi, as the following may suggest. In discussing the Ideas Benjamin takes up the distinction, familiar from Schelling and Schopenhauer, between a 'real ground' and a 'cognitive ground', which is another way of putting Jacobi's contrast of 'the true' with 'knowledge':[44]

> Are the Ideas pre-given as the cognitive or the real ground (*Seinsgrund*) of things? As cognitive ground the Idea would have to be determined by its relations; because cognition is relational (*ein Relationsverhältnis*). ... The Idea, though, does not enter into any relation (*Relations-beziehung*). (ibid.)[45]

The Idea is therefore a real ground of the 'essence of truth' (GS I 1 p. 210). In these terms the problem with scientific truth is that it always leads to the demand for a completed relational 'context of deduction' if all truths are to have equivalent status. This leads in turn to the regress we have been considering all along: 'With every realm of particular science new pre-suppositions that cannot be deduced introduce themselves' (ibid. p. 213), which was also the problem for Schlegel's eclectic. The problem, in Benjamin's terms, lies in the attempt to suggest that the different sciences could be philosophically legitimated in the same way. Scientific theory contends, on the one hand, that the problems of these unlegitimated pre-suppositions are, given the supposed truth of the results of a particular science, actually already solved; on the other hand, the theory also contends that the resolution of these problems could never be finally achieved because the continuing process of scientific discovery alters the status of previous truths. This is, then, as Adorno will later also remark, in fact a version of the problem of induction, which Benjamin is trying to solve via a non-scientific conception of truth. The net result of these reflections is that truth in Benjamin's sense – which cannot, on pain of complete mean-inglessness, be endlessly deferred – must be prior to and independent of relational contexts. This is precisely what the notion of the Idea as 'real ground' is supposed to establish.

The point of the Preface being a preface to a book about *Trauerspiel* only becomes apparent when Benjamin finally says that '*Trauerspiel* in the sense of the art-philosophical essay (*kunstphilosophische Abhandlung*) is an Idea' (ibid. p. 218). Even though the Idea can only be *represented* by 'an ordering of thingly elements in the concept' (ibid. p. 214), the Idea *exists* prior to the things which are configured when it is represented. Benjamin uses the very problematic analogy of a stellar constellation's (= the Idea) relations to the actual stars (= the thingly elements) in the constellation. The Ideas are that which 'salvages/saves' the 'phenomena' (for example, the literary works) by 'crystallising' (GS I 3 p. 946) them as elements of a totality in 'history'. Stars without constellations are a merely indeterminate aggregate of objects, the constellation enables one to *name* stars so that they have an identity which would not exist without the constellation.[46] The idea would again seem to be close to what Heidegger means by being, in the sense of 'being true', because the stars are presumably disclosed via the 'as structure'. Whereas literary history reveals the multiplicity of the historical phenomena that can be subsumed in the category '*Trauerspiel*', the Idea of *Trauerspiel* presupposes the unity of the phenomena which are salvaged by being configured to represent the Idea: it presupposes that unity, of course, because the alternative is another regress. The 'Idea does not determine any class' (GS I 1 p. 218), so the truth is not a result of the correct application of a concept to phenomena, which raises the problem of the regress of judgements, but rather 'an intentionless being, formed out of Ideas. . . . Truth exists (*besteht*) not as a meaning/intending (*Meinen*) which would find its determination via the empirical, but rather as the force which first stamps the essence of the empirical' (ibid. p. 216). In the manner of the structure we have been considering all along we have, then, as an alternative to regress, a kind of absolute beginning. The conception of truth as 'intentionless', which will also be adopted by Adorno, is deeply problematic. Its role is to map out a way of understanding how it is that truth must be context-transcendent, even as it is generated in intentional contexts, but it creates as many problems as it claims to solve.

One obvious aspect of Benjamin's view is that it excludes the subject, the locus of intentionality, from the constitution of truth. In this sense, Benjamin is once again very close to Heidegger's notion that truth is a happening prior to the subject. This conception, though, leaves the problems of how it is that an Idea comes into existence at all, and of how we have access to it, problems which also relate to Heidegger's difficulties in attempting to delineate a history of being. One can argue that Benjamin's later move to Marxism is a function of his becoming aware that this version of the theory of supra-subjective forces which stamp the empirical world of history could never satisfactorily explain the emergence of an Idea, let alone the move from one Idea to another. The move from tragedy to *Trauerspiel* is, as we have already seen, described rather than explained.[47] While it is possible to regard dominant historical ideas (not necessarily in Benjamin's sense) like the rise of Protestantism, which are in one sense prior to the subjects who live within them, as 'stamping the essence' of many peoples' behaviour and thinking, this does not mean that one has to regard them merely as happenings of being. Somebody has to come to see the world in a new way and communicate this way to others: leaving out the dimension of the freedom of the subject in giving an account of the collective adoption of new ideas represses as much as it reveals.

However one interprets them, Benjamin's assertions necessarily entail a version of ontological difference, in which the ground of truth is different from the empirical world of conditioned conditions. But how *do* we gain access to the 'force' in question? Benjamin continues, again leading us back to the questionable territory of the essay 'On Human Language': 'The being which is removed from all phenomenality, to which alone this force [that 'stamps the essence of the empirical'] belongs, is the being of the name' (ibid.). He once more directs his arguments against the notion of language as 'communication', in order to suggest that the job of philosophy must be a kind of anamnesis which goes back to the 'primal hearing' of words (ibid. p. 217). Benjamin says in a letter that the Preface is 'a sort of second – I do not know whether better – stage of the early work on language' (GS I 3 p. 882). Although Heidegger would reject both the Platonic link in the form Benjamin makes it and the obvious theological provenance of the conception, there are clear analogies in Benjamin's formulation to Heidegger's later remark that 'Thinking is at the same time thinking of being, to the extent that thinking, in belonging to being, listens to being' (Heidegger 1949 p. 8). Benjamin's formulations also echo the structure of Jacobi's claim that 'Listening presupposes what can be listened to; reason presupposes the *true*: it is the capacity to presuppose the true' (Jacobi 1799 p. 27). The question is whether the theory of the Idea and the name take us any further than his earlier theory of the name and the Word in giving a defensible account of Benjamin's claims.

Benjamin's methodological concern is, then, to avoid the 'whirlpool' of 'scepticism' (GS I 1 p. 221) which results if one tries to categorise phenomena like *Trauerspiel* via an inductive procedure of the kind that leads to the problems of philosophical legitimation for natural science outlined above. The establishing of just what *Trauerspiel* is would have in this view to be derived from an arbitrary designation of certain plays as belonging to a category whose content is derived from those plays in the first place, which is precisely the problem of induction. Benjamin's Idea, on the other hand, is supposed both to individuate the uniqueness of things and yet also bring out their truth, because they become part of a totality of which they are the irreducible 'monadic' splinters. The term 'monad' is used in Leibniz's sense, in that Benjamin's monads all have the truth of the world in them, like broken pieces of the same mirror, but they cannot communicate because that would reduce them to their relations, thus denying their individuality. Benjamin's goal, as it will be for Adorno, is a way of preserving individuality together with truth. However, as is fairly obvious, Benjamin's conception involves a fair degree of metaphysical contortion of the kind that the Romantics actually foresaw in their attempts to suggest the need to get away from foundational conceptions. Benjamin's conception can in this form only lead, like Jacobi's, to the move from philosophy to theology.

The underlying methodological problem is, therefore, very clearly related to the problems with which I began in Chapter 1. The Idea is supposed to stop the danger of regress, without the starting point being merely the product of the 'intending' imagination (see Chapter 2 above), by setting up a realm of truth prior to the empirical that is inherent in 'language' in the sense we saw in Benjamin's earlier essays. Rather than accepting a fallibilistic pragmatic starting point or model upon which one hermeneutically builds one's analyses – which is what Adorno at his best will suggest is all we can do – Benjamin wishes decisively to overcome the problem of regress. Whether we need to take on Benjamin's approach is, however, pretty doubtful: only if one thinks the truth of an Idea like *Trauerspiel* has to be taken out of history does its generic significance become so important in the first place. The reasons for Benjamin's own need to adopt such a strategy are, though, fundamental: they have to do with questions of theology, language, time and history. These questions turn out, if we take his later reflections on history not to be completely in contradiction to his Marxist work, to form the core of nearly all his work.

Benjamin's constant underlying preoccupation is a search for ways of redeeming the past. The politicisation of this preoccupation will lead to his famous remark about documents of culture always being also documents of barbarism and thus in need of salvaging for the present. Now any kind of concern with the past might be said to be redemptive, because it tries to stop things disappearing into oblivion, but this is why it is vital to specify Benjamin's position in an adequate manner. The aim of his form of philosophical 'critique' is to represent the truth which history threatens to dissolve into an inherently endless and random series of transient relations between phenomena. To this extent he now also abandons the Romantic notion of critique seen in the dissertation, for which the notional goal of interpretation was the 'making absolute' of the work, which can never finally be achieved. The 'origin' (*'Ursprung'*) of the *Trauerspielbuch*'s title is, as a consequence, 'not a becoming of what has emerged (*des Entsprungenen*) but rather a jumping out (*Entspringendes*) from becoming and passing away' (ibid. p. 226). This constitutes a different kind of temporality by 'saving' the phenomena from being merely arbitrary. Benjamin explicitly connects this notion of origin with Goethe's notion of the *'Urphänomen'*, the primal form of the organism, which is manifested in the differing concrete instances of the organism and is therefore not subject to temporality in the same way as the individual organisms. The radicality of this conception will affect his work to the very end. For those, like myself, who see any escape from the nihilism of history as itself inherently transient and who must regretfully take on the consequence that much that happens is therefore at very best imperfectly redeemable, Benjamin's work will therefore remain attached to an indefensible theology.

Although what he tries to do will turn out to be a failure, Benjamin's project is still challenging because it highlights the effects of modern temporality in a variety of important contexts. The understanding of temporality in the *Trauerspielbuch* is summed up in an abstract submitted to one of the projected examiners, Adorno's and Horkheimer's teacher Hans Cornelius:

> It is the object of philosophical critique to show that the function of the form of art – of which *Trauerspiel* is an instance – lies precisely in making objective historical content, which lies at the base of every significant work, into philosophical truth-content. This re-constitution of objective content into truth-content makes the decay of the effect, in which, from decade to decade, the appeal of the earlier charms diminishes, into the ground of a new birth, in which all ephemeral beauty completely falls away and the work asserts itself, so to speak, as a ruin. In the allegorical construction of baroque *Trauerspiel* such ruined forms of the redeemed (*gerettet*) work of art always clearly show themselves. (GS I 3 p. 952: parts of this passage are repeated in the text of the book, i.e. GS I 1 pp. 357–8)

Some of this is relatively self-explanatory. Many works of art will possess an appeal within their own historical context for reasons solely to do with an immediate interest or enjoyment generated by the transient concerns of that context. Their survival as significant works must, though, somehow transcend the context: this is the point of Benjamin's notion of 'philosophical truth-content'. How, then, is the notion of 'philosophical truth-content' cashed out? Benjamin intriguingly sees it in the case of *Trauerspiel* as the work's becoming a 'ruin'. Why a ruin?

The answer to this lies in Benjamin's concept of allegory. A large part of the *Trauerspielbuch* is taken up with an account of allegory, which must here be reduced to a very few points. We have anyway already considered the main arguments in tracing the route to the *Trauerspielbuch*. Allegory in Benjamin's sense has to do above all with the separation of 'sound' and 'meaning' which is characteristic of the baroque, thus with a conception of language of the kind we saw in the essay 'The Meaning of Language in *Trauerspiel* and Tragedy'. There language moved away from the 'pure word', whose meaning resides in a metaphysical order which transcends temporality, to a situation where meaning is constantly transformed and where language becomes connected to music, the temporal form of art *par excellence*. In order to make clear the notion he opposes, Benjamin cites Goethe's view of allegory. Goethe's allegory results when the 'poet seeks the particular for the universal'; Goethe contrasts this with symbol, in which 'whoever grasps this particular in a living manner also receives the universal with it' (Goethe quoted in GS I 1 p. 338). In symbol there is a metaphysical continuity between the particular and the universal. Benjamin, in line with his opposition to the 'bourgeois' conception of language as convention, rejects Goethe's idea of allegory as a means for expressing a universal concept in an image dictated by convention, asserting that allegory is not a means of what he earlier termed 'communication'. Allegory is instead the expression of the essential modern form of temporality, in which 'History, in everything about it which is from the very beginning intemperate, full of suffering, mistaken, expresses itself (*prägt sich aus*) in a face – no, in a death's head' (ibid. p. 343). Because nature is 'always under the spell of death it is always allegorical' (ibid.): 'meaning' and death are thus inextricably linked. Meaning is only ever connected to that which passes away, which changes the very status of language, because there is nothing which now remains fundamentally stable. This is the basic point of modern allegory and of the link to music, the temporalised, non-semantic form of articulation.

The explosion of metaphor and allegory characteristic of the beginning of modern literature – think of Shakespeare's use of metaphor, or metaphysical poetry – is in Benjamin's terms an indication of an ontological change in language, in which 'Every person, every thing, every relationship can arbitrarily mean something else. This possibility passes a devastating but just judgement on the profane world: it is characterised as a world in which details are not strictly that important' (ibid. p. 350). In certain ways this view of language in modernity is the one which I have suggested is common to aspects of the Romantics and to the Davidson of 'A Nice Derangement of Epitaphs' (and, for that matter, to aspects of Derrida). For all these thinkers it becomes clear that one can get any word to mean anything if one uses it in the appropriate way in a context. The difference lies in the consequences drawn by Benjamin on the basis of his theological concerns. He claims that the arbitrariness of the elements of signification does mean that the possibility of establishing such relations 'lifts [profane things] to a higher level' (ibid. p. 351), but his main interest is the arbitrary aspect of baroque allegory. The decisive fact is that allegory is both 'convention and expression; and both are inherently opposed to each other' (ibid.). This model echoes many of the tensions between rule-bound and hermeneutic conceptions that concerned us in earlier chapters, although Benjamin takes it in his own direction.

The essential tension is initially between the 'allegorical' rigidification of language in written language and the 'symbolic' power of the image. Benjamin relates allegory to the Romantic sense of the fragmentary nature of all finite attempts to articulate the infinite, and symbol to the classical ideal of a final match of image and idea, finite and infinite. There is for Benjamin, though, no decisive dialectical 'mediation' of such extremes which would lead to a higher stage. His concern is with the consequences of the dissolution of a metaphysically substantial link between image and truth which he assumes to have been present in the symbol. Allegory is 'script/writing' (*Schrift*) and thus a 'schema': as schema it is 'an object of knowledge . . . a fixed image and a fixed sign in one' (ibid. p. 359). The argument goes through a whole series of complex twists, but the main point is that in the baroque the word becomes a 'thing that may be allegorically exploited' because it is

> emancipated from every received connection with meaning [in the substantial metaphysical sense associated with a fixed world order]. . . . Pulverised language has, in its pieces, ceased to serve mere communication, and places, as a newly born object, its dignity next to that of Gods, rivers, virtues and similar natural forms which shimmer into the allegorical. (ibid. pp. 381–2)

One moves here from a representation of the infinite by the finite means of language to the idea of the 'materiality of the signifier' (see Roberts 1981), in which language is initially no different from any other entity. It is, of course, possible to move from this view to a materialist theory of language as materially embodied praxis of a kind that will play a role in some of Benjamin's later work, to aspects of the earlier Heidegger's pragmatist hermeneutics, or even to Rorty's behaviourist contention that a concept is just 'the regular use of a mark or noise' (Rorty 1991a p. 126). Whichever approach one adopts, Benjamin's argument is clearly in line at this point with anti-metaphysical conceptions of language in modern philosophy. The odd thing, which connects to his desire to combine extremes, is that his ultimate intentions with regard to language are so obviously theological. It is when Benjamin considers these issues in relation to music that things come together somewhat more clearly, if not, in the last analysis, more convincingly.

The separation of sound and meaning, which is part of the separation of the word from a metaphysical order of meaning that we observed in the earlier essay on language and *Trauerspiel*, makes 'music the opponent of speech, which is loaded with meaning' (GS I 1 p. 385). At the end of the seventeenth century this leads, Benjamin maintains, to the 'dissolution of *Trauerspiel* into opera' (ibid.). Despite his critical assessment of opera itself, as a 'product of the decay' of *Trauerspiel*, he regards music as inextricably related to *Trauerspiel*. The question is once again the relationship of language to nature, which is now couched in terms of the opposition between music (as semantically unstable temporalised articulation) and metaphysically grounded 'meaning'. In the Introduction I cited Michel Foucault's claim that the opposition in question is one in which 'words cease to intersect with representations' (Foucault 1970 p. 304), which he situates at the beginning of the nineteenth century and connects to the emergence of 'literature'. Foucault wishes thereby to make a division between 'Classicism' and 'modernity'. Benjamin's point about temporality and language is, however, that the essential aspect of modernity actually *precedes* the kind of Classicism he associates with Klopstock's 'overcoming of the baroque' in a 'reconciliation of sound and meaning' (GS I 1 p. 384).[48] An answer to the question of language's relationship to the nature of which it is a part – a question which he regards as being posed most effectively by

Ritter – would lead 'far beyond . . . untheological philosophising' (ibid. p. 388) back, sadly, to the theory of the Word.

In the light of the modern failures of attempts to get beyond philosophy to theology, what can be salvaged from these ideas? The conclusions of the argument about music are indefensible. However, the attempt to explore, via music, the historical shift in language associated both with the rise of new approaches to allegory and metaphor, and with the related process of secularisation does offer some insights. The elements in Benjamin's argument are the 'thesis' of 'sound-language' (*Lautsprache*), the 'synthesis' of 'written-language' (*Schriftsprache*), for which music, the 'last language of all people after the building of the tower', takes the 'central position' of 'antithesis' (ibid.). Written language, Benjamin maintains, does not emerge directly from spoken language, but via the mediation of 'music'. Music, as that which is inherently opposed to fixed meaning, has to be both temporal and never finally determinate. Having already considered Benjamin's underlying conception of language, this apparently incomprehensible conception should actually be reasonably clear.

It begins with the idea that, as Ritter puts it, 'all of creation is language and thus literally created by the word' (cited ibid.), which is the idea we considered earlier in relation to Scholem. For language to change its status in becoming writing, thereby moving away from a fixed metaphysical order of meaning, there must be a separation between sound and meaning. This is the source of the mediating role of music, which, as sound, is articulated like language, is expressive, and yet is transient and not semantic. The crucial aspect of language manifested in allegory lies in the tension, again derived from the Romantics, between the impetus for language to determine things and the sense that any such determination is merely a passing subjective imposition which leads away from the 'name', thereby making language 'a *mere* sign' (GS II 1 p. 153). The truth sought via the attempt to name things transcends subjective intention, but what Benjamin terms the 'knowledge of evil' – which is explained by the references to the Fall and the plurality of languages we saw in the earlier essays – means that the 'triumph of subjectivity and the dawn of an arbitrary dominion over things is the origin of all allegorical contemplation' (GS I 1 p. 407). The argument once again bears striking similarities both to Heidegger and to Schelling's 'Freedom' essay.

In Schelling's essay 'evil' is associated with subjectivity's attempt to deny that it is grounded in a nature over which it has no final dominion, a denial which appears in the form of the perversion of subjective reason itself. For Schelling, before there is reason there can be no evil, merely a meaningless cycle of the replacement of one state of being by another.[49] This idea is important beyond any possible theological connotations because it suggests the basic structure of what Horkheimer and Adorno will later, partly in the light of Benjamin, term the 'dialectic of enlightenment', as well as opening up the kind of questions about modern philosophy's relationship to subjectivity and art we observed in Heidegger. We here reach a crucial aspect of Benjamin's position, from which major aspects of his later work, and his influence on Adorno follow. One aspect of his argument can be put aside: the assumption of a 'language of names in which man in paradise (*der paradiesische Mensch*) named things' (ibid.), which is 'concrete' and which is left behind by the 'abstract' language of subjective judgement, is simply another way of trying to theologise truth. The interesting question is how to arrive at a theory that does justice to the sense that there *are* problems about truth in modernity, which result from secularisation and the rise of modern science, and to which a new perception of art is one vital response.

The main factor in the defensible aspect of Benjamin's conception is the simultaneous incompatibility and co-existence of 'convention' and 'expression' in allegory. We can convert the core argument with little difficulty into an argument about the changed status of objects in modernity, of the kind we have already encountered in Heidegger. The notion of 'arbitrary dominion over things' is both a way of seeing technology and a way of considering the effects of the commodity system in subjecting all objects to the conventions of exchange value.[50] Convention is necessarily linked to abstraction, because it can never relate directly to the particularity of what is designated: this can now be seen as perhaps the only moment of truth in Benjamin's suspicion of the 'bourgeois' conception of language. It is also why convention is linked by Benjamin to inherently subjective 'judgement', much in the sense that Heidegger's 'metaphysics' relates to 'entities'. Expression tries to reach the particularity of things, but threatens to dissipate itself because pure particularity becomes incomprehensible and requires a stable counterpart to be manifest at all. The essential problem was already inherent in the question of schematism in Kant and in many of the Romantic ideas about aesthetics and language we have explored. Underlying the critical version of all these approaches is the need for that which would, in the manner of Kant's notions of 'dignity' – that which is 'without price' – and of the intrinsic value of the work of art, overcome the 'allegorical' modern world of determined relationships within arbitrarily constituted systems. Any attempt to find a way out of the dilemmas involved leads to problems of grounding of the kind we have repeatedly encountered and will encounter again in Chapter 9.

The model of a possible response to the issue of convention and expression can, for orientation's sake, briefly be suggested here, and will be further explored in Chapter 9. Essential elements are, once again, the attempt to sustain individuality without losing truth, the desire to salvage the past, and the perception of the significance of art. Adorno shows that some of the greatest music in modernity relies upon a 'redemption' of apparently dead objectified conventions, such as the Lydian mode used by Beethoven in the slow movement of the String Quartet Opus 132 to express the deepest individual feelings. The very combination of the extremes of convention and expression turns out here to result in something which mediation or compromise would have failed to achieve. It may be, of course, that Beethoven's success is a possibility which is only present at a particular historical moment and only in the medium of autonomous art. Our assessment of the use of aesthetics as the source of an adequate conception of truth will depend upon how to evaluate this question. For the moment the fundamental point is that modern culture, despite its apparent diversity, increasingly moves towards merely schematic repetition, rather than redemption of convention of the kind suggested in the example from Beethoven. This move to repetition is, for Adorno, a mark of a deep crisis in the concept of truth. Issues which arose in relation to Romantic philosophy hereby become directly connected to the great ideological battles of modernity. How, then, does Benjamin approach these battles in his move to direct political engagement?

REDEMPTION OR ILLUSION?

During the writing of the *Trauerspielbuch* in 1924 Benjamin becomes more directly concerned with politics through his meeting with the Russian revolutionary Asja Lacis and reading Lukács' *History and Class Consciousness*. He finds in Lukács propositions 'which are very familiar or confirming ['*bestätigend*', in the sense that they confirm his own epistemological reflections]' (GS I 3 p. 879) in relation to the *Trauerspielbuch*. Benjamin's editors claim it is impossible that Lukács' arguments should have done this, because there is no trace of Marxism in the Preface (ibid.). However, they fail to see the extent to which a Marxist epistemology based on a critique of commodity structure, of the kind present in Lukács, relies upon the Romantic structures we have been considering all along, which also inform the *Trauerspielbuch*.[51] In a preparatory text for his Marx-inspired work on Baudelaire and Paris in the nineteenth century Benjamin claims, for example: 'The allegorical manner of perception (*allegorische Anschauungsweise*) is always built upon a devalued world of appearance. The specific devaluation of the world of things which is present in the commodity is the foundation of the allegorical intention in Baudelaire' (ibid. p. 1151). Although there is evidently a hiatus between the theological side of the *Trauerspielbuch* and some of Benjamin's Marxist reflections on aesthetics, his own coming to terms with that hiatus remains in many ways the motor of his subsequent work. The fact is that there *is* a very substantial continuity between the earlier and the Marxist Benjamin, which has both positive and negative aspects. In 'On the Concept of History', which is effectively his last work, he claims, for example, via the image of the chess-playing automaton which wins games because a hunch-backed dwarf is concealed within it, that '"historical materialism" can win against anybody if it takes theology, which these days, as is well known, is small and ugly and has to stay out of the way, into its service' (GS I 2 p. 693). The question is just what sort of theological help is required: his answer to this will not be convincing. As I stated at the beginning of this chapter, there is no space here really to engage with Benjamin's Marxist work. I want therefore to try to characterise as briefly as possible some essential aspects of what remains the same and what changes in the later work, before moving to an investigation of some of Adorno's responses to these issues.

It is, of course, not just the influence of Brecht, Lacis, Lukács, or, for that matter, anyone else, which changes the face of Benjamin's work. The period from the First World War to the end of Nazism in Europe gave an intellectual like Benjamin the choice between the attempt to turn away from the history which threatened to and eventually did engulf him, and the acknowledgement that, if his deepest intuitions were to remain live theoretical options, they would have to be sustained in a manner adequate to the nightmare of history. The sense of desperation evident in the chiliastic side of 'On the Concept of History', which wishes to 'explode the continuum of history' (ibid. p. 703) in order to redeem the past in times of emergency, is disturbingly vivid. This text is at least partially a result of the demise of the exaggerated hopes for political transformation via the left-wing use of modern technology for cultural purposes that are present in works like the 1936 'The Work of Art in the Age of Its Mechanical Reproducibility'. At the same time, making Benjamin's later work merely a function of the history that killed him does justice neither to what he was trying to do, nor to the ways in which his ideas, despite their evident and serious failings, can still be used in new ways for contemporary purposes.

How, then, does Benjamin himself use his earlier work, in the light of his realisation of the *political* nature of the understanding of modernity present in the dissertation and the *Trauerspielbuch*? The changes in language analysed in the reflections on allegory, where words become things like all other things, can be read both as informing his view of Baudelaire and as the basis of the 'Work of Art' essay. The broad notion of language we have seen in Benjamin allows language to play the role of the medium in which sense perception is organised that is the key to the essay:

> *Within large historical periods, along with the whole manner of being of human collectives, their manner of sensuous perception also changes.* The manner in which human sensuous perception organises itself – the medium in which it takes place – is not only determined by nature but also by history. (ibid. p. 478)

The refusal to see the truth of art and history in terms of 'intention' and thus in terms of a subject–object structure is now carried over in a more worked out way into the idea that the means of communication in a society, be it print, film or commodity exchange itself, are always also inextricably involved in what it is to be a subject in that society. In modernity communications media function more and more independently of the reflexive awareness of those who experience the world via those media. They thereby threaten to return members of modern societies to the kind of world characteristic of an unreflective mythological culture. At the same time the dominant political forces in modern societies are equipped with the sort of technological means of really achieving goals which were only symbolic projections for cultures based on mythology. Given the catastrophic economic developments of the period, this link between forms of communication and technology seemed in Benjamin's context to lead almost inevitably to the destructive use of those technological means, via the combined mobilisation of mass communication and mass destruction.

There is, then, a danger that this theory can become merely fatalistic, which is one source of Benjamin's utterly radical, but failed attempt at a solution. The complexity involved in theories concerning the political functioning of the mass media and modern technology can usefully be suggested by a more recent example. Television is for us the best example of what Benjamin is concerned with in the 'Work of Art' essay. The fact is that there was a spell, from the 1960s onwards, where television may well have temporarily become a rational means, in the Western world, of helping prevent war (see e.g. the preface to Anders 1980). Now, however, mass communications in their new privatised forms seem to be leading to new kinds of mythological nightmare, if the cultural level and the political effects of the products of supposedly free access to those media in the USA are anything to go by. Whereas the actuality of Benjamin may have diminished when television had evidently progressive effects, he now again seems all too actual, and his insistence on rejecting a merely nostalgic view still has lessons for us: we still lack ways of coming to terms with the realities of new media. The need which Benjamin already saw is for social and political forms which allow those media to function in ways which do not lead to irrationalism. At the same time, his own ways of coming to terms with these realities in the 'Work of Art' essay return us to problems we considered in Chapter 5.

What Benjamin termed the 'philosophical truth-content' of the work of art now comes to be seen in terms of the unmasking of a work's ideological potential for influencing society. This unmasking need not, Benjamin claims in the essay, just be conceived of as a form of negative critique, because there are forms of art, like film, whose ideological potential can be politically legitimated. This is an arguable case, but Benjamin's theory is not much help. He thinks the reason film can be politically important is that, via its reproducibility, it destroys 'aura'. Aura is the residually sacred aspect of the work of art which he regards as a vital mystifying aspect of the reception of art in the nineteenth century. Benjamin's Brecht-influenced approval of this destruction is a result of his desire to demystify a rather diffusely defined 'nineteenth century notion' of art, whose

> ideological character is to be seen in the abstraction in which it defines art in general via magical ideas without taking account of art's historical

construction . . . the [nineteenth-century] conception of art becomes all the more mystical the more art is distanced from real magical usefulness. (GS I 3 p. 1050)[52]

The destruction of aura contributes to the discovery of the truth-content of art, by understanding art in terms of the non-linear temporality we examined earlier in this chapter. In a letter to Scholem in 1935 about his work of that time Benjamin says that 'These thoughts anchor the history of art in the nineteenth century in the recognition of its contemporary situation which is experienced by us' (ibid. p. 983). He also writes to Adorno in 1938 that 'the critique of the attitude of the philologist' who tries to make the work part of a completed context in the past 'is internally identical with the critique of mythology' (ibid. p. 1104). The point is not that we should abandon the historical consideration of art. Instead the truth of art has to do with the ways art concerns us now, and not with 'feeling one's way into' a mythologised past that leads to an illusory escape from the present. Given the links between art and ideology, the question arises as to whether any significant connection between art and truth can really be sustained. In a letter of 1936 Benjamin writes to Adorno that 'through all the years I have tried to make an ever more exact and ever more uncompromising concept of what a work of art is' (ibid. p. 1023). The fact is, as we have seen, that a radicalisation of such questions can lead to the notion that there is no such thing as either literature or any other form of art. It is only if we, like Benjamin, confront the extreme versions of this notion that we can do justice to the theoretical questions he raises.

The influence of Brecht's and others' theories of the political and social usefulness of art in Germany in the period after the First World War are very apparent here. Only by relating art to a wider political project, by politicising it, Benjamin now maintains, can the danger of 'aestheticising' politics in the manner of the Fascists be avoided.[53] Assessing such a theory without taking into account the specific context of its emergence in the cultural politics of the time can only lead to an abstract failure to grasp the nature of the dilemma which Benjamin faced. A questionable theory of the kind Benjamin proposes is one of the few possible options for a radical thinker in the context of the rise of fascism and of the rigid forms of cultural organisation that emerge on the left in the wake of the initial wave of creativity after the Russian revolution. The basis of Benjamin's diagnosis remains valid because it gives a framework for asking the most important questions about the real functioning of art in an increasingly media- and commodity-dominated era. At the same time the notion of the truth-content of art which can transcend immediate contexts and relations seems to be abandoned, in favour of the need for art directly to intervene in the emergencies of history. Whatever one thinks of the theory in question, there is now no doubt that, as Adorno will later say, at the beginning of *Aesthetic Theory*: 'in relation to art nothing is straightforward any more, neither in art, nor in its relationship to the totality, not even art's right to exist' (Adorno 1973b p. 9).

The dubious interventionist view of the 'Work of Art' essay, of which Adorno, as we shall see in Chapter 9, will be highly critical, is not Benjamin's last word on the question of art, truth and modernity. His final, uncompleted work, the *Arcades-Project*, which investigates the nature of modernity via the example of nineteenth-century Paris, contains some of his most important reflections upon the status of art and truth. These are expressly intended to find a rational way through the mythological irrationality of commodity-based societies, which are exemplified by nineteenth-century Paris. The real consequences of this irrationality become apparent for Benjamin in fascism: hence the 'allegorical' use of nineteenth-century Paris to talk about the situation of Benjamin's own increasingly traumatic world. Links to the *Trauerspielbuch* are now, unlike in the 'Work of Art' essay, very explicit: 'In an analogous manner, but more clearly than the baroque-book illuminates (*belichtet*) the 17th century via the present, here the 19th century must have the same thing happen to it' (Benjamin 1983 p. 573). The Marxist aspect is evident in Benjamin's concern with the links between economics and culture, but rather than Marx's (supposedly) 'causal connection between economy and culture' the focus of attention is 'the context of expression. What is to be represented is not the economic emergence of culture, but rather the expression of economy in culture' (ibid.), which we can perhaps best understand these days via the nature of contemporary advertising. Behind this lies Marx's view of 'commodity fetishism', in which relations between people become reified into relations between things. The key for Benjamin is the relationship of the consumer to the commodity, in which the consumer comes to 'feel his way into' the *exchange* value of the commodity, not its use value (GS I 3 p. 1106):[54] 'Feeling one's way into their exchange value makes even canons into the object of consumption which is more pleasing than butter' (ibid.). In these terms the subject–object relationship becomes increasingly dominated by the desire to be on the object side of the relationship, to be taken up by the 'soul of the commodity' (ibid. p. 1136). This is the source of what he terms the 'phantasmagoria' of commodity society. What he means becomes apparent in ever more extreme forms in the contemporary replacement of modern visual art by the images of advertising, and in the concomitant obsession with labels and fake novelty. Although being murdered for a pair of trainers of a specific label is not in any way explained by such a theory, the theory does suggest dimensions of collective change which mean that such a crime is not just like any other form of murder for the purposes of acquisition of property. Without consideration of such dimensions of its culture any analysis of capitalist modernity will be seriously deficient.

The conception in the *Trauerspielbuch* that words become things like everything else – which already points to aspects of the digital era's manipulation of language and the contemporary intensification of commodification

– is thus extended into a more concrete analysis of a generalised historical process of allegorisation in which autonomous subjects no longer play a role. Despite the problem I shall suggest in the extreme version of this conception, the literary examples of Flaubert and Baudelaire cited by Benjamin are ideal illustrations of the way in which the world of things comes to affect the figures who inhabit that world. Art itself radically changes in this respect – though how this is to be interpreted is crucial. The very nature of poetic language is clearly altered by the incursion of the commodity structure: think of Flaubert's divorce, via his particular mode of narrative, of the events and objects of his novels' world from any real sense of connection to the internal lives of the figures in that world (see Bowie 1984, Culler 1974). This change in poetic language is, though, itself a way of *opposing* what such language can reveal. The challenge of Flaubert's style is not exhausted by explaining that its historical condition of possibility is the rise of the commodified world: it is actually able to reveal something of the experience of that world which transcends merely subjective impressions. The survival of Flaubert's novels as a vital source of historical insight and the revealing historical changes in the interpretations of Flaubert's work make this apparent, as does its continuing aesthetic fascination. It is precisely this dimension of the truth of art which Adorno will be concerned to preserve.

Perhaps somewhat surprisingly, the vocabulary Benjamin uses in relation to these issues is that of the *Trauerspielbuch*, which is combined with that of Marxian political economy: he even talks at one point of 'grasping an economic process as an intuitable primal phenomenon (*Urphänomen*)' (Benjamin 1983 p. 574). His framework is once again the relationship between 'convention' (this time in the form of relational connections of the kind present in commodity exchange) and 'expression'. Getting to the truth of the historical situation, as in the *Trauerspielbuch*, depends on the exclusion of 'intention'. He now seeks to achieve this, in some senses in Romantic fashion, via literary montage: 'I have nothing to say. Only to show. . . . I want to allow the rags, the waste . . . to be legitimated' (ibid.) by being presented in a configuration, in the manner familiar from many literary works in the post-First World War period, such as Döblin's *Berlin Alexanderplatz*, or in the radical use of montage in film. The related theory of non-linear temporality is also mobilised. Benjamin wishes to overcome nihilistic history by creating 'dialectical images' that make sense of the present and the past in a non-causal manner, in which the images 'come in a specific period to be interpretable' (ibid. 577) via the emergence of new relationships of past and present. This approach is another version of what Benjamin meant from very early on in his work by 'messianism', but the theory has now been filtered through ideas of redemptive time in psychoanalysis.

In the same way as Freud says that happiness is the fulfilling of a childhood wish, Benjamin thinks historical time can be 'contradicted' (ibid. p. 600) by realising buried possibilities in 'the awakening of a not yet conscious knowledge of what has been' (ibid. p. 572). History is not always comprehensible, as it is assumed to be in traditional historiography, and it is only in the light of configurations of meaning which are beyond the control of the individual thinker, and which suddenly emerge in the work of the most disparate thinkers, that history can become momentarily intelligible and thereby illuminate the present. The task of the theorist is to show these configurations and the form of his work is determined by the need, via the combination of already existing material, to avoid mere subjective impression. The fact is, though, that the success or failure of this method, which, despite all, must rely on the quality of the judgement of the theorist, can only be assessed in terms of the ability of the new configurations to command assent via their capacity for revelation. Benjamin's *Arcades-Project* is consequently very uneven, combining ludicrous associative claims with deep insights into historical interrelations with the present.

In the light of the growing accumulation of historical disasters, the only sense that can be made of history for Benjamin now lies in the escape from sequential temporality that can be achieved by a radical approach to culture: 'For a piece of the past to be affected by actuality, there must be no continuity between them' (ibid. p. 587). Continuity is part of the world of 'conditioned conditions', in which progress is measured by scientific and technical accumulation, not by what this accumulation means for real human beings. Truth is what happens when continuity is interrupted by insight into the fact that history remains a brutal disaster, even though the technical means are already present to alleviate its worst consequences. At this level Benjamin offers an apt diagnosis of the failure of the modern world to develop morally in the same way as it develops technologically, which is perhaps the vital unifying – and essentially Marxist – theme of Frankfurt School Critical Theory. He goes wrong when he suggests that a total transformation of the historical world could redeem this situation. His critique of 'progress' effectively extends the justified critique of an Enlightenment 'grand narrative' of moral amelioration to the idea that, because there is no 'real' progress in history, we must escape history altogether. In making such suggestions he tries to lift phenomena which are part of the meaning of individual lives – in the form of intuitive insights into the truth experienced in psychoanalysis or in the reception of art (Proust's sense that art redeems temporality plays a vital role here) – on to a collective level. The source of his aberration in this respect is again his lurking theology, which makes him seek a new ground for truth in the way we have observed throughout this chapter. The deeper problem is that by using theology and metaphysics as means of understanding collective developments in mass society, Benjamin loses sight of the remains of individual autonomy which are still also part of modernity. He does so in favour of a view which, while wishing to escape irrationalist assumptions about mass society, actually tends to reintroduce such assumptions by making the effects of collective phenomena, like the means of communication, function wholly beyond the control of those within them. As in the later Heidegger there is a chronic tendency, despite all Benjamin's empirical investigations, for him to reduce history to the history of philosophy and to covert theology. Benjamin's chiliastic vision of 'interrupting history' is in this sense a mistaken result of his obliteration of all possibility of autonomy on the part of subjects in history. At the same time his aim in all this is the admirable desire not to surrender the oppressed to the oblivion of history. Important differentiations must therefore be made here.

Answering Horkheimer's contention in a letter from 1937 that 'those who have been struck dead are really dead' and are thus beyond redemption, Benjamin ponders whether the 'corrective of these thoughts lies in the consideration that history is not just a science but no less a form of remembrance (*Eingedenken*)' (ibid. p. 589). As such, history can 'modify' what science has 'established' as fact. This is 'theology' (ibid.). But what is missing from this conception are the individual subjects: such remembrance wishes, really against all the odds, to arrive at a way of counteracting the transience and horrors of history. It actually does so in a manner which is congruent with certain questionable aspects of recent Heidegger-derived literary theory, though that theory would clearly not share Benjamin's conclusions. The fact is that the popularity of Benjamin in the light of recent theory often results from his manner of privileging language, in his broad sense, over individual subjects.[55] This privileging of language, though, is the source of the ultimately futile theory proposed here. That the past can be altered by new ways of writing history is a vital fact in the modern perception of temporality, in which literature plays a central role, from Proust's *In Search of Lost Time* and Mann's *Magic Mountain*, to Alexander Kluge's *New Histories: The Uncanniness of Time* (see Bowie 1982, 1986). However, this should not lead us to think that new approaches to history which circumvent linear temporality make sense of tragically lost lives for those who lost them. For this to succeed there really would have to be a redemptive end to history: signs of this seem to me, sadly, thin on the ground.

The perspective which also informs the best of Adorno's responses to the facticity of individual tragedy is suggested by Horkheimer in a passage which is the most effective refutation of the aspect of Benjamin that was doomed to failure from the outset. It is worth quoting at length:

> Whatever has happened to the people who have perished will not be healed by the future. They will never be summoned in order to be blessed in eternity. Nature and society have done their work on them and the idea of the Last Judgement into which the longing of the oppressed and the dying has entered is just a remainder of primitive thought which fails to recognise the trivial role of mankind in the history of nature, and thus humanises the universe. In the midst of this measureless indifference human consciousness is the only location in which injustice which

has been suffered is negated (*aufgehoben*), the only authority which will not be satisfied with injustice. The all-powerful goodness which was supposed to sort out suffering in eternity was from the beginning just the projection of human participation in the impassive universe. Art and religion in which this dream found its expression are just as much testimonies to this dissatisfaction as they have become, on the other hand, means of deception in the hands of the rulers in every period. Now, when trust in eternity must disintegrate, the writing of history (*Historie*) is the only way in which present day humankind – itself transient – can still pay attention to the accusations (*Anklagen*) of past humankind.

(Horkheimer 1980 p. 341)

Benjamin offers, via his politicised work on aesthetics, vital new resources, which are deeply influenced by literature, for the writing of history, but he does so only if we surrender those theological aspects that Horkheimer makes devastatingly clear can only perpetuate illusions in ways Benjamin himself actually wished to avoid.[56] The idea that one could move from Horkheimer's sense of the remorselessness of history to a total transformation generated by collective insight into the horror that is history is itself as mythological as what it opposes. The real question is whether there are other ways of coming to terms with these issues. Adorno's response to these problems is inextricably bound up with his conception of art, which both depends on ideas from Benjamin and departs from Benjamin in crucial respects. The question I have deliberately left unanswered here, namely the status of Benjamin's rejection of the notion of the autonomous work of art and its relation to truth, will provide the link to Chapter 9.

9 The culture of truth
Adorno

ADORNO AND BENJAMIN: PARADIGMS OF MODERN AESTHETICS

The extent to which Romantic hopes for art in modernity come in the twentieth century to be threatened by historical developments that put the very notion of art into question was evident in Benjamin's Marxist work in the 1930s. T.W. Adorno's work on aesthetics is in this respect the most radical attempt to salvage, rather than abandon, the Romantic heritage. In this chapter I want to highlight certain aspects of Adorno's work in the light of our concerns so far: I shall not undertake anything remotely resembling an exhaustive account of Adorno. Rather than get lost in generalities it is, in line with Adorno's own assumptions, better to engage in detail with a few key aspects of his work within the framework we have already established. This will entail concentrating upon his route to his more elaborated positions, rather than giving an analysis of *Negative Dialectics* (ND) and *Aesthetic Theory* (AT) themselves.[1] Adorno's work is so complex and so uneven that any attempt either to give a characterisation of, or to pass a verdict on, his philosophy 'as a whole' is likely to conceal more than it reveals. An account which simply takes up some of what Adorno says concerning certain major questions, of the kind volunteered here, may in fact do Adorno's thought more justice. Many of the most influential and important responses to Adorno, such as those of Wellmer and Habermas, are concerned to locate him in a particular theoretical space, which is then shown to be untenable. This creates a specific Adorno, such as the philosopher who reveals by his failure the aporias of a philosophical model which his critics wish to abandon. In the process other Adornos tend to be neglected, at the cost of some vital insights. Although it is crucial to try to establish the predominant conceptual assumptions in Adorno's texts, careful reading of the best of those texts often reveals that those assumptions do not finally govern how the texts can best be understood. I have no firm idea how consistent one can make 'Adorno', though I am pretty sure he is often not wholly consistent. On the other hand the competing Adornos are one of the vital reminders in modern thought that there should be no comfortable position from which to judge the most important philosophical issues.

In the history of modern thought there are moments when the whole focus of a major debate emerges in a disagreement between major thinkers. Adorno's and Benjamin's disagreement in the mid-1930s over the status of art has in these terms the same status, for example, as the later Schelling's and Hegel's incompatible approaches to the creation of a system of modern philosophy. However much subsequent thinkers may claim to reject the terms of such debates, the later arguments (including many of Adorno's own arguments) keep turning out to be in part another replay of some essential aspect of what was said in the initial debate.[2] What is in question between Adorno and Benjamin is the very validity and significance, in relation to the growing historical catastrophe with which both are striving to come to terms, of the concept 'work of art'. The fact is that in order to understand Adorno's work one must be able to see how the theoretical bases of his arguments against Benjamin inform his whole approach to art and truth (on this see Buck-Morss 1977). At the same time the debate between the two offers vital perspectives on the question of literature as ideology which has become such a central issue in contemporary literary theory.

What is at stake here can be suggested by looking at two of the more extreme statements about the nature of modern art made by Benjamin during the 1930s:

> As soon as an object is looked at by us as a work of art it can no longer function as such. People today can experience the specific effect of the work of art . . . far more in objects which have been removed from their context of functioning . . . than in certified works of art. (GS I 3 p. 1046)

Benjamin refers in this context to surrealism – the argument actually works better in relation to Dada – but he thinks that what has led to this situation for art is a nineteenth-century phenomenon, which is manifest in Baudelaire's obsession with 'the new':

> The new as the conscious goal of artistic production is itself no older than the nineteenth century. In Baudelaire it is not a question of the attempt which is decisive in all the arts to bring new forms to life or to gain a new perspective on things, but rather it is a question of the object which is completely new, whose power consists solely in the fact that it is new, however repulsive and dreary it may be. (ibid. p. 1152)

The obsession with the new in this form is a reaction to the notion of the 'ever-same', which is central to the *Arcades-Project*'s analyses of the nineteenth century. The currency of the notion in the nineteenth century is largely a result of an influential perception of the success of causal explanation in the natural sciences, which relates to Jacobi's fears about the 'nihilism' of the world of conditioned conditions. If everything is indeed determined in the 'Spinozist' manner there would seem in this view to be no reason why the same chains of conditions might not recur endlessly.

This would mean there is never anything finally new at all. The 'ever-same' appears most notably in Nietzsche's 'eternal recurrence', the basic idea of which Benjamin discovers had been developed in a fit of despair about the futility of history ten years before Nietzsche by the French anarchist Blanqui. For Benjamin, the point is not that the idea of 'eternal recurrence' can be construed as just another questionable metaphysical conception: it is anything but plausible, either in scientific terms or in philosophical terms.[3] His claim, in line with a central contention of *The German Ideology*, is that the real source of such ideas and the location of their real importance is concrete social reality.

Benjamin maintains that the rise of the world of the commodity is the social condition of possibility of ideas of the ever-same. While apparently generating endless novelty, the commodity structure in fact reduces the object-world to one underlying form of identity, to which every particular 'new' thing can be reduced: its exchange value. This reduction can also be analogised to the mathematisation of the cosmos in modern science that was suggested in the *Trauerspielbuch*'s dictum that mathematically-based science involves the 'renunciation of the realm of truth which is meant by languages' (GS I 1 p. 208). In Benjamin's terms, therefore, language is not wholly subservient to the systematic determination which applies to the rest of the natural world. This makes language either into the possible means of salvaging theology, as in his conception of the 'Word', or into the location of a truth which cannot be rendered verifiable in the manner of the truths of the natural sciences: the truth located in art. The links Benjamin makes between speculative thinking and socio-historical reality are the basis of his concern with the changed status of the art object in modernity, of which Baudelaire's demand for novelty is one of the most striking manifestations. In order to explain why the idea of eternal recurrence did not occur until the nineteenth century it is, then, necessary to look at what is particular to the reality of the nineteenth century, rather than merely at abstract speculation in the history of metaphysics. Only in a configuration which links together factors from political economy, philosophy and natural science does it become apparent that the ideology of progress and the mythology of recurrence are, in their hollowing out of the unrepeatable truths of history, inseparable. Such relationships between speculative theoretical ideas and concrete historical contexts will be vital in Adorno, as the source both of major insights and, particularly in *Dialectic of Enlightenment*, of some questionable reductive arguments he derives from the question of identity.

In the commodity world even the apparently new is therefore really only the repetition of forms which are, in Benjamin's (and Adorno's) terms, mythological. Benjamin's aim is to show that modernity is actually a form of 'primitive history', manifested in what he terms a collective 'dream', from which his work is to bring about the awakening. His presupposition is that the ways in which the modern world is ordered do not, despite the development of technological resources to solve many of its major practical problems, lead to greater human happiness, because modern forms of order create new kinds of mythology. Mythology is, then, a vital determining factor in history, which Benjamin regards as an ongoing catastrophe that needs to be 'interrupted' by a truth which overcomes the mythical. Awakening from the 'dream' would be the means of averting the continuation of the catastrophe. As the arguments of Marx, in the theory of commodity fetishism, Max Weber, in the theory of rationalisation, and Lukács in the (Marx- and Weber-derived) theory of reification in *History and Class Consciousness* suggest, the commodity structure brings about the reduction of the world to economically and technically manipulable forms of identity which create new social antagonisms even as they dissolve traditional ones. The functioning of the commodity system must, as we saw, be understood in terms of what Benjamin called the 'expression of economy in culture': the information conveyed by newspapers, for example, is a commodity whose value as commodity has nothing to do with the orientation it may provide in people's lives (see, for example, his essay 'The Storyteller'). Commodification is perhaps most obviously manifest in the employment of beautiful images in advertising. If it is to escape incorporation into forms of repressive identity, of the kind present in advertising images, the really new in art can no longer be beautiful in the received sense, because it would thereby risk simply being part of the reproduction of the mythical forms against which Benjamin's theory is directed. Just how apt theories which link these forms of identity in modernity really are will concern us later. The danger they entail lies in their reduction of commodity exchange to a totalising principle of identity which blocks access to the real complexity of the effects – not by any means all negative – of new forms of identity in modernity.

It is in the light of this particular constellation of forms of identity that the increasingly problematic status of the aesthetic in modernity becomes the central focus of aesthetic theory for both Benjamin and Adorno. If the Romantic connection of art and truth is as important as I have tried to suggest it is, this will clearly be the point at which the idea is subjected to its most severe tests. The mythical forms reveal their underlying nature for Benjamin in the futurist Marinetti's celebration of the 'beauties' of war, and were, to take a recent example, also all too apparent in the widespread public admiration of video film of the effects of new weapons technology in the Gulf War. Benjamin's notion of a new form of truth to be disclosed by art is therefore based on what appears irredeemable because it is of no use for generating collective assent to the forms and images which simultaneously determine and conceal the oppressive nature of modern societies. Now many of the historical structures with which Benjamin is concerned will act as a revelation of a whole new way of thinking about philosophy for Adorno, as we shall see later in this chapter. This can already be suggested by Adorno's enthusiasm in their correspondence for

242 The culture of truth: Adorno

Benjamin's idea of the need for 'liberation of things from the curse of being useful' (Adorno in Lonitz 1994 p. 138).[4] However, his refusal to accept Benjamin's wholesale rejection of the notion of 'autonomous art' reveals a vital difference between them.

The basis of Adorno's criticisms is suggested by his remarks to Benjamin on the fact that the latter adopts Marxist categories in his work on Paris in the nineteenth century which do not follow from the immanent development of his position. The origins of Benjamin's position have much to do with the attempt, suggested in the notion of the 'liberation of things from the curse of being useful', to mobilise potential from theology for historical materialism. This liberation grants a new kind of 'sacred' status to things, which derives from a self-legitimating ground of value. The sacred status depends on the fact that the thing cannot be rendered identical with other things in a relational system. In modernity this kind of self-legitimation is, as we have seen, often exemplified in Kant's notion of rational beings as ends in themselves, and in the sense that the value of the work of art is self-legitimating, whether because it is the source of Kantian disinterested pleasure or because of its non-instrumental revelation of truth. Adorno shares Benjamin's concern to mobilise theological potential for secular purposes. However, he wishes to do so by taking seriously the potential in aesthetics in a way that Benjamin, under the influence of Brecht, seems at this time to repudiate.

In Benjamin's analyses, Adorno claims:

> only too often the Marxist concepts stand all too abstractly and in an isolated manner, have the effect of *dei ex machina* and turn into something which is aesthetic in a bad way (*ins schlecht Ästhetische*). . . . I am very inclined to believe that we are all the more real the more thoroughly and consistently we remain true to the aesthetic origins, and that we are aesthetes only when we deny those origins. That this, coming from my mouth, is not said in the name of salvaging decayed resources does not need to be said – for I believe that the liquidation of art can only be undertaken in an adequate manner from a position within the aesthetic.
>
> (ibid. p. 113)

What Adorno means by the 'liquidation of art' and why this should be carried out from within the aesthetic will become clearer later via his reflections on truth. He is aiming, like Benjamin, to establish a theory which can confront the extremes of the phenomena in question. Without understanding the connection of the most reified social and economic phenomena to the most important modern art, any claim that art can reveal significant truth in modernity would be vacuous. This assumption will lead Adorno to the sometimes questionable idea that it is when the extremes meet that the most important modern art results.

Adorno insists in a later letter that his concern is not 'insular attempts to save autonomous art' and that 'A restitution of theology or rather a radicalisation of the dialectic right into the theological glowing core would have to mean the most extreme sharpening up of the social-dialectical, indeed of the economic motive' (ibid. p. 143) in analyses of capitalist culture. The combination of theology and historical materialism can only succeed if the most extreme differences between them can be incorporated into a theory which really confronts the collective historical changes that philosophy must now try to comprehend. Benjamin's conception of the 'dream' in modernity is based on the collective 'content of consciousness' of the masses in commodity society. For Adorno, this brings him too close to Jung's and Klages' mystification, via their vitalist notion of the 'collective unconscious', of the social and historical structures which actually produce commodity society and its mythological effects. The analysis should there-fore really be based on the fact that the 'fetish-character of the commodity is not a fact of consciousness but dialectical in the emphatic sense that it produces consciousness' (ibid. p. 139). Life in societies dominated by the cultural results of commodity exchange renders people increasingly unable to value things for their particularity and for their intrinsic worth. The task is therefore to work out a way of getting from exchange structures that have undoubted effects on consciousness – which can be revealed in a Marxian analysis of the commodity as both intended human product and as beyond the reach of fully conscious intention – to exactly what the effects of those structures may be.

For Adorno, such effects are not adequately dealt with by the notion that they are a 'dream' based on a collective unconscious, unless this is merely a metaphor to be cashed in via a rational social theory. The effects of the fetish-character of the commodity involve what Adorno will – in my view unfortunately (see Bowie 1995b) – later term the 'primacy of the objective'. It is worth once more remembering here that the sense in which conscious-ness is 'produced' by the structures that mediate it offers a way of linking language to the commodity form. In both cases the potential for reduction of the individuality of the object and for cognitive impoverishment of the subject is a result of a primacy of the system before what it is regarded as subjecting to itself. Modernist literature is often usefully understood in this perspective as the attempt to reach a language for which this reduction of particularity would be impossible. As we shall see in the Conclusion, this raises complex questions of the kind we already raised in earlier chapters about the subject's relationship to language.

Given the theorist's inability to step wholly outside the society which, in the terms of this theory, also produces her consciousness, the problem for Adorno is now the location from which an analysis of fetishisation can be undertaken. We are here back on familiar territory. The question of the ground of social criticism is actually a version of what Heidegger revealed in his account of the necessarily circular structure of interpretation, which Adorno connects to the question of ideology. In order to find a location from which critical analysis of the production of (false) consciousness and reification is possible one must first find a way of showing that the commodity structure does not in fact wholly determine the consciousness of all the members of a society: otherwise that location is simply not available. This location must be intelligible to the subjects of real societies if reification is not to be assumed to be total, which is why the idea of the truth claim inherent in art will be so important for Adorno. The fact is, of course – and Adorno is not always clear about this – that the very idea of total reification is actually unintelligible: there must be a contrasting term with which we are already acquainted for us to be aware of reification as an issue at all. I have argued throughout that such awareness requires the assumption of the freedom of the subject: nothing about the systems that produce reification would, of itself, make us aware of reification. Some of Adorno's later paradoxical formulations result from the implication that the only possible access to the 'other' of reification must either be in terms of something totally different from the world as it already is, or at least in terms of something which, though constituted with the material of the reified world, yet embodies a complete negation of that world. The totalising notion of reification will, as we shall see, sometimes lead Adorno to make impossibly theological demands upon the work of art.

However, even if one rejects the more metaphysical version of the critique of reification, it remains the case that what opposes reification cannot, given the other assumptions of the theory, simply be identified in conceptual terms. These terms, which rely on forms of identification, are subject to the suspicion of complicity with the commodity structure and with the predominantly instrumental nature of modern rationality. Only if there is a way in which what is repressed is really manifested *within* society can this problem be overcome. The work of art is so vital for Adorno because he thinks it is able, via its autonomy, to resist commodification, at the same time as being a social fact, produced by a subject, which yet transcends the subject's intentions. The truth which is communicable through art is a result of this dual status. In the case of a literary text, for example, the question will be whether the text is able, via its re-articulation of already existing linguistic material, to circumvent or negate the meanings which contribute to the structures of domination within a society.

Adorno's most important objections to Benjamin's position in the mid-1930s are set out in a letter of 18 March 1936, concerning the latter's 'Work of Art' essay. What he says goes beyond the contingent and pretty self-evident failures of Benjamin's attempt in this particular essay to map out a positive revolutionary conception of 'post auratic' art based on the cinema and on the imagined laid-back critical members of Brecht's proletarian audience.[5] The crucial terms in Adorno's discussion are 'technique' and 'autonomy' in the work of art:

> You know that the object 'liquidation of art' has been behind my aesthetic endeavours for many years and that the insistence with which

I advocate the primacy of technology, above all in music, is to be understood strictly in this sense. . . . You have in your writings, whose great continuity the most recent text seems to me to take up, separated the concept of the art work as a configuration (*Gebilde*) from both the symbol of theology and the magic taboo. I now find it questionable, and here I find a very sublimated remainder of Brechtian motifs, that you now without more ado transfer the concept of the magic aura to the 'autonomous art work' and straightforwardly attribute a counter-revolutionary function to the latter. (ibid. pp. 168–9)

While not ignoring the 'magical' element in bourgeois art, Adorno thinks that it is inseparable from the 'sign of freedom' (ibid. p. 169) in the same works. The revelation of the consequences of this dual aspect of art will be Adorno's essential concern throughout his mature work on aesthetics. The 'sign of freedom' will, though, consist more and more in the works' refusal to communicate in the dominant terms of their own society, and not in a liberation and expansion of existing semantic possibilities. In AT, written after the catastrophes of the 1940s, Adorno will maintain that 'The popular notion of art as multi-layered is the falsely positive name for art's puzzle-character' (Adorno 1973b p. 192): without this puzzle-character, which constitutes its resistance to interpretation rather than its semantic richness, modern art just slips back into being magical.

What Benjamin misses, which Adorno sees particularly in his own musical experience, is the fact that 'precisely the most extreme consistency in the following of the technological law of autonomous art changes this art and brings it closer to the state of freedom, to what can be produced, done consciously, rather than closer to making it taboo and fetishising it' (Lonitz 1994 p. 170). The combination of technology and freedom, which will remain central to all Adorno's writings on aesthetics, is the dominant characteristic of the great bourgeois works of autonomous art. Via their radical assumption of the modern need for innovation these works embody Adorno's refusal to be nostalgic about the art of the past. He illustrates the point of such works via Mallarmé's dictum that poems are 'not inspired, but made out of words' (ibid.). Elsewhere the idea is illustrated by Beethoven's assertion that what people find mysterious and disturbing in his music is just the result of his skilful new deployment of the diminished seventh chord.[6] In one sense the point is very simple: Adorno wishes to sustain the – for him at least – self-evidently exceptional status of such works as those of Mallarmé and Beethoven without rendering them thereby mysterious, or merely reducing them to their explanation or interpretation. The great works' proximity to the normal and the habitual suggests their importance in revealing a truth which is always already a potential of even the most apparently banal aspects of the world. This idea was, of course, already present in *Monologue*: Mallarmé may wish to 'purify the words of the tribe', but what he carries out is a transformation of the words we already possess by placing them in new configurations.[7] Similarly Beethoven may use essentially the same musical material as others, but he reorganises it according to the most developed technical possibilities, so that it is transformed.

The decisive term in Adorno's disagreement with Benjamin is 'dialectic'. His use of the notion of 'dialectic' relies initially on the German Idealist idea that negativity is the motor of the positive. For a theory concerned to unmask the ideological functions of cultural forms in a commodified world, things which appear negative and in need of criticism should not just be rejected, but 'salvaged', there always being ways in which re-contextualising something can render it meaningful. This is another reason why both Adorno and Benjamin think theology can be rendered serviceable in a 'profane' manner for historical materialism. Benjamin is prepared to salvage the remainders of everyday life which are transformed by the praxes of surrealism or Dada – think of Kurt Schwitters' use of old bus tickets, etc. – but seems prepared to jettison autonomous art. Adorno, on the other hand, thinks that 'as little as the reification of the cinema is completely beyond salvaging, just as little is that of the great work of art' (ibid. p. 171). The extremes of commercial cinema and Schönberg 'are both halves of the whole freedom which have been torn apart, but this freedom cannot be made by adding the two halves together' (ibid.). Benjamin's view, Adorno maintains, leads merely to a rejection of autonomous art because of its failure to possess 'immediate use value' (ibid.). The attempt to demystify art in terms of the destruction of aura means that any truth-content works of art may involve when they are understood via their relationship to human freedom is simply ignored. This happens in the name of the idea that only art which is politically useful can be valid in the present historical circumstances.

I suggested in both the Introduction and Chapter 5 that the basic position adopted here by Benjamin leaves the problem of finding ways to understand the freedom which the revolutionary transformation is to bring about, otherwise it is likely just to reproduce another version of what is already there. The fact is that the 'utopian' images of freedom which would legitimate modern revolutions must always transcend the abolition of hunger, penury and physical repression. Non-commodified aesthetic images are vital in this respect because they suggest human potential which cannot be assimilated into the immediate satisfaction of needs. Anyone in doubt about what is meant by commodified images should ponder how many formerly aesthetic images have been taken over by advertising, to the point where it increasingly seems that images can no longer have truth in Adorno's sense at all. Looked at in this perspective, his Kantian attachment to the ban on images of the deity in Jewish theology, as a way of thinking about how modern art can be true, makes more sense than is sometimes thought. That Benjamin himself was ambivalent about the semantic resources in modern autonomous art which cannot be replaced by anything else has often been noted: the essays on the 'Storyteller' and on Kafka are, for example, much closer to Adorno's position.

The urgency apparent both in Adorno's criticisms and in Benjamin's extreme positions is a result both of the philosophical connection of art to truth with which we have been concerned all along and of the particular historical circumstances of the time. Adorno maintains that one should not surrender one's critical intelligence in allying oneself with the proletariat, 'who need us for knowledge as much as we need the proletariat so that the revolution can be carried out' (ibid. p. 174). The relationship between intellectuals and proletariat is vital for the 'further formulation of the aesthetic debate, for which you [Benjamin] have provided a splendid inaugural address' (ibid.). In the period following the writing of his letter, events in the Soviet Union and in European politics move in ever more catastrophic directions. Adorno comes to realise that world-revolutionary hopes, even in the more differentiated forms he wished to support, are themselves largely illusory, a verdict which subsequent history will only underline. It is not that Adorno therefore ceases to think the oppression inherent in class divisions is an issue. The problem is that the new trans-formations of social structures seem to lead to other forms of oppression, without there being any obvious decisive way beyond this situation. What happens, then, to his theory of art and politics, if his hopes for revolution-ary political transformation turn out to have no basis in concrete historical reality?

Adorno claims in his letter that 'if there is an auratic character then it is a property of films in the most emphatic and most questionable manner. ... Schönberg's music is certainly *not* auratic' (ibid. pp. 172–3). The very idea of the use of culture for political transformation therefore entails a disturbing aporia. Hollywood films watched by a mass audience demon-strably militate against an active critical attitude towards social reality, not least because the spectators, quite understandably, welcome such films as a release from the demands of the work process. This is the case in any society in which the demands of the work process leave little space for developing judgement that is adequate either to the truth-potential of major art or to the complexity of modern socio-political life.[8] Brecht's theories are so problematic precisely because they underestimate the difficulties at issue here. Understanding Schönberg or Proust or, for that matter, Brecht can be 'too much like hard work' for those who do not have sufficient time.[9] A widespread critical and aesthetic engagement with the truth-content of radical modern art would therefore itself depend upon a transformation of the work process that enabled people to engage with and produce such art. Attempting to use art itself to help *bring about* such a transformation leads in the period in question to the danger, evident in Hollywood, and also in both Nazi and Soviet cultural politics, of restoring new forms of mythology, to which art must, in Adorno's terms, be immune. Adorno's insistence upon an uncompromising view of this possible role of art leads him to reject Ernst Bloch's desire, given the success of the Right in doing so, for the Left to use more aesthetic modes of communication in politics. The dilemma is that if the Left does not employ such modes the Right gains political advantages, but the employment of such modes means the Left gets dragged into the territory of the Right. Given the very broad social implications of the issue of mass communication, the very attempt here to frame these questions in terms of kinds of art might seem to put too much weight upon what Adorno means by autonomous art. His position would, however, only be indefensible if there were no evidence that modernist art can be, even despite its perhaps limited reception, significant in the ways he suggests.[10] Consideration of whether the significance Adorno attaches to modernist art as a source of truth about society is in fact justified will form the underlying agenda of much of the rest of this chapter. To begin to answer these questions we need now to locate certain aspects of Adorno's philosophical project more exactly.

Before setting off on that path, however, one vital orienting idea should be introduced. It is easy to be sceptical about the enormous role attributed to art by Adorno even as he announces the probable historical demise of that role. The best way to gain an initial purchase on issues which he probably articulates better than any other modern thinker is to ponder the following point. Most people will tend, given half the chance to engage with it, to appreciate the music of Mozart, Beethoven or Schubert. The same people will tend to have difficulty with Schönberg or other major modernist composers. Among those who dislike Schönberg the more reflective will, though, generally also be aware of the impossibility of a serious composer wanting to write music in the manner of Mozart or Beethoven, even though there are technically no obstacles to doing so. In some important way such music can no longer be 'true', in much the same way as the employment of the narrative forms of nineteenth-century 'realist' fiction also do not 'ring true' as responses to contemporary reality, however much the historical facts such narratives contain may be accurate. Adorno takes what is behind these issues as germane to the question of truth in modern philosophy.

'DREAMLIKE ANTICIPATION': ADORNO'S EARLIEST PHILOSOPHY

In a letter to Ernst Bloch in 1962 Adorno remarks that 'Very much of what I wrote in my youth has the character of a dreamlike anticipation, and only from a certain moment of shock onwards, which probably coincides with the beginning of Hitler's Reich, do I really think I did what I did right' (Adorno 1973a p. 384). He begins his work in the 1920s as a successful music theoretician and critic, and only publishes his first major specifically philosophical work, the *Habilitation* on *Kierkegaard: Construction of the Aesthetic*, in the inauspicious year of 1933. His philosophical work in the 1920s is fairly narrowly academic, and it will be his encounter with Benjamin that first gives him a deep sense of philosophical adventure. It is important to note, however, that the early work influenced by his undistinguished academic teacher of philosophy, Hans Cornelius, does already touch on familiar issues, as well as pointing to Adorno's later theories. The continuity of concerns within the Romantic tradition being reconstructed here is, as I have tried to suggest, quite striking.

Adorno's doctoral dissertation of 1924 is entitled 'The Transcendence of Things (*des Dinglichen*) and of the Noematic in Husserl's Phenomenology', which already suggests a degree of proximity to Heidegger, who will soon have an important influence on Adorno's thinking. Adorno, though, is here nowhere near Heidegger's philosophical level. In the dissertation what Adorno terms the separation of 'being as consciousness' and 'being as reality', which is his questionable way of renaming Husserl's differentiation of 'noesis' and 'noema' (ibid. p. 74), is criticised in the name of a version of transcendental idealism. The problem he wishes to solve is that of the 'thing in itself' in its phenomenological guise, which Adorno claims to obviate by 'completely eliminating the noema' and replacing it with 'the concept of the immanent thing in itself', a thing being defined, rather like Kant defines an 'object', as a 'law-like connection of appearances' (ibid. pp. 75–6). In the *Habilitation* dissertation on 'The Concept of the Unconscious in the Transcendental Doctrine of the Soul' of 1927, which he withdrew, later submitting the Kierkegaard book in its place, Adorno similarly conjures away any sense that the thing in itself is a problem. He does so by asserting philosophy's inescapable need for the 'acknowledgement of the immediately given', which is 'a final and undeducible fact' (ibid. p. 95). This dogmatic assertion, which cannot be substantiated in the form he proposes, is made in order to criticise the ways in which the thing in itself is used in the nineteenth century by thinkers like Schopenhauer to establish a realm of the unconscious based on a conceptually inaccessible 'spontaneity' which underlies the world of knowable appearances.[11] The problems involved here are central concerns of German Idealism: we saw them illustrated, for example, by Jacobi's question about the nature of the 'causality' of Kant's things in themselves (the realm of spontaneity) in relation to 'intuitions' (the realm of appearance, of 'noesis'). It was, of course, Schelling's development of the problem of the ground of appearances revealed by Jacobi that was the major influence on Schopenhauer.

Despite the crude idealism of Adorno's philosophical conclusions in the withdrawn *Habilitation*, one important aspect of his argument points both to a major concern of the present book and to his own later concerns. Adorno rejects any position 'to the extent to which it thinks that, with the concept of the unconscious, it possesses the absolute ground of its assertions' (ibid. p. 305). He thereby already hints at the Romantic antifoundationalism which will come to form the core of his most important later philosophy. Even if there were an 'intuitive' knowledge of unconscious facts, 'this knowledge would require confirmation by scientifically discursive knowledge' (ibid.). This is impossible if the unconscious is in any way transcendent, as it must be in theories which take the unconscious to be an absolute ground. In 1940 Adorno, surprisingly in line both with the early Sartre and with his early philosophical self, will suggest to Benjamin that using Freudian theory to interpret Proustian 'involuntary memory' leaves 'The terribly difficult problem . . . of the unconsciousness of the basic impression, which should be necessary for the basic impression to be allotted to *mémoire involontaire* and not to consciousness. Can one really talk of this unconsciousness? Was the moment of tasting . . . really unconscious?' (Adorno in Lonitz 1994 p. 417). The simple question is, as Adorno realises: what is it that one is *re-membering*, if one was never conscious of it at all in the first place?[12] Although his overall theory of consciousness in the early dissertation has, via its dogmatic scientism, passed into justified oblivion, the conjunction of these two related epistemological examinations of the unconscious is important. It shows how Adorno is concerned from the outset with those areas of modern thought that do not think philosophy can provide a final ground for truth, at the same time as he, like the Romantics, refuses to take an irrationalist path. This refusal will be vital for his developed theories of art and for the theory of 'negative dialectics'.

In this early work Adorno tries in a basically positivistic manner to skirt major philosophical problems by finding a theoretical ground that will incorporate the insights of 'scientific' psychology, which, perhaps surprisingly, includes aspects of psychoanalysis. However, at the end of the withdrawn *Habilitation*, Adorno suddenly and radically changes tack. It is as though a different person comes into the room. The initial reason for his taking up the theme of the unconscious was to see how it related to vitalist theories of 'intuition'. This examination of vitalist theories now leads him to the meta-reflection that 'The function of a theory in social reality is itself always social' (Adorno 1973a p. 317), and thence to a startling change of perspective. He maintains that the very popularity of irrationalist theories of the unconscious in a world which is ever more economically rationalised indicates that the aim of such theories 'is to complete what is lacking in reality' (ibid. p. 318), and that they thereby function as ideology.

The intensity of Adorno's interpolated critique of the social roots of vitalism should be seen against the background of the actions of intellectuals like Georg Simmel who, in an intellectual betrayal almost on a par with that of Heidegger and Nazism, welcomed the First World War as a restitution of vital forces which commodity forms had repressed (see Simmel 1917, Bowie 1979). In Adorno's view the appeal to unconscious forces to account for apparently irrational events is in fact an excuse to conceal the fact of 'uncontrolled egoistic exploitation' and 'the most fatal plans of imperialism' (Adorno 1973a p. 319) as the thoroughly accessible source of such events. It should be clear from this both why Adorno later objects to Benjamin's temporary enthusiasm for Jung and Klages, and why he has such misgivings concerning the idea of the compensatory, as opposed to the critical, truth-revealing function of art in modern societies. Adorno is circumspect in this latter respect not least because the theme of 'intuitive' access to the unconscious had been, since the Romantics, associated with art. The idea of such intuition was based on a misreading of Schelling's 1800 *System of Transcendental Idealism*, where the notion of 'unconscious activity' plays a vital role. Schelling's view of intuition is in fact anything but irrationalist. He actually sees art as a way of rationally coming to terms with those 'intuitive' aspects of ourselves which cannot be rendered into complete discursivity. This gives art a vital political function, in that it is to communicate both abstract 'ideas of reason' and ways of coming to terms with sensuousness in universally accessible forms, in what Schelling terms a 'mythology of reason' (see Lypp 1972, Bowie 1990, 1993). Aesthetics had tended, though, not least via Schopenhauer's and Nietzsche's irrationalist appropriations of Romantic positions, to become part of right-wing ideology, a fact which is still part of the suspicion that fuels theories of art as ideology (e.g. in Eagleton 1990). Given the tendency for some of the most extreme versions of vitalism to use music as the representative form of art, and given Adorno's own highly developed practical and theoretical involvement with music, the importance of these matters to his wider project should now be apparent. Much of Adorno's philosophy is devoted to wresting the deepest questions of aesthetics from right-wing ideology while not landing in the position of the Benjamin of the mid-1930s. This is why he, and not the irrationalists, must be regarded as the legitimate heir to the Romantic thinking which I have been trying to salvage in the present book.

THE 'DISSOLUTION OF WHAT HAS UP TO NOW BEEN CALLED PHILOSOPHY'

Although it is only when he moves away from some of Benjamin's questionable positions that he reaches his most important insights, Adorno's own philosophical voice evidently emerges because of his fascination with Benjamin's work, particularly the *Trauerspielbuch* (see Buck-Morss 1977). Concentrating on the earlier Adorno helps to sustain a historical continuity which might be lost were we to move directly to the major post-war works. Adorno had no doubts that even his very early dissertation on Husserl contained ideas germane to his later work. In the case of the three short pieces from the early 1930s, considered below, as suggesting many of the major directions of his thought – 'The Actuality of Philosophy' (AP), 'The Idea of Nature-History' (INH) and the 'Theses on the Language of the Philosopher' (TLP) – there is no doubt at all that they are crucial for his later work. In a remark appended to *Negative Dialektik* (ND), which was written between 1959 and 1966, Adorno refers, for example, to INH as a key source (Adorno 1975 p. 409).

AP, which was Adorno's inaugural university lecture, begins by stating the most radical Romantic position, namely the renunciation of the ambition of grasping 'the totality of the real by the power of thought' (Adorno 1973a p. 326). This renunciation is elucidated by the remark that

> If philosophy must learn to renounce the question of totality, then that means from the outset that it must learn to get by without the symbolic function, in which up to now, at least in Idealism, the particular appeared to represent the universal. (ibid. p. 336)

The idea derives from the *Trauerspielbuch* and from Lukács' *The Theory of the Novel*, both of which Adorno refers to frequently both in this period and subsequently. Lukács, like Benjamin, relies heavily on the Romantic notions of irony and of allegory as responses to a world which he sees as no longer possessing immanent significance of the kind that is supposedly embodied in the symbol.[13]

Much of the rest of AP is really a repetition in a more accessible form of the argument of the Preface to the *Trauerspielbuch*.[14] There is, though, an important difference of emphasis. Adorno talks of philosophy bringing 'elements which it receives from the sciences into changing constellations' which form into a 'figure' – the notion is related to Benjamin's 'Idea' – that solves the immediate problem in question (ibid. p. 335), such as that of the 'thing in itself'. The difference between philosophy and the natural sciences is that 'the idea of science is research, that of philosophy interpretation (*Deutung*) ... philosophy must always interpret with the claim to truth, without ever having an assured key for the interpretation' (ibid. p. 334). One of the 'figures' that would result from this interpretation would be – here Adorno initially follows the Lukács of *History and Class Consciousness* – the 'commodity form' (ibid. p. 337). This form establishes a world of identities that are constituted by what I have termed, following Jacobi, chains of conditions, and it creates the realm of illusion which historical materialist philosophy wishes to unmask. Adorno does not, though, as does Lukács, think that this 'figure' solves the *philosophical* problem of the thing in itself by revealing that the ground of commodified or reified appearances is in fact living human labour. The proletariat for Lukács is, in these terms, the real 'subject-object' of history. Adorno even denies that the commodity form reveals the socio-economic 'conditions of possibility' of the problem. Instead, he maintains, the philosophical problem might 'simply disappear' (ibid.) via the establishing of the figure. It is only if one presupposes the commodity form that many of the most fundamental social and economic phenomena in modern history become intelligible: to this extent Benjamin's attempt to stop the regresses of induction with the Idea makes pragmatic sense because the 'figure' produces serious results. The task of philosophical interpretation, then, is to locate problems like the thing in itself in a constellation that reveals the historical truth-content of the problem, there being for Adorno no timeless problems and, more importantly, no timeless solutions. Lukács' approach is, then, regarded as leading to difficulties of the kind we have repeatedly encountered, which

Lukács unfortunately tries to resolve by having the proletariat and the party as the ground which stops the regress of explanations.

The vital point for Adorno, which will inform all his major work, is to change the very nature of theoretical arguments, in order to escape the structures of regress and the false totalisations entailed in attempts finally to ground theoretical claims. He now suggests that, by contextualising it in a particular manner, the apparently supra-temporal philosophical problem can be revealed as the mystification of a soluble social problem. This should not, though, be read as a reduction of philosophical problems to sociology: Adorno will bitterly oppose precisely this kind of reductionism in Karl Mannheim's 'sociology of knowledge' at the time he is writing AP. He is therefore not outlining an a priori universal method, but instead describing a praxis of investigation. The aim is to circumvent the metaphysical problems, rather than offering another metaphysical alternative. Benjamin's 'Ideas' and 'dialectical images' are here interpreted as 'instruments of human reason itself even where they seem, as magnetic centres, to direct objective being objectively onto themselves. They are models' (ibid. p. 341). As the word 'model' suggests, they have a more pragmatic status for Adorno than they do for the theologically inspired Benjamin. That this is a central tendency of Adorno's thought will be confirmed in ND, first published in 1966, where he maintains in relation to the idea of 'disclosing objects via constellations' that 'one does not at all need to begin with investigations which are metaphysical in terms of their own content, like Benjamin's *Origin of German Trauerspiel*, which grasp the concept of truth itself as a constellation' (Adorno 1975 p. 166). The success of a model for AP lies in its capacity both to reveal and to obviate the theoretical dilemma involved in a real historical problem. This new pragmatic aspect is vital to an adequate understanding of Adorno, as the following also shows.

One of the main points of orientation of AP is the Vienna Circle. Adorno is anything but dismissive of the arguments of logical positivism, and pointedly rejects the kind of opposition to it which 'wishes to defend philosophy against the claim of exclusive scientificity and yet itself also acknowledges this claim [of scientificity]' via a 'concept of philosophical literature (*Dichtung*) whose non-binding relationship before the truth is only topped by its philistinism ['*Kunstfremdheit*' in the sense that it is 'alien to art'] and aesthetic inferiority' (ibid. p. 332). The core of Adorno's thinking is manifested in his insistence on the primacy of truth against such aestheticising positions: 'one ought simply to liquidate philosophy and dissolve it into individual sciences rather than to try to help it out with an ideal of literature which means no more than a bad ornamental dressing-up of false thoughts' (ibid.). At the same time Adorno sees through logical positivism's verificationist rejection of any statements that have no empirical basis in what has since become the standard manner, suggesting that positivism is 'itself philosophically by no means as lacking in presuppositions as it pretends' (ibid.). The assertion that only statements which can be verified can be truth-determinate cannot itself be verified. This is, in fact, another version of what was entailed by Jacobi's distinction of 'the true' from 'knowledge'. Despite his rejection of the essential foundational claim of the Vienna Circle, Adorno thinks that the truth of such positions as logical positivism lies in the way that they still reveal central theoretical problems of the present.

This defence of logical positivism may, given Adorno's later work, appear very odd. However, his bitter opposition to 'positivism' after the war is by no means incompatible with this stance. Once logical positivism becomes, after its enforced emigration to the USA, an institutionalised discipline whose goal, within a system of power relations that includes the military-industrial complex, is the philosophical legitimation of the natural sciences, it no longer carries out the critical demystifying function it did in Europe prior to the Nazi take-over (see d'Acconti 1995). This change in the significance of philosophical theories is *exactly* the kind of phenomenon with which Adorno is concerned in AP and elsewhere in his subsequent work. The 'extraordinary importance' of the Vienna Circle lies, he maintains, not in its success in 'turning philosophy into science' (Adorno 1973a p. 333), i.e. not in the truth of its claims as judged in its own terms or in supposedly universal philosophical terms, but rather in its excluding 'all questions which, as specifically scientific questions, are appropriate for individual sciences and which cloud philosophical questioning' (ibid.). What, then, are the specifically philosophical questions now to be?

Adorno here comes very close to the anti-foundational aspect of Richard Rorty and the pragmatist tradition, and to the Romantic philosophy we considered in earlier chapters:

> the idea of philosophical interpretation does not shy away from the liquidation of philosophy which appears to me to be signalled by the collapse of the last philosophical claims to totality. For the strict exclusion of all ontological questions in the received sense, the avoidance of invariable universal concepts – including, for example, that of man – the exclusion of every idea of a self-sufficient totality of mind, including of a self-enclosed '*Geistesgeschichte*'; the concentration of philosophical questions on concrete historically immanent complexes from which they should not be separated: these postulates become very similar to a dissolution of what has up to now been called philosophy. (ibid. p. 339)

It should not now be surprising that this position – which has echoes in both Schlegel and in Rorty's contentions that philosophy is a 'kind of literature', rather than a foundational discipline – should have led Adorno to the kind of concerns we observed in Romantic '*Poesie*'.

In INH Adorno gives an over-condensed model of his philosophical procedure by deconstructing the supposedly a priori difference between the idea that 'history' is the realm in which 'the qualitatively new appears' and the idea that 'nature' is the realm of 'pre-given being' (ibid. p. 346) –

of what we have termed, following Putnam, the 'ready-made world'. Many of the ideas in the essay rely on questions of allegory and mythology we examined in the *Trauerspielbuch* and Benjamin's earlier essays. Adorno suggests that the apparently new is in fact an aspect of 'primitive history', and that the line between nature and history cannot be finally established. This is most disturbingly apparent in the fact that nature itself appears as transient, thus in the form associated with history, and therefore cannot be said to be 'ready-made'. While the understanding of the temporality of nature is historical, as is evident in the changed aspect of nature that emerges in the baroque and plays a role in *Trauerspiel*, history itself, particularly in the recurrences of mythical thinking, takes on forms associated with nature when nature is conceived of as the 'ever-same'. This deconstructive approach is an example of what Adorno will later term, against Hegel, 'negative dialectics'. Despite the proximity of the revelation of the interdependence of opposed terms to central ideas in Hegel's *Logic*, there is in INH no dialectical resolution of nature and history into the 'identity of identity and difference'. Such a resolution would entail a position at the end of the system, of the kind familiar from the 'absolute Idea' of the *Logic*, in which all the differences become intelligible as aspects of a self-related and self-grounding totality: this was Hegel's attempted answer to the problems of grounding and regress suggested by Jacobi. Instead, Adorno's essentially Romantic idea, which will later be echoed in the best work of Derrida, is that the foundational categories which philosophy tries to establish turn out never to be finally distinguishable from each other, but are also never finally identical.[15] The categories employed must therefore be understood in terms of the way they can be reconfigured to generate new insight, rather than as grounding concepts. As Novalis put it: 'There is no absolute beginning – it belongs in the category of imaginary thoughts' (Novalis 1978 p. 699). Hegel may not have an absolute beginning, but – which in Adorno's terms is far worse – he has an absolute reconciliation at the end of his philosophy that performs the same function.[16]

Adorno also undertakes his deconstruction of the opposition of nature and history in INH as a way of countering what he sees as the early Heidegger's basically Fichtean subjectivism and Heidegger's tendency simply to replace traditional fixed ontological categories with other equally static categories, such as 'historicity'. He thereby prefigures some of Derrida's (at times questionable) attempts to deconstruct Heideggerian notions like 'presence' (see Chapter 6, this volume), as Adorno's proximity to Rorty's refusal of fixed ontological categories would also suggest. There is no space here to go into the deeply problematic question of Adorno's understanding of Heidegger,[17] though a few of the essential questions will be touched on in what follows. Instead let us now look at TLP, which takes up some of the main questions of the present book in the light of issues outlined above.

WORDS PUT IN QUESTION

TLP gets off to a problematic start; Adorno offers a version of Benjamin's theory of the 'name':

> For a thought which grasps things exclusively as functions of thought, names have become arbitrary: they are free positings (*Setzungen*) of consciousness. . . . For a thought which is no longer prepared to acknowledge autonomy and spontaneity as the ground of justification of cognition, the contingency of the significative attribution of language and things becomes radically problematic. (Adorno 1973a p. 366)

In the early Benjamin the theory of the name was expressly theological. The objection to the theory of the name was that, despite its apparent opposition to the metaphysics of 're-presentational thinking', it covertly involved the idea of a ready-made identity between word and thing, thereby failing to take into account that the very idea of a word finally saying what a thing is leads to insoluble methodological dilemmas. Cognitive truth about objects is articulated in the predication of 'x as something', and not in the naming of the object as (identical with) itself. To this extent any objection to the arbitrariness of the names of things would seem essentially meaningless and thus only salvageable if one is prepared to take on the theology which informed Benjamin's argument. It is worth mentioning at this point that some of Adorno's later aesthetic questions concerning the notion of 'identity', which underlie this issue, will show that the relationship between language and an intelligible world may have dimensions which are inadequately articulated both by theories of predication, and, for that matter, by theories of the 'name'. It will, crucially, be in literature and music that the idea of a possible non-arbitrary status of language can be rendered philosophically interesting.

In TLP Adorno does not argue in an expressly theological manner, but he does rely, in the manner of Lukács' *The Theory of the Novel*, upon the problematic idea that there have been historical periods when language and the world were not arbitrarily related:

> In a homogeneous society the comprehensibility of philosophical language is never demanded, in all cases (*allenfalls*), however, it is pre-given: if the ontological power of words extends so far that they possess objective dignity in society. . . . Without an integrated/closed (*geschlossene*) society there is no objective, thus no truly comprehensible language.
> (ibid. p. 367)

The story of modern hermeneutics we have been reconstructing is implicit in this version of the move away from the sense of the 'Word' as a reflection of a theologically ready-made world, but the story appears in a mystified guise. Adorno seems here (later the question becomes more complex) to hanker after a world in which form and content mirrored each other. He relies on the premise that historical understanding of language could reveal such a mirroring, which is, though, now no longer possible. Adorno thereby seems to reject any sense that the breakup of this notional, and thus in one sense ideological, identity is also a liberation of human possibilities, of the kind suggested in the emergence of the Romantic notion of *Poesie*.[18] He does so in the name of a story which in fact differs little from the later Heidegger's totalising conception of modern 'metaphysics'. Modern changes in the understanding of language cannot, however, simply be assimilated to the idea of the new emergence of language as a manifestation of the growing domination of subjective intention. The very realisation that language in modernity *can* become a form of domination itself depends upon the new freedom which allows us to *reflect* in a secular manner upon our relationship to language, a freedom which can and at times does lead to our going silent rather than extending our supposed linguistic dominion. Furthermore, the status of the language in which it can now intelligibly be stated and understood that the form and content of language used to mirror each other is, in Adorno's account, anything but clear. It is not obvious, for example, whether the account is about societies in which people did not come to question language's relationship to the world because of their theological faith in the Word, or whether it is instead an ontological state- ment about language's changed relationship to being, of the kind we saw in Heidegger. Probably the only source of a persuasive interpretation of what is in question here will, as we shall see below, be via questions of language and music in modern art.

That there is a major shift in ideas about language in the modern period is beyond doubt: Romantic philosophy and the rise of modern hermen- eutics are unthinkable without it. The question is whether Adorno offers a convincing account of the shift. His further premise in TLP, which remains constant in his later work, is that we are faced in modernity with 'an atomised, disintegrated society' (ibid.), of which the philosophical manifes- tation – although he does not in this particular case name it as such – is Kant's schematism. Because it is grounded in the spontaneity of the subject, schematism is the epitome of what Adorno terms 'idealist' thinking: 'If multiplicity's unity is subjectively impressed on it as form, such form is necessarily thought of as separable from the content' (ibid. p. 366). The best aspects of Adorno's mature theory of negative dialectics will result not least from the realisation that, even as it may indeed be the case that there is a deep philosophical problem here, a theoretical determination of the location from which the significance of this separation could be articulated may not be possible. Although the work of art cannot give a philosophical explanation of why the separation of form and content is important, it can perhaps point to a sense of what it means for this separation not to be 'the last word' on the relation of language to being.

The issue of scheme and content is, significantly, still very much part of contemporary philosophy. Rorty's and Davidson's pragmatic alternative to

Adorno's worry about form and content is to deny that there is any real problem at all. For them the Kantian scheme/content distinction – a distinction which both Rorty and Adorno, like Nietzsche and Heidegger, see as already present in Plato's separation of the forms from unreliable empirical reality – is the classic example of the metaphysics we need to renounce if we are not just to keep getting caught in the aporias of Western philosophy. Adorno's anti-foundational, pragmatic remarks cited earlier therefore suggest an important ambivalence in his work, between the idea that there is a definitive way, from either an idealist or a materialist perspective, of explaining how and why such shifts in conceptions of language take place, and the idea that this whole level of philosophical argument should be abandoned because it just reproduces the insoluble problems entailed in attempting to overcome divisions between appearance and reality, subject and object, ideal and real, etc. Adorno's relevance for contemporary philosophy and literary theory is not least a result of his refusal to conjure away this ambivalence.

The perspective adopted in TLP locates Adorno, *avant la lettre*, in some of the same territory as the later Heidegger, of the 'Letter on Humanism' cited in Chapter 7, for whom 'language under the domination of the modern metaphysics of subjectivity almost continuously falls out of its element' (Heidegger 1949 p. 10), so that it becomes 'an instrument of domination over entities' (ibid.). In both cases what is required for the existence of truth happens in a way which is independent of subjective intention, so that words are found which correspond to the 'state of truth' in the available language (Adorno 1973a p. 367). Adorno's critique of the idea that truth is generated by the subject's spontaneity interprets this spontaneity merely as the subject's capacity for domination of the object, which means that the subject–object split is, in his terms, invalidly resolved in the direction of 'idealism'. The subject in 'idealism', or what Adorno also terms the 'autonomous *ratio*', dominates from the side of 'history' (in the undeconstructed sense) rather than of 'nature'. This account of truth, he maintains, obscures the fact, fundamental to psychoanalysis, that how subjects think also has to do with their location in 'objective' contexts – including the fact that they themselves are also 'nature' – which are, in turn, also never finally objectifiable. A similar model will recur in *Dialectic of Enlightenment*, in the idea that the subject both dominates nature by its separation from it in technological manipulation, and is most subjected to nature precisely when it seems to be most separate from it.[19]

Adorno's task is to find a way of sustaining a strong conception of truth once the traditional models of grounding truth have been abandoned. The truth in question, the meaning of which is, it must be said, anything but explicit, would seem to relate to Benjamin's 'force' that 'stamps the essence of the empirical', or to Heidegger's 'clearing', both of which attempt to give an account that is neither pre-Kantian and dogmatic nor 'Fichtean' and subjectivist: 'In relation to received words and language-less subjective intention, configuration is a third option (*ein Drittes*)' (ibid. p. 369). For the philosopher, Adorno maintains, thereby actually opening up what will be a much more promising perspective, 'there is no hope but to place the words around the new truth so that their configuration alone results in the new truth' (ibid. p. 369). The very concern with the configuring of words leads, of course, in the direction of 'literature'.

From the above it should be clear that, in common with other major twentieth-century thinkers, Adorno regards language as playing a decisive role in undermining the idea that the ground of truth is the 'self–present' spontaneity of the subject. In the Kierkegaard book, written at much the same time as TLP, he claims: 'If language is the form of communication of pure subjectivity and at the same time paradoxically presents itself as historically objective, then, in language, objectless inwardness [which is supposed by Kierkegaard to constitute the subject's resistance to transient external historical developments] is reached by the external dialectic' (Adorno 1979 p. 53).[20] As we saw both in Chapter 3 and in Benjamin's account of the Romantics, the idea of the subject as the self-transparent ground of truth was already undermined by Schlegel and Novalis, not least via their theories of language and *Poesie*. Adorno's view of truth in TLP is, though, to be construed in terms of the lost 'name', in which form and content are not contingently related, which is somehow to be restored by the avoidance of 'intention'. In the form in which it appears here the idea is not really much more enlightening than it was in the worst aspects of Benjamin or of the later Heidegger. However, there is another way of interpreting Adorno's conception: this approach follows from remarks in the ninth thesis of TLP.

Adorno introduces the notion of a philosophical 'critique of language':

> words are to be put in question as to their ability to carry the intentions imposed upon them, the extent to which their historical power is extinguished, and the extent to which that power can perhaps be con-figuratively preserved. The criterion of this is essentially the *aesthetic* dignity of the words. (Adorno 1973a p. 370)

The '*aesthetic* dignity' of words does not lie in the beauty of their combination, but rather in their capacity to be true:

> Powerless words are recognisable as those which in the linguistic work of art – which alone preserved the unity of word and thing against the scientific duality – conclusively fell prey to aesthetic critique, whereas they up to now were able unrestrictedly to enjoy philosophical favour.
> (ibid.)

In these terms 'art gains the character of cognition: its language is aesthetically only right ['*stimmig*', which has something of the sense of 'fitting', 'being in tune'] if it is "true"' (ibid.). We are now at the heart of Adorno's philosophical concern with literature and other art: he also asserts similar things about the power of musical material and of techniques in the plastic arts. But what does he mean by the 'cognitive' capacity of literature, as opposed to the philosophy which employs language which is now 'power-less'? The explanation offered in the TLP – that art is true 'if its words are existent according to the objective historical situation (*Stand*)' (ibid.) – is no explanation at all, and is just another – dogmatically Marxist – precursor of Heidegger's idea of a happening which completely transcends the subjects who bring it about. The very use of 'objective' either pre-supposes something that much of the rest of the position would seem to exclude, or it makes the argument circular.

Any conception which relies on particular *words* as the bearers of truth must fall prey to the Romantic insight that truth depends upon particular *relations* of linguistic elements, not upon anything intrinsic to the elements themselves. Clearly certain words may indeed come to play a historically central role in the thought or the literature of a period, and names can come to have what seems a more than arbitrary relationship to who or what bears the name, but the point of holist theories is that this role for the particular word is only possible via its relations to other words in a par-ticular world. Any attempt to avoid this conclusion in a decisive manner leads merely to a theology of the Word. We therefore need to reconstruct a more convincing argument ourselves, using Adorno's later work and some related ideas.

In the essay 'On the Present Relationship between Philosophy and Music' of 1957, which is one of the best and most concise statements of his more fully worked out conceptions, Adorno claims, again referring to Benjamin, that 'As language, music moves towards the pure name, the absolute unity of thing and sign, which is lost in its immediacy to all human knowledge' (Adorno 1984a p. 154). Music, note, only 'moves towards' this unity, and can never reach it. We cannot, of course, 'know' a priori that this is the case, because that would entail the self-contradictory claim that we can have access to what is supposed to be inaccessible – i.e. the 'absolute unity'. This 'knowledge' would also imply that, as Hegel thought, music fails to articulate something which philosophy succeeds in articulating. For Adorno, then, Novalis' comment (discussed in Chapter 3) that the 'Absolute which is given to us can only be known negatively, by our acting and finding that no action can reach what we are seeking' (Novalis 1978 p. 181), is exemplified in the experience of music. However, as Novalis also thought, this is not something that can be positively validated as a philo-sophical assertion. This tension between the aesthetic and the philosophical is decisive for Adorno: the vital question is how, given their common concern with truth, one deals with their differences.

Great music does indeed seem to enact the sort of meaningfulness suggested in the idea of the 'name': the compelling nature of the articu-lation of the material suggests that the work can say all it wants to say. Adorno's standard – and apt – example for this is Beethoven's Eroica

Symphony. At the same time music says what it says via means of articulation which are, with the exception of certain proto-semantic elements, such as 'the echo of march- and war-music in the great symphonies' (Adorno 1984a p. 157), strictly meaningless:

> As a sphinx [music] makes a fool of the spectator by continually promising meanings – and even intermittently granting meanings – which are for it in fact only, in the truest sense of the word, means towards the death of meaning, and in which [meanings] it for that reason never exhausts itself. (ibid. pp. 154–5)

Were it to exhaust itself in 'intended' meanings, in the acts of spontaneity which gave rise to it, the musical work could be replaced by a true verbal account of the work. In this way the lack of semantically decidable meaning in music, which 'kills' communicable meaning, implies that music cannot be hermeneutically exhausted. At the same time, however, the lack of semantically decidable meaning points to music's own inherent lack qua philosophical means of communicating truth. The power of this position lies precisely in its refusal to renounce either music, literature or philosophy as possible sources of truth. Adorno might seem here to be overloading the significance of music, which he claims is closest of all the arts to philosophy, but one can make serious sense of his position if it is connected to questions of textual interpretation.

Probably the most persuasive way of interpreting the idea of the 'unity of word and thing' that is 'preserved' in literature and sundered by science appears in Wittgenstein's apparently unassuming remarks in *Philosophical Investigations* on the understanding of a sentence or proposition (*'Satz'*):

> We talk about understanding a sentence in the sense in which it can be replaced by another sentence which says the same thing; but also in the sense in which it cannot be replaced by any other sentence. (As little as one musical theme by another.)
>
> In one case it is the thought of a sentence which is common to differing sentences, in the other something which only these words in these positions express. (Understanding of a poem) (Wittgenstein 1971 p. 227)

He also maintains that 'Understanding a sentence in language is much more related to understanding a theme in music than one thinks' (ibid.). The parallel of music and language is familiar from *Monologue*, and from Schleiermacher's remarks about the role of rhythm in the communication of meaning. What is in question here is not representational relationships between words and things, but rather forms of language which have a binding status that prevents them from being both substitutable like commodities and, in the manner of information which can be represented algorithmically, indifferent to the specific configuration of the words in which they appear. Wittgenstein's distinction between the 'thought' (the 'proposition' which can be expressed by different sentences) and that which is 'expressed' depends, of course, upon Kant's distinction between 'determining judgement', for the sentence that can be replaced by another, and 'reflective judgement', for the combination of words for which there is no prior rule.

The reasons why a sentence is irreplaceable are philosophically crucial, because they open up territory on which aesthetics, epistemology and semantics cease to be analytically separable. It is this territory that is one of Adorno's primary aesthetic and philosophical concerns. In the notes for his sadly never completed book on Beethoven, Adorno makes a remark about music which is, importantly, equally applicable to literature (I have added the relevant words in square brackets):

> The difficulty of every musical [literary] analysis consists in the fact that the more one analyses and recurs to the smallest units, the more one approaches the mere note [word], and all music [literature] consists of mere notes [words]. The most specific becomes the most general and the most abstract in a bad way. But if one gives up such detailed analysis then the contexts/connections (*Zusammenhänge*) are lost. Dialectical analysis is an attempt to sublate both dangers into each other.
>
> (Adorno 1993 p. 22)

The difficult task, as we have seen, is to say exactly how literature is more than 'mere words'. Gadamer, linking *Dichtung* to what the later Heidegger tries to achieve in the notion of 'thought' as opposed to 'philosophy' (by which he means 'metaphysics' in the later Heidegger's sense), maintains that:

> What the language of thought has in common with the language of *Dichtung* is . . . that here as well nothing is just meant and thus can be designated in this way or some other. The word of *Dichtung* like the word of thought does not [semantically, in the sense of rule-boundedness] 'mean' anything. In a poem nothing is meant that is not there in its linguistic constitution and cannot be there in any other linguistic guise.
>
> (Gadamer 1987 p. 227)

Gadamer, though, here obscures the dialectical tension which is vital for Adorno because he ignores the sense that, even as their configuration makes them something else, the words also remind us that they are just the same words as we use all the time. Without this reminder the point of the new configuration becomes hard to understand. Despite this important difference both Gadamer and Adorno do agree that it simply cannot be 'right' to replace a poem with its paraphrase, unless one has a solely instrumental purpose.

Charles Taylor talks of the difference in language, even before one gets anywhere near what one could call art, between a 'simple task account of rightness' which reduces the linguistic sign to being efficient 'for some nonsemantic purpose', and the many cases of language where the rightness of use 'can't be cashed out' (Taylor 1995 p. 105). This sense of 'rightness' – which Adorno calls '*Stimmigkeit*' – already became apparent when Schleiermacher showed in his account of style that there can be no final way of drawing a line between replaceable and irreplaceable sentences. In some contexts an apparently replaceable instrumental sentence may be irreplaceable, as it is in Beckett's employment of reified language in *Krapp's Last Tape* or *Endgame*, when the rhythm and '*Stimmigkeit*' of a scene depends upon the particular clichéd form of words. Taylor's distinction between the instrumental use of language and the notion that the realm of humanly significant communication must always entail more than instrumental reason will be crucial to my interpretation of Adorno's often questionable account of the relationship between truth in art and 'instrumental reason'.

The essential point is that articulations of truth in real historical contexts are inherently more than a series of particular discrete assertions that can supposedly be abstracted from all contexts. Like 'nature' and 'history', the form of the articulation and its content are neither totally opposed nor totally identical.[21] Adorno wants to understand what sort of a thought it is that wishes to make its true sentences *inherently* substitutable. It is not that he denies the truth-content in its own terms of the science which renounces the 'unity of word and thing': on what arguable grounds would one do that, short of doing the science oneself and getting other results? Although natural sciences are inseparable from social and historical contexts which help give rise to the structures via which they work, they are not merely reducible to such structures, because truth claims of any kind rely on transcendence of context. What really interests Adorno is why natural science, which is able to reduce suffering, so often does the opposite. This cannot possibly be explained from within science and must be dealt with via the ways science relates to the rest of human culture, for example, via the kinds of reduction of difference to identity that it shares with the commodified world.

Without a historical context there are no a priori grounds for suspecting the schematism (in the most general sense) which is the condition of possibility of any workable scientific theory. The real problem is that one culmination of schematic reduction – and this will be the source of Adorno's most emphatic later positions – will later be the scientific experiments carried out upon victims in the concentration camps. Some of the results of these experiments were bought after the Second World War, along with those who perpetrated them, by the American and other governments, in the name of extending 'scientific knowledge'. It is in relation to such examples of what one might term the modern 'culture of truth' that one must try to understand Adorno's increasing suspicion of schematism and of truth claims which are wholly indifferent to the forms in which they are articulated. A theory which wishes to abstract the truth-content of a scientific theory from all contexts is, for Adorno, likely to be complicit with the suffering that is inseparable from the theory. Even science whose results seem unambiguously positive must, in the light of the often catastrophic role of natural science in real history, come under scrutiny for what it represses.

Clearly there are serious dangers in making any links of this kind, but the blank refusal even to countenance such connections simply represses phenomena that will not go away. Rather than rush into hasty judgements on such fraught topics, then, let us, always with this in mind, pursue the reconstruction of Adorno's position with regard to language and truth. In the passage cited above Wittgenstein limited his remarks on understanding to single sentences. Adorno extends the argument to larger texts, where it is not just the position of the words in a sentence but also the relationships of the sentences to each other which play a role in the happening of truth. Adorno's experience of music obviously informs his conception: the most successful music makes us aware of the vital significance of the complex, non-rule-bound interrelations of parts for its success. Adorno's dissatisfaction with attempts by philosophers to reduce the complexity of the interrelations between forms of communication generates both his intricate manner of writing and the theory which informs it. In this sense, form and content of his own texts enact crucial aspects of what he also sees as important in art. The suggestion has rightly been made that *Aesthetic Theory*'s title, which has no article, plays with the idea that the theory itself is in one sense aesthetic.

Given Adorno's ethical concerns, how does he come to terms with the view of the aesthetic which sees it as constituted in terms of the refusal of 'closure' which informs much post-structuralist thinking? Hermeneutic questioning of a reductive semantics of 'meanings', of the kind I illustrated by the example of Dummett in Chapter 5, was based on the regresses that result from the endless possibilities of context for particular words and sentences. The extreme alternative to the semantic view is to let the possibilities of re-contextualisation render meaning undecidable. Adorno's position rejects radical undecidability via its concern with historical context and its demand to understand the – temporalised – truth-content of the text. The point of Adorno's 'configuration' which attempts to reach a 'unity of word and thing', in the manner of a poem giving new life to the words that we require to articulate something significant,[22] is that it can focus attention on things which may otherwise be obscured, rather than just producing another endless series of possible connections. The truth which emerges in the configuration cannot be made accessible via a generalised theory of 'truth in configurations', but neither is it simply an insight into the undecidability of interpretation.

The crucial difference between Adorno's account of truth and a purely deconstructive approach to truth, in the manner of some of the work of both Nietzsche and Derrida, therefore becomes apparent in Adorno's concern to sustain differences between philosophy and literature, at the same time as he rejects any final separation of the two.[23] Despite his undoubted debts to Nietzsche's perspectivism, Adorno wishes to get beyond both a pluralism of undecidable interpretations and the reduction of truth to being a means of human self-preservation. At the same time he wishes to avoid the traps of a new foundationalism. The form of truth that concerns him is not conceived of as a reductive schema for particular truths, of the kind exemplified in positivism's concern with observation sentences and with verification, but as a configuration which opens up access, in a phenomenological manner, to the matter in question itself. That matter is, in dialectical and holist fashion, not simply separable from the configurations via which it becomes accessible. This means that truth cannot claim to be timeless, but neither is it to be seen as the endless deferral of 'true presence' or as the latest manifestation of the 'will to power'. The literary text is supposed to be a model for what Adorno means, in the manner I have tried to suggest via Wittgenstein's remarks. How, though, does one now distinguish the philosophical import of a text from the 'truth' of a text as literature? Is one, as Rorty suggests, to see philosophy itself merely as a kind of literature? Furthermore, if one does this, what happens both to the notion of truth and to Adorno's insistence on the importance of autonomous art for philosophy?

ART, SCHEMATISM AND PHILOSOPHY

Adorno offers no easy answers to questions about philosophy and literature. At its best his work is to be read as a series of engagements which, precisely via their concern to avoid problems of grounding, must keep their central concepts open to reinterpretation, without simply making this stance into another grounding principle. This explains the frustrating experience of trying to extract clear 'philosophical' arguments from his work. Adorno's *Habilitation* on *Kierkegaard: Construction of the Aesthetic*, for example, begins, taking up themes from AP, as follows:

> Whenever one sought to grasp the writings of philosophers as literature (*als Dichtungen*) one failed to reach their truth-content. The law of form of philosophy demands interpretation of the real in the appropriate context (*im stimmigen Zusammenhang*) of concepts. Neither the announcement of the subjectivity of the one who is thinking nor the pure internal coherence of the configuration (*Geschlossenheit des Gebildes*) are decisive for its character as philosophy, but only: whether reality (*Wirkliches*) entered the concepts, proves itself in them and grounds them in a convincing way. The conception of philosophy as literature is in contradiction to this view: by wresting philosophy from being binding in terms of the criterion of reality it removes the philosophical work from adequate criticism. But only in communication with the critical spirit can the work test itself historically. (Adorno 1979 p. 9)

If philosophy is not to be seen as literature, what has happened to the idea that 'art gains the character of cognition' in literature? It all depends on how the terms are being employed. Adorno's opposition to apriorism, and his holism with regard to language, which were suggested in the idea of the configuration, mean that context determines the meaning of words. In this particular case Adorno is clearly arguing against the idea that the literary aspect of Kierkegaard should be excepted, as it was by many critics at the time he writes the text (and since), from the kind of rigour used in judging the truth claims of philosophical texts. This does not, though, obviate questions about the relationship of art and truth, literature and philosophy, not least because Adorno wishes to apply the same kind of rigour to aesthetic texts as well. We now need to move to later work for his responses to these questions.

Thus far I have concentrated mainly upon Adorno's work before the Second World War and before the Holocaust. Too often the image of Adorno's philosophy is summed up in (sometimes misquoted) slogans like 'no poetry after Auschwitz' and his work is assumed to express an all-enveloping cultural pessimism. In the light of the growing suspicion in Western societies of the destructive consequences of the technological advances of modernity, much of the reception of Adorno has come to be based on the idea that his fundamental thought is a verdict on the failure of Enlightenment 'reason' which appears in *Dialectic of Enlightenment* (DoE), the book written with Max Horkheimer during the War, published in 1947. There is no denying that large parts of DoE do simply repeat something like Heidegger's most global versions of the 'subjectification of being' in Western metaphysics, which DoE puts in terms, again echoing Jacobi and Schelling, of the 'subordination of everything natural to the arrogant subject' (Horkheimer and Adorno 1971 p. 5).

This story gives rise to another version of a structural problem we have already encountered in such arguments, namely the location from which we as subjects can even talk about what Anke Thyen terms the 'state of primary lack of separation' between subject and nature (Thyen 1989 p. 102) that precedes the rise of the self-preserving, dominating subject. Even more questionably, the greater part of DoE, which Foucault, late in his career, said could have saved him a lot of effort, relies on a critique of a reductive Nietzschean equation of knowledge and power which tends to concede so much to this position that the point of the critique itself starts to get lost. Habermas calls DoE the authors' 'most black book' (Habermas 1985 p. 130). Interpreted as a whole, though, especially including the more empirically oriented notes and sketches at the end of the book, and in the light of its Schlegel-inspired subtitle, 'Philosophical Fragments', the view of the book only based on its most 'philosophical' universal claims looks somewhat less compelling.

Habermas claims that the authors of DoE 'surrendered themselves to an unrestrained scepticism with regard to reason, instead of pondering the grounds which make one doubt this scepticism itself' (ibid. p. 156). How-ever, the (essentially Romantic) dialogue in 'Contradictions', for example, that deals with real-life situations in which a priori principles lead to cruelty or absurdity, does not entail an affirmation of 'unrestrained scepticism' with regard to reason. Instead the dialogue reveals in a thoroughly rational manner the sheer impossibility of escaping ethical ambiguities, given the structures within which moral actors must function in the modern world. In the light of other such sections of the book and of some of its remarks on art, DoE cannot *just* be a piece of apocalyptic philosophical foundation-alism. DoE becomes this if one reads it as metaphysics and as a purely 'philosophical' book; read with the eyes of the Romantic literary theorist some of the book has more to offer.

It is worth citing here a later, more defensible view of probably the most contentious issue in DoE. This is put forward by Adorno in theses for a discussion in 1957, under the title 'Reason and Revelation'. The passage opens up more interesting perspectives than those allowed by Habermas' universalising 'philosophical' verdict on DoE's critique of reason. Habermas too often extends this verdict to Adorno's work as a whole (for a critique of this view see Bradbury 1993), not least in order to make Adorno part of the story which sees modern philosophy as needing to escape the 'paradigm of subjectivity' and to move towards a model based on intersubjectivity. Adorno's later, more differentiated account of a dialectic of enlightenment is, though, often compatible with Habermas' own views on modern rationality:

> Because too much thinking, unswerving autonomy makes adjustment to the managed world difficult and creates suffering, countless people project their suffering, which is in fact dictated by society, onto reason as such. It is supposed to be reason which has brought suffering and misfortune over the world. The dialectic of enlightenment, which must indeed also name the price of progress, must name all the ruin which rationality gives rise to qua progressing domination of nature, is, so to speak, broken off too early, according to the model of a state of affairs whose blind closure seems to block the way out. Desperately and deliberately it is not recognised that the excess of rationality about which the educated stratum complains and which it registers in concepts like mechanisation, atomisation ... is a lack of rationality, namely the intensification of all calculable apparatuses and means of domination at the cost of the purpose, the rational organisation of humankind, which is left to the unreason of pure constellations of power, to which consciousness, obscured by continual attention to existing positive circumstances and the given, no longer has any trust at all to raise itself. ... Instead of either positing rationality or negating it as an absolute, reason must try to determine it as a moment within the whole, which has admittedly made itself independent in relation to the whole. Reason

must become aware of its own naturalistic character (*ihres eigenen naturhaften Wesens*). (Adorno 1969 pp. 22–3)

The distinction between reason and merely instrumental rationality is one which Adorno at times fails to make explicit, but if it is sustained significant parts of his work take on a different aspect from the one presented by Habermas. Reason's relationship to a nature which is not separated from it in the way that material nature and the intelligible are separated in Kant (but not in Romanticism) is a vital underlying theme of nearly all Adorno's reflections on metaphysics (see Wellmer 1993 Chapter 7), especially when they are concerned with art.

Adorno's methodological difficulty is that a critique of the instrumental domination of the object world needs to invoke a perspective within which instrumental reason, the exclusive concern with the 'how', can be related to the aim of bringing about a society in which instrumental reason would contribute to the reduction of suffering rather than its increase. As we have already seen, the genuine work of art is for Adorno a model of rationality that gives access to an approach to the world which is not merely instrumental, and which thereby gives back to the world a sense of intrinsic value. It is here that secularised theological resources can legitimately come into play, especially if they are linked to what I in Chapter 3 termed the 'hermeneutic imperative'. Adorno held on in the 1930s, against Benjamin, to the idea that great bourgeois art does still retain a potential for liberation via its ability to reveal utopian possibilities which the reality of the modern world obscures. In DoE, though, he and Horkheimer have to come to terms with the fact that this sphere of relative freedom from commodification is now, far more than it was in the nineteenth century, invaded by the commodity form. This leads to what they term the 'culture industry', in which the utopian images in a society are more and more the results of socially manipulated desires for commodities.

The colonisation of hope in the terms of already existing reality will be a central reason why Adorno, in his later writings on aesthetics, often talks of the ban on images in Jewish theology which we already encountered in the discussion of Benjamin and Adorno. He thereby reinterprets the move from symbol, as positive representation of the Absolute, to allegory, as the failure of representation, which was a central part of Romantic thought. As Adorno says in AT: 'No existing, appearing work of art positively has power over what is not (*ist des Nichtseienden positiv mächtig*). . . . In works of art what is not is a constellation made out of what is' (Adorno 1973b p. 204). Utopian images must, like allegories, draw on what is already there, even as they negate it. Art in modernity can therefore no longer promise anything determinate, and must therefore, in the name of truth, break Stendhal's 'promise of happiness' (ibid. p. 205) which was implied in the notion of the symbol. The images of the commodity world render images of happiness untrue and art must therefore renounce them.

Adorno's insistence that real art has truth-content will from now on lead him more and more to a position in which most, but not all, of the traditional legitimations of art must be abandoned. This move was, as we have seen, already prepared by the Romantic move away from representational conceptions of art and truth.

The chapter in DoE on the culture industry undoubtedly generalises too rapidly from certain features of American capitalist culture in the 1940s to an overall verdict on modern culture based on theoretical reflections of the kind which begin in Romanticism. One of the reasons for this is that the authors think that the only sphere of culture which appeared to offer resistance to the commodity form is now becoming like everything else. DoE presents this situation in terms of a model that we have been tracing from the very beginning of the book, which we last observed in relation to Adorno's view of language. This time, however, the model involves almost as much lack of 'mediation' as Adorno found in Benjamin's reductions of culture to political economy in the 1930s:

> The contribution which Kantian schematism had still expected from the subjects, namely the initial relating of the sensuous manifold to the fundamental concepts, is now taken away from the subject by industry. It carries out schematism as the first service to the customer.
>
> (Horkheimer and Adorno 1971 p. 112)

In the same way as the fetishism of the commodity 'produces consciousness', the standardised forms of film and music production now carry out this function by reducing imagination and spontaneity to being merely the consumption of images and sounds based on market research, thereby revoking their status as autonomous art. We are here in the realm of reductive polemic that borders at times on self-parody, but there are grounds for taking at least some of this very seriously, even though one should also keep in mind that the question of schematism and identity is, as we shall see, far more complex than it is made out to be here.

The sad and disturbing fact is that Horkheimer and Adorno's flawed and often merely irritating polemic is, with regard to the 'popular culture' of Western democracies – which increasingly assimilates and invades all other cultures via the new (and old) media – far more appropriate now than when it was first written. It is simply ludicrous to maintain, for example, that the real jazz of the period of DoE – we are at the beginning of the era when Charlie Parker in particular produces music which can be measured against the greatest modern music, and which had little immediate commercial success – fits the model of the culture industry.[24] On the other hand, the contemporary multinationally owned rock music industry fits large parts of Horkheimer and Adorno's characterisation.[25] Much the same applies to Hollywood, the paperback fiction industry, as well as to some of the established, particularly Anglo-Saxon, literary world, in which concern with the marketable aspects of the life and opinions of the author has largely

270 The culture of truth: Adorno

taken over from critical engagement with the work. In the sphere of politics aesthetically manipulated images have, especially in America, long since come to play a more determining role than rational debate.[26] We might seem here to have come a long way from the issue of a philosophical conception of truth, but this is not in fact the case. These are all issues to do with the nature of modern rationality's relationship to schematic reduction, and with the 'culture of truth' in modern societies.

If truth is, as it is in theories based on the natural sciences, to be understood in terms of schematised identity, there are grounds for *linking* – but, importantly, not for *reducing* – truth in modern societies to other ways that human articulations become schematised and standardised. This approach becomes particularly valid when putatively scientific models are ideologically employed in areas where only non-schematic evaluation can really get at the complexity of the issues in question. We live in a culture of measurement, from IQ tests, to psychometrics, to the imbecility of new managerialism, where the truth determinate has come to be equated with what can be quantified or rendered in algorithms. The resources of the Romantic tradition are vital here. Two points must be kept in mind: on the one hand, as Heidegger showed, any equation of truth and quantifiability cannot be grounded without circularity, and, on the other – which is one of the main implications of the work of Jacobi – the very ability to suggest that schematism is a danger requires a sense of truth which cannot itself be reduced to schematism. This latter position is the source of the hermeneutic positions which I have tried to suggest are the valuable philosophical core of Romantic thinking. The question for Adorno is once again the role that works of art, which seem to offer a way beyond what is merely schematic, play in his critique of modern culture. He thinks that art can 'institute' truth, but how does it do so in the face of the industrialisation and 'schematisation' of culture? Let us take one view of this issue from DoE – a view which, in its sustaining of conceptual tensions, again gives the lie to the totalising image of this text.[27]

Adorno maintains that 'style', which is fundamental to any serious conception of literature, is 'the negation of style' in the culture industry, because

> it has no recalcitrant material upon which to test itself. . . . The reconciliation of universal and particular, of rule and specific claim of the object, in the carrying out of which alone style gains content, is annulled because it no longer ever comes to a tension between the poles: the extremes which touch have gone over into murky identity. (ibid. p. 116)

Style can communicate truth by configuring elements of language which disclose the world in a manner that established forms cannot. It does so because the order it institutes is achieved by organising material that resists integration most obstinately, at the same time as still respecting the integrity of that material. Erich Auerbach's account in *Mimesis* of the slow

and often tortuous incorporation into European literature of serious
concern with lower-class language and life can suggest what is meant here.
Adorno's concept of style depends upon a notion of 'authentic' style
derived from art works of the past. However, in the manner particularly
characteristic of his mature work, Adorno also subjects the concept of
authentic style to remorseless interrogation, revealing both its truth and
what it hides. The notion of a universally binding style or styles, which is
indispensable for the communication of aesthetic discrimination, is shown,
via what is revealed in the levelling of the tension between universal and
particular in the culture industry, also to be a form of ideology. This is one
of the major reasons why the most important modern art can no longer
communicate the sense of reconciliation against all the odds which makes
the great bourgeois works enduringly powerful.

The tension between expression and convention we considered in the
last chapter leads Adorno to a decisive insight, and introduces the vital
theme of suffering, which is probably the central concern of his thought
(see Bradbury 1993):

> The greatest artists were never those who embodied style in the most
> unbroken and complete manner, but rather those who took up style
> as resistance (*Härte*) against the chaotic expression of suffering, as
> negative truth. In the style of the works expression gained the force
> without which existence dissolves unheard. Even those works which are
> called classical, like Mozart's music, contain objective tendencies which
> intended something different from the style which they embody.
>
> (Horkheimer and Adorno 1971 p. 117)

The position is summed up in a remark which helps us to grasp a recurrent
structure in Adorno's work on aesthetics and truth: 'The promise of the
work of art to institute truth by imprinting shape (*Gestalt*) into socially
transmitted forms is as necessary as it is hypocritical' (ibid.). By using forms
derived from society as it already is in order to articulate utopian possibilities, art is always also in complicity with what it opposes, and, as such,
ideological. However, the difference of this view from the position we considered at the end of Chapter 5 is that art is not *just* ideological. Without
their using the recalcitrant material of a society based on commodification
and oppression works of art would be merely false reconciliations of social
antagonisms, of the kind that appear when composers today attempt to
produce music that appeals in the manner of Mozart, the real world being
too ugly to 'imprint shape' into its forms. Because authentic works of art use
material derived from unjust societies,[28] they cannot and should not finally
escape the fact that they can only exist as 'negation of social purposiveness.
... The pure works of art which already negate the commodity character
of society by the very fact that they follow their own law, were always
at the same time also commodities' (ibid. p. 141). In such analyses
Adorno combines an approach which relies on the claim of works of art

to a truth which is not to be dissolved into the endless possibilities of re-contextualisation – that would take them wholly into the realm of the commodity – with a deconstructive refusal to accept that art's difference from its other could be total.

This approach offers deep insights into the question of why so many modernist works of art are either ugly or resist being meaningful. Think, for example, of the plays of Heiner Müller: repellent as they may appear to be, for those prepared to engage with them they are often as compelling as a cognitive truth claim. Without also involving that which they oppose, works of art can have no contact with the reality whose transformation they also demand: 'It is precisely the works which conceal the contradiction, instead, like Beethoven, of taking it up into the consciousness of their own production, which fall prey to ideology' (ibid. p. 142). If we now highlight the interrogation of language, qua 'material' of the literary work of art, in the formulation of these issues, Adorno's work raises extreme versions of the questions we have been concerned with in preceding chapters. These questions will lead us to a very provisional Conclusion: the most that can – and probably should – be achieved here is a prolegomena to further investigation on the basis of my attempts to salvage the truth-content of Romantic philosophy.

LITERATURE, TRUTH AND THE CRITIQUE OF 'IDENTITY'

The first thing to remember here is that the material of 'literature' must, in one important sense, be the 'same' language which everybody uses and understands. This fact is the motivation of Kafka's wonderful last story, 'Josephine the Singer or the Mouse People', in which the question is posed by Kafka – on his deathbed – as to whether there is anything such as art at all. The artist, Josephine, seems just to make a show of doing what everyone else is doing all the time anyway. Kafka's story is not, despite appearances, the perfect illustration of Eagleton's thesis that there is no such thing as literature. The fact that the interrogation of the notion of literature takes the form of a story about mice, told by a narrator whose own epistemic status is splendidly unclear, raises questions which a discursive account of the problem of literature like Eagleton's cannot begin to raise. The demands of discursive argument place limits on the interrelation of 'form' and 'content',[29] whereas the success of Kafka's story depends precisely on the unique discrepancy between its theoretical ideas and their context in the world of mice.[30] Any theory which claims that there is no reason to sustain a special status for the literary will inherently lack convincing ways of understanding the opacity to interpretation of major aspects of literary works. The question is exactly why Adorno should regard the opacity to interpretation characteristic of many of the great works of literary modernism as being so important.

The borderline between the literary and the non-literary becomes increasingly fraught for Adorno. He even comes to suspect the semantic dimension to the point where it sometimes seems as if modern literature can only emerge via a complete negation of the everyday functioning of communication. The roots of Adorno's extreme position lie in Romanticism's discovery of the new relationship of language to freedom. In Chapter 3 I cited Novalis' remark on 'Poems, just pleasant sounding and full of beautiful words, but also without any meaning or context ... like fragments of the most diverse things', the possibility of which was a result of the Romantic sense of a liberation of language from the demands of re-presentation. From Adorno's perspective, though, many twentieth-century versions of the aesthetic move away from language as the medium of re-presentation of the ready-made world are the result of historical trauma. Attempts of the kind seen in Dada to create sound poems that avoid all determinable semantic content can also be understood as a rejection of the very use of existing language, and not just as an exploration of language's possibilities for play. The everyday use of language in modern societies is regarded by people as disparate as the Dadaists, Karl Kraus and Adorno as often being in collusion with the irrational and destructive aspects of modern technological civilisation. Adorno's later animus against the exclusive concern with everyday usage in the analytical philosophy of language can be understood as a reaction to the fact that supposedly harmless everyday usage can indeed be a source of appalling inhumanity.[31] In this context the demand, within certain areas of analytical philosophy in particular, for complete transparency and clarity begs the question as to whether transparency is the ultimate linguistic virtue. Great modernist literature is often anything but semantically transparent, and music is anyway not semantic in any direct sense at all. This does not, though, entail any sort of advocacy of the obscure or mysterious: Adorno insists that the configurations in great modernist works possess a clarity and technical rigour of a different kind, without which the works do not achieve the status of art.

The fact is that this whole area is riddled with misunderstandings and confusions, which have bedevilled much recent literary theory and have led to much talking at cross-purposes within differing theoretical traditions. These confusions are, though, in one sense, inevitable. Attempts to question the very means of human interchange must always face the fact that the means of interchange are being employed to question themselves. The problem of the ground beckons once more here: we have no form of communication which can unproblematically assert of itself that it is free of complicity in creating deception. Romantic insights into the simultaneous freedom and lack of total self-transparency of the subject offered positive new creative possibilities for our self-understanding and for our understanding of language. At the same time they helped to open up the space which, in the context of a society increasingly dominated by the reification of human relations, leads psychoanalysis to its questioning of the very possibility of subjective authenticity in language. This characterisation might seem to imply that there was a state of society prior to this where communication was inherently authentic. However, the point at issue is not such a mythical situation, but rather the undoubted change in human self-understanding of which psychoanalysis is a key manifestation. The power of the idea of the subversion of the subject in psychoanalysis *presupposes* the Romantic emancipation of the subject from pre-given orders which is characteristic of modernity, otherwise there would be no reason to see psychoanalysis as such a disruption of our self-understanding. Adorno's view of language and art is located within the tension between these two views of language and the subject in modernity: the move from Goethe to Beckett or from Beethoven to Schönberg is paradigmatic in this respect.

Confronting the depths of cruelty and destruction, which are at the very least contributed to by language's relationship to modern forms of identification, raises serious problems for philosophical reflection on language. The resources of a merely classifying analytical approach, even one which includes the awareness of performativity present in speech-act theory, are simply inadequate. Can there, though, be a philosophically adequate means of confronting these questions that leads neither to what Adorno criticises in referring to 'A semantic taboo [on unclear concepts] which strangles questions of the real (*Sachfragen*) as if they were just questions of meaning' (Adorno 1975 p. 213), nor to incoherence and to a hasty conflating of different issues caused by the failure at least to outline the sense of core concepts? In the same passage Adorno himself insists that the semantic critique of unclear concepts cannot be 'lazily ignored', because the impossibility of what it demands is still necessarily a part of how we try to get to the bottom of an issue. Adorno plays a key role here, because his focus of attention is primarily the sources of suffering and cruelty in what appears, via the dominant instrumental and linguistic forms of the modern world, to be 'rational' and connected to the everyday sense of truth. His remorseless pursuit of these issues leads him to a generalised suspicion of complicity in suffering which even extends to most forms of literature: once the demand to see art in terms of truth is made there is no comfortable position left for the critic.

For some of his critics Adorno's remorselessness actually leads him into incoherence, so that his suspicion of the very nature of language and the dominant forms of truth in modernity has been dismissed from an analytical perspective as being based on a logical misapprehension. This is, though, not just an issue for analytical philosophy. Given Habermas' sometimes excessive admiration of the clarificatory resources offered by analytical philosophy,[32] such judgements reinforce his tendency to concentrate on the aporetic aspects of Adorno's thought, rather than on the resources Adorno still offers. The idea that one can already invalidate Adorno on semantic grounds is usefully summed up in Raymond Geuss' judgement in a review of ND that 'the original error in this whole theory, is Adorno's conviction that all predication is identification' (Geuss 1975 p. 172). Adorno

supposedly thinks that the very attempt to predicate something of something inherently entails subjectification and reification, because it represses
the irreducible difference of anything intended by a singular term from any
other such thing by subsuming it under a general term.

There are certain parts, particularly of DoE, but also of ND and AT,
which allow this reading. If one does interpret Adorno in this way, only
forms of language which have no immediately accessible propositional
content could be an appropriate response to the world of system-generated
delusion, the world of what Benjamin saw as a 'dream'. Non-predicative
forms of articulation here take precedence over language which tries to
communicate determinate propositions, which suggests one reason for
the centrality of music for Adorno. The aim of non-predicative forms of
articulation can be seen as the expression of the individual experience
of suffering that cannot be attained in a language whose terms are general.
Even in this highly problematic version such a view of language does tell
us something valid about the nature of the relationship of the subject to
poetic language in modernity. Adorno says of Hölderlin, for example:[33]

> To the extent to which it is conceptual and predicative language is
> opposed to subjective expression, it levels what is to be expressed down
> to something pre-given and known because of its generality. The poets
> protest against this. They continually would like to incorporate, even
> to the point of their destruction, the subject and its expression into
> language. (Adorno 1965 p. 192)

However, he also insists that Hölderlin 'knows of language not just as
something external and repressive, but also knows its truth': this truth is
dependent upon the freedom of the subject characteristic of modernity,
but it is 'raised above the subject' (ibid. p. 193). Getting to this truth
demands the transcendence of mere subjective expressivity. The fact is that
the nature of language inherently takes one beyond subjective intention
because even its aesthetic forms depend in part upon collective interactions
within society that are prior to and irreducible to the individual subject.
Furthermore, the ability of the subject to render its works collectively
significant cannot, as we saw in Schleiermacher, be merely internal to its
'feeling'. This transcendence of language over intention has a dual aspect.
Language is supra-subjective in a negative manner when it is mere ideology
generated by reified forms of human interchange; on the other hand,
the demands imposed by working in a literary form entail the obligation to
seek what is beyond both ideology and contingent subjective intention. The
question here is once again the location from which one judges whether
language is functioning as ideology or as a medium of truth. What, then, is
the role of the philosophical interpretation of art in Adorno's project?
Given that interpretation inherently requires predication, and that large
parts of his work are devoted to interpretation, is Adorno not simply
trapped in an aporia that threatens his whole critical project?

If even works of music or non-representational art could be rendered semantically determinate via the predicative structure, the point of their resistance to such 'identification' would presumably be obviated and we could eventually obviate the aesthetic. This problem was apparent in relation to Kafka's story. On the other hand, the complete exclusion of the attempt to say what works of art mean would lead to a surrender of the cognitive potential of art or to the worst kind of 'culinary' consumption of art. Adorno is quite clear in his rejection both of what one can term 'semantic reduction', and of what is basically aestheticism. This dual rejection leads him into the uncomfortable position which is actually the source of many of his major insights. He asserts in 'On the Present Relationship between Philosophy and Music' that 'If philosophy were able, as it admittedly must keep on trying to do, and which art itself requires it to do, to determine the raison d'être of art, then art would indeed be completely dissolved by cognition and thus in the strictest sense overtaken' (Adorno 1984a p. 153). The fact is, though, that philosophy cannot finally do this, even though he insists that it is its duty to try to do so. Adorno may seem here to give philosophy a certain – Hegelian – primacy over art, but his approach in fact closely echoes the Romantic positions outlined in Chapter 3. By bringing out both the tensions and the necessary interrelations between art and philosophy, Adorno echoes aspects of *Monologue*. The reason he makes more of the separation of philosophy from art has to do with the failure of Romantic hopes for their creative interaction and with his fear of surrendering the resources required for the critique of the culture industry. If philosophy is as important to art as Adorno maintains, can it really be the case that he thinks that all predication is identification?

Taking up a clarification of this issue by Herbert Schnädelbach, Anke Thyen has usefully shown that much of the confusion over the understanding of Adorno's position results from his own unfortunate tendency to conflate the notions of 'identifying *with*' (which would imply that predication really is identification) and 'identifying *as*' (which would not), even though the strengths of his theory depend precisely upon separating the two notions. One way of making the separation, that establishes a further structural link between many of the positions with which we have been concerned, is – despite Adorno's objections to Heidegger – via the version of Heidegger's ontological difference I outlined in Chapter 6. 'Identifying with' is 'ontic', in that it is necessarily secondary to the 'ontological' 'as-structure'. The assertion of the identity of two commodities with each other, for example, two bottles of wine of the same price, can (loosely) be cashed out in the form that 'There is an x such that x is a bottle of wine and there is a y such that y is bottle of wine' and 'There is an x which is an exchange value and there is a y that is an exchange value, such that the exchange value of x and the exchange value of y is the same'. However, even though, both as 'bottle of wine' and as 'exchange value', x and y are 'the same', they can, as something else, also be different: one may be a useful offensive weapon because it is made of strong glass, the other not; one may be good, the other not, and so on. The prior structure is, then, the 'ontological' form of disclosure, which allows an unlimited number of predicative possibilities for all entities, and it is only after 'ontological' disclosure that 'identifying with' is possible at all.[34] Heidegger's crucial insight here was into the fact that there is no theoretical way of going back behind this prior disclosure. The disclosure was best understood via the work of art, which opens spaces of intelligibility that are obscured by established means of articulation.

If 'identifying as' is not the same as 'identifying with', the idea that the commodity-determined 'context of delusion' is total cannot be sustained. Why should a commodity not also be something which permits an utterly individual use or possesses aesthetic value, even though this possibility is indeed denied to much of the world of monopoly capitalism? In these terms the assumption in DoE, for example, that all rationality is instrumental reason, which is based on the Nietzschean idea that all conceptual thought entails the reduction of difference to identity, must be false. The assumption relies on the idea that rationality is the identification of things *with* each other, in terms of the Hobbesian subjective purposes for which they can be used. These purposes thus become, in a 'Fichtean' manner, the ground both of scientific cognition and of the commodity form. The tradition of aesthetics derived from Schelling and the Romantics was precisely directed against such a ground. As such, the account of identity in DoE lacks a whole dimension that is present in the best arguments of ND and AT. Thyen suggests, citing ND, that:

> Cognition which wishes to experience the non-identical in the object is not directed against identity, but against identifications. 'To this extent the non-identical would be the own identity of the thing (*Sache*) against its identifications' (Adorno 1975 p. 164).... Cognition of the non-identical aims at the identity of the object; it identifies it *as* something, but it announces reservations against identifications in the sense of 'identifying *with*'. (Thyen 1989 p. 205)

The distinctions involved in clarifying these issues are also germane to philosophical approaches to literary and other works of art, which exemplify what Adorno means by the 'non-identical'.

Adorno's position can be construed in these terms as exemplifying the hermeneutic opposition to 'identifying' semantics which reconstructs 'Platonist' rules for what we already do (ibid. p. 124 and Chapter 5, this volume), and to the idea that philosophy should give a binding account of the application of linguistic rules which could extend to literary texts. Both Wittgenstein's distinction between the two ways of understanding and Gadamer's point about the 'language of *Dichtung*' implied that the interpretation of a literary text should not (and could not) equate the text's meaning with the sentences via which we attempt to say predicatively what it means. The aesthetic import of the text lies in the particular arrangement of its linguistic material. This arrangement cannot be exhausted by even the most sophisticated semantic (or 'stylistic') account of its component sentences: that was already the point of Schleiermacher's particular notion of style. The real problem, which has played a part in many of the controversies over deconstruction, is how to sustain a critical, analytical perspective, given that the possibilities of 'identifying as' with regard to a literary text are inherently unlimited. This is made even more difficult by the fact that the structure of predication makes the possibilities of predication in theory unlimited for *any* object at all, aesthetic or not.

In this perspective Adorno's recurrence in relation to literature and music to the theory of the name, qua 'unity of word and thing', can be understood as a way of attempting to overcome the apparent randomness which ensues from the lack or loss of a determinable ground for meaning. This attempt is also apparent in his talk of the 'mimetic' in art, as 'the non-conceptual affinity of what is subjectively produced to its other, which is not posited by the subject' (Adorno 1973b pp. 86–7), which can appear in the unique 'configuration' of the elements of the work. To the extent to which these terms merely point back to Benjamin's theology they are of no serious theoretical use any more. Adorno, though, does not limit himself to this perspective. The very desire to configure language in ways which reveal the world anew is motivated by a suspicion of the substitutability of the linguistic elements we use all the time. In a Romantic perspective the striving for what would be achieved by the name is doomed to failure, but also in a sense inescapable, if the truths which make human lives meaningful are not to be swallowed by dead forms of identity. For Adorno, the seriousness of our historical situation is manifested in the fact that the pursuit of this unity can no longer lead to works that possess the beauty of the period exemplified by Goethe and Beethoven, when art still seemed able to promise hope for a better future.

In the essay on philosophy and music Adorno sums up the position which I want to use to lead us into the Conclusion: 'The aesthetic special sphere, itself no Apriori, can also in no way sustain itself a priori, and the historical movement of all art takes place not least via that instability of the aesthetically pure. In literature that is obvious' (Adorno 1984a p. 157). It is obvious because the line between the literary and the non-literary, like the line between nature and history in INH, is not a line between two ready-made opposing quantities, but rather a line which is constituted precisely by the changing interactions of those notional quantities. The revelation occasioned, for example, in the second half of the nineteenth century by Zola's incorporation of working-class vernacular into the technically sophisticated literary prose developed by Flaubert later becomes, for critics like Roland Barthes, an ideological form of linguistic condescension. It thereby gives rise to the demand for new ways of configuring proletarian language that will really do justice to it as the language of the oppressed. The discovery in this century of the text of Büchner's *Woyzeck*, written in the 1830s, which offers other revealing ways of configuring proletarian language, can itself render aspects of Zola's texts ideological, and thus poses a new literary challenge.

The question that follows from this is whether the emergence of its ideological character takes a work out of the realm of the literary or whether the work's truth-content should be said to be 'instituted' by its historical role in changing the then established canon of the literary. In either case the truth of the text is inherently connected to temporality and to history, but is not reducible to them. If one were to be able to identify this truth conceptually, the work would 'die' – literary history is full of such dead works, which can, though, in the right circumstances, be revived by new readings. On the other hand, the renunciation of the attempt to get at the truth of the work would betray the work qua work of art. In the essay on Hölderlin Adorno claims that both literary works and philosophy aim at truth-content: 'One is led to it by the contradiction that every work wishes to be understood purely from within itself, but no work can be understood from within itself' (Adorno 1965 p. 158). As he puts it in AT, the work is both 'autonomous' and a 'social fact': without the interaction and contradiction between these two statuses there could be no truth conveyed by works of art.

The very attempt to negotiate between the literary and the non-literary, the aesthetic and the non-aesthetic, takes place, as Romanticism suggested, in a 'space of reasons' where evaluative decisions must be made which cannot rely on rule-based criteria. If one could rely on such criteria the goal of theory would be the state in which the cognitive and semantic would liquidate the aesthetic and hermeneutic: 'identification with' would replace 'identification as'. This is precisely what Adorno will not allow, even though he insists on the importance of the cognitive in the constitution of the truth-content of literature. The vital question is, then, as Novalis suggested, the understanding of a text *as* literature, not its identification *with* other reputedly literary texts: 'Criticism of literature (*Poesie*) is an absurdity. It is already difficult to decide, yet the only possible decision, whether something is literature or not' (Novalis 1978 p. 840). The vigilance required for such a position keeps philosophy open to forms of world-disclosure which it can lose sight of if truth becomes based solely on 'identification with', at the same time as preventing art from becoming a mere object of culinary enjoyment.

For there to be literary texts that can subsequently be identified with each other there must already be texts which are understood as aesthetically significant. These cannot, though, be identified via conceptual classification: this could be said to be the secular moment of truth in Benjamin's notions of the name and the Idea. Christoph Menke rightly observes that 'there are no predicates which could designate aesthetic qualities in a direct manner' (Menke 1991 p. 31). The same aesthetic quality in one text can be an 'aesthetic' disaster in another, and thus no aesthetic quality at all: the crucial aspect is the place of the elements in the configuration, not the predicates attributable to the elements themselves. Given the fact both that the elements of any natural language are relatively fixed, and that the rules of grammar and syntax impose inescapable constraints, what is decisive in literary texts is the way in which the same elements are re-configured in order to disclose truths which would otherwise be inarticulable. This can sometimes be achieved precisely by not writing in a received 'literary' manner. Adorno suggests that Hölderlin 'inaugurates the process which ends in Beckett's report-sentences that are empty of sense' (Adorno 1965 p. 194). Hölderlin does so because he is already aware of the crisis in subjective expression that threatens to take it away from any claim to truth. Even in early modernity the linguistic means for subjective expression are already becoming hollowed out by what will later become the culture industry. The destruction of received linguistic forms in Hölderlin's most difficult verse thus conveys a vital truth about the threats to the emancipation of language from convention in commodified societies. For Adorno, the question for modern art is how, in the face of the capacity of modern forms of identity to absorb and defuse forms of aesthetic innovation, to prevent freedom from just generating new forms of delusion and constraint.

It is Adorno's achievement to have been able in his best work to reveal the contradictions that emerge in every one of these issues. Underlying them all is the question which has been our central theme from the outset: how is the modern relationship between what is revealed by art and what is revealed by philosophy to be understood? It is this question which, I would contend, should inform the future of both philosophy and literary theory. In the Conclusion I want use some of Adorno's other reflections on these issues as a model for understanding the state of contemporary theory.

Conclusion

It should be evident from the preceding chapters that even the most radical versions of recent literary theory are responses to questions about language, truth, art and interpretation which are intrinsic to modern philosophy, rather than a complete novum. The fact that debates over literary theory have been so controversial has, especially in the English-speaking world, not least to do with two intellectual failures.[1] The analytical tradition of philosophy has until recently failed to assimilate any of the insights of hermeneutics into the importance of aesthetics for questions of language, truth and interpretation. At the same time traditional forms of literary study have also failed to engage with philosophical resources which, in the case of Jacobi, Novalis and Schlegel, were even produced by authors whose literary texts are deemed appropriate objects of academic study. The disparate nature of these disciplines itself suggests a divide which literary theory has rightly begun to question. If approaches to meaning and communication exclude either the literary in the name of a scientistic conception of semantic explanation, or the philosophical in the name of the uncritical common-sense assumption that there are no serious methodological – as opposed, say, to historical or biographical – problems involved in understanding works of art, the result is a completely unrealistic image of how problems of meaning and communication emerge in real societies. These problems, as the Romantics already realised, inherently involve dimensions which must draw on the whole range of resources from philosophy and literary studies, and the best contemporary literary theory has now again begun to realise this.[2]

It is, of course, not just in literary theory that there have been attempts to make good the consequences of the omissions that result from rigid disciplinary boundaries. Ideas which emerge from Romantic philosophy's connections of art and truth have recurred in contemporary holist approaches to semantics. In this sense, what I mean by Romantic philosophy offers a series of important possibilities for creating dialogue between hermeneutics, post-structuralist influenced literary theory, and those contemporary analytical approaches to philosophy which have moved away from semantic and other foundationalism. To this extent, it seems to me that

Rorty's claim that there are essentially different enterprises at issue here – the analytical tradition being concerned with the idea, derived from a certain perception of the natural sciences, that 'metaphor is a distraction from [ahistorical] reality', the continental tradition with the anti-realist idea that metaphor is 'the way of escaping from the illusion that there is such a reality' (Rorty 1991a p. 23) – is now in need of a certain amount of relativisation. Although Rorty's schematic judgement is probably *de facto* still true of much of the contemporary institutionalised philosophical scene, the present attempt to write a history which might also shed a different light on the analytical/continental divide has, I hope, already suggested new ways of deconstructing that divide.

However, the fact is that, despite the convergence of interests which links philosophers like Davidson and Putnam to a tradition that was widely thought until recently to have little if anything to do with their concerns, the influence of the literary theory associated with 'post-structuralism' has in some areas tended to widen the divide between philosophy as it is practised in the greater part of the English-speaking world and what is loosely termed 'continental philosophy'. The reasons for this have to do with responses to questions of truth. Within the main traditions of continental thought a very crude, but useful, separation can be made. On the one hand, there are the positions which try to undermine the notion of truth, which include certain forms of Nietzschean, Freudian and Marxist 'hermeneutics of suspicion' and theories of ideology, as well as the deconstructive critiques of 'presence'. On the other, there are the positions, exemplified by Schleiermacher, and, in another way, by the best work of Adorno, Gadamer and Habermas,[3] which try to show in differing ways that truth is not adequately dealt with by the attempt either to reduce it to something else such as power, or to reveal that it depends upon the illusion of 'presence', or to equate it with rule-based meaning. The Nietzschean versions of the first position are sometimes associated with an idea of the need for a 'transvaluation of all values', including truth qua value, which is linked to a farewell to the repressive nature of reason's reduction of difference to identity in modernity. This is the case, for example, in Derrida's affirmation of the kind of interpretation which, rather than seek a ground for interpretation, 'affirms play and tries to go beyond man and humanism' (Derrida 1967b p. 427) that I have cited at various times. The second position, that Derrida himself has increasingly come to espouse in recent years, sees truth as an ethical obligation inherent in communication with the Other, which leaves space to connect truth to what can be revealed by aesthetic modes of articulation.

Nietzsche's conception of truth as a merely metaphorical illusion, which underlies many positions of the first kind, was always going to cause more methodological trouble than it is worth. Nietzsche himself is torn between trying to legitimise the idea of truth as domination of one manifestation of the will to power by another, and the sense that it is literally nonsensical to try to construct a theory out of such an idea, because the very statement of the theory is self-refuting. As I have suggested elsewhere (in the Conclusion of Bowie 1993) the first of these alternatives, which is mimicked in many areas of literary theory and in the worst aspects of DoE, is the result of an over-dramatised attack on the representational conception of truth. Attacks of this kind must rely on intuitive access to something which grounds truth, such as the subject's desire for self-preservation against the other. As Rorty has suggested, this position is therefore itself just another representational theory, because it assumes reference and representation are '*illusions* (as opposed to being notions which, in certain contexts, might usefully be dispensed with)' (Rorty 1991a p. 5). If they are illusions, the criteria for identifying them as such cannot themselves be illusory, on pain of a by now hopefully familiar regress.

The Romantic conception of *Poesie* is a much better alternative for questioning representational conceptions, both because of its insistence on 'beginning in the middle' and because of what was suggested by Novalis' rejection of 'the belief in true complete representation – and relation of the picture and the original – of appearance and substance' and of 'the inference from external similarity to complete inner correspondence and connection', thus of 'the confusions of subject and object' (Novalis 1978 p. 637). In Romantic terms the serious Nietzschean questions about the value of truth are already implicit in the demand to do justice to whatever is to be understood, rather than to 're-present' it, that I have termed the 'hermeneutic imperative'. It is not least for these reasons, as I suggested in the Introduction, that the present book, against the trend of much literary theory, deliberately consigned Nietzsche to a subordinate role.[4]

New perspectives for the future of literary theory seem to me now to require at least a partial move away from increasingly repetitive deconstructions of decidability in interpretation and from – often questionable – repetitions of post-Romantic critiques of representational thinking and of 'Western metaphysics'. We need to move instead towards the development of new strategies for interpretation that are alive to the need to salvage already existing resources for the generation and transformation of meaning. These resources are too often regarded in literary theory as part of a 'modern' past which we need to escape in order to be open to 'post-modern' possibilities. Within the more recent manifestations of the traditions examined in the present book Adorno's attempts to take seriously the Nietzschean suspicion of truth, at the same time as sustaining the idea that truth and art must be connected, still have much to tell us. Despite his obvious failings, Adorno most tenaciously defends – and questions – the heritage with which we have been concerned. I want therefore to conclude by taking a final look at a few of the issues dealt with in the rest of the book in relation to certain questions in Adorno. In subsequent work I intend to take up in more detail some of the more contemporary developments that emerge from the move from Romanticism to critical theory: this will have to stand as my excuse for the schematic and incomplete nature of my final reflections.

Adorno's potential contribution to perspectives for the future of literary theory are indirectly encapsulated in a characterisation, written in 1968, of the interpretative achievement of Wilhelm Furtwängler, which I cite below.[5] The characterisation of Furtwängler is thoroughly apt to Adorno's own approaches to art and philosophy and it touches upon many of the central themes of the preceding chapters. I also cite it because Furtwängler's performances of some of the greatest music we have and Adorno's discursive interpretations both of that music and of other great works of art embody what certain forms of contemporary literary and cultural theory are often in danger of relinquishing.

The assertion that there is such a danger inevitably involves an appeal to tradition, which can too easily become a merely conservative attempt to avoid real engagement with the present. However, it is fundamental to Adorno's approach that he employs concepts in such a way that they always remind the reader both of their inescapability and of their inherent inadequacy to their object. His appeal to tradition – in contrast, for example, to Gadamer's sometimes too comfortable reliance on the supposedly shared interpretative horizons in which we are always already located – makes awareness of the repressions and fissures in the notion of tradition central to the very use of the notion:

> If I wanted to try to formulate Furtwängler's idea in a word – I mean the objective idea, not what he wanted, but rather what realised itself through him – then I would have to say that he was concerned with the salvaging (*Rettung*) of something which was already lost, with winning back for interpretation what it began to lose at the moment of the fading of binding tradition. This attempt to salvage gave him something of the excessive exertion involved in an invocation for which what the invocation seeks is no longer purely and immediately present.
>
> If his idea was the salvaging of music which sinks away (*entsinkt*) from consciousness, then it is up to us, in the same spirit, to salvage the image of music which was once more alive in him.
>
> (Adorno 1984b p. 469)

Salvaging the image of art which was once more alive in Adorno is a crucial task for any serious literary theory, however much it must depart from the idiosyncrasies and indefensible theoretical totalisations we observed in chapter 9.

Some of the resources for avoiding the problems Adorno often creates for himself are present in the work of the Romantics and Schleiermacher that we have already examined. Although we must now read the Romantics rather as Furtwängler interprets the great works of bourgeois music, that does not mean we cannot salvage elements of their thought which can contribute more to our self-understanding than many of the contemporary theoretical alternatives. It is time that illusions of complete novelty and of a new era beyond the restrictions of metaphysics, which are characteristic of some of the worst forms of literary theory, gave way to a more sober critical engagement with already existing resources that are far from exhausted.

The terms in which Adorno formulates his account of Furtwängler echo the underlying framework of the preceding chapters. The difference between what the subject wants and what realises itself through the subject is the source of the reflections on the relationships between truth, art, the subject and language that develop via Kant and Jacobi in Romanticism; the problem of interpretation in the face of the loss of binding traditions is the problem of modern hermeneutics; the invocation of what is no longer immediately present informs those aspects of modern art which, as Novalis and Schlegel do, regard the Absolute as a normative goal that is only accessible via the ongoing failure to achieve it; the notion of 'salvaging' is both the secularised reaction in art to modern temporality, which continually threatens to consign all truths to oblivion, and a reaction to the appropriation of culture for the commodity world and reactionary politics. In all these areas the point of orientation is some notion of truth, not the dissolution of truth into perspectivism, ideological context or mere undecidability.

If great bourgeois art – or, remembering Novalis' dictum that 'the only possible decision is whether something is literature or not', any work which is judged to be art – is reduced to its identifiable historical and ideological determinations or made into the repeated demonstration of interpretative undecidability, rather than also being understood in terms of its challenges to what we think we know, to what we think is worth doing, and to what we can hope for, our self-understanding will be immeasurably impoverished. Those aspects of modern culture upon which Adorno concentrates, like the works of Kafka or Mahler, succeed in combining the articulation of truths that are only accessible in an unrepeatable autonomous form with a sense of the loss that results from the decline of collectively binding theology and from the admission of the failure to find totalising alternatives to theology. Engagement with such works must always take account of the tendency even of great art towards ideology, but it will not see its task as merely the revelation of the barbarism that underlies all culture. Sustaining the tension between the critical and the aesthetic moments is the challenge for all theory in this area. This can only be achieved via the intrinsically normative demand that the concepts we employ be appropriate to the object in question. Decisions on the appropriateness of those concepts cannot be arrived at by a prior theory, but must rather, as Adorno shows, be the result of the always fallible attempt to arrive at constellations which do justice to their object.

If we renounce the lessons to be learned from great works of art, including, as Adorno shows, from their ideological entanglements, we conspire with a world whose tendencies are those of the culture industry. Although Heidegger's notion that, in the face of the domination of the world by the principle of subjectivity, we need primarily to 'listen' to great works and Gadamer's idea that we become part of the 'happening of tradition' in subjecting ourselves to great art both rely on an untenable model of the subject's relationship to language and on an invalid abridgement of the history of modern philosophy, the moment of truth in their conceptions has become apparent through some of the failings of recent literary theory. The claim that there are no essential differences between great art and contemporary popular culture is a betrayal of art works – including those which are not yet an acknowledged part of any tradition – whose resources for rendering life more meaningful have been hardly tapped, let alone exhausted by the contingencies of their reception up to now by conservative, liberal or Marxist critics. In a secular world which increasingly demands conformity of evaluative perspectives, the imaginative, subversive and affective resources in art remain the location of possibilities which the rest of society tends to forget or dismiss. The ability of art to bring about productive 'cognitive dissonance' still remains a possibility in any half-way functioning public sphere.

The really difficult problem here is that the great autonomous works seem, as was suggested in Adorno's characterisation of Furtwängler, increasingly to be a thing of the past. One of the vital tasks for contemporary theory is therefore to ask how what was offered by the great autonomous works, from Hölderlin to Beckett, and from Beethoven to Schönberg, manifests itself in contemporary culture, where the very notion of the 'work' is now a problem.

Peter Bürger (e.g. in Bürger 1983) assumes that the contemporary erosion of the category of the autonomous work of art means that the resources offered by art should be brought back into everyday life. Now it would be wholly mistaken to maintain that the use of aesthetic resources could not make life more humane and tolerable in almost any area of contemporary society. However, Bürger's position is more a sign of his own failure to appreciate what was at issue in the development of aesthetic autonomy against the increasingly instrumental tendencies of modern societies than an adequate assessment of what is meant by the erosion of the autonomous work. Albrecht Wellmer rightly suggests against Bürger that 'without the paradigmatic creations of "great" art, in which the fantasy, the accumulated knowledge and ability of obsessively specialised artists objectify themselves, democratically universalised aesthetic production would presumably decay into mere arts and crafts' (Wellmer 1985 p. 39). The very fact that the innovations of great art will be assimilated and watered down by the culture industry, even as they contribute to new insight, suggests the need for the kind of exacting critical perspective adopted by Adorno and by major artists. Even the maintaining of the great traditions of art requires relentless renewal. To take two examples close to Adorno: Beethoven is all too rarely played in a manner which communicates the truth of his works, and Kafka is almost invariably hermeneutically travestied via the failure to engage adequately with his aesthetic achievement.

A whole series of important questions arise here. Adorno's own avowed preparedness to countenance the end of art's role as a bearer of substantial truth is predicated upon an extreme, Benjamin-inspired utopianism, in which the reconciliation that took the form of appearance in art would in fact be realised in actual human societies. The fact is, though, that in a world where totalising utopian hopes now increasingly appear merely as residues of dead theology, Adorno's insistence that great works of art are no more than appearance no longer seems wholly convincing. As more and more of the world is rendered explicable in scientific terms, the experiences generated by 'pleasure in that which cannot be recognised or identified' (Menke 1991 p. 29), which Menke sees as germane to Adorno's view of aesthetics, take on a different importance. The insights offered by great art into ways of temporarily redeeming those aspects of finitude which are finally irredeemable constitute in many ways quite 'realistic' responses to our facticity. Bürger's idea that this post-theological aspect of art should be dissolved into a new social function for art, which comes down to art being a means of articulating insights that are already also accessible in other forms, fails to grasp the nature of the aesthetic experience which is central to Adorno. Adorno's justified suspicion of a direct social function for art need not, though, be construed as an argument for political quietism. The point – which was what lay behind many of Adorno's objections to Benjamin – is that linking art directly to politics can create simplifying illusions of the kind which great art inherently undermines via its revelation of the need to accept complexity and fallibility as part of the modern experience of truth.

There are no easy answers in relation to any questions concerning art and politics, but some contemporary approaches seem to me to misjudge the significance of major art in this respect. The abandonment, in the name of the assertion of a wholly different cultural identity, of the resources available in the great works of modern Western art, which is taking place in many areas of literary and cultural studies, involves a failure to realise that those works can also be salvaged for new perspectives and new cultural identities.[6] Their truth consists precisely in this recurrent possibility and it is the continuing task of interpretation to show how they can be salvaged, rather than how they merely conspire with repression. Western art has undoubtedly been used as a means of cultural repression. However, this should not obscure the emancipatory possibilities of that art: the failure to appreciate this is one of the most damaging misunderstandings in contemporary theory.[7]

Interpretative models which lead to a dismissal of works in terms of their supposed ideology merely confirm their own premises: an interpretation which begins by looking for the ideological function of the work of art is unlikely to see what can be learned from the work which is not merely ideology. The understanding of time to be gained, for example, from listening to the expansions and contractions in the musical elements of pieces by Webern, or from Proust's articulation of the experience of time in the rhythm of his sentences and the larger rhythms of his novel can undoubtedly be analysed in terms of the wider social functioning of modern time or in terms of philosophical approaches to time. However, theories of the commodification of modern time and theories of time in modern physics, and the articulation of time in works of art are quantities which cannot be reduced to each other. Adorno's best analyses of major art works, which exemplify some of the workable aspects of his theory of 'non-identity', do not exclude socio-historical approaches to the work, but they insist that one can only understand the theoretical issues appropriately if one also undertakes a thorough immanent engagement with the work. The truth-content of the work consists, as Romantic philosophy suggested, not least in its involving more significant possibilities than any theoretical account could exhaust. The fact is that works of art make hermeneutic demands which cultural materialism in particular too often simply ignores or represses: hence the revealingly Oedipal sense in such theory that the works must now be put in their ideological place, rather than acknowledged as continual challenges to our self-understanding.

The other most widespread false alternative in this area are those types of literary theory which regard aesthetic experience, or experience of the sublime, as an escape from modern rationality. What such theories fail to see is that one of the main tasks of rationality, as Adorno suggested in the passage cited in Chapter 9 from 'Reason and Revelation', is not to repress what is not conceptually articulable but rather to search for ways of articulating what cannot be said discursively. There is, for example, a fundamental difference between the real irrationality of insanity and the access to a non-reductive *understanding* of insanity made possible by certain pieces of music or by texts like Büchner's *Lenz*. Such understanding does not re-present insanity: that, one must assume, is inherently impossible. Neither, though, does it reduce insanity to an explanation which ignores its resistance to discursivity. Adorno's theoretically defensible positions rely, as did the best Romantic theories, on a rejection of irrationalism as a basis for aesthetics: hence his insistence on the idea of the truth-content of art. His stress on the recalcitrance of great art to easy assimilation is a manifestation of the 'hermeneutic imperative': it keeps the tension alive between what can be said discursively and what may only be available metaphorically, without necessarily privileging one over the other or asserting an absolute distinction between the two. This tension goes right to the heart of the contemporary relationship between philosophy, literary theory and literature itself. As we have seen, Romantic philosophy is at its most convincing when it shows ways of both sustaining and questioning these divisions.

Adorno insists that, even though art is affected by commodification and other modern forms of identification, this is no reason to adopt, in relation to art, the evaluative levelling which is itself the basis of the commodity form. He does so not least because art offers a location from which we can glimpse utopian possibilities, even if those possibilities are, in art, in one sense merely appearance. As I suggested above, I think Adorno actually overplays the sense of art as mere appearance because of his Benjamin-derived utopianism. The sense of reconciliation at the end of a Bruckner symphony or of Proust's *À la recherche* may be in one sense ideological, because it seems to promise what real societies and real life do not provide, but it can also be a way of sustaining and arousing motivations and hopes which otherwise have no form of articulation and would thus be threatened by oblivion. Even in this more individualised and particularistic sense autonomous art allows us to be critical of social developments which destroy possibilities of reconciliation, because it is never reducible to being a function of those developments. This is one reason why art is still a 'sign of freedom' and why repressive governments still take the trouble to try to keep it under control or to weaken its social role.

One of the vital questions for theory is, then, how to think about the freedom of which art is a sign, which is neglected in many of the dominant contemporary conceptions. As we have seen, the Romantics' rejection of the questionable aspects of the early Fichte enabled them to avoid the idea that the freedom of the subject consists merely in the ability to dominate its other. Many of the recent Heideggerian critiques of metaphysics, which assume that modern metaphysics inherently involves domination by the subject, and which try to dethrone the subject via the revelation of its dependence on language, are therefore demonstrably invalid. Adorno also has a tendency to remove freedom to a location which is beyond any form of articulation, on the assumptions that the world of the culture industry has no place for such freedom and that the individual creative subject or the individual interpreter in such a world is inherently suspect. In these terms even major contemporary works of art are seen as lacking any positive expressive capacity beyond their resistance to identification in the terms of society as it is at present. This extreme stance relies, as we have seen, upon Adorno's most questionable assumptions, some of which he shares with Heidegger and with aspects of post-structuralism, for example when these positions invoke such notions as a 'language of metaphysics'.

As Schnädelbach has argued, a reduction of everything determinate to being part of the 'universal context of delusion' is a function of the indefensible side of Adorno's linking of 'idealist' philosophy (which largely corresponds to Heidegger's 'Western metaphysics') to the commodity world:

> Adorno philosophically . . . identified the critique of idealism [the critique of a world understood merely as 'conditioned conditions'] and the theory of society with each other; Hegel's absolute idea, which appeared to him as the essential paradigm of 'identity' and the social totality were for him two forms of the same whole, which is the untrue.
>
> (Schnädelbach 1987 p. 202)

This identification has highly problematic consequences for Adorno's view of the work of art and therefore for any literary theory that wishes to sustain a position which takes the aesthetic seriously. It is important to disentangle the conflations of differing issues it involves, not least because similar conflations sometimes play a role in theories whose concern is with the attempt to acknowledge alterity without repressively reducing it to identity.

Even though truth and untruth cannot be said to be symmetrical – the possibility of asserting what is false presupposes an understanding of truth, but not vice versa (on this see e.g. Tugendhat 1992) – the whole can as little be justifiably said to be the true (Hegel) as it can be said to be the untrue (Adorno). Novalis' assertion that 'The essence of identity can only be established in an apparent proposition (*Scheinsatz*). We leave the identical in order to represent it' (Novalis 1978 p. 8) makes it clear that any proposition concerning the whole is inherently problematic: that is the point of the Romantic conception of the Absolute and of the links of the Absolute to art. Adorno's claim results in paradoxes because it involves the assertion – which entails a truth claim – that it is indeed the case that the whole is the untrue. This means, given the statement's role as part of the whole, that the whole cannot in fact be the untrue (if the assertion that it is could actually be made intelligible anyway). Instead of just accepting that this was not the appropriate way to theorise the repressions involved in modern forms of identification, Adorno is often tempted into trying to make logical issues concerning identity into a direct function of the social world's constitution in terms of forms of identity, forms which are in fact irreducibly different from each other.[8] He thereby conflates 'identification with' and 'identification as' in the way which was criticised in Chapter 9. What, then, especially in the light of the generalised suspicion of identification as repression of the other in many areas of literary theory, is one to do with questions of truth that are conceptualised in terms of a critical attitude to identity?

The model which links metaphysical systems, language conceived as a system of differences and the commodity world of negatively related exchange values, which all leave the particularity of the individual elements outside the system while identifying them under a general concept, could only be valid as a unified model, rather than as series of contingently connected analogies, if the theory which links them together could be definitively grounded. Schnädelbach argues that '[Adorno] could only make his thesis of universal mediation which is critical of idealism into an argument which grounds itself if he succeeded in showing the social basic-antagonism [the foundation of value in exchange value] as the foundation in all logical variants of non-identity' (Schnädelbach 1987 p. 200). If this programme is to succeed it would have to turn the absolute ground which Jacobi sought in theology into a totalising insight into the way reality is socially mediated. The foundation of the world of conditioned conditions, from natural science, to language, to the commodity system, would have to be fully accessible from within society itself. This access was what Lukács sought in his conception of the relationship of the proletariat as the subject-object of history to the revolutionary party, what Benjamin tried to accomplish via the combination of a critique of language as identification with the theological idea of a language which allowed things really to be themselves, and what the later Heidegger sought in the idea of the 'sendings of being', of which the link between metaphysics and technology was the most recent manifestation. Benjamin and Heidegger develop these theories as a way of sustaining an emphatic philosophical conception of truth which does not depend upon a systematic metaphysics. The alternative to this emphatic conception is often seen as some version of the Nietzschean reduction I described above. Are these, though, the only real alternatives? The crucial issue here is the understanding of subjectivity.

Although he at times comes close to both Benjamin and Heidegger, Adorno himself, as we have seen, is ambivalent about the possibility of grounding a totalising critique, despite his sporadic adherence to the idea of the name and despite the more extreme versions, especially in DoE, of the critique of subjectivity in the name of its supposed inherent domination of the Other. In *Minima Moralia* he summarises a key aspect of the Romantic position whose often subterranean history has been a major concern of the present book:

> Today nothing less is demanded of the thinker than that he should be at every moment in the things (*Sachen*) and outside the things – the gesture of Münchhausen who pulls himself by his own hair out of the bog becomes the schema of every cognition which wants to be more than an assertion or a project. And then the official philosophers come and reproach us with having no firm standpoint. (Adorno 1978 p. 91)

In this passage Adorno comes close to the Romantic hermeneutic maxim of 'beginning in the middle', which renounces the attempt definitively to ground philosophy either in the power of the subject or anywhere else. As I suggested at the end of Chapter 7, though, this renunciation by no means removes questions about the subject from contemporary theory, because the subject need not be conceived as a final ground in the manner of the early Fichte. This fact gives rise to some of the most problematic issues in Adorno's account of the relationship of art to truth.

Both Adorno's account of the links of art and truth and many of the most influential recent philosophical attempts to arrive at new approaches to interpretation involve a significant theoretical deficit, because their account of the role of subjectivity in understanding and world-disclosure is inadequate. Manfred Frank has made vital contributions to overcoming this deficit by his reminder that the model of subjectivity which leaves only the alternative between either the Cartesian self-presence that results in the domination of the Other, or the subordination of the subject to linguistic and other determinations, fails to deal with central Romantic insights into the nature of subjectivity.

The crucial aspect of Frank's theory is a development of the Romantic conception of a subject which is never fully transparent to itself, but which is also not merely subjected to the linguistic and other systems into which it is inserted. The innovation most apparent in aesthetic production, but which is actually a potential in any act of communication, cannot in these terms be regarded as *meaningful* innovation unless a subject's creative and interpretative individuality is regarded as its source: otherwise language itself takes over the role of the subject. The fact that meaning cannot, as Schleiermacher showed, be explained by the existence of prior linguistic rules, thus in terms of language conceived of as a 'code', means that questions of subjectivity are inherently connected to questions of the generation of new truths, including in art (on this topic see Frank 1992 in particular). Such a position does not imply a complete control of the subject over the new articulations it generates, but it does imply that our understanding of those articulations must take account of what Schleiermacher theorised in terms of style, of the individuality of combination which cannot be derived from the existing forms and rules of language and which can reveal new aspects of the world. The questions involved here are highly complex, and I just want to sketch a model of a key theoretical dilemma, rather than explore them in detail.

The theoretical tensions generated by Frank's account of subjectivity, which refuses to reify the subject into being what is in fact the object of its language, become very apparent if one wishes to retain a substantial link of art to truth, as both Adorno and Frank wish to do. In AT, Adorno claims, for example, that 'The particular individual human subject is hardly more than a limit, a minimum which the work of art needs in order to crystallise itself' (Adorno 1973b p. 250). This in one sense just echoes some of the indefensible aspects of Benjamin and Heidegger, because it reifies the subject at the same time as making the work itself, in the way Gadamer also does, into a kind of subject. Gadamer asserts, for example, that 'The "subject" of the experience of art, that which remains and persists, is not the subjectivity of the person who experiences it, but the work of art itself' (Gadamer 1975 p. 98). How do we avoid this sort of reification, without also surrendering the conception of truth in art?

Clearly any sense in which works of art are bearers of truth must rely on their transcending of inner subjective intention. Novalis maintains that 'The artist belongs to the work, and not the work to the artist' (Novalis 1978 p. 651), precisely as a way of coming to terms with the fact that the truth of the work must be more than what gave rise to it in the first place. Adorno's whole project of rendering art a source of insight into aspects of modern society which are not adequately articulated in more discursive forms depends upon the ability to move from what is the product of the individual to a significance that transcends the individual. At the same time, if it is the case, as Adorno also insists, that artefacts can only possess the status of art if they are fundamentally non-substitutable, the source of their uniqueness must be located. While a computer can configure verbal, musical or visual articulations in randomly novel ways, the sense of the *meaningfulness* of that which cannot be interpreted or brought into existence via existing rules can only be the result of the spontaneous initiative of the subject, either as producer or as interpreter (see Chapter 5, this volume, and Frank 1992). How, then, can spontaneity and truth be reconciled without falling back into an essentially 'Fichtean' viewpoint, of the kind Adorno is so concerned to avoid?

The vital problem here is the relationship between the generality of the material of articulation and the individuality required for aesthetic articulation. The Romantics wished to avoid the Fichtean view of absolute spontaneity, without at the same time delegating the meaningfulness of art merely to the linguistic and other material in which it is manifested. Adorno admits that the works of art which sustain their revelatory capacity seem to do so not least because they cannot be replaced by anything else. This suggests an interesting dialectic which Adorno does much to elucidate, but which also involves aspects he tends to ignore. The really universal *works* seem to be precisely those which are most individual: they are also nearly always those in which previous forms of subjectively generated articulation have both been assimilated most effectively and yet have been 'destroyed' in their previous form. Kafka, for example, needs traditional story-telling and techniques from the literature of his time, even as he makes them into something else. The individuality of the *artist* also only becomes significant, and thus plays a role in the possible articulation of truth, if the objectified – but still subjectively produced – general aspects of the process of aesthetic production, such as the rules of harmony or the craft of story-telling, have been both assimilated and transcended into something which those rules cannot generate.

The further significant difficulty here is that the historical accumulation of the objective means in a form of art can render the task of producing significant art more and more difficult: this is one of Adorno's indispensable insights into the problem of modern art. Theory must now try, therefore, to take on board Frank's demonstration of the ways in which many existing theories fail to deal with the necessary role of the subject's innovative capacity in art; at the same time, it must acknowledge Adorno's powerful insights into the difficulties for contemporary artists who seek, in the face of the accumulated objectivity of existing aesthetic forms, to produce works which have truth-value in the way in which the great bourgeois works had (and can still have) such value.

Is this whole approach, though, as Rüdiger Bubner (Bubner 1989) has claimed, merely a misapprehension of the nature of literature and other art, because it seeks to force a 'philosophical' conception of truth on to art? Bubner maintains, in thoroughly Hegelian fashion, that 'Questions of truth are posed by theory, and not in any way by art on its own behalf, even though theory talks itself out of trouble by using aesthetic analogies if there are problems with the concept' (ibid. p. 120). If the power of the Romantic tradition lies in its linking of aesthetics to truth, how can we account for the differences between philosophy and literature without falling prey to Bubner's objection? The most troubling aspect of the story I have been constructing will lie for many readers in my avowedly cavalier use of the word 'truth'. What, then, *is* the 'truth' to which I have repeatedly referred?

When Thomas Kuhn, in *The Structure of Scientific Revolutions*, used the word 'paradigm' in whatever number of different and undefined senses he was supposed to have used it,[9] many people regarded this as grounds for rejecting his whole enterprise. This rejection exemplifies precisely the attitude which misses the theoretical point of a hermeneutic position. How can one conclusively reject the still developing effects of a book which disclosed an anti-empiricist way of thinking about what science is to a world-wide audience that had largely lost touch with such ideas?[10] Only those completely attached to the idea of a ready-made world that can be mirrored in true propositions could think that the lack of ambiguity in key concepts is the sole route to truth. It is clearly vital to explore and differentiate the senses of a key term like 'paradigm', but one should not regard this as the sole aim of the theoretical enterprise: semantics can assist hermeneutics, but it cannot replace hermeneutics.

One does not need to move wholly outside the analytical tradition to realise that the reduction of truth to regulist semantics and its exclusion from questions of aesthetics is not even a good idea for the natural sciences. In his often remarkably Romantic *Ways of Worldmaking*, which exemplifies in important respects how the analytical and hermeneutic traditions are beginning to be able to communicate, Nelson Goodman maintains:

> Insofar as a version [of a world] is verbal and consists of statements, truth may be relevant. But truth cannot be defined or tested by agreement with 'the world'; for not only do truths differ for different worlds but the nature of agreement between a version and a world apart from it is notoriously nebulous. . . . Truth, moreover, pertains solely to what is said, and literal truth solely to what is said literally. We have seen, though, that worlds are made not only by what is said literally but also by what is said metaphorically, and not only by what is said either literally or metaphorically but also by what is exemplified and expressed – by what is shown as well as by what is said. . . . On these terms, knowing cannot be exclusively or even primarily a matter of determining what is true. (Goodman 1978 pp. 17–21)

If one moves away from an exclusively semantic conception of truth, be it by, as Goodman does, making it secondary to 'rightness' (ibid. p. 19) – his counterpart of Adorno's *Stimmigkeit* – or by adopting something like Heidegger's view of disclosure, vital issues remain accessible which a narrowly propositional view can exclude. The use of the word 'truth' may here run the risk of underplaying the value of the clarifications of the post-Tarskian use of the word in analytical philosophy, but if truth and meaning are connected in the ways Davidson and Heidegger suggest, then there are perhaps grounds for keeping a more open-textured sense of the word. It is obvious that Heidegger, Adorno and Gadamer, for example, do not see truth as an exclusively semantic category.[11]

The interpretation of the role of truth in Adorno is revealing in this respect because he combines aspects of a pragmatism not so far from that of Goodman and others with a sense that the aim of a truth of the kind suggested in the Romantic notion of the Absolute should not be finally renounced. The latter position sometimes regresses into the theory of the name, but, as we have seen, there are other ways of thinking about the Absolute. The tension between a predominantly pragmatic sense of truth and one which sustains the more emphatic normative sense suggested by the Romantic conception of the Absolute points to a fundamental tension in contemporary philosophy, exemplified, for example, in the differences between Rorty and Putnam. I think this tension needs to be sustained, and not conjured away as Rorty often attempts to do.

In Chapter 3 I cited Manfred Frank's remark that the Romantic Absolute 'exists as that which, in the divisions and fragmentations of our world of the understanding, yet creates that unity, without which contradiction and difference could not be shown as such' (Frank 1989b p. 340). The loss of an epistemological or theological ground is in these terms not merely the occasion of playful liberation but also of a normative motivation which, although it cannot be satisfied with allowing conflicting positions a purely relativistic co-existence, also acknowledges that there is no ready-made world and thus no determinate final philosophical answer to the question of the unity which grounds contradiction. Art works are, in this respect, one location of our sense of the unity to which Frank points, even as they are, as Adorno reminds us, also suspect for that very reason.

Adorno insists that 'art works are not themselves an Absolute, neither is it immediately present in them' in the manner of the symbol: 'they have it and do not have it. In their movement towards truth works of art need the concept which they keep away from themselves for the sake of their truth' (Adorno 1973b p. 201). The refusal to separate art from truth would seem, though, to lead here to mere paradox: 'Art wants that which did not yet exist, but all that art is already did exist' (ibid. p. 203). Art for Adorno is, as we have seen, only appearance, which is dependent upon social reality even as it negates it, and is thus not the true realisation of the happiness art seemed to promise before the promise was broken. The almost impenetrable section of AT on the 'truth-content' of art from which these statements are cited suggests how problematic this issue is for Adorno, and I do not think one can finally do a great deal with the repeated dialectical shifts involved in his account. What is at issue is, however, vital for the future of the Romantic tradition in philosophy and literary theory.

The paradigmatic question in the present context emerges when Adorno insists earlier in the section of AT on 'truth-content' that art relies upon the assistance of philosophy: 'Genuine aesthetic experience must become philosophy, otherwise it does not exist' (ibid. p. 197). The Romantic position we considered in preceding chapters suggested that philosophy must become 'art', in the sense of that which is not bound by rules, because of the impossibility of philosophy grounding itself and thereby establishing a decisive difference of itself from other forms of discourse. Both positions share the idea that what is being sought is a new understanding of truth beyond a theory of correspondence, but can they be reconciled? Given Adorno's rejection of foundationalism, how are we to understand the assertion from AT?

A great deal is at stake here, and I have no easy answers. The most impressive and influential response to Adorno's problems has been the suggestion, in the 'second generation' of critical theory, that we can move beyond Adorno's problems by changing philosophical paradigm from 'subject philosophy' or 'philosophy of consciousness' to a philosophy of intersubjectivity based predominantly on the linguistic turn in analytical philosophy.[12] In this way the idea in DoE that rationality has been revealed as the 'subordination of everything natural to the arrogant subject' (Horkheimer and Adorno 1971 p. 5) can be overcome by the realisation that the subject cannot be conceived of as merely that which relates to its object other, because of its relationship to language and of its concomitant intersubjective constitution.[13] The problems I have shown in Adorno's conception of identity can thereby supposedly be dissolved into the analysis of the linguistic forms in which we communicate about what things are, what they are for, and whether we value them in themselves.

In a justly celebrated essay on Adorno's aesthetic theory, many of whose conclusions are very persuasive, Albrecht Wellmer says of the issue implicit in the relationships between art, truth and philosophy: 'If one wanted analytically to separate that which Adorno thinks together dialectically, then one could differentiate truth as aesthetic rightness from truth as objective truth' (Wellmer 1985 p. 16). He goes on to infer from this that 'Adorno can only think the appropriation of the truth of art in the sense of a transformation of aesthetic experience into philosophical insight' (ibid. p. 31). The question is once again, though, how one conceives of the difference between what is articulated by art and what is articulated by philosophy.

Wellmer, like Habermas, invokes the separation between truth as disclosure, and the cognitivist position which sees propositional truth as a 'validity claim which we connect with a statement by asserting it' (Habermas 1984 p. 129). He does so as a way of avoiding some of Adorno's aporetic positions, which he regards as leading to a situation where 'art and philosophy together map out the form of a negative theology' (Wellmer 1985 p. 14). In Wellmer's terms art and philosophy become analogous to negative theology in Adorno because the reconciliation of word and thing demanded in the idea of the 'name' is inherently impossible. It is, however, important to ponder whether Adorno's refusal to make a definitive separation of kinds of truth is adequately explained by Wellmer's claim that 'art works fulfil their enlightening, cognitive function precisely not on the level of philosophical *knowledge*' (ibid. p. 30). This raises problems of grounding of the kind we have repeatedly encountered: what kind of knowledge is it that distinguishes philosophical knowledge from any other knowledge? In Chapter 7 I cited, against Habermas, Manfred Frank's notion of 'truth-qua-comprehensibility', which is prior to propositional truth, and which is closely analogous to the defensible side of Heidegger's conception of disclosure. The point of the notion was to prevent a rigid division between kinds of truth and to allow an interplay between the ways in which we make worlds, of the kind suggested in Romanticism and in the passage from Goodman cited above.

In *Style in Philosophy* Frank insists that the attempt to establish a generic difference between philosophy and literature is doomed to failure, because one can as easily gain 'philosophical' insight from, say, reading Musil, as one can gain 'literary' insight from reading Plato. Following Schleiermacher, Frank maintains that the difference between a philosophical and a literary text is constituted within a continuum of forms of linguistic usage of which the wholly propositional and the wholly innovative and metaphorical are the notional extremes, which never anyway appear in their pure form. This question is further complicated if one moves, as Adorno suggests one must, from the level of sentences as articulators of truth to the larger-scale world-making formal aspects of texts, which have clear analogies to musical forms of organisation.

Wellmer's assertion about 'philosophical knowledge' is based on the assumptions that 'one can only talk of the truth in art if we already know how one can talk of truth independently of truth in art' (ibid.), and that 'philosophical' knowledge is therefore straightforwardly propositional. This is a foundational claim of the kind Adorno clearly avoids, even in the passage Wellmer cites from AT, and it involves a problem we have repeatedly considered. We may indeed, as Jacobi suggested, have to presuppose truth, but for Jacobi that meant we could have no *explanatory* account of what truth is that does not end in a regress. This was the reason for the Romantic turn to *Poesie*, which is therefore, as I have argued, a key direct and indirect source of modern insight into truth.

Art in the Romantic and Adornian view resists all forms of closure which would convert it into discursivity, so that any determinate claim as to its meaning, while being in one sense potentially part of its meaning, is always negatable via further determinations. Truth here becomes the ongoing normative obligation to do justice to the object, which must rely upon what Heidegger meant by disclosure. It is more than arguable that this is, on a holist view, the best way to see truth about any object of our concern. In Wellmer's terms, though, we know what truth is on the basis of the 'everyday concept of truth'. He derives his account of the everyday concept from Habermas' analyses of the forms of truth in 'normal speech', which try to make categorial divisions between forms of validity claim. Truth is, then, to be understood via a version of semantics which is filtered through the theory of communicative action, thus through a classifying speech-act theory which separates spheres of validity.

My objection to this position in Chapter 7 was that the status of the theory itself was questionable, because it is not clear to which sphere of cognitive, ethical or aesthetic validity it belonged: the theory itself seems to be required to ground the difference between the spheres in the first place. Unless, as Anke Thyen suggests, one *already* presupposes the change of paradigm from 'philosophy of consciousness' to the paradigm of communication, the divisions the theory regards as constitutive cannot be legitimated by the theory itself. This is yet another version of the problem of grounding which was the source of Romantic philosophy. The further problem was that Habermas' theory did not give an adequate account of the individual subject's relationship to the happening of truth, which Schleiermacher showed, via his refusal to exclude aesthetic considerations of reflective judgement from their accounts of meaning, still to be a major issue in this area.

Goodman suggests why we need to be more careful in separating out forms of validity, when he maintains that

> The scientist who supposes that he is single-mindedly dedicated to the search for truth deceives himself. He is unconcerned with the trivial truths he could grind out endlessly; and he looks to the multi-faceted and irregular results of observations for little more than suggestions of overall structures and significant generalisations. (Goodman 1978 p. 18)

Even the scientist, in this view, builds the kind of model which Adorno saw as central to truth in the early philosophical essays and which also plays a role in the notion of constellation in ND. He also works in terms of the consequences that Schleiermacher saw as ensuing from Kant's reflective judgement.[14] Adorno is indeed, as Wellmer maintains, led to dilemmas by his attachment to the idea of the name, to a reconciliation between word or concept and thing, of the kind also suggested in the notion of the mimetic. It is not clear in Adorno's account, though, just what the truth *is* that philosophy is supposed to tell us about art. The work of art is, as we saw, characterised for Adorno by its resistance to being replaced by something else. Were its truth merely to be that which philosophy told us, then this status would be lost in the process of identifying its conceptual content. Often, though, Adorno evidently does not mean that the truth of the work is what philosophy tells us, as is clear from his remark that 'No proposition could be squeezed out of Hamlet; its truth content is no less for that' (Adorno 1973b p. 193). Adorno's own account of these matters is quite often of little help, but one can suggest that Wellmer's objections look less convincing if, in the manner of Frank and the Romantics, one keeps the relationships between art and its interpretation in philosophy more open.

It is precisely because the border between what is revealed by art and what is revealed by philosophy needs to be constantly re-negotiated that a simple division, on the basis of a classification of speech acts, between the propositional and the aesthetic is inappropriate. As Frank suggests (Frank 1992 p. 69), the difference between a philosophical and a literary text is a difference of degree, not a difference of principle: one can, for example, learn more about the philosophy of self-consciousness from a reading of Proust than from many philosophical texts on the subject. The ways in which art and the attempt to interpret art in aesthetics and literary theory can contribute to reflections on truth all relate to the sense that theories of truth which remain at the level of propositionality exclude too many of the differing modes of articulation via which we understand ourselves and the world. This was one of the key insights of Romantic theory and is, I suspect, one of the underlying reasons for the success of literary theory in redefining the concerns of so many areas of the contemporary humanities.

Instead, therefore, of separating the issue of truth from art we need to begin to analyse more adequately how contending notions of truth in contemporary philosophy and literary theory contribute to our self-understanding. If one admits the necessity of transitions between Habermas' – in my sense – merely heuristic spheres of validity, of the kind suggested in Romantic philosophy, and in Adorno's ambivalences about the relationship of art to philosophy, then one must make communication between the spheres more open. The failure to do this reduces the significance of art to what can be said about it in the other spheres, and its potential contribution to cognitive and ethical insight is diminished. The reduction of art to the ways it can be theorised is also inherent in Eagleton's rejection of the notion of literature, which I think has unfortunate consequences for the contemporary direction of the study of literature, despite the important reminder it gives us of the need to be vigilant if the study of literature is to be more than what goes on at Plato's 'wine parties of second-rate and commonplace people'. It is, then, more promising to maintain the tension between theoretical attempts to determine truth via formal semantics or a theory of communicative action, and the subversion of such determination which is most vividly sustained in the experience of autonomous art, than to lose sight of essential aspects of the experience of truth via a separation of the spheres of validity of the kind proposed by Habermas. In this sense the Romantic heritage still has much to offer which has yet to be adequately assimilated into contemporary philosophy. The very survival of literary theory as a viable discipline will depend upon its readiness to engage with other philosophical approaches which too many of its practitioners still seem to think they can ignore. Much the same also applies, though, to many areas of contemporary analytical philosophy. It is perhaps appropriate to conclude, without comment or analysis, with two Romantic views of such matters:

> The poem of the understanding is philosophy – It is the greatest impetus which the understanding gives to itself beyond itself – Unity of the *understanding* and of the *imagination*. Without philosophy humankind

remains divided in its essential powers – There are two people – One who knows (*Ein Verständiger*) – and a poet.

Without philosophy incomplete poet – Without philosophy incomplete thinker – incomplete judge (*Urtheiler*). (Novalis 1978 p. 321)

Mere philosophy without philology constitutes only *half the logical education* of a man. (Schlegel 1988 (5) p. 175)

Notes

INTRODUCTION: RENEWING THE THEORETICAL CANON

1 It should perhaps be added here that I attach no importance to my concentration upon a particular national tradition: the simple fact is that Kant and his contemporaries and successors, who founded the most significant strands of modern philosophy, were located in what we think of as German geographical space. *Why* they were German does not really interest me here, and I am not even sure if it is a meaningful question. 'Germany' did not exist in any serious sense at that time anyway.

2 I have already suggested some of the ways in which this is the case in Bowie (1990). This book will deal with these issues from other perspectives, so the two books should complement each other.

3 I shall return to this issue later: these developments in fact begin as early as the first half of the nineteenth century, as I suggest in relation to Schleiermacher and Bernard Bolzano in Chapter 4. Clearly there are enormous differences between these traditions, but the 'driving of thoughts out of consciousness' which is so central to Frege's enterprise is compatible in important ways with a literary theory which does not rely on authorial intentionality: both can be seen under the heading of 'understanding an author better than she understands herself' (see Chapters 4 and 5).

4 'Disclosure' is, then, not an uncovering of some kind of already present essence, but is instead an event in which something comes to be seen as something in a new way – Heidegger himself sometimes suggests that disclosure reveals some kind of primordial essence of 'being', but the idea is much more convincing if we avoid this appeal to 'origins'. I shall frequently return to these ideas in what follows.

5 On this see, for example, Kluge 1986. Eagleton's kind of analysis may, though, just involve an overestimation of the widespread ideological effect of literary texts on real human beings in particular historical contexts. The danger of this kind of overestimation will be considered later, in relation to twentieth-century Marxist approaches to literature and ideology. The obvious fact today is that film and television are far more important as sources of ideology in Western societies than literature, for reasons to do with the possibilities of dissemination via the mass media.

6 Any text at all will, of course, do this, if read in an appropriate context. The important question, though, is whether and how it matters that ambiguity can function in differing ways.

7 Certain works may be said to initiate ideological expectations, although, interestingly, they tend to be regarded as of less literary value than the works which survive and become part of the 'canon'.

8 Accepting, as one must, that there is no way of arguing with true fundamentalists anyway, because the argument can only be carried on in their terms, which would

be no argument at all. The task is to try to render the point at which it is either me or you as distant as possible.

9 I show how the reorientation in the notion of Greek tragedy usually associated with Nietzsche begins with the Romantics and Schelling in Bowie (1990).

10 My argument here is close to Gadamer's contentions in *Truth and Method*: I shall briefly consider some of my disagreements with Gadamer's position in the Conclusion.

11 See e.g. Putnam's 'Is Water Necessarily H_2O?' (Putnam 1990 pp. 54–79).

12 The doubts in some areas of analytical philosophy whether *any* words are finally synonymous mean that any text may not ultimately be paraphrasable. The fact that this is pragmatically usually not a problem, whereas it is a problem in relation to 'literary' texts, is what counts here. The borderline between what can and cannot be paraphrased is obviously fluid, but this does not mean that such borderlines do not matter. The same applies to the borderline between the literary and the non-literary: see Chapter 5 and Chapter 9.

13 Lest this sounds silly, it is worth citing the frequently heard claim by older figures in traditional kinds of literary studies to those planning to do literary research – this was said to me as a potential research student – that there is 'really not a lot left to do'.

14 The other is the 'new critical' attention to the endless ambiguity of the 'verbal icon'. This model fails to come to terms with the vital issues concerning art and truth which are raised in the traditions to be examined here.

15 In one sense it can be argued that Hegel's view of the 'end of art' corresponds to this analysis, because philosophy's ability to say propositionally what art can only say via images is seen by Hegel as a crucial advance in thought, which has already rendered art pointless as a means of articulating the *highest* truth (see Bowie 1990 Chapter 5).

16 Whatever this last phrase might actually mean – when or how do we ever encounter or could we know we have encountered the 'bare linguistic medium'? The assumption seems to be that there is 'language', the 'bare linguistic medium', and then there is that which 'developed' in order to bypass its limitations. However, what 'offsets' or 'bypasses' the medium is presumably itself still the medium. Was there ever a time when one could claim there was language bare of all elaboration? Such a language would have to be the mythical metaphor-free language towards which philosophy has sometimes been understood as striving (Bertrand Russell and others, for example, at one point wanted a logically purified language) and which Derrida in particular has done so much to discredit, rather than the form of language which literature is supposedly to escape. As I shall later argue, it is increasingly apparent that the notion of language as some kind of entity or medium is one of the biggest obstacles to an appropriate account of understanding anyway (see Chapter 5 in particular).

17 If this sounds too far from our more pragmatic contemporary conceptions to make any sense, it is worth remembering that the young John Dewey, whose influence on the work of Rorty, Putnam, and other major contemporary thinkers has been enormous, saw his intellectual project as linked to idealism's (and by extension Romanticism's) 'assertion of the unity of intelligence and the external world' that needed to 'secure the conditions of its objective expression' (cited in R. Bernstein 1992 p. 231).

18 A conception which is later echoed in Freud's conception of artistic production as the sublimation of instinctual drives, as well as being echoed in certain conceptions of mythology.

19 Eagleton would not necessarily claim anything to the contrary, but his position does not give sufficient weight to what this fact implies.

20 On the successes and failures of Romantic science see Cunningham and Jardine

(1990); on the continuing relevance of Romantic thought to contemporary philosophy see Bowie (1993).
21 Cf. Derrida's perhaps rather melodramatic attack – but one which is clearly in the spirit of Romanticism – on those concerned with rigid demarcation of intellectual disciplines, in a response to criticisms of a piece of his which attacks racism:

> In short, you are for the division of labour and the disciplined respect of disciplines. Each must stick to his role and stay within the field of his competence, none may transgress the limits of his territory. Oh, you wouldn't go so far as to wish that some sort of apartheid remain or become the law of the land in the academy. Besides you obviously don't like this word.... No, in the homelands of academic culture or of political action you favour instead reserved domains, the separate development of each community in the zone assigned to it. Not me. (Cited in Bernstein 1991 pp. 195–6)

22 Eagleton has subsequently devoted an important book to the topic of aesthetics, which, while giving much more time to the positive implications of the aesthetic, as that which provides images of new human possibilities, still fails in my view to make an adequate distinction between the aesthetic and the ideological: see Eagleton (1990), and my review (Bowie 1991). The book is, of course, entitled *The Ideology of the Aesthetic*.
23 I shall be returning to this issue in the course of this book, hence the very reductive account of it here.
24 Davidson is aware that 'convention-T', as Tarski's convention is termed, does not give one a *concept* of truth, because it cannot show how differing cases of the convention in differing languages could be shown to have the same significance. This is why Davidson thinks what he terms 'radical interpretation' is inescapable in establishing any kind of truth. This brings him, as we shall see, particularly in Chapter 5, very close to the hermeneutic traditions to be discussed in this book.
25 Acknowledgement of the importance of this structure in analytical philosophy has been apparent in the realisation of the disruptive effects of metaphor both on the attempt to circumscribe a theory of meaning and on new approaches to scientific discovery. See e.g. the work of Davidson, Mary Hesse, Nelson Goodman, Max Black and others on metaphor, Mulhall 1990, and the discussion below.
26 On this see Dahlhaus (1978).
27 See also Bowie (1990) on this topic in more detail.
28 The further advantage of this approach is that it does not attempt to make meaning something which can be attached to an individual word. I shall continue to use the word 'meaning' in a more general sense here, despite the heuristic usefulness of Rorty's restriction: when I am using the word in the Rortyian sense I shall use inverted commas. The problem with this conception of meaning lies in the attempt to distinguish it from metaphor, on the assumption that 'literal' meaning and metaphor can be finally separated, because literal meaning is established via knowledge of the conditions in which an utterance is held true (Rorty is ambiguous on this question). Against this conception, see Taylor (1985 Vol. 1 pp. 282–92), and my discussions in subsequent chapters. Taylor's argument explicitly derives from Romantic philosophy, beginning with Herder.
29 I am aware this begs a whole series of questions, some of which will be dealt with in subsequent chapters.
30 The extreme position here would be that in one rather strict sense no meaning can be semantically determined, because of meaning's inherent contextuality. See Chapters 4 and 5.

31 One does not need to maintain, with regard to the new approaches to language in question here, that there is, in a broader sense, no referential or representational aspect of language. It is just that this aspect cannot be shown to be the key to understanding language as a whole.

32 The sense of 'modernity' intended here will become clearer later: it basically corresponds to the sense given to it by Jürgen Habermas (1985), for whom modernity is defined by Kant's assertion of the autonomy of human reason, via which we 'give the law' both to nature, in cognitive judgements, and to ourselves, in moral decisions, and thus no longer derive the law from a divine authority.

33 Cf. Davidson on metaphor: 'I hold that the endless character of what we call the paraphrase of a metaphor springs from the fact that it attempts to spell out what the metaphor makes us notice, and to this there is no clear end. I would say the same for any use of language' (Davidson 1984 p. 263).

34 See my piece on 'Aesthetic autonomy' (Bowie 1992b).

35 Obviously this potential has in a certain sense always existed, and is inherent in language *per se*, in that recontextualisation can create new possibilities of meaning all the time, be it in the Bible or Thomas Mann. What matters here is the fact that at a certain point in history this potential becomes a central aspect of a new reflexive understanding of language, because of the decline of theological ideas about language, and in opposition to the rise of the assumption that language can be circumscribed in a science. Once this has happened there is no problem in reading Aeschylus as 'literature', even if the assumptions upon which the writing of his plays were based had little or nothing to do with modern assumptions about 'literature'.

1 PHILOSOPHICAL ORIGINS: KANT, JACOBI, AND THE CRISIS OF REASON

1 See the discussion in Lyotard 1979 of the 'grand narratives' of Enlightenment which Lyotard uses to define his conception of modernity.

2 A good, if at times merely historicist, account of this period in German philosophy is Beiser (1987), which offers more of the historical detail behind some of the theoretical points I wish to outline here in order to make the roots of later theories more apparent.

3 I do not, of course, think all Marxist accounts of these issues are necessarily reductive.

4 The path from these theorists to Derrida and other contemporary thinkers can be seen in two ways. In the first one can show how certain conceptual structures recur in differing manners, whether because of influence or not; in the second one can show that this recurrence is the result of demonstrable influence. I shall try to show both these paths at various points in what follows.

5 The term 'nihilism' emerged most publicly in a text called 'Metaphysics in Despair between Kant and Wizenmann' by Jacob Hermann Obereit in 1787, the same year as the second edition of the *Critique of Pure Reason* (see Hammacher 1971 pp. 80–1). Whether this was its source for Jacobi is unclear: the term, or something close to it based on the same Latin root, was used in various intellectual movements of the time. It is, then, anything but Nietzsche's invention, and was certainly brought into wider currency by Jacobi.

6 Kant himself still sees his new approach as leading to a new version of truth as adequacy to the object, albeit in his new sense of object, but once the new foundations he proposes have been revealed as questionable the non-representational implications of what Kant maintains come to the fore. As we

shall see in Chapter 2, this will become the main Kantian legacy for literary theory.

7 In T.J. Reed's terms I am, redundantly, 'talking epistemology' (see Reed 1992 p. 203). However, underestimating the implications of epistemological issues for the study of literature is one of the sources of the platitudes of much traditional literary criticism. Influential recent attacks by Rorty and literary theorists on the very notion of epistemology (including in Kant's non-dogmatic sense), as the attempt to establish foundations of knowledge, should not obscure the fact that the perceived need for epistemology in a particular historical context may be more significant than the subsequent failure to arrive at the foundations epistemology seeks.

8 The other most obvious candidate was J.G. Hamann (see Bowie 1990, Introduction and Chapter 6).

9 I discuss the analogy of this to Saussure's conception of the signifier, which is also defined negatively in terms of its relations to other signifiers, in Bowie (1993 Chapter 1). See also below.

10 See Bowie (1993) for an account of how this problem both founds German Idealism and leads to its demise in the work of the later Schelling.

11 For those readers worried about our apparent continuing distance from questions of literature, the fact is that Friedrich Hölderlin also arrived, probably influenced by Jacobi, at a closely related insight, which demonstrably fed into his literary creations and thereby also into subsequent philosophy, most notably into the work of Schelling, and much later, via Schelling, into the work of Heidegger (see Bowie 1990, 1993, Henrich 1992).

12 See e.g. Beiser 1987, Frank 1989b, Sandkaulen-Bock 1990, Henrich 1992, Bowie 1993, 1996a. The importance of Jacobi's contribution has often been ignored because the opposition to what he was saying was so virulent. The fact is, though, that the virulence of the attacks of Friedrich Schlegel, Hegel and Schelling cannot disguise their ultimate failure to find a satisfactory way around Jacobi's key insight. Schlegel, for example, takes an even less convincing theological way out than Jacobi himself in his later (1822) essay on Jacobi (Schlegel 1988 Vol. 4 pp. 242–50). See also Benjamin's remarks on Schlegel and Jacobi cited in Chapter 8, this volume.

13 On this see Beiser 1987, Christ 1988. See also Bowie (1993) for how this relates to German Idealism and Schelling in particular.

14 How fraught the question of atheism was at the time is apparent in the fact that in 1799 Fichte lost his academic job because of the accusation that he was an atheist. The political explanation of this incident is, of course, at least as important, if not more important, than the religious and philosophical explanation. Fichte was regarded as a Jacobin.

15 The idea of 'self-presence' itself, one should remember, goes at least as far back as Saint Augustine, who, in remarkable proximity to the much later arguments of Descartes, talks of the mind's self-knowledge as 'true presence (for nothing is more present to it than itself)' (Przywara 1936 p. 12).

16 Spinoza, though in many respects located in the tradition of Cartesianism, does not think the idea of a creator God makes sense and therefore thinks of God as substance and first cause. He still, however, adheres to a version of the ontological proof (see Allison 1987 pp. 59–60).

17 How far Jacobi has been neglected can be suggested by the fact that in a recent book on Heidegger (Dreyfus 1991 p. 3), the inversion of *cogito, sum* is attributed to Kierkegaard, thereby distorting the historical context of Heidegger's work. Kierkegaard's inversion of the *cogito* is clearly derived from his familiarity with Schelling's critique of Descartes. Schelling arrived at it via the combined influence of Jacobi and Hölderlin: see the Introduction to Bowie (1993). Sadly,

of course, a lot of work in literary theory thinks the decentring of the subject is a recent philosophical event.

18 He also, of course, refutes the ontological proof on this basis in the first *Critique*.

19 I shall outline Heidegger's most important contentions in more detail in Chapter 6. Dreyfus (1991) and Okrent (1988) are the best philosophical introductions to the early Heidegger. See also Tugendhat 1992, and my review in Bowie 1994b.

20 By 'philosophy' he essentially at this time means Spinoza's self-contained system. Later, as we shall see, he comes to regard Fichte's attempt to complete Kantian philosophy as the embodiment of 'philosophy'.

21 Heidegger's *Der Satz vom Grund* ('The Principle of Sufficient Reason') (Heidegger 1957) points out at great length the significance of the difficulty involved in translating *Nihil est sine ratione*. The argument of Heidegger's work on the principle of sufficient reason is initially identical with Jacobi's key argument, as we shall see in Chapter 6.

22 Jacobi had a great fear, which began even in childhood, of the idea of a boundless universe and of human transience.

23 We shall see Davidson making much the same point in Chapter 6, which will help make a further link between Davidson and the hermeneutic tradition.

24 Heidegger makes the same point in *Being and Time*, when he suggests that *all* interpretation and *all* cognitive claims inherently involve circularity, because we must already have understood what we wish to interpret, so that 'The decisive thing is not to get out of the circle but to get into it in the right way' (Heidegger 1979 p. 153). I shall consider the circular structure of interpretation below and in later chapters.

25 Beiser (1987 pp. 89–90) claims Jacobi's notion of *Glaube* rests on a confusion between what we *know* to be true, such as the a priori axioms of geometry, and what we *believe* to be true. Jacobi, though, like Heidegger and Davidson, thinks 'holding as true' (*Fürwahrhalten*) is a structure which is prior even to axiomatic truths, in that the *understanding* of truth cannot be demonstrated, even by the statement of identity, A=A, or by Tarski's convention which we considered in the Introduction. The real question for Jacobi is the relationship between demonstration and what cannot be demonstrated, which is apparent in the problem of demonstrating the relationship of a priori truths to the world. We can generate an infinity of necessary mathematical truths from axioms, but this does not tell us how these truths relate to the world outside these axioms. This problem is the core of what Jacobi wishes to argue, not the apparent conflation of knowledge and belief. Had Beiser been more aware of the historical context of the use of the word '*Glaube*' he would have avoided this evident misunderstanding.

26 The theological move is central to the Protestant philosophical tradition which leads to Kierkegaard, whose stress on faith, because of the failure of reason to ground itself, is directed against Hegel's attempt to solve the problem Jacobi revealed. The mediating figures here are Schelling (see Bowie 1993) and Schleiermacher (see Chapter 5).

27 With the difference that Nietzsche often seems to think that the pragmatic needs of human beings are sufficient to unmask 'truth' as simply the product of the need for instrumental control of nature. Jacobi is in many ways closer to Heidegger. Despite his indefensible claim that our cognitive world is 'completely unlike the real world' – which involves the usual problems of how he is able to know this – he thinks that all truth requires an irreducible prior world-disclosure over which we have no final influence and which therefore cannot be explained in terms of something which we know. On Nietzsche in this connection see the Conclusion of Bowie 1993.

28 For a more detailed account see Bowie 1990, 1993, Neuhouser 1989.
29 Kant is routinely cited as claiming that Fichte's system was 'totally indefensible'. However, in the *Opus Postumum*, he says things like the following, which hardly differ from the claims being made by Fichte: 'Transcendental philosophy is the act of consciousness whereby the subject becomes the originator of itself and, thereby, also of the whole object of technical-practical and moral-practical reason in one system – ordering all things in God, as in one system' (Kant 1993 p. 245). Given how seriously Kant seems to have taken such arguments it is hardly good enough, as so many people do, merely to repeat his initial rejection of Fichte.
30 It is this final consequence that Schelling and Hegel will attempt to overcome – before Schelling realises that it cannot be overcome within a system of philosophy and therefore tries to incorporate theology into a new kind of 'Philosophy of Revelation' (see Bowie 1993 Chapters 5 and 6).
31 See Hegel's 'Belief and Knowledge', which contains his critique of Jacobi, in Hegel 1970 Vol. 2. See Bowie 1993 for a more detailed account of Hegel's conception.
32 As I show in Chapter 5, Schleiermacher is familiar with the texts at issue here.
33 Hegel's system can be understood as the most developed and impressive attempt to avoid both these alternatives, by having a presuppositionless system, in which infinite regress is avoided by showing how the system is bound only by itself. Schelling's critique of this model leads, as I have shown (Bowie 1993), to the tradition of Heidegger and Derrida, as well as having effects in the Marxist and pragmatist traditions (see Frank 1975).
34 The relation of this to the intuitive aspect of truth discussed above in relation to Davidson is a major area of discussion in contemporary philosophy, where Heidegger's notion of the world which makes meaning possible is closely linked to Davidson's and others' 'holism'. See Chapters 6 and 7.
35 Fichte himself was deeply affected by it: following this time he increasingly becomes disturbed by the ontological issues Jacobi has raised. In 1800 he asks, for example, 'And do I really think or do I just think a thinking of thinking? What can stop speculation acting like this and continuing asking to infinity?' (Fichte 1971 II p. 252). He becomes convinced that only theology would enable one to escape this problem.
36 As Dieter Henrich has shown, Fichte had already begun to see the problems of his initial conception of the I even before Jacobi's letter: after *circa* 1797 he assumes:

> an active ground existing prior to the active Self (*Ich*), a ground which explains the equiprimordial unity of the factors in the Self, but is not itself present in the Self. The term 'Self' refers not to this ground, but only to its result. For 'Self' means to be for oneself. However, the Self does not focus explicitly on what makes its unity possible, even though this latter is its source. (Henrich 1982 p. 30)

Manfred Frank has developed aspects of this position in order to criticise the post-structuralist subversion of the subject, by showing that the notion of Cartesian self-presence does not apply to such a model of the I (see Frank 1984).
37 The complex route from these issues to Derrida and others can be traced in a variety of ways: whichever way one chooses, it is evident that there are clear paths of influence, for instance via Schelling, to Franz Rosenzweig, Heidegger and Emmanuel Levinas (see Bowie 1993). See also Chapter 8, this volume, on Benjamin.
38 See Frank (1977), Bowie (1990 Chapter 6) for the refutation of the standard

misinterpretation of Schleiermacher, by Gadamer and others, which effectively assumes that Schleiermacher's position is Ast's position. See also Chapter 5, this volume.

39 It can be argued, as Lacan does, that the subject could not even *be* a subject without the medium of the 'symbolic order', so that the interior and the exterior of the subject cannot be separated in this manner. This does, though, leave unanswered a whole series of questions concerning the subject's relationship to language. See Frank 1984, 1991.

40 The work of Claude Lévi-Strauss, which sees differing mythologies from wholly unconnected societies as being structurally related, depends upon this assumption. Schelling's *Philosophy of Mythology* works on a similar basis, in that it sees the process of myth-production as essentially like an unconscious natural process, which is only transcended when people become able to reflect critically on the meaning of myths, via the demise of polytheism and the rise of Judaeo-Christian monotheism. The question is how one explains the unconscious functioning of the myth, and therefore of the unconscious aspect of meaning production in general.

41 The links of Saussure to the Romantic tradition of linguistics have yet to be exhaustively analysed, but he was clearly aware of the work of Humboldt, Schlegel and others.

42 It will, of course, be the early Schelling and Hegel who think they can integrate the Spinozist and Fichtean positions, thereby answering Jacobi's objections. Schelling attempts in 1800 to suggest that art can give us access to what Jacobi means by the true. Hegel's views on the 'end of art' follow from his conviction that philosophy can integrate the two positions: the contrast of Hegel's position with the Romantic position can be used to define a fundamental aspect of modern philosophy which underlies literary theory. On this see also Frank 1989a, 1989b, Bowie 1990, 1993.

43 On this issue in relation to Romanticism see Frank (1989c), where he considers the broader implications of the Romantic metaphor of the 'cold heart', which values gold, the means of exchange, over the people who are the real repositories of value.

44 Kierkegaard's prioritising of existence is undoubtedly derived from Schelling's critique of Hegel and his division of philosophy into 'negative', systematically complete philosophy, and 'positive' philosophy, which is concerned with existence and thus cannot ever be completed merely by abstract thought itself. Kierkegaard was fascinated by Schelling, which led to his attending Schelling's lectures on the *Philosophy of Revelation* in Berlin in 1841. The influence of Schleiermacher on the idea of the 'individual' which cannot be reduced to the system is also central to Kierkegaard, and Schleiermacher was aware of Jacobi's arguments as we shall see in Chapter 5 (see also Bowie 1990, 1993, particularly Introduction and Chapter 6, and Frank 1975, 1977).

45 This was not Saussure's own view, but has come to be seen as such, given the way his editors tried to convert his theory into a merely structuralist enterprise. Many approaches to language in the wake of Frege's 'driving thoughts out of consciousness' in analytical philosophy and in certain parts of hermeneutics have, of course, insisted that meaning can be understood independently of particular language users. We shall encounter this issue in subsequent chapters.

46 I would maintain that the success or otherwise of Tarski's attempt to clarify a notion of truth at a formal level which we saw in the Introduction has no ultimate bearing on the problem of truth as it is understood here. Tarski himself is sometimes clear that he is not concerned with natural languages: it is Davidson who attempts to apply Tarski's idea to them.

2 SHIFTING THE GROUND: 'WHERE PHILOSOPHY CEASES LITERATURE MUST BEGIN'

1 See Behler 1993 for a good account of why one refers to *early* German Romanticism (see also Benjamin 1980 I (1) p. 10). When I refer to 'Romanticism' it is important to remember that I will always mean only the early Romanticism of Friedrich Schlegel, Novalis and, in certain respects, Schleiermacher. Behler gives a very detailed historical account of Romantic literary theory, including accounts of the less philosophically oriented aspects of that theory: my aim here is to demonstrate the philosophical power of the Romantic ideas, which Behler touches on but does not really explore.

2 Why this has come about cannot be considered here, nor can the vexed question of how much of Romantic theory ever fully became part of public debate. Some of Schlegel's best work never saw the light of published day until after the Second World War. On the other hand, the wealth of insight in Walter Benjamin's Ph.D. on the Romantics, written in 1919, suggests that enough was available at least by then to give a clear picture of the most important insights. It is evident that as the nineteenth century progressed Romantic philosophy was increasingly ignored in mainstream science and philosophy, especially following the demise of Hegelianism, but the effects of Romantic philosophy in the first half of the nineteenth century are still evident in many areas. The fundamental question, however, is why this philosophy should now seem so relevant to our contemporary concerns: as such I wish to consider its best arguments, even if their dissemination at the time of writing was sometimes quite limited.

3 Translating '*Poesie*' is a problem for which there is no single solution: at times I leave it in German, at others I translate it as 'literature'. The main aspect of the word is of course its link, via its Greek origin, to creativity, and it can be used to refer to any form of art. I return to this issue in Chapter 3.

4 In 1796 Schlegel claims 'Jakobi [sic] is an empirical mystic. He is finished. His philosophical achievement was to have given rise to Fichte' (Schlegel 1963 p. 3). As Benjamin points out (1980 (I) 1 p. 46) – see Chapter 8 below – Jacobi was often used as a scapegoat for problems which others also could not solve.

5 Although the Romantics help to establish the main divisions of intellectual labour, they are very suspicious of what happens when these divisions become rigid. An analogous suspicion lies, I would maintain, behind the renewed contemporary interest in Romantic approaches to science, and in the echoes of Romantic thought in some contemporary philosophy. On the role of Romantic thinkers in the new German universities see e.g. Cunningham and Jardine 1990.

6 Many of these arguments can be applied against Habermas' own position which, as I suggest in Bowie 1993 and in Chapter 7, this volume, itself tries to make the division of these spheres too rigid.

7 On this see Bowie 1990 and 1993, where I discuss Schelling's version of this position in the *System of Transcendental Idealism*, which puts forward a position in many ways analogous to that of Schlegel (see below).

8 Which does not, one should add, mean that we cannot make true judgements in a pragmatic sense. Wittgenstein deals with the same problem in the *Philosophical Investigations*, where he, like Kant, suggests that the chain of rules for rules must be broken by the *practice* of judgement, which cannot be further grounded. See Bell 1987, Caygill 1989, Brandom 1994 and Chapter 5, this volume, where I show how Schleiermacher is the first to make explicit the insight usually attributed to Wittgenstein.

9 For a somewhat over-dramatised but important view of this issue in relation to Romantic literary theory see Lacoue-Labarthe and Nancy 1988 pp. 132–3. The over-dramatisation of their account of the issue is a result of the authors'

excessive reliance on Heidegger's questionable version of the history of philosophy and the meaning of that history.

10 The shifts between the words 'art', 'technique', and terms derived from them tell one much about the formation of the modern conceptions of art and literature in this period. Kant insists in the third *Critique* that art, in the new sense of the product of 'genius', must entail more than just technique, which can be learned, whereas art cannot (see Bowie 1990, Chapters 1 and 6).

11 The function of schematism is actually more complex than this, because of its connection to the question of time. On this issue see Heidegger 1973 and Chapters 5 and 6, this volume.

12 Schleiermacher usefully terms the schema an 'intuition which can be shifted within certain limits'. We shall consider his position in Chapter 5.

13 The 'Schematism Chapter' has frequently been regarded as flawed in both the analytical and European traditions: Heidegger, however, sees it as the 'core of the whole' *Critique of Pure Reason* (Heidegger 1973 p. 108). See also David Bell's splendid piece on it (Bell 1987). As Stephen Mulhall has shown (Mulhall 1990), analogous issues to those confronted by Kant are central to the later Wittgenstein. Furthermore, Nietzsche will try to use a similar argument to undermine the very notion of truth, by seeing truth as the repressive imposition of structures of identity on what Adorno later terms the 'non-identical'. The importance of this development of the problem of the schema for contemporary literary theory's concern with 'difference' or 'alterity' and the avoidance of 'closure' should thereby already be apparent.

14 This is why the schema plays such an important role in Heidegger's understanding of Kant. The schema is vital to what Heidegger means by 'being', the fact of the world's intelligibility (see Chapter 6, this volume).

15 I shall show in Chapter 8 how this issue is crucial to Walter Benjamin's work on *Trauerspiel*.

16 The complexity and richness of Kant's position is not adequately dealt with by this characterisation, but the essential point for Romantic philosophy lies in the aspects which I have highlighted. I have dealt with the aesthetic aspect of reflective judgement in Bowie 1990 Chapter 1. The crucial point is that aesthetic pleasure points to a way in which the world of appearing, deterministic nature and the 'intelligible' aspect of the subject (the realm of freedom) may actually be connected. The notion of 'free play', which for Kant defines the aesthetic, is also central both to Romantic literary theory and to what so irritates people about some contemporary conceptions of meaning, from Derrida to Davidson.

17 Whether one can finally establish such a literal sense seems to me more and more questionable (see e.g. Bowie 1993 Introduction, Taylor 1985 Vol. 1 pp. 282–92).

18 See Ricoeur 1986, whose view of this topic is very close to what is being suggested here, though he does not make the link to Romanticism in any developed manner.

19 The phrase 'world-making' has become part of recent philosophy via Nelson Goodman, but what is meant clearly derives from Romantic philosophy. 'World-making' is not to be understood in analogy to theological ideas of creation, but in terms of how we can make what there is intelligible in new ways.

20 I have discussed Hamann in more detail elsewhere (Bowie 1990 Chapter 6); see also Beiser 1987. The importance of the idea of a 'general philosophical language' can be gauged by its relationship to the notion of a 'translation manual' in the work of W.V.O. Quine: see the discussion of 'holism' in Novalis and contemporary semantics in Chapter 3 and the discussion of Davidson and Schleiermacher in Chapter 5.

21 I am thinking both of the interest in literary translation, exemplified by the (August Wilhelm) Schlegel-Tieck translation of Shakespeare, and of the interest in the theoretical implications of translation.

22 Just how early in the modern period philosophically serious questioning of the divine origin of language becomes a major issue cannot concern us here. The important point is the sense in the latter half of the eighteenth century that language is an issue *sui generis*, rather than one dependent upon theology or epistemology, as it had been, for example, for Locke or Hobbes. For Locke, words are merely the instruments for designating already existing ideas. Hobbes gives a classic model of the approach which is rejected by the thinkers at issue here in *Leviathan* of 1651, when he claims: 'The first author of Speech was *God* himself, that instructed *Adam* how to name such creatures as he presented to his sight; for the Scripture goeth no further in this matter' (Hobbes 1968 p. 100). Even though Babel intervenes, the underlying assumption about language in relation to truth is that it is grounded in the divinity. The story of Babel still leaves the source of truth as the divinity who brings about the loss of the one true language. The relation of language to rational theology will concern us in Chapter 4.

23 Hamann, of course, held a thoroughly theological (and Locke-influenced) conception of language, but his important claim in this context was that the multiplicity of languages could not be reduced to a common language by *philosophy*.

24 These seminal positions are splendidly set out by Herder himself in his *Essay*. See also Behler 1993 pp. 265–8.

25 Paul de Man's analysis of this passage in *Blindness and Insight* stylises it into a unique rejection of the idea of meaning as 'presence' (of signified to signifier), but ignores the way in which it is part of a more general shift in the understanding of language at this time, away from the notion of presence or representation (see Bowie 1990 pp. 188–94). In non-representational visual art, the conceptual foundation of which is established in this period, the relationship of image to object also no longer depends upon a notion of correspondence.

26 This does not mean, which would be absurd, that prior to this period it was thought that language simply gave one direct access to the truth because of its divine source – the Ancients' concern with questions of interpretation and rhetoric makes this evident – but the dominant assumption prior to the modern period was that language was at least potentially a reflection of the ready-made world, though it could be misused via the 'art of persuasion'; hence the frequent claim that rhetoric was a perversion of language.

27 Whether one need accept the idea that 'seeing-as' necessarily depends on language is these days less certain than has often been thought (see e.g. Frank 1991, and aspects of the following chapters). This does not mean that one thinks that words mirror ideas, but rather that not all awareness is propositional.

28 This conception of the subject's relationship to language will be considered in relation to Schleiermacher in Chapter 5 (see also Frank 1977, Bowie 1990 Chapter 6).

3 THE PHILOSOPHY OF CRITIQUE AND THE CRITIQUE OF PHILOSOPHY: ROMANTIC LITERARY THEORY

1 On the question of 'literature' see Lacoue-Labarthe and Nancy (1988 p. 83), who claim that 'literature as its own infinite questioning and as the perpetual positing of its own question, dates from romanticism and as romanticism'. This is in many ways an apt characterisation, though the largely Derridean

consequences they draw from the position seem to me to be based on a misunderstanding of the question of truth, which they tend to see only in terms of the failure of representation, rather than in terms of the new temporalised conception of truth suggested in *Monologue* and other texts.

2 It would clearly be mistaken simply to equate the conceptions of Novalis and Friedrich Schlegel, and there is not space here even to attempt to outline their differences: my account is an attempt to synthesise some of the most important ideas of both thinkers into what I believe to be a coherent version of a few of their most vital insights. I would maintain that my 'synthetic' procedure here is congruent with their own positions. It should also be clear that I have omitted huge areas of Romantic concern, some of which seem to me now to be of only historical interest.

3 The difference of the Romantic view from the Idealist view, which Manfred Frank has done the most to elucidate, lies in the Romantics' eventual conviction that a self-grounding system of philosophy is impossible: the aim of German Idealism is such a system.

4 Kant was evidently aware of this question, as the notion of reflective judgement showed and as his discussion of the 'transcendental ideal' makes apparent (see Bowie 1993 Chapter 5), but the epistemological side of his enterprise was devoted to establishing stable forms which ground determinate knowledge claims. There is, by the way, no reason to suggest that the Romantic position in question here rejects the insights of natural science: its concern is to grasp the significance of those insights in relation to the broader question of the world's intelligibility. Whether the Romantic position must be construed as scepticism is too major an issue to consider here, though I touch on it in the discussion of the Absolute (see below and Chapter 8).

5 Lacoue-Labarthe and Nancy suggest that 'romanticism is neither mere "literature" (they invent the concept) nor simply a "theory of literature" (ancient and modern). Rather, it is *theory itself as literature* or, in other words, literature producing itself as it produces its own theory' (Lacoue-Labarthe and Nancy 1988 p. 12), a view which is in many ways an echo of the view presented in Walter Benjamin's dissertation on the Romantics (see Chapter 8, this volume). This useful characterisation again needs to be complemented by a more developed consideration of the issue of truth.

6 I am aware that the following parallel ignores significant differences between the Romantic position and the contemporary positions. However, the connections Malpas establishes between Davidson and Heidegger make it clear that the parallel must have substance. I have already suggested how Heidegger's hermeneutics is rooted in the issues of this period, and this will become even more apparent in subsequent chapters. *Why* this parallel has emerged cannot be adequately dealt with here: I attempt to address this question at various points later.

7 It should be clear from the rest of my argument that I do not share either Quine's essentially behaviourist conclusions from his version of the question of translation or his conviction that the ultimate grounding is provided by the discoveries of physics.

8 Much the same idea is present in Derrida's accounts of *différance*, which in this perspective look less and less earth-shaking or scandalous, and more and more part of a general philosophical reorientation of the kind begun by the Romantics. I shall consider other aspects of this question in later chapters.

9 It is odd how often positions based on a certain kind of faith in scientific explanation lead to assumptions which are ultimately theological, because they are based on the idea of the ready-made world which is grounded in absolute causality. The recurrence of versions of Fichte's arguments in the arguments of

the contemporary philosophy of mind against positions such as that of Fodor can suggest another way in which this parallel is philosophically substantial (see e.g. Frank 1991).

10 In this context it is worth remembering both Davidson's contention that metaphors are meaningless, because the only 'meaning' a word has is its literal meaning, and Taylor's suspicion of the very notion of literal meaning.

11 This is roughly what Kant intended with his concept of 'genius', who can redefine the rules of art, but not by *conscious* creation of new rules: the 'rules' emerge spontaneously by deviation from existing artistic praxis, and only become rules when they are understood and applied by others.

12 I will leave for later the discussion of whether Benjamin in fact wishes for the return of a 'mimetic' 'language of names' that would overcome the gap between signifier and signified, which he sees in the early essays and the *Trauerspielbuch* as having nihilistic consequences of the kind we have considered in relation to Jacobi.

13 The question of how language may be inherently ideological, given its formation within the history of human oppression, will concern us later, when we look at questions of literature and ideology. It will be clear that such a theory is indefensibly reductive, because there is no position available from which it could be stated without entailing a performative contradiction: how can someone truthfully say that their own means of communication is inherently ideological, without invoking a non-ideological level of communication on the basis of which the claim is made?

14 In Chapter 6 we will consider Donald Davidson's almost identical claim, which links to Jacobi's conception, namely that: 'our only evidence for a belief is other beliefs; this is not merely the logical situation, but also the pragmatic situation. And since no belief is self-certifying, none can supply a certain basis for the rest' (Lepore 1986 p. 331). In this way the very beginning of modern hermeneutic philosophy already prefigures the contemporary convergence of semantics and hermeneutics.

15 It was this problem which led Leibniz, for example, to assert that all true statements were 'analytical' or a kind of tautology.

16 See Frank 1991 for a detailed demonstration of the importance of this argument in a wide variety of contexts. See also Schelling (1994 pp. 47–8).

17 See Bowie 1993 Chapter 4. As we saw, Jacobi thinks these positions actually mirror each other.

18 It should be noted that this does not mean that truth and error are symmetrical (see my reply to Alan White in Bowie 1994a).

19 The Romantics do use the notion of 'longing', but it means the desire for and pursuit of truth that cannot finally be fulfilled, not the surrender to indeterminacy.

20 On the failure of Hegel's attempt to salvage a position from which philosophy could encompass this relativity, see Bowie 1993. Hegel was familiar with the work of Schlegel in question here. On Schlegel's conception see also Behler (1993 pp. 71–2).

21 The first part of this passage appeared on the London Underground in 1994, to advertise exhibitions and events about German Romanticism: the reversal in the second part of the passage was omitted, suggesting, sadly, that Romanticism has still not been adequately grasped.

22 Clearly there can be true assertions about oneself, but they do not cover all that one is, because major aspects of self-conscious life may not be articulable in propositions.

23 Proust's *À la recherche du temps perdu* can be interpreted as echoing this philosophical model in novel form.

24 Davidson now explicitly rejects a coherence view of truth, but one need not hold to an explicitly coherentist position to accept the rejection of correspondence and the assumption of holism.

25 This interpretation of Schlegel's view is the core of Benjamin's argument in his dissertation on *The Concept of Art-Critique in German Romanticism* (see Bowie 1990 Chapter 7, and Chapter 8, this volume).

26 See Hegel's *Aesthetics* and Kierkegaard's *The Concept of Irony*.

27 The alternative to this, as I have already suggested, is Hegel's system, which tries to articulate a culminating final position in the form of the 'absolute idea' which resolves the contradiction between the finite and the infinite.

28 It should be mentioned here that Schlegel does later fall into the arms of the Catholic Church, thereby looking for the kind of ground decisively renounced in his earlier work. This issue is far too complex for consideration here.

29 This creates the regress in which the second being can also be the means for another being's ends, and so on, leaving the need for a being who is not thus subjected if ends are to be legitimate rather than arbitrary. Kant essentially thinks we should all be this being.

30 This does not mean that aesthetic experience cannot have cognitive and moral effects, but that those effects, because they are not based on intrinsic value, are not what defines the experience as aesthetic. The real question, though, is whether one can draw the lines between these areas in a definitive theory (see the last section of Chapter 7, this volume).

31 Such a view is in line with the growing sense in contemporary philosophy that truth is a normative issue and thus inseparable from ethical and aesthetic considerations (see e.g. Brandom 1994, Putnam 1995). I shall return to this issue in subsequent chapters.

4 INTERPRETATIVE REASONS

1 It would be unfair to Herder to suggest that this consequence was one which he would have found desirable: after all, his whole enterprise should be understood as giving new value to languages other than his own, once the notion of the divine origin could no longer be invoked to valorise a language.

2 As I suggested in Chapter 1, this distinction is already prepared by some of the key conceptual moves made by Jacobi: the possible historical link will be shown later, via the work of Schleiermacher.

3 Nietzsche's philosophy tends to work by exploring the tension between these two poles, refusing finally to attach itself to either. Both Benjamin's and Adorno's work, as I shall suggest, also centres around this tension.

4 I have already given a substantial account of Schleiermacher in Bowie 1990: the present account is necessarily more selective, and will concentrate on issues defined by the questions we have already begun to investigate, as well as on Schleiermacher's precursors and certain questions in contemporary semantics. It should, as such, complement rather than repeat what is said in my earlier account, which contains more of the basic detail of the structure of Schleiermacher's philosophy.

5 On this see e.g. Birus 1982, who gives a useful bibliography, Frank's introduction to Schleiermacher (1977), Bruns 1992, and the classic essay 'The Origin of Hermeneutics' in Dilthey 1990 pp. 317–38. The literature on the history of hermeneutics is now enormous, though relatively little of it deals substantively with the links to the analytical tradition I want to show here.

6 See Foucault 1970, who gives a fascinating account of the significance of this doctrine.

7 The manner of this insistence is strangely reminiscent of Davidson's contention that the only meaning a word has is its literal meaning, whereas what metaphors (in Aquinas' case allegories) do is to make us notice things, there being no 'metaphorical meaning'. Davidson's rigid distinction seems to me a residue of his attachment to a certain semantic conception which the best of his work, parts of which will be considered in the following chapters, has now come to question.

8 The question will be, though, whether interpretation, even of individual words, is not in fact holistic, dependent upon the context of the utterance, including the context of the world of the utterance. See e.g. Putnam 1995 p. 63, who refuses to accept that there are any facts separable from interpretations.

9 I mention this aspect here because it will concern us later, when we come to Benjamin's reflections on allegory, where the realisation of the uncontrollability of allegory evident in the fact that anything can be made to stand for anything else is seen as leading in baroque *Trauerspiel* to the disintegration of the meaningful world of resemblances. Benjamin sees this realisation as having a major effect on the significance of music and the rise of autonomous art in the modern period, as well as being a 'just verdict on the profane world'. Many of the major questions in Benjamin's view of language relate to the significance of allegory.

10 A theological version of this would see God's word in the Scripture as a living word which transcends the person who records it: hence Luther's conception described above.

11 Kant probably saw the issue from an Enlightenment perspective – he was trying to show what Plato should have said if his argument were to be consistent – but the effects of his claim actually exemplify what the Romantic position suggests, in that it assumes a kind of non-identity between author and text which is the space of exploration of most modern interpretative theory, from hermeneutics to psychoanalysis, to analytical philosophy.

12 'Cartesian' only in the sense that the phenomena of my present consciousness are incorrigible at the moment of their occurrence, though I can come to recognise a delusion after the event. On the problems of Cartesian 'self-presence' and the Romantic rejection of it see Bowie 1990 Chapter 3 in particular, and Frank 1990, 1991.

13 Evidently this is the space in which psychoanalysis operates – and key concepts of psychoanalysis already develop in Romanticism (see Bowie 1990 Chapter 3) – but the issues are not confined to psychoanalysis, as the Romantic notion of 'unconscious creation' makes clear.

14 On this see Bowie 1990 Chapter 6. The consequences of this argument still lie behind much of contemporary hermeneutics and have, for example, recently been used by thinkers like Putnam to argue against the claims of functionalist reductions of language to processes reproducible by computers. See also Chapter 5, this volume, in relation to Schleiermacher and Davidson.

15 This clearly relates to the question of the 'schema' looked at in Chapter 2: I shall first of all develop some of the other implications of this issue before looking again at the schema in Schleiermacher in Chapter 5.

16 The division can be crudely mapped on to the differences between the first and the third critiques, though Kant is aware of the problem which leads to modern hermeneutics even in the first critique. The third critique rarely, if ever, plays a significant role in the semantic tradition.

17 One is tempted to see Hegel's 'owl of Minerva' here: when a tradition becomes aware of itself as a tradition it has already ceased to be a completely living option and needs to move in new directions. That is the point most of the present account will try to suggest. It should be added that I think it is mistaken to think of a monolith called analytical philosophy, although certain of the

logical and semantic concerns at issue here do recur in a wide variety of approaches.

18 Coffa stresses the largely subterranean influence of Bolzano, which was also the case for a long time in this century for Frege. It is worth remembering that something similar might now be said to apply both to Saussure and to the Romantics, including Schleiermacher, given the failure, even of their more favourable readers at the time and since, to articulate some of the major implications of what they were saying. The fact is that a Saussure-derived structuralist literary theory and certain varieties of analytical philosophy actually share some quite similar notions about the working of language (see Frank 1984 on what he calls the 'code model'). I shall return to these issues in subsequent chapters.

19 See Dummett 1981 pp. 41–5 for an account of Frege on the 'realm of sense'.

20 For an interesting, if questionable, account of the problems of Husserl's phenomenology with meaning, see Tugendhat 1976. More and more analytically oriented philosophers, such as Dummett, are turning again to Husserl and the phenomenological tradition, which suggests the problems indicated here are far from obviated.

5 THE ETHICS OF INTERPRETATION: SCHLEIERMACHER

1 Manfred Frank (1977, and in many subsequent works) was the first to reveal to what extent this is the case, and my account owes much to his, although my focus is somewhat different.

2 The linking role between Jacobi and the existential tradition is also evident in this case. The influence of Jacobi on Schleiermacher leads to the latter's vital role for Kierkegaard, who himself, of course, becomes important for Heidegger.

3 Jacobi, as we saw in Chapter 1, put this as follows:

> For even if according to [Kantian philosophy] it can be *admitted* that a transcendental something *may* correspond as *cause* to these merely subjective beings (*Wesen* [by which he means 'appearances']), which are only determinations *of our own being*, it yet remains hidden in the deepest obscurity *where* this cause and what the nature of the relation it has to its effect is. (Jacobi 1787 p. 224)

4 The immediate object of Schleiermacher's hermeneutics is the Bible, particularly the New Testament; as so often in Schleiermacher, however, the ideas of the text need have no direct application to theology.

5 This is one of the sources of Schleiermacher's theology, which was primarily based on the 'feeling of absolute dependence' of ourselves as finite beings who are not the ground of who we are.

6 It is not possible here to discuss the substantial differences between Schlegel and Schleiermacher: my concern is with the potential of their best theories. Suffice to say I do not think they are quite as far apart as Behler (1993) and Hörisch (1988) suggest, simply because Schleiermacher was well aware of the limits of understanding.

7 The boundaries of the 'linguistic' and the non-linguistic here should not necessarily be drawn just in terms of words and texts: rhythm and music play a major role in Schleiermacher's conception of language, as the discussion of 'feeling' below will show. The semantic tradition significantly fails to make such connections between language and music until the later Wittgenstein (see Chapter 9).

8 He also shares the assumption that 'The proposition (*Satz*) as a unit is also the smallest thing that can be understood or misunderstood' (Schleiermacher 1977

p. 98), a thought which he connects with the idea of a 'speech act' (ibid. p. 89). The significance of the orientation to the proposition will be explored in Chapter 6 in relation to Heidegger.

9   In the space available here I shall not attempt to delineate stages in the development of Schleiermacher's hermeneutics, which would lead one into ongoing disagreements about the relative importance of the varying aspects of his hermeneutics at various times in his life (see e.g. Frank's Introduction to Schleiermacher 1977). There is enough consistency in Schleiermacher's texts to construct ideal types of his major insights, a process of which he would also have approved, given his acknowledgement of the need for pragmatic decisions in actual interpretation.

10 The implications of this thorny question are most evident in experiments with chimpanzees, who seem capable of correct responses to and even the employment of words in ways that may not be wholly conditioned: the underlying question is how 'externalist' one thinks one can be about interpretation. The *locus classicus* of this issue is Quine's discussion of the 'field linguist's' attempt to understand an alien language in *Word and Object*. Understanding, I would argue, against Quine, Dummett and many others, must involve a moment to which only a subject can have access, namely the certainty (which may, of course, turn out to be mistaken) at a particular moment that I know what something means in a real-world situation. Vital to this is the question of how individual linguistic innovations are ever understood at all by others or, for that matter, by the innovator. On this see Taylor 1995 pp. 84–5.

11 My use of Davidson will be very selective: I am interested in those aspects of his thought which converge with hermeneutics. There is no space here to deal with the other dimensions of such a complex and important thinker.

12 See Chapter 2, the discussion of schematism below, and the discussion of Heidegger in Chapters 6 and 7.

13 Dummett's position evidently involves far more complexities (and powerful arguments) than this, but his essential assumption against Davidson (and by extension against Schleiermacher) is that there is such a thing as a language which is a social praxis common to a group of people, and that this thing is more than just a heuristic regulative idea we need to guide any attempt at systematic insight into the utterances of language-users, because it is amenable to being explained by a complete theory. Derrida's views of language are also not so far from the Schleiermacher/Davidson view (see Samuel Wheeler's essay in Lepore 1986).

14 There are endless questions here which I cannot deal with, such as whether the 'primitive' status attached to truth by Davidson entails a redundancy theory, in which knowing the truth conditions of an utterance is just understanding it, 'true' meaning no more than this. My feeling is that there *is* more to it than this, and that Heidegger and others have suggested why. I shall return to the underlying issue in subsequent chapters.

15 The rejection is prefigured by key arguments in Schlegel and Novalis, and fully developed by the later Schelling (see Bowie 1993, 1996b, Schelling 1994).

16 This is also the source of the links of critiques of Hegel to deconstructive rejections of the structuralist project: in both cases the idea is that, contra Hegel, the system cannot be self-grounding (see Bowie 1993, Frank 1984).

17 This is obviously unfair to Hegel. It is only at the level of the system as a whole that this link is valid: at the level of the system Hegel is, as Dieter Henrich suggests, a kind of dynamised Platonist; at other levels Hegel can be and increasingly is seen as fitting a pragmatic model (see e.g. Brandom 1994).

18 Ast admittedly tries to dissolve the regress in the manner of German Idealism, by seeing whole and part as grounding each other, but his teacher Schelling will later realise that this will not be successful (see Bowie 1993).

19 It is a sad comment on the state of philosophical communication between the traditions when in Brandom's excellent 700-page book 'hermeneutics' does not even appear in the index – this in a work that expressly links itself to Hegel by someone who has written on Heidegger. The book is entitled *Making It Explicit*; 'explicate' is the best translation of the word '*auslegen*', which the hermeneutic tradition often uses for 'interpret'.

20 It is arguable that the semantic tradition is only just beginning to discover the *Critique of Judgement*: one still encounters illuminating engagements with Kant like that of John McDowell (1994) which ought to lead in the direction of the *Critique of Judgement* but seem to assume that the text itself does not exist (see Bowie 1996b).

21 The difference within the semantic tradition stylised and reduced here to that between Dummett and Davidson will be further apparent later in the chapter when Davidson's notion of a 'passing theory' will be seen as a kind of reflective judgement. It can be argued that Quine's rejection of the analytic/synthetic distinction is another version of the realisation that reflective judgement is universal in semantics, which is essentially Schleiermacher's position.

22 The *Ethics* is a remarkable text because it gives a generative anthropological account of the ethical, which sees it in thoroughly historicised terms, leading from animal nature to the forms of human organisation, that are not always so far from Marx. There is no room here to explore this, but it is important to note the context of the remarks on hermeneutics and language from the *Ethics* cited here if one is to appreciate the scope of Schleiermacher's project, which is often regarded as predominantly theological. Theology plays a wholly subordinate role in the *Ethics* and is, as already suggested, in many ways also peripheral to his hermeneutics.

23 Bolzano uses the term '*Vorstellung*' when talking of 'objective representations', but it seems clear that Schleiermacher here means something very close to what Bolzano means.

24 This will be one of Heidegger's key insights in parts of his conception of truth, as we shall see in Chapter 6. Schleiermacher's position is in this respect close to Bakhtin's and Voloshinov's Marx-inspired view of language as praxis.

25 I do *not* mean by this that the differing possibilities of approaching such utterances can be theoretically circumscribed. Aesthetic aspects of communication cannot, I believe, be finally separated out by a theory in the manner that, for example, Habermas would wish, but this is no reason just to dismiss as insignificant the kind of discriminations people make all the time anyway. Too much radical theory in this area assumes that unless there is absolute certainty there is no possibility of validity. Once one gives up on Platonism, as most major contemporary positions have, this is not the central issue.

26 It is indisputable that irreconcilable beliefs held by a religious fundamentalist and a liberal pragmatist are a deeply serious political problem, but the question for Lyotard is how much work his philosophical version of the issue can really do here, given its flawed premises.

27 There is evidently a role for questions about the ways in which certain forms of articulation block any possible understanding or point to what we may be as yet unable to say: the question of avant-garde art is central here, as we shall see in particular in relation to Adorno. However, to be avant-garde always requires presupposing the meanings one wishes to destroy or transcend: without the enemy there is no sense in the notion of avant-garde. *Absolute* otherness is unrecognisable as such.

28 The crudest theories of language in artificial intelligence work with something like this model, which links to the behaviourist position examined above.

29 Frank interestingly links this to Sartre's method of interpretation in the Flaubert book (see Frank 1989a).
30 Assuming I am not lying, which itself presupposes knowledge of what I hold true. Holding true is the condition of any kind of understanding at all, so truth and lies are not polar opposites, because the latter must always presuppose the former, but not vice versa.
31 Rorty makes this point against Paul de Man's over-inflated claims about literature in Rorty 1991a p. 132.
32 Davidson himself is not entirely convinced that what is at issue could be called a 'theory': this relates again to the general problem of literal meaning in Davidson which will recur when we look at Heidegger.
33 I suggest how Schleiermacher's *Aesthetics* opposes this conception in Bowie 1990, Chapters 6 and 7. I shall look at a few aspects of the *Aesthetics* later in this section. Some of the questions raised here will be further considered in Chapter 9 and in the Conclusion.
34 In this sense Rorty's 'nominalism', the rejection of any approach to language and understanding which entails the non-propositional or the sub-propositional, is thoroughly Hegelian. My objections to this position should become apparent both here and in subsequent chapters, and are already suggested by what Schleiermacher means by 'feeling'.
35 Sometimes the move is admittedly fairly easy, as in the predominance of the use of the masculine pronoun for non-gender-specific cases. It is very rarely as obvious as this, and any general claim in this respect is best avoided, not least because the position from which the claim is made must itself claim more than its own premises ought to allow.
36 The Nazi judgements rely, of course, on such notions as 'Jewishness' in music.
37 Which does not, therefore, mean 'empathy', as the standard misinterpretation of Schleiermacher suggests (see Bowie 1990 Chapter 6, Frank 1977, 1989a).
38 The fact that Schleiermacher (and Schelling) were major influences on such materialist thinkers as Feuerbach and Marx (and, in a different perspective, on Kierkegaard) is too rarely appreciated, and was often concealed by the later thinkers anyway. Much the same applies to the effects of German Idealism on neo-Kantianism, and on such figures as Helmholtz.
39 The vital book which fills in the philosophical history that cannot be dealt with here is Schnädelbach (1984), which has too often been ignored in debates in this area.

6 BEING TRUE: DILTHEY, HUSSERL AND HEIDEGGER (1)

1 I have dealt with other aspects of Heidegger's not fully acknowledged debts to the past in Bowie 1993, 1994a, 1996a.
2 To some extent Benjamin can be regarded as part of the Frankfurt School, but this raises problems that do not actually do much theoretical work. In certain obvious senses Benjamin does not belong to any school.
3 In contrast, for example, to Furtwängler, who is often seen as an analogous case. Despite grave failings and at times almost unbelievable political naïveté, Furtwängler did at least make some efforts to counter the worst of what he saw going on and would not have dreamed of joining the NSDAP.
4 The exception to this rule tends to be *Being and Time*, where Heidegger's sustained development of a new vocabulary makes interpretative life more difficult: other texts could at times almost have been written by an early analytical philosopher and are far clearer than, say, much of Wittgenstein's *Tractatus*. I shall not attempt to give a historical account of when Heidegger's

later work begins, and shall rely on the fairly obvious shift of emphasis which starts at some point in the 1930s from the primacy of Dasein as the locus for the understanding of being to Heidegger's insistence on the primacy of being before subjectivity.

5 The obvious historical link is via the work of Dilthey, which Heidegger regarded as vital to his own philosophical development.

6 Translating Heidegger's '*Sein*', or in some texts '*Seyn*', is always a problem: what appears to be a noun is actually incomprehensible if it is analysed as a noun. 'Being' is often capitalised in English, but I see no real advantages in this. The main point is to be able to make a distinction between '*Sein*' and '*Seiendes*', which I translate here as 'being', and 'entities', or on certain occasions, following a frequent habit of Heidegger translators, 'beings' (which does function as a noun, albeit one whose plural status is sometimes problematic): where there is the possibility of confusion I shall attempt to explain why in context.

7 There are obvious divergences between the two (see e.g. Mulhall 1990) but it is the convergences which are more important here. It can also remain open as to whether this view entails a realist ontology: Davidson changes his position on this every few years, and I think the point that matters here does not require one to make a commitment to realism or anti-realism (the debate between which seems to me to get more and more confused anyway). One should also note that neither Heidegger nor Davidson pays any serious attention to the fact that the interpretation of non-rule-bound utterances, or the production of new utterances that cannot be understood by rules, would only seem possible in terms of the interpretative and productive acts of a subject, as Schleiermacher suggested. I shall return to this issue later.

8 In Chapter 7 I will try to show that the question of self-consciousness is necessarily linked to this conception, albeit not in any of the manners in which Heidegger or Davidson consider. The question will be how to explain that individuals can disclose a new aspect of the world which can become truth-determinate, even though it may only begin, say, as a metaphor which is the result of an individual imaginative articulation.

9 The story is obviously far more complex than this. Helmholtz was expressly interested in Fichte and in the aesthetics of music, for example, but the effects of Helmholtz lay far more in his scientific success and his clear rejection of the systematic side of Idealist *Naturphilosophie*.

10 If one reads Nietzsche as a hermeneuticist, then he should in many ways be considered alongside Dilthey, although the direction of his work was very different.

11 I shall not translate the term, which is by now largely familiar, its literal meaning being 'sciences of the mind/spirit'. An adequate account of how to translate the term would have to answer many of the questions concerning science, art and truth at issue in this chapter. The initial point is that the word refers to the pursuit of truths which are not within the domain of natural science because they can only exist via the activity of *Geist*, thus of that which produces articulations that have to be 'understood', rather than 'explained' in a law-like manner.

12 I do not mean to suggest a rigid distinction between the two, but if one accepts the sense that modernist art has to do with crises of meaning and human identity which are articulated in disruptive formal experiments, then it seems fair to suggest that the differences between Proust and Balzac have some more general significance, even if one can find disruptive elements in Balzac of the kind associated with modernism.

13 Metaphysical assumptions concerning the nature of scientific truth clearly do, though, form part of the unconscious background which helps to determine the

nature of inquiry. Such metaphysical questions will again become a more overt part of the natural sciences in the wake of relativity and quantum theory. In the main, though, the contribution of philosophy to natural science will be most evident from the second half of the nineteenth century onwards in the new developments in mathematics and logic undertaken by and in the wake of Frege and Russell, not in contributions to epistemology. What one thinks of this issue does, admittedly, very much depend where and how one draws the boundaries of the natural sciences.

14 Exemplified, for example, in the opening of Musil's *The Man without Qualities*.

15 The beginnings of such an approach are what leads Schelling to develop what he terms 'positive philosophy' against Hegel's conception of a philosophical system (see Bowie 1993 Chapter 6).

16 This is not, though, to say that Hegel's manner of overcoming their apparent separation is in fact wholly successful.

17 Kierkegaard took over this criticism from Schleiermacher – and from Schelling – in his critique of Hegel, and it plays a significant role in Heidegger.

18 Whether 'the mind' is an entity like any other object of science is more than dubious, and many of the false (and often perverse and cruel) approaches to psychology that develop at this time are in one sense a result of bad metaphysics.

19 This is also not so far in certain ways from a view like that of Dummett, when he claims that 'words have meanings in themselves, independently of speakers' (Lepore 1986 p. 473).

20 I should add that I do not think the question of solipsism with regard to semantics is a non-issue: aspects of Schleiermacher's account of 'feeling' can suggest why there is an aspect of language which may indeed only be available to each speaker as they use an expression.

21 Clearly such an account is impossible in these terms because the immediacy of the facts of consciousness, and mediated cognition according to the principle of sufficient reason are concepts of a different order from each other. Jacobi, the Romantics and Hegel were already quite clear about this.

22 The structuralist aspect of this is apparent if one makes language one of these systems.

23 I may, of course, be taking some perception-altering substance, but we do not take this as the norm for how we find our way round the world or how we arrive at what we hold to be true: my ability to be aware of the contrast between my everyday and altered states is the key here. The choice is between a crazy scepticism (there are, one should add, other very important kinds of scepticism) and the fact that we always already work in a world on the intuitive basis of holding certain kinds of things as unquestionably true. One cannot even begin generally to question the veracity of what we believe without having certain beliefs which are not open to question, otherwise we would also have no way of coming to doubt anything either. As we have seen all along, the key question is how and whether we can attribute certainty to that which has to be presupposed: in many ways this is still Heidegger's basic question.

24 There is more to the issue than this, but for the moment it is best not to get involved with the question of whether this is all there is to the structure of self-consciousness.

25 See Chapter 1. Husserl's continued attempts to give an adequate account of a transcendental subject are precisely what Heidegger comes to wish to avoid in more and more radical ways. The reasons for this are already prefigured in Jacobi's critiques of Kant and Fichte.

26 Derrida applies this basic critique to both Husserl and Hegel (see Derrida 1967a, 1967b).

27 It is important to remember that these aspects of logic formed an essential part of the development of analytical philosophy via Frege and Russell. The fact that Heidegger was fully aware of the importance of new developments in logic has until fairly recently been all but ignored by analytical philosophers. The obvious exception in this respect is Ernst Tugendhat.

28 Note that Heidegger, as elsewhere at this time, has no qualms about equating Dasein with the I, or the subject. Only later will he consistently try to avoid the notion of subject because he thinks it leads to the problems of metaphysics which in their modern form begin with Descartes' *cogito*.

29 See, for example, Derrida's evasive footnote in *Positions* (Derrida 1972a pp. 79–80). The case of Lacan is much more complex, as Peter Dews has shown (see Dews 1987). Derrida's treatment of Lacan raises the same problem I have already suggested, because it becomes unclear how it is we understand truth at all, so concerned is Derrida to equate truth with a metaphysically grounded notion of 'presence'.

30 A similar realisation is possible via Frege's distinction between the logical status of 'arguments' and 'functions' (though that is not necessarily how Frege himself sees it) (see Bowie 1994a for an account of this issue in relation to Schelling's critique of Hegel, with which Heidegger must have been familiar). See also Chapter 9 below, where these distinctions are used to clarify one of Adorno's crucial confusions.

31 Tugendhat is probably right when he shows (Tugendhat 1992) that the attempt to give a unitary sense to the word 'being' founders on the fact that the 'is' of existence, predication, identity and the 'veritative "is"' do not form any unified wider sense of 'being'. Whether this means that it is wrong to see 'being' as involved every time we understand something is another question, which depends on whether we think all understanding is propositional. See my review of Tugendhat (Bowie 1994b) and some of the discussion that follows.

32 On this see in particular Frank 1990, who shows in great detail how the Romantics had already temporalised Kant's atemporal I that is supposed to 'be able to accompany all my representations'.

33 It is worth remembering in this context, in order to counter the frequent assumption in literary theory that it took until Nietzsche and Heidegger for truth to become temporalised, that Schelling was saying things like the following in the 1820s:

> All is just a product of time and we do not know what is absolutely true, but just what the time allows within which we are enclosed. We are beginning to grasp that eternal truths are really only propositions which are abstracted from the present state of things. (Schelling 1990 p. 16)

34 This does not mean that, having seen the problems with this version of subjectivity, which do not apply to the best Romantic theories, Heidegger works out a more convincing account of self-consciousness (see Frank in Wood 1992). I will suggest in Chapter 7 that this failure puts significant parts of his larger story into question.

7 THE TRUTH OF ART: HEIDEGGER (2)

1 The usual translation, *The Origins of German Tragic Drama*, does not get the sense that what is being referred to is a very specific form of drama – mainly German baroque drama – which Benjamin emphatically differentiates from tragedy. I shall refer to the book in question as the '*Trauerspielbuch*'. Gillian Rose has suggested the translation 'Mourning Play' for '*Trauerspiel*', which seems apt, but would be clumsy when referring to the book in question.

2 He cites *Monologue* in *On the Way to Language*, for example, and Hölderlin, who can be thought of as a Romantic thinker, is obviously vital, but there is no sustained engagement with the ideas which come closest to his own.

3 The fact is that, although individual natural scientists may be interested in philosophical reflections concerning how they validate their theories, most scientists tend to work with the notion that they are building models to deal with the facts they encounter, and the structure within which they work already dictates most of what they do. Otherwise the global nature of scientific research becomes inexplicable. Putnam has observed that 'rationality in the "nomothetic" sciences is just as vague and just as impossible to formalize as "Verstehen"' (Putnam 1983 p. 299), which, if true, means that the philosophical attempt to do so becomes fairly otiose, given science's success in its own terms. The real philosophical question is to ask exactly what science is, as Heidegger in fact does.

4 As I have shown in Chapter 6 of Bowie 1993, Schelling makes similar moves in the 1820s in a brilliantly argued rejection of the premises of transcendental idealism, which he will subsequently apply in a different form in his critique of Hegel (see Schelling 1994). The main point of the move is to deconstruct the apparent primacy of the subject in the generation of truth, by revealing the subject's dependence upon a being with which it can never be in direct contact. Schelling's later work, like that of the Romantics, is immune to most of the later Heidegger's claims that all previous philosophy since Descartes has depended upon the dominance of subjectivity (see also Bowie 1996a).

5 If one takes the Kantian line on values – exemplified in his sense of the intrinsic value of that which has 'dignity' and, importantly, in the work of art – which sees values as self-grounding, I suspect that one ought to say that exchange values are not necessarily values at all. The Marxian distinction would thereby become a distinction between the ethical and the non-ethical, in the sense that use-values are constituted by our being in the world and in the intersubjective *acknowledgement* of how values are thereby generated.

6 Exactly where Heidegger locates the beginning of 'Western metaphysics' varies between texts: he seems to suggest in the very late work that metaphysics goes all the way down, given its links to natural science from the very beginning.

7 The first to make such a link explicit was probably Schelling, who at much the same time as he was developing a philosophy of nature with expressly ecological concerns writes texts which see art as central to philosophy (see Bowie 1990, 1993).

8 Translating Heidegger now becomes an art in itself: I shall generally be as literal as possible, and where absolutely necessary give the German, usually with a commentary. Given that much of the sense of the texts depends upon (often questionable) etymologies, this is, of course, a compromise. I do think, though, that there is a tendency among writers on Heidegger to fetishise his use of language, by assuming that he really does enact something fundamentally new in his way of using language. This in itself raises important questions about the relationship of philosophy to literature.

9 Dasein is itself always regarded as an entity, albeit one with a particular relation to its being.

10 In this respect Heidegger makes, as we shall see him doing in other respects, moves similar to the later Schelling. Schelling is also often accused of merely invoking what he comes to term 'being before anything can be thought'; the fact is, though, that Schelling only arrives at this notion via the breakdown of the attempt to complete a system based on 'reflection', thus upon the failure of the mutual determination of the aspects of the system to ground the system in the way Hegel would wish (see Frank 1975, Bowie 1993).

11 The assumption is that both idealism and materialism are in these terms equivalent as forms of grounding.

12 Though not as obviously as it seems to do to Heidegger and later to Gadamer: the point of Kant's supposedly subjectivised aesthetic judgements is that they are based on the attempt to reach universal consensus. To this extent they are not necessarily more random or subjective than any other kind of judgement, if one assumes that truth is, as, for example, do both Schleiermacher and Putnam, idealised consensus.

13 In his own terms he does not necessarily need to: if the changes in the history of metaphysics are, as he will later put it, 'sendings of being', they are inherently beyond any explanation in historical or other terms anyway.

14 The suggestion is that they were probably van Gogh's own boots: see Derrida's *La vérité en peinture* (Derrida 1978). There is no space here to go into whether Derrida's reflections on art and truth in this book get us much further than his other rather meagre reflections on the topic of truth.

15 Much of the debate between materialists and anti-realists in the philosophy of mind revolves around the question of this primacy: if all our thinking is really brain functions, from what perspective can this actually be stated in a manner which is not viciously circular?

16 This is not to say that the idea expressed via the example of the van Gogh painting is *per se* invalid on the grounds, as we are frequently reminded by post-structuralists, that essentialist claims about what something means are inherently problematic because of the contextuality of meaning. The real question, as Gadamer shows, is why certain works keep demanding our attention in new ways, which he, I think justifiably, sees as having to do with their being true. The question is how we should theorise this truth.

17 The unfortunate English seems necessary in order not to give false connotations to what Heidegger is saying.

18 Schelling rejects Jacobi's work at various points, but there is no doubt that Jacobi's key thoughts which have been highlighted so far were precisely Schelling's main preoccupations: most of his work is an ongoing battle with Spinozism, for reasons not unlike those of Jacobi (see Bowie 1996a).

19 Heidegger, as one can see, is by no means the first to philosophise by explicit use of etymology.

20 Or does one? A man who is as dishonest about his own life as Heidegger was should not lead us to expect from him in one area what he did not offer in another.

21 Manfred Frank has suggested that Heidegger's conception is also prefigured in Schelling's own view of art in the *System of Transcendental Idealism* (see Frank 1989b, Bowie 1990, 1993).

22 The word is '*Wesen*', which used also to be used as a verb, and which therefore connects to the ambiguity about the grammatical status of '*Sein*'. The word is untranslatable, but has something to do with the idea that what used to be seen as a-temporal is in fact 'essentially' temporal: this idea is already present in Hegel's use of the word.

23 Given the frequent accusation that Schelling is an irrationalist, it is important to stress that he would not have dreamed of such a conception of the renunciation of reason at any stage of his philosophy.

24 There are worse passages in Heidegger than those in the work of art essay, notably the overtly Nazi passages of *Introduction to Metaphysics*, but these have been widely discussed and are not germane here.

25 One has to remember here that the most momentous scientific version of this process in this century is the development of nuclear physics.

26 The influence of Hölderlin, which is decisive for much of the later work, is apparent in the phrase '*ins Offene*'.

27 Heidegger never really makes up his mind on this important issue: one reason for this is his dismissal of all forms of philosophy concerned with the question of consciousness as part of 'Western metaphysics'.

28 If anyone is in any doubt about this interpretation, they should consult Habermas (1985 p. 186), where Habermas cites Heidegger using, and not just once, exactly the vocabulary in question here in support of Hitler.

29 I shall return to the specific issue of the relationship between art and technology in Chapters 8 and 9, hence my cursory treatment of it here.

30 It is vital to remember, as some of his critics do not, that the 'ideal speech situation' may never actually take place. The point is that we can still understand the idea of such a situation by the very fact of trying to achieve consensus in discourse. The Kantian aspect of the idea is clear. Kant suggests in the *Foundation of the Metaphysics of Morals* that it may be that there never is an actual moral act because there are always conflicting motives for real individuals in any situation, but he is clear that this does not mean we cannot understand what we think a moral act ought to be. At the hermeneutic level, as I suggested in Chapter 3, this seems to me a defensible position.

31 Derrida, one should add, is now becoming more and more like Habermas all the time: his primary concern now seems to be the ethics of law and communication, and Marx is again an issue.

32 For a rather more sympathetic view see Taylor 1995.

33 He associates this idea of identity with the Romantics, but this is not the case for that side of the Romantics which I have tried to highlight. The danger of adopting Schnädelbach's loose use of the term 'Romantic' is that it simply reinforces the existing picture, which is in some ways justified but threatens to obscure the side of Romanticism which goes well beyond that picture.

34 It is worth noting here, as Gadamer has pointed out, that Paul Celan, whose poetry itself is deeply concerned with the question of silence, visited Heidegger after the war, despite what had happened to his family in the Holocaust.

35 We may seem to have forgotten the importance of the question of being which concerned us in earlier chapters. For Jacobi, and more explicitly for the later Schelling, the question subverted any attempt at epistemological grounding of the kind Hegel wished to establish. It was not important for establishing a positive philosophical answer to the problems of metaphysics. The primacy of being is the result of the failure of philosophy to ground itself, and leads either to the attempted restitution of theology in the manner of Jacobi, the later Schelling, Kierkegaard, Rosenzweig, and others, or to a fallibilist hermeneutic pragmatism which attends to those forms of articulation that are not exhausted by what can be said about them in propositional terms. This will become clearer in what follows.

36 This not to say that there is nothing important in later Heidegger – there is much – but the faults really need to be looked at first, before trying to extract what is of value.

37 This is in some degree confirmed by the fact that Karl-Otto Apel, whose influence on Habermas has been in many ways decisive, ends up with a position with more than a few similarities to that of Reinhold, in that both see no alternative to what is effectively an absolute proposition. (I owe this observation to Manfred Frank.)

38 The ground here is not a ground in a positively articulable sense, in that it is where one arrives via the failure of reflection: this is the point of the Romantic position I have tried to trace via Jacobi, which is best worked out by Schelling (see Bowie 1993 Chapter 6). I shall not attempt here to deal with Tugendhat's objection to Heidegger, namely that truth as disclosure/comprehensibility gives one no criteria for validating propositional claims in terms of assent or denial.

It would seem to me that the choice of the criteria themselves would require a prior judgement based on how one had understood the articulation in question. The question is whether semantic truth is prior or whether it is, as Heidegger would claim, always secondary to a happening upon which it depends. The *locus classicus* of the discussion is, however, Heidegger (1969 pp. 76–8), where Heidegger actually says that *aletheia* is not the same as 'the natural concept of truth', thereby apparently reserving truth for propositional truth, while still regarding it as secondary to the happening of *aletheia*. I am aware that this leaves open more problems than it resolves, but see the Conclusion to this volume, where I suggest how one might try to avoid the rigid distinction Heidegger seems to accept here.

39 Rorty has, though, no time for the question of subjectivity in these terms, because of his rejection of non-propositional forms of understanding (and because of his 'eliminativist' materialism, which regards notions of the 'mental' as merely adding unnecessary entities to ontology). See the Introduction above for the suggestion that Rorty's way of talking about art and science may itself introduce another problematic metaphysical distinction.

40 This does not, of course, mean that we cannot use meta-language: we do so all the time. The point is that we cannot have a meta-language to characterise the relationship between language and language about language without either landing in another regress or having to assume a grounding philosophical language.

8 UNDERSTANDING WALTER BENJAMIN

1 In what follows, reference to 'the dissertation' will always be to this work.
2 In a recent collection of essays on *Walter Benjamin's Philosophy* (Benjamin and Osborne 1994) it warrants only one mention, for example, and even that gives no indication as to the content of the dissertation. Eagleton (1990) does not mention the work at all.
3 Benjamin committed suicide on the French–Spanish border in order to escape being caught by the Nazis: had he waited he would almost certainly have survived.
4 His admiration for Carl Schmitt and Ludwig Klages does suggest a certain kind of ideological ambiguity characteristic of the 1920s, when, as Thomas Mann rather clumsily suggests in *The Magic Mountain*, radical critiques of culture from left and right sometimes coincided.
5 Just how appropriate it is to term Benjamin a Marxist remains controversial. What I mean here – wishing to avoid what I think is now an arid dispute – is that Benjamin comes to address many of the problems which are, particularly in the light of Lukács' *History and Class-Consciousness*, central to twentieth-century Marxism.
6 Clearly the context of the Romantics is in one sense anything but indirect, in that Benjamin wrote about them: the question is what contexts one finds for understanding Romanticism, which is where a straightforwardly hermeneutico-historical approach would be of little help, as I have been trying to suggest. It is also the case that putting Benjamin in this context *is* wrenching him from the contexts in which he is often considered.
7 I give references in this form for greater brevity and clarity. The edition is *Walter Benjamin: Gesammelte Schriften* (Benjamin 1980).
8 I can think of no way of effectively translating the word, apart from explaining its meaning in the contexts in which I discuss it.
9 Benjamin here sees the Bible in terms of 'fulfilled time', presumably because

the events narrated in the Bible have a ground which gives them their meaning beyond their place in a sequence. Benjamin's last works, the *Arcades-Project* and 'On the Concept of History', will return to the issue of sequential time and the meaning of history. The difference between unfulfilled and fulfilled time will also be echoed in the difference between 'information' and 'story' in 'The Storyteller'.

10 As we have seen, this is a vital aspect of both Hegel's and Heidegger's approach to the truth of art, as well as being the central aspect of Nietzsche's *The Birth of Tragedy*.

11 There are analogies of this view of art, language and modernity to Lukács' account of the rise of the novel, an equally 'unclosed' form, in *The Theory of the Novel* of 1914. Benjamin and Adorno will both be great admirers of this text.

12 The German title is '*Über Sprache überhaupt und über die Sprache des Menschen*': the meaning of '*überhaupt*', which can be literally but inelegantly translated as 'in general', will become clear in the course of the analysis of the essay.

13 This link also connects to the idea that tragedy is often about the historical move from one order of law to another, as in the *Oresteia*.

14 How far this echo is based on actual knowledge of Schelling's work is not clear. Benjamin's relationship to Schelling is very odd, as the dissertation makes clear by hardly mentioning him. See Menninghaus (1987) for an interesting but questionable view of this issue, which fails to see the tension in Schelling between an idealist and a Romantic conception.

15 It is therefore quite clear where Schopenhauer got his conception of music from, as it is known that he read some of the work of the Schelling in question.

16 In which case the obvious objection, of which Schelling was thoroughly aware, is that we could have no perspective from which to establish whether such mirroring was taking place.

17 It is also unclear whether what is at issue is language in modernity as it is, say, for the Lukács of *The Theory of the Novel*, or language in virtually any human society.

18 Leaving aside the question as to exactly what a proposition is: that way lies a re-run of the whole history of analytical philosophy and of the problem of 'meanings' suggested by Quine.

19 In the later essays of 1933–5 on 'The Doctrine of the Similar' and 'On the Mimetic Capacity' he links this question to onomatopoeia, where he manages to make a bit more sense of it via further reflection on the relations between differing words in differing languages which stand for the same things and the very intelligibility of the things they designate. He bases the theory, though, on the problematic notion of a 'non-sensuous similarity' (GS 2 1 p. 208) between the differing words and the thing they designate in common (see Bowie 1995a).

20 Novalis does suggest that nature may be looked at in such a way that patterns caused by electric charges or manifested in organisms be considered as 'language', but this need not be read in theological terms.

21 Schelling shows the way in which these two systems are ultimately equivalent in Schelling 1994.

22 But remember Benjamin's remark that Schlegel 'turned against Jacobi in order to castigate his own defects in public'.

23 Novalis carries out a much more detailed investigation of the problem in his 'Fichte Studies' at exactly the same time, but Benjamin had no access to this text, even though much of what he says is confirmed by Novalis' analysis. Novalis and Schlegel were, of course, in frequent contact (see Bowie 1996b).

24 The source of Jacobi's critique should thereby be clear: as we saw, in 1800

Fichte asks, 'And do I really think or do I just think a thinking of thinking? What can stop speculation acting like this and continuing asking to infinity?' (Fichte 1971 (Vol. 2) p. 252).

25 There is obviously much more to Fichte than this, but the early versions of the *Wissenschaftslehre* can be read in these terms, as Heidegger in fact did read them, thereby seeing Fichte as the epitome of Western metaphysics' subjectification of being. Benjamin in many ways shares aspects of such a view, as his later antagonism to giving subjectivity a serious role in philosophy can suggest.

26 Benjamin already opposed a notion of Romanticism and intuition in very early writings: in an essay of 1913 'Romanticism – the Answer of the Uninitiated' he says, in Nietzschean vein, suggesting links between art and truth: 'Art should not be morphium against the will which suffers in a painful present' (GS 2 1 p. 47). Benjamin was politically active as a student, but in the politics of education. At the time of the dissertation the biographical evidence confirms that there is no direct sense that his later politics are playing any role in his work. The opposition to 'intuition' will be repeated by the early Adorno: see Chapter 9.

27 Benjamin is in this way at odds both with positivistic tendencies to reduce all truth to science while condemning art to 'meaninglessness', and with irrationalist forms of cultural critique which regard scientific enlightenment as the real threat to 'intuition'. He shares this suspicion of theories of the unconscious with Adorno's early work.

28 I have given a somewhat different interpretation of these ideas in Bowie (1990 Chapter 7): my worry there is that Benjamin's argument, like Derrida's, may not give one an answer to how it is that the differential articulations of language become meaningful at all. This requires a description of self-consciousness which takes account of some of Fichte's arguments, even if it rejects their most extreme consequences. Benjamin's relationship to individual subjectivity is not much less problematic than Heidegger's, though he does not share the latter's philosophical indifference to human suffering.

29 Benjamin arrives at these positions well before Heidegger, but I do not know of any possible influence. The reason for the link seems to be the common relationship to a reinterpretation of Romantic ideas.

30 Obviously this is true of any text: the question is whether the completion is merely pragmatic or, in the case of an aesthetic text, part of a process which continues as long as the work is 'true' in the temporalised sense we have seen in Heidegger that comes later to be shared by Gadamer.

31 Similar ideas, albeit couched in different terms, are present in Schleiermacher, as we saw in Chapter 5.

32 This will be a source of Benjamin's later interest in Freud's theory of the unconscious, which he will try to transfer to the collective level as a way of understanding historical changes of which the actors in history cannot be reflexively aware. It is also a source of his interest in Klages and Jung, although, especially in the latter case, he will come to realise that the notion of a 'collective unconscious' not explained via the concrete historical factors that lead to collective phenomena is merely irrationalist. Jung was, one should remember, for a time at least, enthusiastic about the Nazis, and approved of the Aryan as opposed to the Jewish soul.

33 This idea is taken up in this century by Lévi-Strauss (who also, significantly, links it to music). The actual source of Lévi-Strauss' conception is clearly the Romantics, and particularly Schelling. Lévi-Strauss borrowed much from Jung, who borrowed (and perverted) many of Schelling's insights.

34 As I suggested in the discussion at the end of Chapter 5, such approaches

always run the danger of a reification of what they investigate. I shall look again at this problem in Chapter 9.

35 The preface is termed '*Erkenntniskritische Vorrede*', which involves the notion of a 'critique' of the idea of 'cognition': I can think of no appropriate way to translate this that is not ridiculously cumbersome, so I shall refer just to 'the Preface'.

36 Habermas suggests that Brecht must have been a 'sort of reality-principle' for Benjamin, who led him to drop his esotericism (Habermas 1973 p. 303).

37 In his most esoteric vein, Benjamin gleefully claims that, compared to Ritter: 'Novalis is a demagogue (*Volksredner*)' (GS I 3 p. 876)!

38 Benjamin's interest in Proust and psychoanalysis evidently relates to the way both reject linear temporality in favour of truth-generating conjunctions of past and present.

39 The translation of '*Darstellung*' is a problem: it does not mean re-presentation in the sense we saw undermined by the Romantics. It has rather to do with explication, interpretation which is not systematic and whose form is part of its content: the sense should become clearer in the following discussion.

40 This procedure could give rise to endless interpretative and methodological reflections: it seems to me that the texts help make sense of each other, so those suspicious of the procedure adopted here might regard it as an 'experiment', rather in the sense that Benjamin uses in his dissertation.

41 In the 1924 essay on Goethe's *Elective Affinities* Benjamin says what he says here about truth about beauty.

42 The reasons for this have to do with Schelling's relationship to Schopenhauer, who is the major influence in *The Birth of Tragedy*.

43 This maps, somewhat schematically, on to the difference between Fichte (spontaneity) and the Romantics (contemplation) in the dissertation. 'Reflection', which might at first sight appear to be equivalent to mediation, is in fact connected to the 'Idea', because it is not a result of grounded systematic relations, but rather of non-systematic integration into what Benjamin will term a 'configuration'.

44 Schelling uses this distinction against Hegel (see Bowie 1993 Chapter 6 and Bowie 1994a).

45 Both the German terms mean literally 'relation of relation', but the sense is rendered without the duality.

46 There are so many obvious ways in which this analogy can cause trouble – different cultures see different constellations, etc. – and confuse the argument that I will leave it at this, and try to elucidate the point in other ways.

47 Foucault's Heidegger-influenced notion of 'episteme' in *The Order of Things* gives rise to similar problems, both with regard to how it is that a move from one episteme to another can take place and with regard to the perspective from which one can delineate an episteme at all.

48 It is worth remembering, as a way of understanding the kind of connections with which Benjamin is concerned, that the *Trauerspielbuch* itself is also, as Benjamin makes clear (see GS I 3 p. 879), unthinkable without German expressionism. Expressionism again made transience, allegory and decay a central factor in the self-understanding of modernity.

49 See Bowie (1993 Chapter 5), where I argue that Schelling's 'evil' is therefore effectively the same as the later Heidegger's 'metaphysics', in the sense used in Chapter 7, this volume.

50 Prefiguring this, Schelling says in 1806 of Fichte's philosophy of subjectivity:

> in the last analysis what is the essence of his whole opinion of nature? It is this: that nature should be used . . . and that it is there for nothing more than

to be used; his principle, according to which he looks at nature, is the economic teleological principle. (I/7 p. 17)

51 It is fairly clear, incidentally, that *Being and Time* was influenced by the reading of *History and Class Consciousness*.

52 Although he is not explicit about this, it would seem that he does not include the Romantics in this conception: the whole point of his approach to Romantic theory, as we saw, was to discredit the very notion of Romanticism as a philosophy of mysterious hidden origins.

53 See Welsch (1993 p. 153) for a clarification of exactly what kind of aestheticisation Benjamin was rejecting.

54 Benjamin attributes this version of the idea to Adorno (ibid. p. 1102).

55 Along with this adherence to subjectless conceptions of language, Lyotard, for example, also shares some of Benjamin's ideas about non-linear history (see Lyotard 1977).

56 I have tried to show in Bowie (1982) that Alexander Kluge's prose writings provide one model of how Benjamin's ideas in this area can be made fruitful as a model for writing 'New Histories' without falling into the theological traps.

9 THE CULTURE OF TRUTH: ADORNO

1 Given the growing amount of secondary literature which usefully outlines the concerns of these texts (e. g. Buck-Morss 1977, Rose 1978, Jay 1984, Thyen 1989, Zuidervaart 1991, Bernstein 1992, among many others), it seems timely to offer a different perspective.

2 It should already be clear from the rest of what I have said that I do not think the almost simultaneous Brecht–Lukács–Bloch 'Expressionism debate' – however important it may be in other respects as a model for questions in cultural theory – has the same kind of wider philosophical significance.

3 If the notion has any substance at all in Nietzsche (which I doubt), it would seem to lie in its being an imperative really to live in the present, instead of always hoping for the world eventually to be different.

4 Most of the key passages from the correspondence cited here are also in the Benjamin *Gesammelte Schriften*. The importance of the full edition of the letters lies not least in its final laying to rest of any suspicion that Adorno and the Institute for Social Research did not offer Benjamin real assistance in the troubles that led to his tragic death. The detailed and objective criticisms by Adorno of Benjamin's work discussed here never put in question his immense admiration for and indebtedness to the latter's ideas, and the letters are a deeply moving testimony to an intellectual friendship which has been wrongly viewed with some suspicion. It is perhaps also worth mentioning, in order to counter another widespread false impression, that both correspondents could be very witty in a wonderfully scurrilous manner.

5 That there might be some members of an audience for whom the model offered by Benjamin (and Brecht) may have applied should not be allowed to conceal the fact that radical cinema and theatre have been shown generally to play a relatively minor role in effective political change. Other factors in economic and social life are clearly more decisive, as Adorno suggests.

6 What Adorno fails to do, though, is to give us convincing ways of understanding how it is that Beethoven does something with such musical material which no one else does (see Bowie 1990 pp. 97–9).

7 Adorno criticises Heidegger in the early 1930s precisely because Heidegger thinks coining neologisms really brings one closer to a truth not available in everyday language (see Adorno 1973a p. 368).

8 That there are plenty of individual empirical exceptions to this should not blind one to the worst effects of capitalism on mass culture.

9 An autobiographical piece of anecdotal evidence is relevant here: as a research student in Berlin, who could largely determine my own use of time, I was able to engage with great profit with the music of Schönberg, Webern, Berg and their successors, not least because cheap – subsidised – public concerts of the highest quality regularly offered their music. Since being in full-time academic employment – which is hardly the most reified form of work – I have in the main returned to the 'First Vienna School', only being able seriously to engage with the 'Second Vienna School' when there were professional reasons and the requisite time for doing so. I suspect this is a common experience.

10 One way that radical art is obviously significant lies in the manner in which it gets assimilated into mainstream art and into commodity culture: were it not to articulate something real there would be no reason for this to take place. Schönberg's positive effects on film music are one example here. The dialectic this gives rise to is the basic problem of the self-consuming nature of the avant-garde, of which Adorno is the greatest theorist.

11 In its suspicion of a grounding spontaneity (though not at all in other ways) the argument is quite close to Benjamin's objections to Fichte in his dissertation on the Romantics.

12 Adorno in 1940 therefore suggests that the vital requirement is a theory of forgetting, a theme which still, incidentally, awaits anything resembling an adequate philosophical treatment.

13 This notion of the symbol was the one employed by Goethe briefly considered in Chapter 8.

14 To the extent that Benjamin very politely insists in a letter that Adorno's initial failure to mention the *Trauerspielbuch* might be corrected (see Lonitz 1994 pp. 18–20).

15 Asserting this as a universal claim would, of course, lead back to familiar problems, because the claim itself seems foundational: the position can only work by its continually being validated in intellectual practice.

16 Adorno's relationship to Hegel is obviously more complex than this: his main enthusiasm is for the deconstructive aspect of Hegel's dialectic, which breaks up static categories and oppositions. It is when this becomes a complete philo-sophical method that he parts company with Hegel.

17 For one view, which suggests how he may have misread one of the most convincing aspects of Heidegger, see Bowie 1995b.

18 Adorno's emphatic affirmation elsewhere of radical modernist art suggests that he is here in fact under the spell of the regressive aspects of both Heidegger and Benjamin: he will later be rather more consistent.

19 See Bowie (1993 Chapter 3), which shows that Schelling already mapped out the reasons for this kind of repressive relationship between the subject and the nature in which it is grounded, as well as suggesting that subjectivity is not *inherently* a principle of domination, because, as Jacobi argued against Fichte, it is not ground of itself.

20 The criticism is, incidentally, much the same as Derrida's critique of Husserl's transcendental ego in *La voix et le phénomène*.

21 This position offers a way of suggesting that the scheme/content model is still serviceable if one has adopted Adorno's deconstructive approach to founding categories. When scheme takes over from content one has the 'autonomous *ratio*', and when content takes over from scheme one has mere empiricism. There is, though, no dialectical resolution of these extremes, except in art, where the problem is then the one observed above in terms of music 'moving towards the name'. There seems to be an answer in the work's combination of

universal and particular, but the analysis of the work cannot finally say what it is.

22 This was what Schleiermacher meant by his concept of 'style', of which there could not be a 'concept', and which therefore did not derive from semantic rules, even though it employed the already constituted rule-bound elements of language.

23 Derrida in particular may well agree with such a position, but there are, as I have suggested, too many times when he seems singularly unconcerned about truth.

24 I think the way to deal with the old problem of Adorno and jazz, which, as a jazz musician with great sympathies for Adorno, I ought briefly to do here, is actually quite simple. The lack in Adorno's writings on jazz of specific analyses of examples of performances by major jazz musicians, and the classification of musicians, like Ted Lewis – whom even Benny Goodman parodied – that no jazz musician would take seriously as jazz musicians, make it clear that Adorno listened to very little that deserves the name of jazz. The texts on jazz suggest that the nearest he got was some of Louis Armstrong's more commercialised efforts (where the awful context anyway sometimes makes it hard to appreciate what one musician was doing), and some of the 1930s big bands. Had Adorno analysed the mature work of Jimmie Noone, Coleman Hawkins, Art Tatum, Lester Young, Charlie Parker and other major jazz improvisers of the time, one might have taken what he said more seriously. There is admittedly a lot of 'schematised' jazz, played even by the greatest musicians, but there is just as much schematised European classical music. Indeed, the latter can lack the articulation of protest and suffering, as well as the inventiveness and energy that are clearly still alive even in relatively run-of-the-mill jazz in the period of Adorno's jazz writings.

25 It is important to avoid Adorno's mistake with regard to jazz here: one *can* make significant evaluative discriminations between better and worse rock music. It is clear, though, that the forms in which rock music is produced are increasingly dictated by the music industry. This also applies, of course, to much of the performance of classical music.

26 This is one of the few areas where the kind of generalised verdict in DoE, that links fascism and democracies based on the mass media, has a degree of hyperbolic validity.

27 I cite these passages from DoE as being by Adorno because they are so much in line with his other work that there is no reason not to; it is well known that the authors divided up responsibility for the differing parts of the book.

28 This need not be read in excessively utopian terms: the point is that Adorno is referring to societies with the already existing financial and technical means to abolish destitution and alienation which do not in fact do so.

29 Adorno deconstructs their difference, as his remarks like 'form is sedimented content' suggest, but he does not think that one should abandon the discriminations that the opposition allows us to make.

30 For a view of the story that sees the story's view of art as superior even to that of AT, see Karl Markus Michel's essay in Lindner and Lüdke (1980).

31 At the same time it is clear that Adorno never engaged in a serious manner with the later Wittgenstein, some of whose aims were not necessarily as far from his own as the remarks on philosophy leaving things as they are might suggest.

32 Adorno's differing judgements on Viennese and American positivism provide a useful model (but no more) here. In a German context one can understand, especially in the light of Heidegger, why Habermas takes this stance; in an Anglo-American context there are reasons for suspecting that the analytical insistence on linguistic transparency is often simply an obstacle to trying to

come to terms with things we already know enough about, even if we cannot finally validate how we talk about them.

33 I shall relegate to this footnote the fact that, along with Kant and Fichte, the decisive philosophical influence on Hölderlin was Jacobi (see Henrich 1992).

34 I suspect that Adorno's confusions here are partly occasioned by his use of Hegel – who tries to dissolve the question of being by equating being with 'nothing' at the beginning of the *Logic*. Hegel thereby makes 'being' a concept like any other, which makes no sense in the terms suggested here: on this see my account of Schelling against Hegel in Bowie (1994a), which deals with this issue in some detail. Adorno also attempts to suggest that what Heidegger means by 'being' is always some sort of reification or appeal to an origin. This suggestion is, as far as the issue of ontological difference in these contexts is concerned, simply mistaken, even though it may be valid in other contexts.

CONCLUSION

1 There are, of course, many other reasons, such as the anti-theoretical bias of the empiricist tradition, as well as complex sociological and historical factors which affect the openness to other intellectual traditions.

2 In this respect the work of Manfred Frank (e.g. 1989a, 1992) is exemplary. This is no coincidence, of course: Frank maintains that 'I was always and still am engaged in an inner dialogue with early Romanticism (including Solger and Schleiermacher)' (Frank 1990 pp. 499–500).

3 The first two of whom sometimes belong to the first position.

4 Nietzsche at his best comes very close to Schlegel and Novalis, but it is precisely when he departs from the Romantic positions that he is philosophically most suspect. I leave to one side the issue of his Social Darwinism, which is much too often simply ignored by his admirers.

5 Adorno already says startlingly similar things about Furtwängler in 1926, which suggests a deep continuity of his views in relation to art that transcends some of his early philosophical vagaries (see Adorno 1984a pp. 453–5).

6 It also involves a repression of the extent to which an individual's involvement in a cultural horizon which has claims to its own validity cannot be obliterated by that individual's desire to reject that horizon.

7 This in no way implies that only great Western art is what is at issue here: it is just that many of our theoretical resources have tended to be developed in relation to that art.

8 This mistaken project derives from Adorno's interest in the work of Alfred Sohn-Rethel. It is highly likely that, as Sohn-Rethel claims, the emergence of logical forms is the result of necessities generated by human interaction with nature and by concrete forms of social exchange. That is, though, no reason to *reduce* them to these origins: the very attempt to give a theoretical account of the grounding of logic in social terms leads to yet another series of regresses or to an absolute presupposition that maintains that 'identity is really "x"'. This is actually another version of the problem Nietzsche has with his attempt to reveal truth as really a form of power, as well as being open to the sort of objections the semantic tradition and Husserl make to psychologism.

9 The very idea that one could enumerate all its senses suggests a misapprehension on the part of the enumerators of how we use concepts and understand their boundaries.

10 There is no general rule to be derived from this example: one might say the same about the dissemination of ideas for witch-finding. The real question is what normative implications are involved in the adoption of anomalous ideas.

11 Heidegger is sometimes ambiguous about this (see Chapter 7 note 38), but his most interesting work depends upon his refusal to reduce truth to propositionality.
12 Aspects of this view were outlined in the account of Habermas in Chapter 7.
13 It should be clear from what has already been said that this notion of subject philosophy cannot be applied to many Romantic positions, which do not involve a rigid subject/object schema.
14 Goodman's key arguments on induction in *Fact, Fiction and Forecast* (Goodman 1983) follow exactly in the tradition of Schleiermacher.

Bibliography

Adorno, T.W. (1965) *Noten zur Literatur III*, Frankfurt: Suhrkamp.
Adorno, T.W. (1967) *Ohne Leitbild: Parva Aesthetica*, Frankfurt: Suhrkamp.
Adorno, T.W. (1969) *Stichworte: Kritische Modelle 2*, Frankfurt: Suhrkamp.
Adorno, T.W. (1973a) *Philosophische Frühschriften* (*Gesammelte Schriften* Vol. 1), Frankfurt: Suhrkamp.
Adorno, T.W. (1973b) *Ästhetische Theorie*, Frankfurt: Suhrkamp.
Adorno, T.W. (1975) *Negative Dialektik*, Frankfurt: Suhrkamp.
Adorno, T.W. (1978) *Minima Moralia*, Frankfurt: Suhrkamp.
Adorno, T.W. (1979) *Kierkegaard: Konstruktion des Ästhetischen*, Frankfurt: Suhrkamp.
Adorno, T.W. (1984a) *Musikalische Schriften V* (*Gesammelte Schriften* Vol. 18), Frankfurt: Suhrkamp.
Adorno, T.W. (1984b) *Musikalische Schriften VI* (*Gesammelte Schriften* Vol. 19), Frankfurt: Suhrkamp.
Adorno, T.W. (1993) *Beethoven: Philosophie der Musik*, Frankfurt: Suhrkamp.
Allison, Henry E. (1987) *Benedict de Spinoza: An Introduction*, New Haven, Conn., and London: Yale University Press.
Anders, Günther (1980) *Die Antiquiertheit des Menschen*, Munich: C.H. Beck.
Behler, Ernst (1993) *German Romantic Literary Theory*, Cambridge: Cambridge University Press.
Beiser, Frederick C. (1987) *The Fate of Reason: German Philosophy from Kant to Fichte*, Cambridge, Mass., and London: Harvard University Press.
Bell, David (1987) 'The Art of Judgement', *Mind* Vol. XCVI, April.
Benjamin, Andrew and Osborne, Peter (1994) *Walter Benjamin's Philosophy: Destruction and Experience*, London: Routledge.
Benjamin, Walter (1980) *Gesammelte Schriften*, Frankfurt: Suhrkamp.
Benjamin, Walter (1983) *Das Passagen-Werk*, Frankfurt: Suhrkamp.
Bernstein, J. M. (1992) *The Fate of Art*, Cambridge: Polity.
Bernstein, Richard (1992) *The New Constellation*, Cambridge: Polity.
Biale, David (1982) *Gershom Scholem: Kabbalah and Counter-History*, Cambridge, Mass., and London: Harvard University Press.
Birus, Hendrik (1982) *Hermeneutische Positionen*, Göttingen: Vandenhoek and Ruprecht.
Bowie, Andrew (1979) *Problems of Historical Understanding in the Modern Novel*, unpublished Ph.D. dissertation, University of East Anglia.
Bowie, Andrew (1982) 'New Histories: Aspects of the Prose of Alexander Kluge', *Journal of European Studies* 12.
Bowie, Andrew (1984) 'Marx, Flaubert and 1848: History and Literature/Literature and History', *Ideas and Production* 2.

Bowie, Andrew (1985) 'Individuality and *différance*', *Oxford Literary Review* 7:1 and 2.

Bowie, Andrew (1986) 'Alexander Kluge: An Introduction', *Cultural Critique* 4.

Bowie, Andrew (1989) 'Music, Language and Modernity', in ed. Andrew Benjamin, *The Problems of Modernity: Adorno and Benjamin*, London: Routledge.

Bowie, Andrew (1990) *Aesthetics and Subjectivity: From Kant to Nietzsche*, Manchester: Manchester University Press. Paperback edition published 1993.

Bowie, Andrew (1991) Review of 'Terry Eagleton, *The Ideology of the Aesthetic*', *Radical Philosophy* 57.

Bowie, Andrew (1992a) 'The Presence of Literary Theory in German Studies', *Oxford German Studies* 20/21.

Bowie, Andrew (1992b) 'Aesthetic Autonomy' in eds D. Cooper, J. Margolis and C. Sartwell, *A Companion to Aesthetics*, Oxford: Blackwell.

Bowie, Andrew (1993) *Schelling and Modern European Philosophy: An Introduction*, London: Routledge.

Bowie, Andrew (1994a) 'The Schellingian Alternative', *Bulletin of the Hegel Society of Great Britain* 30.

Bowie, Andrew (1994b) Review of 'Ernst Tugendhat, *Philosophische Aufsätze*', *European Journal of Philosophy* 2:3.

Bowie, Andrew (1995a) 'Truth, Language and Art: Benjamin, Davidson and Heidegger' in ed. G. Bartram, *New Comparison* 18.

Bowie, Andrew (1995b) '"Non-Identity": The German Romantics, Schelling, and Adorno' in ed. T. Rajan, *Intersections: Nineteenth-Century Philosophy and Contemporary Theory*, Albany: SUNY Press.

Bowie, Andrew (1995c) 'Romanticism and Technology', *Radical Philosophy* 72.

Bowie, Andrew (1996a) 'Re-thinking the History of the Subject: Jacobi, Schelling and Heidegger', in eds Simon Critchley, Peter Dews, *Deconstructive Subjectivities*, Albany: SUNY Press.

Bowie, Andrew (1996b) 'John McDowell's *Mind and World*, and Early Romantic Epistemology', *Revue internationale de philosophie* 197.

Bradbury, Elizabeth (1993) *Social and Aesthetic Theory: A Reexamination of Aspects of the Work of T.W. Adorno*, unpublished Ph.D. dissertation, Cambridge University.

Brandom, Robert (1994) *Making It Explicit*, Cambridge, Mass., and London: Harvard University Press.

Bruns, Gerald L. (1992) *Hermeneutics Ancient and Modern*, New Haven, Conn., and London: Yale University Press.

Bubner, Rüdiger (1989) *Ästhetische Erfahrung*, Frankfurt: Suhrkamp.

Buck-Morss, Susan (1977) *The Origin of Negative Dialectics*, Sussex: Harvester.

Bürger, Peter (1983) *Zur Kritik der idealistischen Ästhetik*, Frankfurt: Suhrkamp.

Cavell, Stanley (1969) *Must We Mean What We Say?*, Cambridge: Cambridge University Press.

Caygill, Howard (1989) *The Art of Judgement*, Oxford: Blackwell.

Chladenius, Johann Martin (1969) *Einleitung zur richtigen Auslegung vernünftiger Reden und Schriften*, Introduction L. Goldsetzer (Reprint of edition Leipzig 1742), Düsseldorf.

Christ, Kurt (1988) *Jacobi und Mendelssohn: Eine Analyse des Spinozastreits*, Würzburg: Königshausen and Neumann.

Coffa, J. Alberto (1991) *The Semantic Tradition from Kant to Carnap*, Cambridge: Cambridge University Press.

Culler, Jonathan (1974) *Flaubert: The Uses of Uncertainty*, London: Elek.

Cunningham, Andrew and Jardine, Nicholas (1990) *Romanticism and the Sciences*, Cambridge: Cambridge University Press.

d'Acconti, Alessandra (1995) *The Genealogies of Logical Positivism*, unpublished Ph.D. dissertation, Cambridge University.

Dahlhaus, Carl (1978) *Die Idee der absoluten Musik*, Munich and Kassel: dtv.
Davidson, Donald (1984) *Inquiries into Truth and Interpretation*, Oxford: Oxford University Press.
Derrida, Jacques (1967a) *La voix et le phénomène*, Paris: Presses Universitaires de France.
Derrida, Jacques (1967b) *L'écriture et la différence*, Paris: Points.
Derrida, Jacques (1972a) *Marges de la philosophie*, Paris: Minuit.
Derrida, Jacques (1972b) *Positions*, Paris: Minuit.
Derrida, Jacques (1978) *La vérité en peinture*, Paris: Flammarion.
Dews, Peter (1987) *Logics of Disintegration*, London: Verso.
Dilthey, Wilhelm (1981) *Der Aufbau der geschichtlichen Welt in den Geisteswissenschaften*, Frankfurt: Suhrkamp.
Dilthey, Wilhelm (1983) *Texte zur Kritik der historischen Vernunft*, Göttingen: Vandenhoeck and Ruprecht.
Dilthey, Wilhelm (1990) *Die Geistige Welt: Einleitung in die Philosophie des Lebens*, Gesammelte Schriften Vol. 5, Stuttgart: Teubner.
Dreyfus, Hubert L. (1991) *Being-in-the-World*, Cambridge, Mass., and London: MIT Press.
Dummett, Michael (1981) *The Interpretation of Frege's Philosophy*, London: Duckworth.
Dummett, Michael (1993) *The Seas of Language*, Oxford: Oxford University Press.
Eagleton, Terry (1983) *Literary Theory: An Introduction*, Oxford: Blackwell.
Eagleton, Terry (1990) *The Ideology of the Aesthetic*, Oxford: Blackwell.
Easthope, Antony (1995) 'Literary into cultural studies', *Radical Philosophy* 70.
Fichte, J.G. (1971) *Werke I*, *Werke II*, Berlin: de Gruyter.
Foucault, Michel (1970) *The Order of Things*, London: Tavistock.
Frank, Manfred (1975) *Der unendliche Mangel an Sein*, Frankfurt: Suhrkamp.
Frank, Manfred (1977) *Das Individuelle-Allgemeine: Textstrukturierung und -interpretation nach Schleiermacher*, Frankfurt: Suhrkamp.
Frank, Manfred (1984) *Was Ist Neo-Strukturalismus?*, Frankfurt: Suhrkamp.
Frank, Manfred (1988) *Grenzen der Verständigung*, Frankfurt: Suhrkamp.
Frank, Manfred (1989a) *Das Sagbare und das Unsagbare*, Frankfurt: Suhrkamp.
Frank, Manfred (1989b) *Einführung in die frühromantische Ästhetik*, Frankfurt: Suhrkamp.
Frank, Manfred (1989c) *Kaltes Herz: Unendliche Fahrt. Neue Mythologie*, Frankfurt: Suhrkamp.
Frank, Manfred (1990) *Das Problem 'Zeit' in der deutschen Romantik*, Paderborn, Munich, Vienna and Zürich: Schöningh
Frank, Manfred (1991) *Selbstbewußtsein und Selbsterkenntnis*, Stuttgart: Reclam.
Frank, Manfred (1992) *Stil in der Philosophie*, Stuttgart: Reclam.
Frank, Manfred (1994) 'Philosophische Grundfragen der Frühromantik' in *Athenäum* 4, Paderborn, Munich, Vienna and Zürich: Schöningh.
Gadamer, Hans-Georg (1975) *Wahrheit und Methode*, Tübingen: J.C.B. Mohr.
Gadamer, Hans-Georg (1986) *Hermeneutik: Wahrheit und Methode 2. Ergänzungen, Register* Tübingen: J.C.B. Mohr.
Gadamer, Hans-Georg (1987a) *Neuere Philosophie 1. Hegel Husserl Heidegger*, Tübingen: J.C.B. Mohr.
Gadamer, Hans-Georg (1987b) *Neuere Philosophie II. Probleme Gestalten*, Tübingen: J.C.B. Mohr.
Gadamer, Hans-Georg and Boehm, Gottfried (1976) *Seminar: Philosophische Hermeneutik*, Frankfurt: Suhrkamp.
Geuss, Raymond (1975) 'Theodor W. Adorno: Negative Dialectics', *The Journal of Philosophy* 72.
Goodman, Nelson (1978) *Ways of Worldmaking*, Indianapolis, Ind.: Hackett.

Goodman, Nelson (1983) *Fact, Fiction and Forecast*, Cambridge, Mass., and London: Harvard University Press.

Habermas, Jürgen (1973) *Kultur und Kritik*, Frankfurt: Suhrkamp.

Habermas, Jürgen (1983) *Moralbewußtsein und kommunikatives Handeln*, Frankfurt: Suhrkamp.

Habermas, Jürgen (1984) *Vorstudien und Ergänzungen zur Theorie des kommunikativen Handelns*, Frankfurt: Suhrkamp.

Habermas, Jürgen (1985) *Der philosophische Diskurs der Moderne*, Frankfurt: Suhrkamp.

Habermas, Jürgen (1988) *Nachmetaphysisches Denken*, Frankfurt: Suhrkamp.

Habermas, Jürgen (1991) *Texte und Kontexte*, Frankfurt: Suhrkamp.

Hammacher, Klaus (ed.) (1971) *Friedrich Heinrich Jacobi*, Frankfurt am Main: Klostermann.

Hegel, G.W.F (1970) *Jenaer Schriften 1801–7*, Werke 2, Frankfurt: Suhrkamp.

Heidegger, Martin (1949) *Brief über den Humanismus*, Frankfurt: Klostermann.

Heidegger, Martin (1957) *Der Satz vom Grund*, Pfullingen: Neske.

Heidegger, Martin (1959) *Unterwegs zur Sprache*, Pfullingen: Neske.

Heidegger, Martin (1960) *Der Ursprung des Kunstwerkes*, Stuttgart: Reclam.

Heidegger, Martin (1961) *Nietzsche 1, 2*, Pfullingen: Neske.

Heidegger, Martin (1969) *Zur Sache des Denkens*, Tübingen: Niemeyer.

Heidegger, Martin (1971) *Schellings Abhandlung Über das Wesen der menschlichen Freiheit*, Tübingen: Niemeyer.

Heidegger, Martin (1973) *Kant und das Problem der Metaphysik*, Frankfurt: Klostermann.

Heidegger, Martin (1978) *Wegmarken*, Frankfurt: Klostermann.

Heidegger, Martin (1979) *Sein und Zeit*, Tübingen: Niemeyer.

Heidegger, Martin (1983) *Die Grundbegriffe der Metaphysik*, Frankfurt: Klostermann.

Heidegger, Martin (1989) *Die Grundprobleme der Phänomenologie*, Frankfurt: Klostermann.

Heidegger, Martin (1990) *Metaphysische Anfangsgründe der Logik*, Frankfurt: Klostermann.

Henrich, Dieter (1967) *Fichtes ursprüngliche Einsicht,* Frankfurt: Klostermann.

Henrich, Dieter (1982) *Selbstverhältnisse*, Stuttgart: Reclam.

Henrich, Dieter (1992) *Der Grund im Bewußtsein: Untersuchungen zu Hölderlins Denken (1794–5)*, Stuttgart: Klett-Cotta.

Herder, Johann Gottfried (1966) *Abhandlung über den Ursprung der Sprache*, Stuttgart: Reclam.

Hobbes, Thomas (1968) *Leviathan*, Harmondsworth: Penguin.

Hogrebe, Wolfram (1989) *Prädikation und Genesis: Metaphysik als Fundamentalheuristik im Ausgang von Schellings "Die Weltalter"*, Frankfurt: Suhrkamp.

Hörisch, Jochen (1988) *Die Wut des Verstehens*, Frankfurt: Suhrkamp.

Horkheimer, Max (1980) 'Zu Bergsons Metaphysik der Zeit', in *Zeitschrift für Sozialforschung* III/1934, Munich: dtv.

Horkheimer, Max and Adorno, T.W. (1971) *Dialektik der Aufklärung*, Frankfurt: Fischer.

Humboldt, Wilhelm von (1973) *Schriften zur Sprache*, Stuttgart: Reclam.

Husserl, Edmund (1992) *Gesammelte Schriften, Band 4. Logische Untersuchungen. Zweiter Band. II Teil*, Hamburg: Meiner.

Jacobi, Friedrich Heinrich (1787) *David Hume über den Glauben oder Idealismus und Realismus ein Gespräch*, Breslau: Löwe.

Jacobi, Friedrich Heinrich (1789) *Über die Lehre des Spinoza in Briefen an den Herrn Moses Mendelssohn von F.H. Jacobi*, Breslau: Löwe.

Jacobi, Friedrich Heinrich (1799) *Jacobi an Fichte*, Hamburg: Friedrich Perthes.

Jameson, Fredric (1990) *Late Marxism: Adorno, or the Persistence of the Dialectic*, London and New York: Verso.
Jay, Martin (1984) *Adorno*, London: Fontana.
Kant, Immanuel (1968) (*KrV*) *Kritik der reinen Vernunft* (Vols III, IV), Frankfurt: Suhrkamp.
Kant, Immanuel (1968–77) *Werkausgabe* I-XII, ed. Wilhelm Weischedel, Frankfurt: Suhrkamp.
Kant, Immanuel (1974) (*KpV*) *Kritik der praktischen Vernunft: Grundlegung der Metaphysik der Sitten* (Vol. VII), Frankfurt: Suhrkamp.
Kant, Immanuel (1977) (*KdU*) *Kritik der Urteilskraft* (Vol X), Frankfurt: Suhrkamp.
Kant, Immanuel (1993) *Opus postumum*, ed. Eckart Förster, Cambridge: Cambridge University Press.
Kierkegaard, Søren (1968) *Concluding Unscientific Postscript*, Princeton, NJ: Princeton University Press.
Kluge, Alexander (1986) 'The Political as Intensity of Everyday Feelings', *Cultural Critique* 4.
Lacoue-Labarthe, Philippe and Nancy, Jean-Luc (1988) *The Literary Absolute*, Albany: SUNY Press.
Lepore, Ernest (ed.) (1986) *Truth and Interpretation*, Oxford: Blackwell.
Lindner, Burkhardt, Lüdke and W. Martin (eds) (1980) *Materialien zur ästhetischen Theorie Th. W. Adornos Konstruktion der Moderne*, Frankfurt: Suhrkamp.
Lonitz, Henri (ed.) (1994) *Theodor Adorno; Walter Benjamin: Briefwechsel 1928–1940*, Frankfurt: Suhrkamp.
Lyotard, Jean-François (1977) *Rudiments païens*, Paris: 10/18.
Lyotard, Jean-François (1979) *La condition postmoderne*, Paris: Minuit.
Lyotard, Jean-François (1983) *Le différend*, Paris: Minuit.
Lypp, Bernhard (1972) *Ästhetischer Absolutismus und politische Vernunft*, Frankfurt: Suhrkamp.
McDowell, John (1994) *Mind and World*, Cambridge, Mass., and London: Harvard University Press.
Makkreel, Rudolf A. (1992) *Dilthey: Philosopher of the Human Studies*, Princeton, NJ: Princeton University Press.
Malpas, J.E. (1992) *Donald Davidson and the Mirror of Meaning*, Cambridge: Cambridge University Press.
Mann, Thomas (1972) *Der Zauberberg*, Frankfurt: Fischer.
Menke, Christoph (1991) *Die Souveränität der Kunst: Ästhetische Erfahrung nach Adorno und Derrida*, Frankfurt: Suhrkamp.
Menninghaus, Winfried (1987) *Unendliche Verdopplung*, Frankfurt: Suhrkamp.
Mulhall, Stephen (1990) *On Being in the World: Wittgenstein and Heidegger on Seeing Aspects*, London: Routledge.
Neuhouser, Frederick (1989) *Fichte's Theory of Subjectivity*, Cambridge: Cambridge University Press.
Nietzsche, Friedrich (1980) *Sämtliche Werke*, eds G. Colli and M. Montinari, Munich, Berlin and New York: dtv.
Novalis (1978) *Band 2 Das philosophisch-theoretische Werk*, ed. Hans-Joachim Mähl, Munich and Vienna: Hanser.
Okrent, Mark (1988) *Heidegger's Pragmatism: Understanding, Being, and the Critique of Metaphysics*, Ithaca, NY, and London: Cornell University Press.
Orth, Ernst Wolfgang (ed.) (1985) *Dilthey und die Philosophie der Gegenwart*, Freiburg and Munich: Alber.
Przywara, Erich (ed.) (1936) *An Augustine Synthesis*, London: Sheed and Ward.
Putnam, Hilary (1981) *Reason, Truth and History*, Cambridge: Cambridge University Press.

Putnam, Hilary (1983) *Realism and Reason: Philosophical Papers Vol. 3*, Cambridge: Cambridge University Press.
Putnam, Hilary (1988) *Representation and Reality*, Cambridge, Mass., and London: MIT Press.
Putnam, Hilary (1990) *Realism with a Human Face*, Cambridge, Mass., and London: Harvard University Press.
Putnam, Hilary (1995) *Pragmatism*, Oxford: Blackwell.
Ramberg, Bjørn T. (1989) *Donald Davidson's Philosophy of Language*, Oxford: Blackwell.
Reed, T.J. (1990) '"Nobody's Master": Goethe and the Authority of the Writer. With a Reflection on Anti-Literary Theory', Oxford: Oxford University Press.
Reed, T.J.(1992) 'Communicating or Theorising? Some Thoughts for Andrew Bowie', *Oxford German Studies* 20/21.
Reinhold, Karl Leonhard (1978) *Über das Fundament des philosophischen Wissens: Über die Möglichkeit der Philosophie als strenge Wissenschaft*, Hamburg: Meiner.
Ricoeur, Paul (1986) *Die lebendige Metapher* (revised German edition), Munich: Fink.
Roberts, Julian (1981) *Walter Benjamin*, London: Macmillan.
Rorty, Richard (1980) *Philosophy and the Mirror of Nature*, Oxford: Blackwell.
Rorty, Richard (1989) *Contingency, Irony and Solidarity*, Cambridge: Cambridge University Press.
Rorty, Richard (1991a) *Essays on Heidegger and Others: Philosophical Papers Volume Two*, Cambridge: Cambridge University Press.
Rorty, Richard (1991b) *Objectivity, Relativism, and Truth: Philosophical Papers Volume One*, Cambridge: Cambridge University Press.
Rose, Gillian (1978) *The Melancholy Science*, London: Macmillan.
Rössler, Beate (1990) *Die Theorie des Verstehens in Sprachanalyse und Hermeneutik*, Berlin: Dunker and Humblot.
Rousseau, Jean-Jacques (1990) *Essai sur l'origine des langues*, Paris: Gallimard.
Ryan, Kiernan (1995) *Shakespeare*, London and New York: Prentice Hall/ Harvester Wheatsheaf.
Sandkaulen-Bock, Birgit (1990) *Ausgang vom Unbedingten: Über den Anfang in der Philosophie Schellings*, Göttingen: Vandenhoeck and Ruprecht.
Schelling references, e.g. (I/10 p. 121), are to Friedrich Wilhelm Joseph Schelling's *Sämmtliche Werke*, ed. K.F.A. Schelling, I Abtheilung Vols 1–10, II Abtheilung Bde 1–4, Stuttgart, 1856–61.
Schelling, F.W.J. (1946) *Die Weltalter*, ed. Manfred Schröter, Munich: Biederstein and Leibniz.
Schelling, F.W.J. (1969) *Initia Philosophiae Universae* (1820–1), ed. Horst Fuhrmans, Bonn: Bouvier.
Schelling, F.W.J. (1990) *System der Weltalter* (1827–8), ed. S. Peetz, Frankfurt: Klostermann.
Schelling, F.W.J. (1994) *On the History of Modern Philosophy*, translation and introduction by Andrew Bowie, Cambridge: Cambridge University Press.
Schlegel, Friedrich (1963) *Philosophische Lehrjahre* (1796–1828) (*Kritische Friedrich Schlegel Ausgabe* Vol. 18), Munich, Paderborn and Vienna: Ferdinand Schöningh.
Schlegel, Friedrich (1964) *Philosophische Vorlesungen* (1800–1807) (*Kritische Friedrich Schlegel Ausgabe* Vol. 12), Munich, Paderborn and Vienna: Ferdinand Schöningh.
Schlegel, Friedrich (1988) *Kritische Schriften und Fragmente 1–6*, Paderborn: Ferdinand Schöningh.
Schlegel, Friedrich (1991) *Transcendentalphilosophie*, ed. Michael Elsässer, Hamburg: Meiner.

Schleiermacher, Friedrich (1974a) *Vorlesungen über die Ästhetik*, ed. Carl Lommatzsch, Berlin and New York: de Gruyter.

Schleiermacher, Friedrich (1974b) *Hermeneutik*, ed. H. Kimmerle, Heidelberg: Abhandlungen der Heidelberger Akademie der Wissenschaften.

Schleiermacher, Friedrich (1976) *Friedrich Schleiermachers Dialektik*, ed. Rudolf Odebrecht, Darmstadt: Wissenschaftliche Buchgesellschaft.

Schleiermacher, Friedrich (1977) *Hermeneutik und Kritik*, ed. Manfred Frank, Frankfurt: Suhrkamp.

Schleiermacher, Friedrich (1984) *Jugendschriften 1787–1796*, ed. Günter Meckenstock, Berlin and New York: de Gruyter.

Schleiermacher, Friedrich (1990) *Ethik (1812/13)*, Hamburg: Meiner.

Schnädelbach, Herbert (1984) *Philosophy in Germany 1831–1933*, Cambridge: Cambridge University Press.

Schnädelbach, Herbert (1987) *Vernunft und Geschichte*, Frankfurt: Suhrkamp.

Schnädelbach, Herbert (1992) *Zur Rehabilitierung des animale rationale*, Frankfurt: Suhrkamp.

Scholem, Gershom (1970) *Judaica 3*, Frankfurt: Suhrkamp.

Scholz, Heinrich (ed.) (1916) *Die Hauptschriften zum Pantheismusstreit zwischen Jacobi und Mendelssohn*, Berlin: Reuther and Reichard.

Simmel, Georg (1917) *Der Krieg und die geistigen Entscheidungen*, Munich and Leipzig.

Spinoza, Benedict de (1955) *The Ethics*, trans. R.H.M. Elwes, New York: Dover.

Taylor, Charles (1985) *Human Agency and Language*, Cambridge: Cambridge University Press.

Taylor, Charles (1995) *Philosophical Arguments*, Cambridge, Mass., and London: Harvard University Press.

Thyen, Anke (1989) *Negative Dialektik und Erfahrung: Zur Rationalität des Nichtidentischen bei Adorno*, Frankfurt: Suhrkamp.

Tugendhat, Ernst (1976) *Einführung in die sprachanalytische Philosophie*, Frankfurt: Suhrkamp.

Tugendhat, Ernst (1992) *Philosophische Aufsätze*, Frankfurt: Suhrkamp.

Tugendhat, Ernst and Wolf, Ursula (1986) *Logisch-semantische Propädeutik*, Stuttgart: Reclam.

Vattimo, Gianni (1990) *Das Ende der Moderne*, Stuttgart: Reclam.

Wellmer, Albrecht (1985) *Zur Dialektik von Moderne und Postmoderne*, Frankfurt: Suhrkamp.

Wellmer, Albrecht (1993) *Endspiele: Die unversöhnliche Moderne*, Frankfurt: Suhrkamp.

Welsch, Wolfgang (1993) *Ästhetisches Denken*, Stuttgart: Reclam.

Wittgenstein, Ludwig (1961) *Tractatus Logico-Philosophicus*, London: Routledge.

Wittgenstein, Ludwig (1971) *Philosophische Untersuchungen*, Frankfurt: Suhrkamp.

Wood, David (ed.) (1992) *Derrida: A Critical Reader*, Oxford: Blackwell.

Zuidervaart, Lambert (1991) *Adorno's Aesthetic Theory*, Cambridge, Mass.: MIT Press.

Index

This index does not include reference to topics such as 'hermeneutics', 'interpretation', 'language', which occur too often and in too many different contexts to be usefully listed.